Game Programming
in C++

Game Programming in C++

Creating 3D Games

Sanjay Madhav

⋏⋏Addison-Wesley

Boston • Columbus • Indianapolis • New York • San Francisco
Amsterdam • Cape Town • Dubai • London • Madrid • Milan
Munich • Paris • Montreal • Toronto • Delhi • Mexico City • São
Paulo • Sydney • Hong Kong • Seoul • Singapore • Taipei • Tokyo

For information about buying this title in bulk quantities, or for special sales opportunities (which may include electronic versions; custom cover designs; and content particular to your business, training goals, marketing focus, or branding interests), please contact our corporate sales department at corpsales@pearsoned.com or (800) 382-3419.

For government sales inquiries, please contact governmentsales@pearsoned.com.

For questions about sales outside the U.S., please contact intlcs@pearson.com.

Visit us on the Web: informit.com/aw

Library of Congress Control Number: 2017964125

Editor-in-Chief
Mark Taub

Executive Editor
Laura Lewin

Development Editor
Michael Thurston

Managing Editor
Sandra Schroeder

Tech Editors
Josh Glazer
Brian Overland
Matt Whiting

Senior Project Editor
Lori Lyons

Production Manager
Dhayanidhi Karunanidhi

Copy Editor
Kitty Wilson

Indexer
Lisa Stumpf

Proofreader
Larry Sulky

Editorial Assistant
Courtney Martin

Cover Designer
Chuti Prasertsith

Compositor
codemantra

To my family and friends: Thanks for the support.

Contents at a Glance

Contents

PREFACE

Today, video games are some of the most popular forms of entertainment. Newzoo's "Global Games Market Report" estimates over $100 billion in revenue for games in 2017. This staggering amount shows how popular this field truly is. Because of the size of this market, game programmers are in low supply and high demand.

Alongside this explosion of games, game technology has become increasingly democratized. A single developer can make award-winning and hit games by using one of many popular game engines and tools. For game designers, these tools are fantastic. So what value is there in learning how to program games in C++?

If you take a step back, you can see that many game engines and tools are, at their core, written in C++. This means that C++ is ultimately the technology behind every game created using one of these tools.

Furthermore, top-notch developers who release some of the most popular games today— including *Overwatch*, *Call of Duty*, and *Uncharted*—still predominantly use C++ because it provides a great combination of performance and usability. Thus, any developer who wants to eventually work for one of these companies needs a strong understanding of programming games—specifically in C++.

This book dives into many of the technologies and systems that real game developers use. The basis for much of the material in this book is video game programming courses taught at the University of Southern California over the course of almost a decade. The approach used in this book has successfully prepared many students to make it in the video games industry.

This book is also heavily focused on real working implementations of code integrated into actual game project demos. It is critical to understand how all the various systems that go into a game work together. For this reason, you should keep the source code handy while working through this book.

At this writing, all the code provided with this book works on both PC and macOS, using the Microsoft Visual Studio 2017 and Apple Xcode 9 development environments, respectively.

The source code for this book is available on GitHub, at **https://github.com/gameprogcpp/code.** For instructions on setting up the development environment for this book, see Chapter 1, "Game Programming Overview."

Who Should Read This Book?

This book is for you if you're a programmer who is comfortable with C++ and wants to learn how to program 3D video games. For readers rusty on C++, Appendix A, "Intermediate C++ Review," reviews several C++ concepts. However, if you have with little or no prior C++ experience, you should learn C++ before jumping into this book. (One option is *Programming Abstractions in C++* by Eric Roberts.) This book also expects you to be familiar with some common data structures, including dynamic arrays (vectors), trees, and graphs, and to have some recollection of high school-level algebra.

The topics covered in this book are applicable to readers in academic environments, hobbyists, and junior- and mid-level game programmers who want to expand their knowledge of game programming. The content in this book corresponds to a little more than a semester and a half of material in a university setting.

How This Book Is Organized

This book is intended to be read linearly from Chapter 1 through Chapter 14. However, in case you are not interested in some specific topics, Figure P.1 shows the dependencies between the chapters.

In the first handful of chapters, the games are in 2D as you learn core concepts. From Chapter 6 onward (with the exception of Chapter 8), the games are in 3D.

The chapters cover the following information:

- Chapter 1, "Game Programming Overview," looks at the fundamental concepts of game programming and how to get an initial game up and running. It also introduces the Simple DirectMedia Layer (SDL) library.

- Chapter 2, "Game Objects and 2D Graphics," discusses how programmers organize the objects in their games and explores additional 2D graphics concepts, such as flipbook animation.

- Chapter 3, "Vectors and Basic Physics," covers mathematical vectors, which are critical tools for any game programmer. It also explores the basics of physics, for use with both motion and collisions.

- Chapter 4, "Artificial Intelligence," looks at approaches to make game characters that are computer controlled, including concepts such as state machines and pathfinding.

- Chapter 5, "OpenGL," explores how to create an OpenGL renderer, including implementing vertex and pixel shaders. It includes a discussion of matrices.

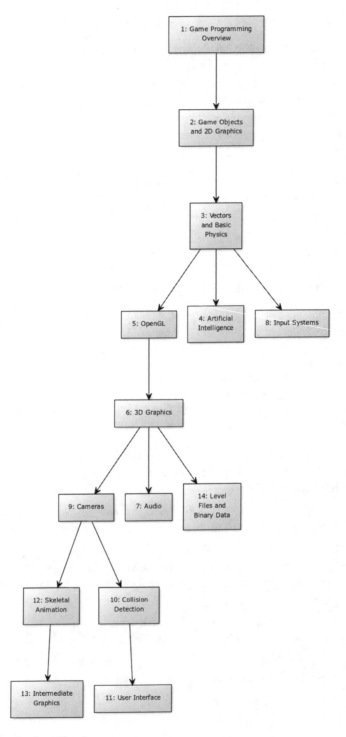

Figure P.1 Chapter dependencies

- Chapter 6, "3D Graphics," focuses on converting the code created so far to work for a 3D game, including how to represent the view, projection, and rotations.

- Chapter 7, "Audio," covers how to bootstrap an audio system using the excellent FMOD API. It includes coverage of 3D positional audio.

- Chapter 8, "Input Systems," discusses how to design a more robust input system for processing keyboard, mouse, and game controller events.

- Chapter 9, "Cameras," shows how to implement several different 3D cameras, including a first-person camera, a follow camera, and an orbit camera.

- Chapter 10, "Collision Detection," dives into methods of collision detection for games, including spheres, planes, line segments, and boxes.

- Chapter 11, "User Interfaces," looks at implementing both a menu system and heads-up display (HUD) elements such as a radar and aiming reticule.

- Chapter 12, "Skeletal Animation," covers how to animate characters in 3D.

- Chapter 13, "Intermediate Graphics," explores a handful of intermediate graphics topics, including how to implement deferred shading.

- Chapter 14, "Level Files and Binary Data," discusses how to load and save level files, as well as how to write binary file formats.

- Appendix A, "Intermediate C++ Review," reviews several intermediate C++ topics used throughout the book including memory allocation and collections.

Each chapter includes a corresponding game project (with source code available, as mentioned), recommended additional readings, and a couple of exercises. These exercises generally instruct you to add additional features to the code implemented in the chapter.

Conventions Used in This Book

New terms appear in **bold**. Code appears in a `monospaced font`. Small snippets of code sometimes appear as standalone paragraphs:

```
DoSomething();
```

Longer code segments appear in code listings, as in Listing P.1.

Listing P.1 Sample Code Listing

```
void DoSomething()
{
    // Do the thing
    ThisDoesSomething();
}
```

From time to time, some paragraphs appear as notes, tips, sidebars, and warnings. Here is an example of each.

> ### note
> Notes contain some useful information about implementation changes or other features that are worth noting.

> ### tip
> Tips provide hints on how to add certain additional features to your code.

> ### warning
> Warnings call out specific pitfalls that warrant caution.

> ### SIDEBAR
> Sidebars are lengthier discussions that are tangential to the main content of the chapter. This content is interesting but isn't crucial to understanding the core topics of the chapter.

ACKNOWLEDGMENTS

Although this is not my first book, writing this one has been an especially long process. I am thankful that Laura Lewin, the executive editor on this book, was especially patient throughout the two years this book was in progress. I would also like to thank the rest of the team at Pearson, including Michael Thurston, the development editor on this book.

I would also like to acknowledge the work put in by the technical editors on this book: Josh Glazer, Brian Overland, and Matt Whiting. The technical reviews were critical in making sure both that the content was correct and that it was accessible for the target audience.

I'd also like to thank all my colleagues at the USC Information Technology Program and especially those who helped shape the curriculum of the games courses I teach: Josh Glazer, Jason Gregory, Clark Kromenaker, Mike Sheehan, and Matt Whiting. Much of the inspiration for this book comes from that curriculum. I would also like to thank all my excellent TAs over the years, who are too numerous to name personally.

I would also like to thank the content creators on sites like https://opengameart.org and https://freesound.org for creating excellent game content released under Creative Commons licenses. These sites were critical to finding assets for the game projects in this book.

Finally, I'd like to thank my parents, as well my sister, Nita, and her family. Without their support, inspiration, and guidance, I never would have gotten here in the first place. I'd also like to thank my friends, like Kevin, who understood when I couldn't go see the latest movie, go to dinner, or really do anything social because I was "working on my book." Well, I guess I have time now.…

ABOUT THE AUTHOR

Sanjay Madhav is a senior lecturer at the University of Southern California, where he teaches several programming and video game programming courses. He has taught at USC since 2008.

Prior to joining USC, Sanjay worked as a programmer for several video game developers, including Electronic Arts, Neversoft, and Pandemic Studios. His credited games include *Medal of Honor: Pacific Assault*, *Tony Hawk's Project 8*, *Lord of the Rings: Conquest*, and *The Saboteur*.

Sanjay is also the author of *Game Programming Algorithms and Techniques* and co-author of *Multiplayer Game Programming*. He has a B.S. and an M.S. in computer science and is pursuing a Ph.D. in computer science, all from USC.

CHAPTER 1

GAME PROGRAMMING OVERVIEW

This chapter first discusses how to set up a development environment and access the source code for this book. Next, it covers the core concepts behind any real-time game: the game loop, how a game updates over time, and the basics of game input and output. Throughout the chapter, you will see how to implement code for a version of the classic game *Pong*.

Setting Up a Development Environment

Although it's possible to write the source code for any program with a text editor, professional developers typically use an **integrated development environment (IDE)**. The advantage of an IDE is that it provides code completion and debugging in addition to text editing capabilities. The code for this book works on both Microsoft Windows and Apple macOS, and the choice of IDE depends on the choice of platform. For Windows, this book uses Microsoft Visual Studio, and for macOS, it uses Apple Xcode. The remainder of this section contains brief instructions on setup of these environments on their respective platforms.

Microsoft Windows

For Windows development, the most popular IDE by far is Microsoft Visual Studio. Visual Studio also tends to be the most popular IDE for C++ game developers, with most PC and console developers gravitating toward the IDE.

This book uses Microsoft Visual Studio Community 2017, which is available as a free download at https://www.visualstudio.com/downloads/. Installation of Visual Studio Community 2017 requires Microsoft Windows 7 or higher.

When you run the installer program for Visual Studio, it asks which "workloads" it should install. Make sure to minimally select the Game Development with C++ workload. Feel free to also select any other workloads or options desired.

> ### warning
>
> **THERE ARE DIFFERENT VERSIONS OF VISUAL STUDIO**   There are several other products in the Microsoft Visual Studio suite, including Visual Studio Code and Visual Studio for Mac. Neither of these products are the same thing as Visual Studio Community 2017, so be careful to install the correct version!

Apple macOS

On macOS, Apple provides the free Xcode IDE for development of programs for macOS, iOS, and other related platforms. The code for this book works in both Xcode 8 and 9. Note that Xcode 8 requires macOS 10.11 El Capitan or higher, while Xcode 9 requires macOS 10.12 Sierra or higher.

To install Xcode, simply go to the Apple App Store and search for Xcode. The first time Xcode runs, it asks if you want to enable debugging features. Make sure to select Yes.

Getting This Book's Source Code

Most professional developers utilize **source control** systems, which, among many other features, keep a history of the source code. With such a system, if code changes cause unexpected or undesired behavior, it's easy to return to a previously known working version of code. Furthermore, source control allows for much easier collaboration between multiple developers.

One popular source control system is Git, originally developed by Linus Torvalds of Linux fame. In Git, the term **repository** refers to a specific project hosted under source control. The GitHub website (https://github.com) provides for easy creation and management of Git repositories.

The source code for this book is available on GitHub at https://github.com/gameprogcpp/code. If you are unfamiliar with the Git system, you can simply click the green Clone or Download button and choose Download ZIP to download a compressed ZIP file that contains all the book's source code.

Alternatively, if you wish to use Git, you can clone the repository via the command line, as follows:

```
$ git clone https://github.com/gameprogcpp/code.git
```

This command works out of the box in the macOS terminal, but Windows users need to first install Git for Windows (see https://git-for-windows.github.io).

The source code contains a separate directory (or folder) for each chapter. For example, this chapter's source code is in the `Chapter01` directory. In this directory, there is a `Chapter01-Windows.sln` file for Microsoft Visual Studio and a `Chapter01-Mac.xcodeproj` file for Apple Xcode. Before moving forward, make sure that you can compile the code for this chapter.

Beyond the C++ Standard Library

The C++ Standard Library only supports text console input and output and does not have any graphics libraries built in. To implement graphics in a C++ program, you must use one of the many available external libraries.

Unfortunately, many libraries are **platform specific**, meaning they work on only one operating system or type of computer. For example, the Microsoft Windows application programming interface (API) can create windows and other UI elements supported by the Windows operating system. However, the Windows API doesn't work on Apple macOS—for obvious reasons. Likewise, macOS has its own set of libraries for these same features that do not work on Windows. As a game programmer, you can't always avoid platform-specific libraries. For instance, game developers working with the Sony PlayStation 4 console must use libraries provided by Sony.

Luckily, this book sticks to **cross-platform** libraries, meaning that the libraries work on many different platforms. All the source code for this book works on recent versions of both Windows and macOS. Although Linux support is untested, the game projects generally should also work on Linux.

One of the foundational libraries used in this book is Simple DirectMedia Layer (SDL; see https://www.libsdl.org). The SDL library is a cross-platform game development library written in C. It provides support for creating windows, creating basic 2D graphics, processing input, and outputting audio, among other features. SDL is a very lightweight library that works on many platforms, including Microsoft Windows, Apple macOS, Linux, iOS, and Android.

In this first chapter, the only external library needed is SDL. Subsequent chapters use other libraries and introduce them when needed.

The Game Loop and Game Class

One of the big differences between a game and any other program is that a game must update many times per second for as long as the program runs. A **game loop** is a loop that controls the overall flow for the entire game program. Like any other loop, a game loop has code it executes on every iteration, and it has a loop condition. For a game loop, you want to continue looping as long as the player hasn't quit the game program.

Each iteration of a game loop is a **frame**. If a game runs at 60 **frames per second** (**FPS**), this means the game loop completes 60 iterations every second. Many real-time games run at 30 or 60 FPS. By running this many iterations per second, the game gives the illusion of continuous motion even though it's only updating at periodic intervals. The term **frame rate** is interchangeable with FPS; a frame rate of 60 means the same thing as 60 FPS.

Anatomy of a Frame

At a high level, a game performs the following steps on each frame:

1. It processes any inputs.
2. It updates the game world.
3. It generates any outputs.

Each of these three steps has more depth than may be apparent at first glance. For instance, processing inputs (step 1) clearly implies detecting any inputs from devices such as a keyboard, mouse, or controller. But these might not be the only inputs for a game. Consider a game that supports an online multiplayer mode. In this case, the game receives data over the Internet as an input. In certain types of mobile games, another input might be what's visible to the camera, or perhaps GPS information. Ultimately, the inputs to a game depend on both the type of game and the platform it runs on.

Updating a game world (step 2) means going through every object in the game world and updating it as needed. This could be hundreds or even thousands of objects, including characters in the game world, parts of the user interface, and other objects that affect the game—even if they are not visible.

For step 3, generating any outputs, the most apparent output is the graphics. But there are other outputs, such as audio (including sound effects, music, and dialogue). As another example, most console games have **force feedback** effects, such as the controller shaking when something exciting happens in the game. And for an online multiplayer game, an additional output would be data sent to the other players over the Internet.

Consider how this style of game loop might apply to a simplified version of the classic Namco arcade game *Pac-Man*. For this simplified version of the game, assume that the game immediately begins with Pac-Man in a maze. The game program continues running until Pac-Man either completes the maze or dies. In this case, the "process inputs" phase of the game loop need only read in the joystick input.

The "update game world" phase of the loop updates Pac-Man based on this joystick input and then also updates the four ghosts, pellets, and the user interface. Part of this update code must determine whether Pac-Man runs into any ghosts. Pac-Man can also eat any pellets or fruits he moves over, so the update portion of the loop also needs to check for this. Because the ghosts are fully AI controlled, they also must update their logic. Finally, based on what Pac-Man is doing, the UI may need to update what data it displays.

> ### note
> This style of game loop is **single-threaded**, meaning it does not take advantage of modern CPUs that can execute multiple threads simultaneously. Making a game loop that supports multiple threads is very complex, and not necessary for games that are smaller in scope. A good book to learn more about multi-threaded game loops is Jason Gregory's, listed in the "Additional Reading" section at the end of this chapter.

The only outputs in the "generate outputs" phase of the classic *Pac-Man* game are the audio and video. Listing 1.1 provides pseudocode showing what the game loop for this simplified version of *Pac-Man* might look like.

Listing 1.1   *Pac-Man* Game Loop Pseudocode

```
void Game::RunLoop()
{
    while (!mShouldQuit)
    {
        // Process Inputs
        JoystickData j = GetJoystickData();

        // Update Game World
        UpdatePlayerPosition(j);

        for (Ghost& g : mGhost)
        {
            if (g.Collides(player))
            {
                // Handle Pac-Man colliding with a ghost
            }
            else
            {
                g.Update();
            }
        }

        // Handle Pac-Man eating pellets
        // ...

        // Generate Outputs
        RenderGraphics();
        RenderAudio();
    }
}
```

Implementing a Skeleton Game Class

You are now ready to use your basic knowledge of the game loop to create a Game class that contains code to initialize and shut down the game as well as run the game loop. If you are rusty in C++, you might want to first review the content in Appendix A, "Intermediate C++ Review," as the remainder of this book assumes familiarity with C++. In addition, it may be helpful to keep this chapter's completed source code handy while reading along, as doing so will help you understand how all the pieces fit together.

Listing 1.2 shows the declaration of the Game class in the Game.h header file. Because this declaration references an SDL_Window pointer, you need to also include the main SDL header file SDL/SDL.h. (If you wanted to avoid including this here, you could use a forward declaration.) Many of the member function names are self-explanatory; for example, the Initialize function initializes the Game class, the Shutdown function shuts down the game, and the RunLoop function runs the game loop. Finally, ProcessInput, UpdateGame, and GenerateOutput correspond to the three steps of the game loop.

Currently, the only member variables are a pointer to the window (which you'll create in the Initialize function) and a bool that signifies whether the game should continue running the game loop.

Listing 1.2 Game Declaration

```cpp
class Game
{
public:
    Game();
    // Initialize the game
    bool Initialize();
    // Runs the game loop until the game is over
    void RunLoop();
    // Shutdown the game
    void Shutdown();
private:
    // Helper functions for the game loop
    void ProcessInput();
    void UpdateGame();
    void GenerateOutput();

    // Window created by SDL
    SDL_Window* mWindow;
    // Game should continue to run
    bool mIsRunning;
};
```

With this declaration in place, you can start implementing the member functions in Game.cpp. The constructor simply initializes mWindow to nullptr and mIsRunning to true.

Game::Initialize

The Initialize function returns true if initialization succeeds and false otherwise. You need to initialize the SDL library with the SDL_Init function. This function takes in a single parameter, a bitwise-OR of all subsystems to initialize. For now, you only need to initialize the video subsystem, which you do as follows:

```cpp
int sdlResult = SDL_Init(SDL_INIT_VIDEO);
```

Note that `SDL_Init` returns an integer. If this integer is nonzero, it means the initialization failed. In this case, `Game::Initialize` should return `false` because without SDL, the game cannot continue:

```
if (sdlResult != 0)
{
    SDL_Log("Unable to initialize SDL: %s", SDL_GetError());
    return false;
}
```

Using the `SDL_Log` function is a simple way to output messages to the console in SDL. It uses the same syntax as the C `printf` function, so it supports outputting variables to `printf` specifiers such as `%s` for a C-style string and `%d` for an integer. The `SDL_GetError` function returns an error message as a C-style string, which is why it's passed in as the `%s` parameter in this code.

SDL contains several different subsystems that you can initialize with `SDL_Init`. Table 1.1 shows the most commonly used subsystems; for the full list, consult the SDL API reference at https://wiki.libsdl.org.

Table 1.1 SDL Subsystem Flags of Note

Flag	Subsystem
SDL_INIT_AUDIO	Audio device management, playback, and recording
SDL_INIT_VIDEO	Video subsystem for creating a window, interfacing with OpenGL, and 2D graphics
SDL_INIT_HAPTIC	Force feedback subsystem
SDL_INIT_GAMECONTROLLER	Subsystem for supporting controller input devices

If SDL initializes successfully, the next step is to create a window with the `SDL_CreateWindow` function. This is just like the window that any other Windows or macOS program uses. The `SDL_CreateWindow` function takes in several parameters: the title of the window, the x/y coordinates of the top-left corner, the width/height of the window, and optionally any window creation flags:

```
mWindow = SDL_CreateWindow(
    "Game Programming in C++ (Chapter 1)", // Window title
    100,    // Top left x-coordinate of window
    100,    // Top left y-coordinate of window
    1024,   // Width of window
    768,    // Height of window
    0       // Flags (0 for no flags set)
);
```

As with the `SDL_Init` call, you should verify that `SDL_CreateWindow` succeeded. In the event of failure, `mWindow` will be `nullptr`, so add this check:

```
if (!mWindow)
{
    SDL_Log("Failed to create window: %s", SDL_GetError());
    return false;
}
```

As with the initialization flags, there are several possible window creation flags, as shown in Table 1.2. As before, you can use a bitwise-OR to pass in multiple flags. Although many commercial games use full-screen mode, it's faster to debug code if the game runs in windowed mode, which is why this book shies away from full screen.

Table 1.2   Window Creation Flags of Note

Flag	Result
SDL_WINDOW_FULLSCREEN	Use full-screen mode
SDL_WINDOW_FULLSCREEN_DESKTOP	Use full-screen mode at the current desktop resolution (and ignore width/height parameters to SDL_CreateWindow)
SDL_WINDOW_OPENGL	Add support for the OpenGL graphics library
SDL_WINDOW_RESIZABLE	Allow the user to resize the window

If SDL initialization and window creation succeeds, `Game::Initialize` returns `true`.

Game::Shutdown

The `Shutdown` function does the opposite of `Initialize`. It first destroys the `SDL_Window` with `SDL_DestroyWindow` and then closes SDL with `SDL_Quit`:

```
void Game::Shutdown()
{
    SDL_DestroyWindow(mWindow);
    SDL_Quit();
}
```

Game::RunLoop

The `RunLoop` function keeps running iterations of the game loop until `mIsRunning` becomes `false`, at which point the function returns. Because you have the three helper functions for each phase of the game loop, `RunLoop` simply calls these helper functions inside the loop:

```
void Game::RunLoop()
{
    while (mIsRunning)
    {
        ProcessInput();
```

```
      UpdateGame();
      GenerateOutput();
   }
}
```

For now, you won't implement these three helper functions, which means that once in the loop, the game won't do anything just yet. You'll continue to build on this Game class and implement these helper functions throughout the remainder of the chapter.

Main Function

Although the Game class is a handy encapsulation of the game's behavior, the entry point of any C++ program is the main function. You must implement a main function (in Main.cpp) as shown in Listing 1.3.

Listing 1.3   main Implementation

```
int main(int argc, char** argv)
{
   Game game;
   bool success = game.Initialize();
   if (success)
   {
      game.RunLoop();
   }
   game.Shutdown();
   return 0;
}
```

This implementation of main first constructs an instance of the Game class. It then calls Initialize, which returns true if the game successfully initializes, and false otherwise. If the game initializes, you then enter the game loop with the call to RunLoop. Finally, once the loop ends, you call Shutdown on the game.

With this code in place, you can now run the game project. When you do, you see a blank window, as shown in Figure 1.1 (though on macOS, this window may appear black instead of white). Of course, there's a problem: The game never ends! Because no code changes the mIsRunning member variable, the game loop never ends, and the RunLoop function never returns. Naturally, the next step is to fix this problem by allowing the player to quit the game.

Figure 1.1 Creating a blank window

Basic Input Processing

In any desktop operating system, there are several actions that the user can perform on application windows. For example, the user can move a window, minimize or maximize a window, close a window (and program), and so on. A common way to represent these different actions is with events. When the user does something, the program receives events from the operating system and can choose to respond to these events.

SDL manages an internal queue of events that it receives from the operating system. This queue contains events for many different window actions, as well as events related to input devices. Every frame, the game must poll the queue for any events and choose either to ignore or process each event in the queue. For some events, such as moving the window around, ignoring the event means SDL will just automatically handle it. But for other events, ignoring the event means nothing will happen.

Because events are a type of input, it makes sense to implement event processing in `ProcessInput`. Because the event queue may contain multiple events on any given frame, you must loop over all events in the queue. The SDL_PollEvent function returns true if it finds an event in the queue. So, a very basic implementation of ProcessInput would keep calling SDL_PollEvent as long as it returns true:

```
void Game::ProcessInput()
{
    SDL_Event event;
    // While there are still events in the queue
    while (SDL_PollEvent(&event))
    {
    }
}
```

Note that the SDL_PollEvent function takes in an SDL_Event by pointer. This stores any information about the event just removed from the queue.

Although this version of ProcessInput makes the game window more responsive, the player still has no way to quit the game. This is because you simply remove all the events from the queue and don't respond to them.

Given an SDL_Event, the type member variable contains the type of the event received. So, a common approach is to create a switch based on the type inside the PollEvent loop:

```
SDL_Event event;
while (SDL_PollEvent(&event))
{
    switch (event.type)
    {
        // Handle different event types here
    }
}
```

One useful event is SDL_QUIT, which the game receives when the user tries to close the window (either by clicking on the X or using a keyboard shortcut). You can update the code to set mIsRunning to false when it sees an SDL_QUIT event in the queue:

```
SDL_Event event;
while (SDL_PollEvent(&event))
{
    switch (event.type)
    {
        case SDL_QUIT:
            mIsRunning = false;
            break;
    }
}
```

Now when the game is running, clicking the X on the window causes the `while` loop inside `RunLoop` to terminate, which in turn shuts down the game and exits the program. But what if you want the game to quit when the user presses the Escape key? While you could check for a keyboard event corresponding to this, an easier approach is to grab the entire state of the keyboard with `SDL_GetKeyboardState`, which returns a pointer to an array that contains the current state of the keyboard:

```
const Uint8* state = SDL_GetKeyboardState(NULL);
```

Given this array, you can then query a specific key by indexing into this array with a corresponding `SDL_SCANCODE` value for the key. For example, the following sets `mIsRunning` to `false` if the user presses Escape:

```
if (state[SDL_SCANCODE_ESCAPE])
{
   mIsRunning = false;
}
```

Combining all this yields the current version of `ProcessInput`, shown in Listing 1.4. Now when running the game, the user can quit either by closing the window or pressing the Escape key.

Listing 1.4 Game::`ProcessInput` Implementation

```
void Game::ProcessInput()
{
   SDL_Event event;
   while (SDL_PollEvent(&event))
   {
      switch (event.type)
      {
         // If this is an SDL_QUIT event, end loop
         case SDL_QUIT:
            mIsRunning = false;
            break;
      }
   }

   // Get state of keyboard
   const Uint8* state = SDL_GetKeyboardState(NULL);
   // If escape is pressed, also end loop
   if (state[SDL_SCANCODE_ESCAPE])
   {
      mIsRunning = false;
   }
}
```

Basic 2D Graphics

Before you can implement the "generate outputs" phase of the game loop, you need some understanding of how 2D graphics work for games

Most displays in use today—whether televisions, computer monitors, tablets, or smartphones—use **raster graphics**, which means the display has a two-dimensional grid of picture elements (or **pixels**). These pixels can individually display different amounts of light as well as different colors. The intensity and color of these pixels combine to create a perception of a continuous image for the viewer. Zooming in on a part of a raster image makes each individual pixel discernable, as you can see in Figure 1.2.

Figure 1.2 Zooming in on part of an image shows its distinct pixels

The **resolution** of a raster display refers to the width and height of the pixel grid. For example, a resolution of 1920×1080, commonly known as 1080p, means that there are 1080 rows of pixels, with each row containing 1920 pixels. Similarly, a resolution of 3840×2160, known as 4K, has 2160 rows with 3840 pixels per row.

Color displays mix colors additively to create a specific hue for each pixel. A common approach is to mix three colors together: red, green, and blue (abbreviated **RGB**). Different intensities of these RGB colors combine to create a range (or **gamut**) of colors. Although many modern displays also support color formats other than RGB, most video games output final colors in RGB. Whether or not RGB values convert to something else for display on the monitor is outside the purview of the game programmer.

However, many games *internally* use a different color representation for much of their graphics computations. For example, many games internally support transparency with an **alpha** value. The abbreviation **RGBA** references RGB colors with an additional alpha component. Adding an alpha component allows certain objects in a game, such as windows, to have some amount of transparency. But because few if any displays support transparency, the game ultimately needs to calculate a final RGB color and compute any perceived transparency itself.

The Color Buffer

For a display to show an RGB image, it must know the colors of each pixel. In computer graphics, the **color buffer** is a location in memory containing the color information for the entire screen. The display can use the color buffer for drawing the contents screen. Think of the color buffer as a two-dimensional array, where each (x, y) index corresponds to a pixel on the screen. In every frame during the "generate outputs" phase of the game loop, the game writes graphical output into the color buffer.

The memory usage of the color buffer depends on the number of bits that represent each pixel, called the **color depth**. For example, in the common 24-bit color depth, red, green, and blue each use 8 bits. This means there are 2^{24}, or 16,777,216, unique colors. If the game also wants to store an 8-bit alpha value, this results in a total of 32 bits for each pixel in the color buffer. A color buffer for a 1080p (1920×1080) target resolution with 32 bits per pixel uses 1920×1080×4 bytes, or approximately 7.9 MB.

> ### note
> Many game programmers also use the term **framebuffer** to reference the location in memory that contains the color data for a frame. However, a more precise definition of *framebuffer* is that it is the combination of the color buffer *and* other buffers (such as the depth buffer and stencil buffer). In the interest of clarity, this book references the specific buffers.

Some recent games use 16 bits per RGB component, which increases the number of unique colors. Of course, this doubles the memory usage of the color buffer, up to approximately 16 MB for 1080p. This may seem like an insignificant amount, given that most video cards have several gigabytes of video memory available. But when considering all the other memory usage of a cutting-edge game, 8 MB here and 8 MB there quickly adds up. Although most displays at this writing do not support 16 bits per color, some manufacturers now offer displays that support color depths higher than 8 bits per color.

Given an 8-bit value for a color, there are two ways to reference this value in code. One approach involves simply using an unsigned integer corresponding to the number of bits for each color (or **channel**). So, for a color depth with 8 bits per channel, each channel has a value between 0 and 255. The alternative approach is to normalize the integer over a decimal range from 0.0 to 1.0.

One advantage of using a decimal range is that a value yields roughly the same color, regardless of the underlying color depth. For example, the normalized RGB value (1.0, 0.0, 0.0) yields pure red whether the maximum value of red is 255 (8 bits per color) or 65,535 (16 bits per color). However, the unsigned integer RGB value (255, 0, 0) yields pure red only if there are 8 bits per color. With 16 bits per color, (255, 0, 0) is nearly black.

Converting between these two representations is straightforward. Given an unsigned integer value, divide it by the maximum unsigned integer value to get the normalized value. Conversely, given a normalized decimal value, multiply it by the maximum unsigned integer value to get an unsigned integer value. For now, you should use unsigned integers because the SDL library expects them.

Double Buffering

As mentioned earlier in this chapter, games update several times per second (at the common rates of 30 and 60 FPS). If a game updates the color buffer at the same rate, this gives the illusion of motion, much the way a flipbook appears to show an object in motion when you flip through the pages.

However, the **refresh rate**, or the frequency at which the display updates, may be different from the game's frame rate. For example, most NTSC TV displays have a refresh rate of 59.94 Hz, meaning they refresh very slightly less than 60 times per second. However, some newer computer monitors support a 144 Hz refresh rate, which is more than twice as fast.

Furthermore, no current display technology can instantaneously update the entire screen at once. There always is some update order—whether row by row, column by column, in a checkerboard, and so on. Whatever update pattern the display uses, it takes some fraction of a second for the whole screen to update.

Suppose a game writes to the color buffer, and the display reads from that same color buffer. Because the timing of the game's frame rate may not directly match the monitor's refresh rate, it's very like that the display will read from the color buffer while the game is writing to the buffer. This can be problematic.

For example, suppose the game writes the graphical data for frame A into the color buffer. The display then starts reading from the color buffer to show frame A on the screen. However, before the display finishes drawing frame A onto the screen, the game overwrites the color buffer with the graphical data for frame B. The display ends up showing part of frame A *and* part of frame B on the screen. Figure 1.3 illustrates this problem, known as **screen tearing**.

Tear

Figure 1.3 Simulation of screen tearing with a camera panning to the right

Eliminating screen tearing requires two changes. First, rather than having one color buffer that the game and display must share, you create two separate color buffers. Then the game and display alternate between the color buffers they use every frame. The idea is that with two separate buffers, the game can write to one (the **back buffer**) and, at the same time, the display can read from the other one (the **front buffer**). After the frame completes, the game and display swap their buffers. Due to the use of two color buffers, the name for this technique is **double buffering**.

As a more concrete example, consider the process shown in Figure 1.4. On frame A, the game writes its graphical output to buffer X, and the display draws buffer Y to the screen (which is empty). When this process completes, the game and display swap which buffers they use. Then on frame B, the game draws its graphical output to buffer Y, while the display shows buffer X on screen. On frame C, the game returns to buffer X, and the display returns to buffer Y. This swapping between the two buffers continues until the game program closes.

However, double buffering by itself does not eliminate screen tearing. Screen tearing still occurs if the display is drawing buffer X when the game wants to start writing to X. This usually happens only if the game is updating too quickly. The solution to this problem is to wait until the display finishes drawing its buffer before swapping. In other words, if the display is still drawing buffer X when the game wants to swap back to buffer X, the game must wait until the display finishes drawing buffer X. Developers call this approach **vertical synchronization**, or **vsync**, named after the signal that monitors send when they are about to refresh the screen.

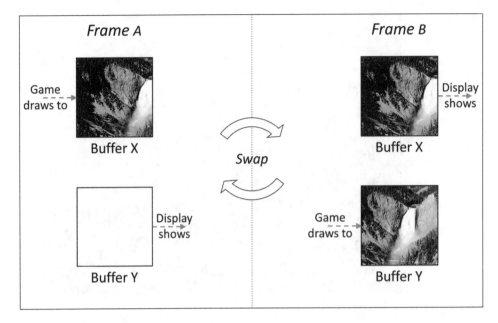

Figure 1.4 Double buffering involves swapping the buffers used by the game and display every frame

With vertical synchronization, the game might have to occasionally wait for a fraction of a second for the display to be ready. This means that the game loop may not be able to achieve its target frame rate of 30 or 60 FPS exactly. Some players argue that this causes unacceptable stuttering of the frame rate. Thus, the decision on whether to enable vsync varies depending on the game or player. A good idea is to offer vsync as an option in the engine so that you can choose between occasional screen tearing or occasional stuttering.

Recent advances in display technology seek to solve this dilemma with an **adaptive refresh rate** that varies based on the game. With this approach, rather than the display notifying the game when it refreshes, the game tells the display when to refresh. This way, the game and display are in sync. This provides the best of both worlds as it eliminates both screen tearing and frame rate stuttering. Unfortunately, at this writing, adaptive refresh technology is currently available only on certain high-end computer monitors.

Implementing Basic 2D Graphics

SDL has a simple set of functions for drawing 2D graphics. Because the focus of this chapter is 2D, you can stick with these functions. Starting in Chapter 5, "OpenGL," you'll switch to the OpenGL library for graphics, as it supports both 2D and 3D.

Initialization and Shutdown

To use SDL's graphics code, you need to construct an `SDL_Renderer` via the `SDL_CreateRenderer` function. The term **renderer** generically refers to any system that draws graphics, whether 2D or 3D. Because you need to reference this `SDL_Renderer` object every time you draw something, first add an `mRenderer` member variable to `Game`:

```
SDL_Renderer* mRenderer;
```

Next, in `Game::Initialize`, after creating the window, create the renderer:

```
mRenderer = SDL_CreateRenderer(
    mWindow, // Window to create renderer for
    -1,      // Usually -1
    SDL_RENDERER_ACCELERATED | SDL_RENDERER_PRESENTVSYNC
);
```

The first parameter to `SDL_CreateRenderer` is the pointer to the window (which you saved in `mWindow`). The second parameter specifies which graphics driver to use; this might be relevant if the game has multiple windows. But with only a single window, the default is `-1`, which means to let SDL decide. As with the other SDL creation functions, the last parameter is for initialization flags. Here, you choose to use an accelerated renderer (meaning it takes advantage of graphics hardware) and enable vertical synchronization. These two flags are the only flags of note for `SDL_CreateRenderer`.

As with `SDL_CreateWindow`, the `SDL_CreateRenderer` function returns a `nullptr` if it fails to initialize the renderer. As with initializing SDL, `Game::Initialize` returns `false` if the renderer fails to initialize.

To shut down the renderer, simply add a call to `SDL_DestroyRenderer` in `Game::Shutdown`:

```
SDL_DestroyRenderer(mRenderer);
```

Basic Drawing Setup

At a high level, drawing in any graphics library for games usually involves the following steps:

1. Clear the back buffer to a color (the game's current buffer).
2. Draw the entire game scene.
3. Swap the front buffer and back buffer.

First, let's worry about the first and third steps. Because graphics are an output, it makes sense to put graphics drawing code in `Game::GenerateOutput`.

To clear the back buffer, you first need to specify a color with `SDL_SetRenderDrawColor`. This function takes in a pointer to the renderer, as well as the four RGBA components (from 0 to 255). For example, to set the color as blue with 100% opacity, use the following:

```
SDL_SetRenderDrawColor(
    mRenderer,
    0,    // R
    0,    // G
    255,  // B
    255   // A
);
```

Next, call `SDL_RenderClear` to clear the back buffer to the current draw color:

```
SDL_RenderClear(mRenderer);
```

The next step—skipped for now—is to draw the entire game scene.

Finally, to swap the front and back buffers, you call `SDL_RenderPresent`:

```
SDL_RenderPresent(mRenderer);
```

With this code in place, if you now run the game, you'll see a filled-in blue window, as shown in Figure 1.5.

Drawing Walls, a Ball, and a Paddle

This chapter's game project is a version of the classic video game *Pong*, where a ball moves around the screen, and the player controls a paddle that can hit the ball. Making a version of *Pong* is a rite of passage for any aspiring game developer—analogous to making a "Hello World" program when first learning how to program. This section explores drawing rectangles to represent the objects in *Pong*. Because these are objects in the game world, you draw them in `GenerateOuput`—after clearing the back buffer but before swapping the front and back buffers.

For drawing filled rectangles, SDL has a `SDL_RenderFillRect` function. This function takes in an `SDL_Rect` that represents the bounds of the rectangle and draws a filled-in rectangle using the current draw color. Of course, if you keep the draw color the same as the background, you won't see any rectangles. You therefore need to change the draw color to white:

```
SDL_SetRenderDrawColor(mRenderer, 255, 255, 255, 255);
```

Figure 1.5 Game drawing a blue background

Next, to draw the rectangle, you need to specify dimensions via an SDL_Rect struct. The rectangle has four parameters: the x/y coordinates of the top-left corner of the rectangle onscreen, and the width/height of the rectangle. Keep in mind that in SDL rendering, as in many other 2D graphics libraries, the top-left corner of the screen is (0, 0), positive x is to the right, and positive y is down.

For example, if you want to draw a rectangle at the top of the screen, you can use the following declaration of an SDL_Rect:

```
SDL_Rect wall{
    0,          // Top left x
    0,          // Top left y
    1024,       // Width
    thickness // Height
};
```

Here, the x/y coordinates of the top-left corner are (0, 0), meaning the rectangle will be at the top left of the screen. You hard-code the width of the rectangle to 1024, corresponding to the width of the window. (It's generally frowned upon to assume a fixed window size, as is done here, and you'll remove this assumption in later chapters.) The thickness variable is const int set to 15, which makes it easy to adjust the thickness of the wall.

Finally, you draw the rectangle with `SDL_RenderFillRect`, passing in `SDL_Rect` by pointer:

```
SDL_RenderFillRect(mRenderer, &wall);
```

The game then draws a wall in the top part of the screen. You can use similar code to draw the bottom wall and the right wall, only changing the parameters of the `SDL_Rect`. For example, the bottom wall could have the same rectangle as the top wall except that the top-left y coordinate could be `768 - thickness`.

Unfortunately, hard-coding the rectangles for the ball and paddle does not work because both objects will ultimately move in the `UpdateGame` stage of the loop. Although it makes some sense to represent both the ball and paddle as classes, this discussion doesn't happen until Chapter 2, "Game Objects and 2D Graphics." In the meantime, you can just use member variables to store the center positions of both objects and draw their rectangles based on these positions.

First, declare a simple `Vector2` struct that has both x and y components:

```
struct Vector2
{
    float x;
    float y;
};
```

For now, think of a vector (not a `std::vector`) as a simple container for coordinates. Chapter 3, "Vectors and Basic Physics," explores the topic of vectors in much greater detail.

Next, add two `Vector2`s as member variables to `Game`—one for the paddle position (`mPaddlePos`) and one for the ball's position (`mBallPos`). The game constructor then initializes these to sensible initial values: the ball position to the center of the screen and the paddle position to the center of the left side of the screen.

Armed with these member variables, you can then draw rectangles for the ball and paddle in `GenerateOutput`. However, keep in mind that the member variables represent the *center points* of the paddle and ball, while you define an `SDL_Rect` in terms of the *top-left point*. To convert from the center point to the top-left point, you simply subtract half the width/height from the x and y coordinates, respectively. For example, the following rectangle works for the ball:

```
SDL_Rect ball{
    static_cast<int>(mBallPos.x - thickness/2),
    static_cast<int>(mBallPos.y - thickness/2),
    thickness,
    thickness
};
```

The static casts here convert `mBallPos.x` and `mBallPos.y` from floats into integers (which `SDL_Rect` uses). In any event, you can make a similar calculation for drawing the paddle, except its width and height are different sizes.

With all these rectangles, the basic game drawing now works, as shown in Figure 1.6. The next step is to implement the `UpdateGame` phase of the loop, which moves the ball and paddle.

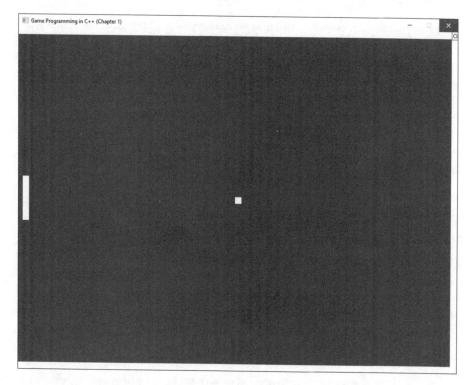

Figure 1.6 A game with walls, a paddle, and a ball drawing

Updating the Game

Most video games have some concept of time progression. For real-time games, you measure this progression of time in fractions of a second. For example, a game running at 30 FPS has roughly 33 milliseconds (ms) elapse from frame to frame. Remember that even though a game appears to feature continuous movement, it is merely an illusion. The game loop *actually* runs several times per second, and every iteration of the game loop updates the game in a discrete time step. So, in the 30 FPS example, each iteration of the game loop should simulate 33ms of time progression in the game. This section looks at how to consider this discrete progression of time when programming a game.

Real Time and Game Time

It is important to distinguish **real time**, the time elapsing in the real world, from **game time**, the time elapsing in the game's world. Although there often is a 1:1 correspondence between real time and game time, this isn't always the case. Take, for instance, a game in a paused state. Although a great deal of time might elapse in the real world, the game doesn't advance at all. It's not until the player unpauses the game that the game time resumes updating.

There are many other instances where real time and game time might diverge. For example, some games feature a "bullet time" gameplay mechanic that reduces the speed of the game. In this case, the game time must update at a substantially slower rate than actual time. On the opposite end of the spectrum, many sports games feature sped-up time. In a football game, rather than requiring a player to sit through 15 full minutes per quarter, the game may update the clock twice as fast, so each quarter takes only 7.5 minutes. And some games may even have time advance in reverse. For example, *Prince of Persia: The Sands of Time* featured a unique mechanic where the player could rewind the game time to a certain point.

With all these ways real time and game time might diverge, it's clear that the "update game" phase of the game loop should account for elapsed game time.

Logic as a Function of Delta Time

Early game programmers assumed a specific processor speed and, therefore, a specific frame rate. The programmer might write the code assuming an 8 MHz processor, and if it worked properly for those processors, the code was just fine. When assuming a fixed frame rate, code that updates the position of an enemy might look something like this:

```
// Update x position by 5 pixels
enemy.mPosition.x += 5;
```

If this code moves the enemy at the desired speed on an 8 MHz processor, what happens on a 16 MHz processor? Well, because the game loop now runs twice as fast, the enemy will now also *move* twice as fast. This could be the difference between a game that's challenging for players and one that's impossible. Imagine running this game on a modern processor that is thousands of times faster. The game would be over in a heartbeat!

To solve this issue, games use **delta time**: the amount of elapsed game time since the last frame. To convert the preceding code to using delta time, instead of thinking of movement as pixels per frame, you should think of it as pixels per second. So, if the ideal movement speed is 150 pixels per second, the following code is much more flexible:

```
// Update x position by 150 pixels/second
enemy.mPosition.x += 150 * deltaTime;
```

Now the code will work well regardless of the frame rate. At 30 FPS, the delta time is ~0.033, so the enemy will move 5 pixels per frame, for a total of 150 pixels per second. At 60 FPS, the enemy will move only 2.5 pixels per frame but will still move a total of 150 pixels per second. The movement certainly will be smoother in the 60 FPS case, but the overall per-second speed remains the same.

Because this works across many frame rates, as a rule of thumb, everything in the game world should update as a function of delta time.

To help calculate delta time, SDL provides an `SDL_GetTicks` member function that returns the number of milliseconds elapsed since the `SDL_Init` function call. By saving the result of `SDL_GetTicks` from the previous frame in a member variable, you can use the current value to calculate delta time.

First, you declare an `mTicksCount` member variable (initializing it to zero in the constructor):

```
Uint32 mTicksCount;
```

Using `SDL_GetTicks`, you can then create a first implementation of `Game::UpdateGame`:

```
void Game::UpdateGame()
{
    // Delta time is the difference in ticks from last frame
    // (converted to seconds)
    float deltaTime = (SDL_GetTicks() - mTicksCount) / 1000.0f;
    // Update tick counts (for next frame)
    mTicksCount = SDL_GetTicks();

    // TODO: Update objects in game world as function of delta time!
    // ...
}
```

Consider what happens the very first time you call `UpdateGame`. Because `mTicksCount` starts at zero, you end up with some positive value of `SDL_GetTicks` (the milliseconds since initialization) and divide it by `1000.0f` to get a delta time in seconds. Next, you save the current value of `SDL_GetTicks` in `mTicksCount`. On the next frame, the `deltaTime` line calculates a new delta time based on the old value of `mTicksCount` and the new value. Thus, on every frame, you compute a delta time based on the ticks elapsed since the previous frame.

Although it may seem like a great idea to allow the game simulation to run at whatever frame rate the system allows, in practice there can be several issues with this. Most notably, any game that relies on physics (such as a platformer with jumping) will have differences in behavior based on the frame rate.

Though there are more complex solutions to this problem, the simplest solution is to implement **frame limiting**, which forces the game loop to wait until a target delta time has elapsed.

For example, suppose that the target frame rate is 60 FPS. If a frame completes after only 15ms, frame limiting says to wait an additional ~1.6ms to meet the 16.6ms target time.

Conveniently, SDL also provides a method for frame limiting. For example, to ensure that at least 16ms elapses between frames, you can add the following code to the start of `UpdateGame`:

```
while (!SDL_TICKS_PASSED(SDL_GetTicks(), mTicksCount + 16))
    ;
```

You also must watch out for a delta time that's too high. Most notably, this happens when stepping through game code in the debugger. For example, if you pause at a breakpoint in the debugger for five seconds, you'll end up with a huge delta time, and everything will jump far forward in the simulation. To fix this problem, you can clamp the delta time to a maximum value (such as `0.05f`). This way, the game simulation will never jump too far forward on any one frame. This yields the version of `Game::UpdateGame` in Listing 1.5. While you aren't updating the position of the paddle or ball just yet, you are at least calculating the delta time value.

Listing 1.5 `Game::UpdateGame` Implementation

```
void Game::UpdateGame()
{
    // Wait until 16ms has elapsed since last frame
    while (!SDL_TICKS_PASSED(SDL_GetTicks(), mTicksCount + 16))
        ;

    // Delta time is the difference in ticks from last frame
    // (converted to seconds)
    float deltaTime = (SDL_GetTicks() - mTicksCount) / 1000.0f;

    // Clamp maximum delta time value
    if (deltaTime > 0.05f)
    {
        deltaTime = 0.05f;
    }

    // TODO: Update objects in game world as function of delta time!
}
```

Updating the Paddle's Position

In *Pong*, the player controls the position of the paddle based on input. Suppose you want the W key to move the paddle up and the S key to move the paddle down. Pressing neither key *or* both keys should mean the paddle doesn't move at all.

You can make this concrete by using a `mPaddleDir` integer member variable that's set to `0` if the paddle doesn't move, `-1` if if the paddle moves up (negative y), and `1` if the paddle moves down (positive y).

Because the player controls the position of the paddle via keyboard input, you need code in `ProcessInput` that updates `mPaddleDir` based on the input:

```
mPaddleDir = 0;
if (state[SDL_SCANCODE_W])
{
   mPaddleDir -= 1;
}
if (state[SDL_SCANCODE_S])
{
   mPaddleDir += 1;
}
```

Note how you add and subtract from `mPaddleDir`, which ensures that if the player presses both keys, `mPaddleDir` is zero.

Next, in `UpdateGame`, you can add code that updates the paddle based on delta time:

```
if (mPaddleDir != 0)
{
   mPaddlePos.y += mPaddleDir * 300.0f * deltaTime;
}
```

Here, you update the y position of the paddle based on the paddle direction, a speed of `300.0f` pixels/second, and delta time. If `mPaddleDir` is `-1`, the paddle will move up, and if it's `1`, it'll move down.

One problem is that this code allows the paddle to move off the screen. To fix this, you can add boundary conditions for the paddle's y position. If the position is too high or too low, move it back to a valid position:

```
if (mPaddleDir != 0)
{
   mPaddlePos.y += mPaddleDir * 300.0f * deltaTime;
   // Make sure paddle doesn't move off screen!
   if (mPaddlePos.y < (paddleH/2.0f + thickness))
   {
      mPaddlePos.y = paddleH/2.0f + thickness;
   }
   else if (mPaddlePos.y > (768.0f - paddleH/2.0f - thickness))
   {
      mPaddlePos.y = 768.0f - paddleH/2.0f - thickness;
   }
}
```

Here, the `paddleH` variable is a constant that describes the height of the paddle. With this code in place, the player can now move the paddle up and down, and the paddle can't move offscreen.

Updating the Ball's Position

Updating the position of the ball is a bit more complex than updating the position of the paddle. First, the ball travels in both the x and y directions, not just in one direction. Second, the ball needs to bounce off the walls and paddles, which changes the direction of travel. So you need to both represent the **velocity** (speed and direction) of the ball and perform **collision detection** to determine if the ball collides with a wall.

To represent the ball's velocity, add another `Vector2` member variable called `mBallVel`. Initialize `mBallVel` to `(-200.0f, 235.0f)`, which means the ball starts out moving −200 pixels/second in the x direction and 235 pixels/second in the y direction. (In other words, the ball moves diagonally down and to the left.)

To update the position of the ball in terms of the velocity, add the following two lines of code to `UpdateGame`:

```
mBallPos.x += mBallVel.x * deltaTime;
mBallPos.y += mBallVel.y * deltaTime;
```

This is like updating the paddle's position, except now you are updating the position of the ball in *both* the x *and* y directions.

Next, you need code that bounces the ball off walls. The code for determining whether the ball collides with a wall is like the code for checking whether the paddle is offscreen. For example, the ball collides with the top wall if its y position is less than or equal to the height of the ball.

The important question is: what to do when the ball collides with the wall? For example, suppose the ball moves upward and to the right before colliding against the top wall. In this case, you want the ball to now start moving downward and to the right. Similarly, if the ball hits the bottom wall, you want the ball to start moving upward. The insight is that bouncing off the top or bottom wall negates the y component of the velocity, as shown in Figure 1.7(a). Similarly, colliding with the paddle on the left or wall on the right should negate the x component of the velocity.

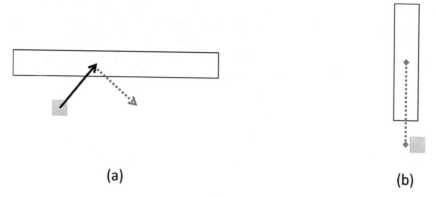

(a)   (b)

Figure 1.7 (a) The ball collides with the top wall so starts moving down. (b) The y difference between the ball and paddle is too large

For the case of the top wall, this yields code like the following:

```
if (mBallPos.y <= thickness)
{
    mBallVel.y *= -1;
}
```

However, there's a key problem with this code. Suppose the ball collides with the top wall on frame A, so the code negates the y velocity to make the ball start moving downward. On frame B, the ball tries to move away from the wall, but it doesn't move far enough. Because the ball still collides with the wall, the code negates the y velocity *again*, which means the ball starts moving upward. Then on every subsequent frame, the code keeps negating the ball's y velocity, so it is forever stuck on the top wall.

To fix this issue of the ball getting stuck, you need an additional check. You want to only negate the y velocity if the ball collides with the top wall *and* the ball is moving toward the top wall (meaning the y velocity is negative):

```
if (mBallPos.y <= thickness && mBallVel.y < 0.0f)
{
    mBallVel.y *= -1;
}
```

This way, if the ball collides with the top wall but is moving away from the wall, you do not negate the y velocity.

The code for colliding against the bottom and right walls is very similar to the code for colliding against the top wall. Colliding against the paddle, however, is slightly more complex. First, you calculate the absolute value of the difference between the y position of the ball and the y position of the paddle. If this difference is greater than half the height of the paddle, the ball is too high or too low, as shown earlier in Figure 1.7(b). You also need to check that the ball's x-position lines up with the paddle, and the ball is not trying to move away from the paddle. Satisfying all these conditions means the ball collides with the paddle, and you should negate the x velocity:

```
if (
    // Our y-difference is small enough
    diff <= paddleH / 2.0f &&
    // Ball is at the correct x-position
    mBallPos.x <= 25.0f && mBallPos.x >= 20.0f &&
    // The ball is moving to the left
    mBallVel.x < 0.0f)
{
    mBallVel.x *= -1.0f;
}
```

With this code complete, the ball and paddle now both move onscreen, as in Figure 1.8. You have now completed your simple version of *Pong*!

Figure 1.8 Final version of *Pong*

Game Project

This chapter's game project implements the full *Pong* game code constructed throughout the chapter. To control the paddle, the player uses the W and S keys. The game ends when the ball moves offscreen. The code is available in the book's GitHub repository in the `Chapter01` directory. Open `Chapter01-windows.sln` in Windows and `Chapter01-mac.xcodeproj` on Mac. (For instructions on how to access the GitHub repository, consult the instructions at the beginning of this chapter.)

Summary

Real-time games update many times per second via a loop called the game loop. Each iteration of this loop is a frame. For example, 60 frames per second means that there are 60 iterations of the game loop per second. The game loop has three main phases that it completes every frame: processing input, updating the game world, and generating output. Input involves not only input devices such as the keyboard and mouse but networking data, replay data, and so on. Outputs include graphics, audio, and force feedback controllers.

Most displays use raster graphics, where the display contains a grid of pixels. The size of the grid depends on the resolution of the display. The game maintains a color buffer that saves color data for every pixel. Most games use double buffering, where there are two color buffers, and the game and display alternate between using these buffers. This helps reduce the amount of screen tearing (that is, the screen showing parts of two frames at once). To eliminate screen tearing, you also must enable vertical synchronization, which means the buffers swap only when the display is ready.

For a game to work properly at variable frame rates, you need to write all game logic as a function of delta time—the time interval between frames. Thus, the "update game world" phase of the game loop should account for delta time. You can further add frame limiting to ensure that the frame rate does not go over some set cap.

In this chapter, you have combined all these different techniques to create a simple version of the classic video game *Pong*.

Additional Reading

Jason Gregory dedicates several pages to discussing the different formulations of a game loop, including how some games take better advantage of multi-core CPUs. There are also many excellent references online for the various libraries used; for example, the SDL API reference is handy.

Gregory, Jason. *Game Engine Architecture,* 2nd edition. Boca Raton: CRC Press, 2014.

SDL API Reference. https://wiki.libsdl.org/APIByCategory. Accessed June 15, 2016.

Exercises

Both of this chapter's exercises focus on modifying your version of *Pong*. The first exercise involves adding a second player, and the second exercise involves adding support for multiple balls.

Exercise 1.1

The original version of *Pong* supported two players. Remove the right wall onscreen and replace that wall with a second paddle for player 2. For this second paddle, use the I and K keys to move the paddle up and down. Supporting a second paddle requires duplicating all the functionality of the first paddle: a member variable for the paddle's position, the direction, code to process input for player 2, code that draws the paddle, and code that updates the paddle. Finally, make sure to update the ball collision code so that the ball correctly collides with both paddles.

Exercise 1.2

Many pinball games support "multiball," where multiple balls are in play at once. It turns out multiball is also fun for *Pong*! To support multiple balls, create a `Ball` struct that contains two `Vector2s`: one for the position and one for the velocity. Next, create a `std::vector<Ball>` member variable for `Game` to store these different balls. Then change the code in `Game::Initialize` to initialize the positions and velocities of several balls. In `Game::UpdateGame`, change the ball update code so that rather than using the individual `mBallVel` and `mBallPos` variables, the code loops over the `std::vector` for all the balls.

CHAPTER 2

GAME OBJECTS AND 2D GRAPHICS

Most games have many different characters and other objects, and an important decision is how to represent these objects. This chapter first covers different methods of object representation. Next, it continues the discussion of 2D graphics techniques by introducing sprites, sprite animations, and scrolling backgrounds. This chapter culminates with a side-scrolling demo that applies the covered techniques.

Game Objects

The *Pong* game created in Chapter 1 does not use separate classes to represent the wall, paddles, and ball. Instead, the `Game` class uses member variables to track the position and velocity of the different elements of the game. While this can work for a very simple game, it's not a scalable solution. The term **game object** refers to anything in the game world that updates, draws, or both updates *and* draws. There are several methods to represent game objects. Some games employ object hierarchies, others employ composition, and still others utilize more complex methods. Regardless of the implementation, a game needs some way to track and update these game objects.

Types of Game Objects

A common type of game object is one that's both updated every frame during the "update game world" phase of the loop and drawn every frame during the "generate outputs" phase. Any character, creature, or otherwise movable object falls under this umbrella. For example, in *Super Mario Bros.*, Mario, any enemies, and all the dynamic blocks are game objects that the game both updates and draws.

Developers sometimes use the term **static object** for game objects that draw but don't update. These objects are visible to the player but never need to update. An example of this is a building in the background of a level. In most games, a building doesn't move or attack the player but is visible onscreen.

A camera is an example of a game object that updates but doesn't draw to the screen. Another example is a **trigger**, which causes something to occur based on another object's intersection. For instance, a horror game might want to have zombies appear when the player approaches a door. In this case, the level designer would place a trigger object that can detect when the player is near and *trigger* the action to spawn the zombie. One way to implement a trigger is as an invisible box that updates every frame to check for intersection with the player.

Game Object Models

There are numerous **game object models**, or ways to represent game objects. This section discusses some types of game object models and the trade-offs between these approaches.

Game Objects as a Class Hierarchy

One game object model approach is to declare game objects in a standard object-oriented class hierarchy, which is sometimes called a **monolithic class hierarchy** because all game objects inherit from one base class.

To use this object model, you first need a base class:

```
class Actor
{
public:
   // Called every frame to update the Actor
   virtual void Update(float deltaTime);
   // Called every frame to draw the Actor
   virtual void Draw();
};
```

Then, different characters have different subclasses:

```
class PacMan : public Actor
{
public:
   void Update(float deltaTime) override;
   void Draw() override;
};
```

Similarly, you could declare other subclasses of `Actor`. For example, there may be a `Ghost` class that inherits from `Actor`, and then each individual ghost could have its own class that inherits from `Ghost`. Figure 2.1 illustrates this style of game object class hierarchy.

A disadvantage of this approach is that it means that every game object must have all the properties and functions of the base game object (in this case, `Actor`). For example, this assumes that every `Actor` can update and draw. But as discussed, there may be objects that aren't visible, and thus calling `Draw` on these objects is a waste of time.

The problem becomes more apparent as the functionality of the game increases. Suppose many of the actors in the game—but not all of them—need to move. In the case of *Pac-Man*, the ghosts and Pac-Man need to move, but the pellets do not. One approach is to place the movement code inside `Actor`, but not every subclass will need this code. Alternatively, you could extend the hierarchy with a new `MovingActor` that exists between `Actor` and any subclasses that need movement. However, this adds more complexity to the class hierarchy.

Furthermore, having one big class hierarchy can cause difficulties when two sibling classes later need to have features shared between them. For instance, a game in the vein of *Grand Theft Auto* might have a base `Vehicle` class. From this class, it might make sense to create two subclasses: `LandVehicle` (for vehicles that traverse land) and `WaterVehicle` (for water-based vehicles like boats).

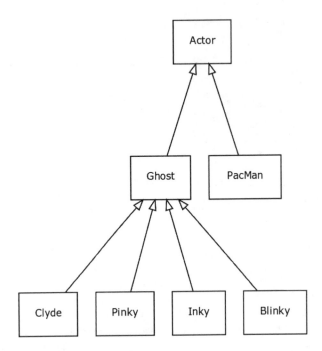

Figure 2.1 Partial class hierarchy for *Pac-Man*

But what happens if one day a designer decides to add an amphibious vehicle? It may be tempting to create a new subclass called `AmphibiousVehicle` that inherits from both `LandVehicle` and `WaterVehicle`. However, this requires use of multiple inheritance and, furthermore, means that `AmphibiousVehicle` inherits from `Vehicle` along two different paths. This type of hierarchy, called **diamond inheritance**, can cause issues because the subclass might inherit multiple versions of a virtual function. For this reason, it's recommended that we avoid diamond hierarchies.

Game Objects with Components

Instead of using a monolithic hierarchy, many games instead use a **component-based** game object model. This model has become increasingly popular, especially because the Unity game engine uses it. In this approach, there is a game object class, but there are no subclasses of the game object. Instead, the game object class *has-a* collection of component objects that implement needed functionality.

For example, in the monolithic hierarchy we looked at earlier, `Pinky` is a subclass of `Ghost`, which is a subclass of `Actor`. However, in a component-based model, Pinky is a `GameObject` instance containing four components: `PinkyBehavior`, `CollisionComponent`, `TransformComponent`, and `DrawComponent`. Figure 2.2 shows this relationship.

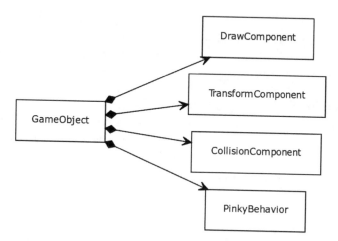

Figure 2.2 The components that make up the ghost Pinky

Each of these components has the specific properties and functionality needed for that component. For example, `DrawComponent` handles drawing the object to the screen, and `TransformComponent` stores the position and transformation of an object in the game world.

One way to implement a component object model is with a class hierarchy for components. This class hierarchy generally has a very shallow depth. Given a base `Component` class, `GameObject` then simply has a collection of components:

```
class GameObject
{
public:
    void AddComponent(Component* comp);
    void RemoveComponent(Component* comp);
private:
    std::unordered_set<Component*> mComponents;
};
```

Notice that `GameObject` contains only functions for adding and removing components. This makes systems that track different types of components necessary. For example, every `DrawComponent` might register with a `Renderer` object so that when it is time to draw the frame, the `Renderer` is aware of all the active `DrawComponents`.

One advantage of the component-based game object model is that it's easier to add functionality only to the specific game objects that require it. Any object that needs to draw can have a `DrawComponent`, but objects that don't simply don't have one.

However, a disadvantage of pure component systems is that dependencies between components in the same game object are not clear. For instance, it's likely that the `DrawComponent` needs to know about the `TransformComponent` in order know where the object should draw. This means that the `DrawComponent` likely needs to ask the owning `GameObject` about its `TransformComponent`. Depending on the implementation, the querying can become a noticeable performance bottleneck.

Game Objects as a Hierarchy with Components

The game object model used in this book is a hybrid of the monolithic hierarchy and the component object models. This is, in part, inspired by the game object model used in Unreal Engine 4. There is a base `Actor` class with a handful of virtual functions, but each actor also has a vector of components. Listing 2.1 shows the declaration of the `Actor` class, with some getter and setter functions omitted.

Listing 2.1   `Actor` Declaration

```
class Actor
{
public:
    // Used to track state of actor
    enum State
    {
        EActive,
        EPaused,
        EDead
    };
    // Constructor/destructor
    Actor(class Game* game);
    virtual ~Actor();

    // Update function called from Game (not overridable)
    void Update(float deltaTime);
    // Updates all the components attached to the actor (not overridable)
    void UpdateComponents(float deltaTime);
    // Any actor-specific update code (overridable)
    virtual void UpdateActor(float deltaTime);

    // Getters/setters
    // ...

    // Add/remove components
    void AddComponent(class Component* component);
    void RemoveComponent(class Component* component);
private:
    // Actor's state
    State mState;
    // Transform
    Vector2 mPosition; // Center position of actor
    float mScale;      // Uniforms scale of actor (1.0f for 100%)
```

```
    float mRotation;    // Rotation angle (in radians)
    // Components held by this actor
    std::vector<class Component*> mComponents;
    class Game* mGame;
};
```

The `Actor` class has several notable features. The state `enum` tracks the status of the actor. For example, `Update` only updates the actor when in the `EActive` state. The `EDead` state notifies the game to remove the actor. The `Update` function calls `UpdateComponents` first and then `UpdateActor`. `UpdateComponents` loops over all the components and updates each in turn. The base implementation of `UpdateActor` is empty, but `Actor` subclasses can write custom behavior in an overridden `UpdateActor` function.

In addition, the `Actor` class needs access to the `Game` class for several reasons, including to create additional actors. One approach is to make the game object a **singleton**, a design pattern in which there is a single, globally accessible instance of a class. But the singleton pattern can cause issues if it turns out there actually need to be multiple instances of the class. Instead of using singletons, this book uses an approach called **dependency injection**. In this approach, the actor constructor receives a pointer to the `Game` class. Then an actor can use this pointer to create another actor (or access any other required `Game` functions).

As in the Chapter 1 game project, a `Vector2` represents the position of an `Actor`. Actors also support a scale (which makes the actor bigger or smaller) and a rotation (to rotate the actor). Note that the rotation is in radians, not degrees.

Listing 2.2 contains the declaration of the `Component` class. The `mUpdateOrder` member variable is notable. It allows certain components to update before or after other components, which can be useful in many situations. For instance, a camera component tracking a player may want to update after the movement component moves the player. To maintain this ordering, the `AddComponent` function in `Actor` sorts the component vector whenever adding a new component. Finally, note that the `Component` class has a pointer to the owning actor. This is so that the component can access the transform data and any other information it deems necessary.

Listing 2.2 Component Declaration

```
class Component
{
public:
    // Constructor
    // (the lower the update order, the earlier the component updates)
    Component(class Actor* owner, int updateOrder = 100);
    // Destructor
    virtual ~Component();
    // Update this component by delta time
```

```
    virtual void Update(float deltaTime);
    int GetUpdateOrder() const { return mUpdateOrder; }
protected:
    // Owning actor
    class Actor* mOwner;
    // Update order of component
    int mUpdateOrder;
};
```

Currently, the implementations of `Actor` and `Component` do not account for player input devices, and this chapter's game project simply uses special case code for input. Chapter 3, "Vector and Basic Physics," revisits how to incorporate input into the hybrid game object model.

This hybrid approach does a better job of avoiding the deep class hierarchies in the monolithic object model, but certainly the depth of the hierarchy is greater than in a pure component-based model. The hybrid approach also generally avoids, though does not eliminate, the issues of communication overhead between components. This is because every actor has critical properties such as the transform data.

Other Approaches

There are many other approaches to game object models. Some use interface classes to declare the different possible functionalities, and each game object then implements the interfaces necessary to represent it. Other approaches extend the component model a step further and eliminate the containing game object entirely. Instead, these approaches use a component database that tracks objects with a numeric identifier. Still other approaches define objects by their properties. In these systems, adding a health property to an object means that it can take and receive damage.

With any game object model, each approach has advantages and disadvantages. However, this book sticks to the hybrid approach because it's a good compromise and works relatively well for games of a certain complexity level.

Integrating Game Objects into the Game Loop

Integrating the hybrid game object model into the game loop requires some code, but it ultimately isn't that complex. First, add two `std::vector` of `Actor` pointers to the `Game` class: one containing the active actors (`mActors`), and one containing pending actors (`mPendingActors`). You need the pending actors vector to handle the case where, while updating the actors (and thus looping over `mActors`), you decide to create a new actor. In this case, you cannot add an element to `mActors` because you're iterating over it. Instead, you need to add to the `mPendingActors` vector and then move these actors into `mActors` after you're done iterating.

Next, create two functions, AddActor and RemoveActor, which take in Actor pointers. The AddActor function adds the actor to either mPendingActors or mActors, depending on whether you are currently updating all mActors (denoted by the mUpdatingActors bool):

```cpp
void Game::AddActor(Actor* actor)
{
   // If  updating actors, need to add to pending
   if (mUpdatingActors)
   {
      mPendingActors.emplace_back(actor);
   }
   else
   {
      mActors.emplace_back(actor);
   }
}
```

Similarly, RemoveActor removes the actor from whichever of the two vectors it is in.

You then need to change the UpdateGame function so that it updates all the actors, as shown in Listing 2.3. After computing delta time, as discussed in Chapter 1, you then loop over every actor in mActors and call Update on each. Next, you move any pending actors into the main mActors vector. Finally, you see if any actors are dead, in which case you delete them.

Listing 2.3   Game::UpdateGame Updating Actors

```cpp
void Game::UpdateGame()
{
   // Compute delta time (as in Chapter 1)
   float deltaTime = /* ... */;

   // Update all actors
   mUpdatingActors = true;
   for (auto actor : mActors)
   {
      actor->Update(deltaTime);
   }
   mUpdatingActors = false;

   // Move any pending actors to mActors
   for (auto pending : mPendingActors)
   {
      mActors.emplace_back(pending);
   }
   mPendingActors.clear();

   // Add any dead actors to a temp vector
   std::vector<Actor*> deadActors;
```

```
for (auto actor : mActors)
{
    if (actor->GetState() == Actor::EDead)
    {
        deadActors.emplace_back(actor);
    }
}

// Delete dead actors (which removes them from mActors)
for (auto actor : deadActors)
{
    delete actor;
}
}
```

Adding and removing actors from the game's `mActors` vector also adds some complexity to the code. This chapter's game project has the `Actor` object automatically add or remove itself from the game in its constructor and destructor, respectively. However, this means that code that loops over the `mActors` vector and deletes the actors (such as in `Game::Shutdown`) must be written carefully:

```
// Because ~Actor calls RemoveActor, use a different style loop
while (!mActors.empty())
{
    delete mActors.back();
}
```

Sprites

A **sprite** is a visual object in a 2D game, typically used to represent characters, backgrounds, and other dynamic objects. Most 2D games have dozens if not hundreds of sprites, and for mobile games, the sprite data accounts for much of the overall download size of the game. Because of the prevalence of sprites in 2D games, it is important to use them as efficiently as possible.

Each sprite has one or more image files associated with it. There are many different image file formats, and games use different formats based on platform and other constraints. For example, PNG is a compressed image format, so these files take up less space on disk. But hardware cannot natively draw PNG files, so they take longer to load. Some platforms recommend using graphics hardware–friendly formats such as PVR (for iOS) and DXT (for PC and Xbox). This book sticks with the PNG file format because image editing programs universally support PNGs.

Loading Image Files

For games that only need SDL's 2D graphics, the simplest way to load image files is to use the SDL Image library. The first step is to initialize SDL Image by using `IMG_Init`, which takes in a flag parameter for the requested file formats. To support PNG files, add the following call to `Game::Initialize`:

```
IMG_Init(IMG_INIT_PNG)
```

Table 2.1 lists the supported file formats. Note that SDL already supports the BMP file format without SDL Image, which is why there is no `IMG_INIT_BMP` flag in this table.

Table 2.1 SDL Image File Formats

Flag	Format
IMG_INIT_JPG	JPEG
IMG_INIT_PNG	PNG
IMG_INIT_TIF	TIFF

Once SDL Image is initialized, you can use `IMG_Load` to load an image file into an `SDL_Surface`:

```
// Loads an image from a file
// Returns a pointer to an SDL_Surface if successful, otherwise nullptr
SDL_Surface* IMG_Load(
   const char* file // Image file name
);
```

Next, `SDL_CreateTextureFromSurface` converts an `SDL_Surface` into an `SDL_Texture` (which is what SDL requires for drawing):

```
// Converts an SDL_Surface to an SDL_Texture
// Returns a pointer to an SDL_Texture if successful, otherwise nullptr
SDL_Texture* SDL_CreateTextureFromSurface(
   SDL_Renderer* renderer, // Renderer used
   SDL_Surface* surface    // Surface to convert
);
```

The following function encapsulates this image-loading process:

```
SDL_Texture* LoadTexture(const char* fileName)
{
   // Load from file
   SDL_Surface* surf = IMG_Load(fileName);
   if (!surf)
   {
      SDL_Log("Failed to load texture file %s", fileName);
      return nullptr;
   }
```

```
    // Create texture from surface
    SDL_Texture* text = SDL_CreateTextureFromSurface(mRenderer, surf);
    SDL_FreeSurface(surf);
    if (!text)
    {
        SDL_Log("Failed to convert surface to texture for %s", fileName);
        return nullptr;
    }
    return text;
}
```

An interesting question is where to store the loaded textures. It's very common for a game to use the same image file multiple times for multiple different actors. If there are 20 asteroids, and each asteroid uses the same image file, it doesn't make sense to load the file from disk 20 times.

A simple approach is to create a map of filenames to SDL_Texture pointers in Game. You then create a GetTexture function in Game that takes in the name of a texture and returns its corresponding SDL_Texture pointer. This function first checks to see if the texture already exists in the map. If it does, you can simply return that texture pointer. Otherwise, you run the code that loads the texture from its file.

> **note**
>
> While a map of filenames to SDL_Texture pointers makes sense in a simple case, consider that a game has many different types of assets—textures, sound effects, 3D models, fonts, and so on. Therefore, writing a more robust system to generically handle all types of assets makes sense. But in the interest of simplicity, this book does not implement such an asset management system.

To help split up responsibilities, you also create a LoadData function in Game. This function is responsible for creating all the actors in the game world. For now these actors are hard-coded, but Chapter 14, "Level Files and Binary Data," adds support for loading the actors from a level file. You call the LoadData function at the end of Game::Initialize.

Drawing Sprites

Suppose a game has a basic 2D scene with a background image and a character. A simple way to draw this scene is by first drawing the background image and then the character. This is like how a painter would paint the scene, and hence this approach is known as the **painter's algorithm**. In the painter's algorithm, the game draws the sprites in back-to-front order. Figure 2.3 demonstrates the painter's algorithm, first drawing the background star field, then the moon, then any asteroids, and finally the ship.

Figure 2.3 The painter's algorithm applied to a space scene

Because this book uses a game object model with components, it makes a great deal of sense to create a `SpriteComponent` class. Listing 2.4 provides the declaration of `SpriteComponent`.

Listing 2.4 `SpriteComponent` Declaration

```
class SpriteComponent : public Component
{
public:
    // (Lower draw order corresponds with further back)
    SpriteComponent(class Actor* owner, int drawOrder = 100);
    ~SpriteComponent();
    virtual void Draw(SDL_Renderer* renderer);
    virtual void SetTexture(SDL_Texture* texture);

    int GetDrawOrder() const { return mDrawOrder; }
    int GetTexHeight() const { return mTexHeight; }
    int GetTexWidth() const { return mTexWidth; }
protected:
    // Texture to draw
    SDL_Texture* mTexture;
    // Draw order used for painter's algorithm
```

```
    int mDrawOrder;
    // Width/height of texture
    int mTexWidth;
    int mTexHeight;
};
```

The game implements the painter's algorithm by drawing sprite components in the order specified by the mDrawOrder member variable. The SpriteComponent constructor adds itself to a vector of sprite components in the Game class via the Game::AddSprite function.

In Game::AddSprite, you need to ensure that mSprites stays sorted by draw order. Because every call to AddSprite preserves the sorted order, you can implement this as an insertion into an already-sorted vector:

```
void Game::AddSprite(SpriteComponent* sprite)
{
    // Find the insertion point in the sorted vector
    // (The first element with a higher draw order than me)
    int myDrawOrder = sprite->GetDrawOrder();
    auto iter = mSprites.begin();
    for ( ;
        iter != mSprites.end();
        ++iter)
    {
        if (myDrawOrder < (*iter)->GetDrawOrder())
        {
            break;
        }
    }

    // Inserts element before position of iterator
    mSprites.insert(iter, sprite);
}
```

Because this orders the sprite components by mDrawOrder, Game::GenerateOutput can just loop over the vector of sprite components and call Draw on each. You put this code in between the code that clears the back buffer and swaps the back buffer and front buffer, replacing the code in the Chapter 1 game that drew the wall, ball, and paddle rectangles.

As discussed in Chapter 6, "3D Graphics," 3D games can also use the painter's algorithm, though there are some drawbacks in doing so. But for 2D scenes, the painter's algorithm works very well.

The SetTexture function both sets the mTexture member variable and uses SDL_QueryTexture to get the width and height of the texture:

```cpp
void SpriteComponent::SetTexture(SDL_Texture* texture)
{
   mTexture = texture;
   // Get width/height of texture
   SDL_QueryTexture(texture, nullptr, nullptr,
      &mTexWidth, &mTexHeight);
}
```

To draw textures, there are two different texture drawing functions in SDL. The simpler function is SDL_RenderCopy:

```cpp
// Renders a texture to the rendering target
// Returns 0 on success, negative value on failure
int SDL_RenderCopy(
   SDL_Renderer* renderer,   // Render target to draw to
   SDL_Texture* texture,     // Texture to draw
   const SDL_Rect* srcrect,  // Part of texture to draw (null if whole)
   const SDL_Rect* dstrect,  // Rectangle to draw onto the target
);
```

However, for more advanced behavior (such as rotating sprites), you can use SDL_RenderCopyEx:

```cpp
// Renders a texture to the rendering target
// Returns 0 on success, negative value on failure
int SDL_RenderCopyEx(
   SDL_Renderer* renderer,   // Render target to draw to
   SDL_Texture* texture,     // Texture to draw
   const SDL_Rect* srcrect,  // Part of texture to draw (null if whole)
   const SDL_Rect* dstrect,  // Rectangle to draw onto the target
   double angle,             // Rotation angle (in degrees, clockwise)
   const SDL_Point* center,  // Point to rotate about (nullptr for center)
   SDL_RenderFlip flip,      // How to flip texture (usually SDL_FLIP_NONE)
);
```

Because actors have a rotation, and you want your sprites to inherit this rotation, you must use SDL_RenderCopyEx. This introduces a few complexities to the SpriteComponent::Draw function. First, the SDL_Rect struct's x/y coordinates correspond to the top-left corner of the destination. However, the actor's position variable specifies the center position of the actor. So, as with the ball and paddle in Chapter 1, you must compute the coordinates for the top-left corner.

Second, SDL expects an angle in degrees, but Actor uses an angle in radians. Luckily, this book's custom math library in the Math.h header file includes a Math::ToDegrees function that can handle the conversion. Finally, in SDL a positive angle is clockwise, but this is the opposite of the unit circle (where positive angles are counterclockwise). Thus, negate the angle to maintain the unit circle behavior. Listing 2.5 shows the SpriteComponent::Draw function.

Listing 2.5 `SpriteComponent::Draw` Implementation

```
void SpriteComponent::Draw(SDL_Renderer* renderer)
{
    if (mTexture)
    {
        SDL_Rect r;
        // Scale the width/height by owner's scale
        r.w = static_cast<int>(mTexWidth * mOwner->GetScale());
        r.h = static_cast<int>(mTexHeight * mOwner->GetScale());
        // Center the rectangle around the position of the owner
        r.x = static_cast<int>(mOwner->GetPosition().x - r.w / 2);
        r.y = static_cast<int>(mOwner->GetPosition().y - r.h / 2);

        // Draw
        SDL_RenderCopyEx(renderer,
            mTexture, // Texture to draw
            nullptr,  // Source rectangle
            &r,       // Destination rectangle
            -Math::ToDegrees(mOwner->GetRotation()), // (Convert angle)
            nullptr, // Point of rotation
            SDL_FLIP_NONE); // Flip behavior
    }
}
```

This implementation of `Draw` assumes that the position of the actor corresponds to its position onscreen. This assumption holds only for games where the game world exactly corresponds to the screen. This doesn't work for a game like *Super Mario Bros.* that has a game world larger than one single screen. To handle such a case, the code needs a camera position. Chapter 9, "Cameras," discusses how to implement cameras in the context of a 3D game.

Animating Sprites

Most 2D games implement sprite animation using a technique like **flipbook animation**: a series of static 2D images played in rapid succession to create an illusion of motion. Figure 2.4 illustrates what such a series of images for different animations for a skeleton sprite might look like.

The frame rate of sprite animations can vary, but many games choose to use 24 FPS (the traditional frame rate used in film). This means that every second of an animation needs 24 individual images. Some genres, such as 2D fighting games, may use 60 FPS sprite animations, which dramatically increases the required number of images. Luckily, most sprite animations are significantly shorter than 1 second in duration.

Figure 2.4 Series of images for a skeleton sprite

The simplest way to represent an animated sprite is with a vector of the different images corresponding to each frame in an animation. The AnimSpriteComponent class, declared in Listing 2.6, uses this approach.

Listing 2.6 AnimSpriteComponent Declaration

```
class AnimSpriteComponent : public SpriteComponent
{
public:
    AnimSpriteComponent(class Actor* owner, int drawOrder = 100);
    // Update animation every frame (overriden from component)
    void Update(float deltaTime) override;
    // Set the textures used for animation
    void SetAnimTextures(const std::vector<SDL_Texture*>& textures);
    // Set/get the animation FPS
    float GetAnimFPS() const { return mAnimFPS; }
    void SetAnimFPS(float fps) { mAnimFPS = fps; }
private:
    // All textures in the animation
    std::vector<SDL_Texture*> mAnimTextures;
    // Current frame displayed
    float mCurrFrame;
    // Animation frame rate
    float mAnimFPS;
};
```

The mAnimFPS variable allows different animated sprites to run at different frame rates. It also allows the animation to dynamically speed up or slow down. For instance, as a character gains speed, you could increase the frame rate of the animation to further add to the illusion of speed. The `mCurrFrame` variable tracks the current frame displayed as a float, which allows you to also keep track of how long that frame has displayed.

The `SetAnimTextures` function simply sets the `mAnimTextures` member variable to the provided vector and resets `mCurrFrame` to zero. It also calls the `SetTexture` function (inherited from `SpriteComponent`) and passes in the first frame of the animation. Since this code uses the `SetTexture` function from `SpriteComponent`, it's unnecessary to override the inherited `Draw` function.

The `Update` function, shown in Listing 2.7, is where most of the heavy lifting of `AnimSpriteComponent` occurs. First, update `mCurrFrame` as a function of the animation FPS and delta time. Next, you make sure that `mCurrFrame` remains less than the number of textures (which means you need to wrap around back to the start of the animation if needed). Finally, cast `mCurrFrame` to an `int`, grab the correct texture from `mAnimTextures`, and call `SetTexture`.

Listing 2.7 `AnimSpriteComponent::Update` Implementation

```
void AnimSpriteComponent::Update(float deltaTime)
{
    SpriteComponent::Update(deltaTime);

    if (mAnimTextures.size() > 0)
    {
        // Update the current frame based on frame rate
        // and delta time
        mCurrFrame += mAnimFPS * deltaTime;

        // Wrap current frame if needed
        while (mCurrFrame >= mAnimTextures.size())
        {
            mCurrFrame -= mAnimTextures.size();
        }

        // Set the current texture
        SetTexture(mAnimTextures[static_cast<int>(mCurrFrame)]);
    }
}
```

One feature missing from `AnimSpriteComponent` is better support for switching between animations. Currently, the only way to switch an animation is to call `SetAnimTextures` repeatedly. It makes more sense to have a vector of all the different textures for all of a sprite's animations and then specify which images correspond to which animation. You'll explore this idea further in Exercise 2.2.

Scrolling Backgrounds

A trick often used in 2D games is having a background that scrolls by. This creates an impression of a larger world, and infinite scrolling games often use this technique. For now, we are focusing on scrolling backgrounds, as opposed to scrolling through an actual level. The easiest method is to split the background into screen-sized image segments, which are repositioned every frame to create the illusion of scrolling.

As with animated sprites, it makes sense to create a subclass of `SpriteComponent` for backgrounds. Listing 2.8 shows the declaration of `BGSpriteComponent`.

Listing 2.8 `BGSpriteComponent` Declaration

```cpp
class BGSpriteComponent : public SpriteComponent
{
public:
    // Set draw order to default to lower (so it's in the background)
    BGSpriteComponent(class Actor* owner, int drawOrder = 10);
    // Update/draw overriden from parent
    void Update(float deltaTime) override;
    void Draw(SDL_Renderer* renderer) override;
    // Set the textures used for the background
    void SetBGTextures(const std::vector<SDL_Texture*>& textures);
    // Get/set screen size and scroll speed
    void SetScreenSize(const Vector2& size) { mScreenSize = size; }
    void SetScrollSpeed(float speed) { mScrollSpeed = speed; }
    float GetScrollSpeed() const { return mScrollSpeed; }
private:
    // Struct to encapsulate each BG image and its offset
    struct BGTexture
    {
        SDL_Texture* mTexture;
        Vector2 mOffset;
    };
    std::vector<BGTexture> mBGTextures;
    Vector2 mScreenSize;
    float mScrollSpeed;
};
```

The `BGTexture` struct associates each background texture with its corresponding offset. The offsets update every frame to create the scrolling effect. You need to initialize the offsets in `SetBGTextures`, positioning each background to the right of the previous one:

```cpp
void BGSpriteComponent::SetBGTextures(const std::vector<SDL_Texture*>&
textures)
{
    int count = 0;
```

```
    for (auto tex : textures)
    {
        BGTexture temp;
        temp.mTexture = tex;
        // Each texture is screen width in offset
        temp.mOffset.x = count * mScreenSize.x;
        temp.mOffset.y = 0;
        mBGTextures.emplace_back(temp);
        count++;
    }
}
```

This code assumes that each background image has a width corresponding to the screen width, but it's certainly possible to modify the code to account for variable sizes. The Update code updates the offsets of each background, taking to account when one image moves all the way off the screen. This allows the images to infinitely repeat:

```
void BGSpriteComponent::Update(float deltaTime)
{
    SpriteComponent::Update(deltaTime);
    for (auto& bg : mBGTextures)
    {
        // Update the x offset
        bg.mOffset.x += mScrollSpeed * deltaTime;
        // If this is completely off the screen, reset offset to
        // the right of the last bg texture
        if (bg.mOffset.x < -mScreenSize.x)
        {
            bg.mOffset.x = (mBGTextures.size() - 1) * mScreenSize.x - 1;
        }
    }
}
```

The Draw function simply draws each background texture using SDL_RenderCopy, making sure to adjust the position based on the owner's position and the offset of that background. This achieves the simple scrolling behavior.

Some games also implement **parallax scrolling**. In this approach, you use multiple layers for the background. Each layer scrolls at different speeds, which gives an illusion of depth. For example, a game might have a cloud layer and a ground layer. If the cloud layer scrolls more slowly than the ground layer, it gives the impression that the clouds are farther away than the ground. Traditional animation has used this technique for nearly a century, and it is effective. Typically, only three layers are necessary to create a believable parallax effect, as illustrated in Figure 2.5. Of course, more layers add more depth to the effect.

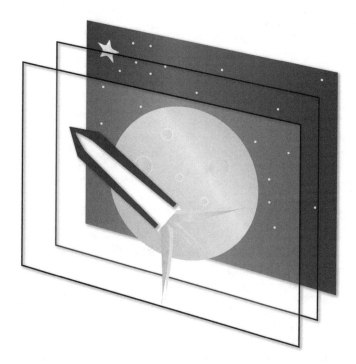

Figure 2.5 Space scene broken into three layers to facilitate parallax scrolling

To implement the parallax effect, attach multiple BGSpriteComponents to a single actor and specify different draw order values. Then you can use a different scroll speed for each background to complete the effect.

Game Project

Unfortunately, you have not learned about enough new topics to make a game with noticeably more complex mechanics than the *Pong* clone created in Chapter 1, "Game Programming Overview." And it wouldn't be particularly interesting to just add sprites to the previous chapter's game. So in lieu of a complete game, this chapter's game project demonstrates the new techniques covered in this chapter. The code is available in the book's GitHub repository, in the Chapter02 directory. Open Chapter02-windows.sln on Windows and Chapter02-mac.xcodeproj on Mac. Figure 2.6 shows the game project in action. Jacob Zinman-Jeanes created the sprite images, which are licensed under the CC BY license.

The code includes an implementation of the hybrid Actor/Component model, SpriteComponent, AnimSpriteComponent, and parallax scrolling. It also includes a subclass of Actor called Ship. The Ship class contains two speed variables to control the left/right speed and the up/down speed, respectively. Listing 2.9 shows the declaration of Ship.

Listing 2.9 Ship Declaration

```
class Ship : public Actor
{
public:
    Ship(class Game* game);
    void UpdateActor(float deltaTime) override;
    void ProcessKeyboard(const uint8_t* state);
    float GetRightSpeed() const { return mRightSpeed; }
    float GetDownSpeed() const { return mDownSpeed; }
private:
    float mRightSpeed;
    float mDownSpeed;
};
```

The Ship constructor initializes mRightSpeed and mDownSpeed to 0, and also creates an AnimSpriteComponent attached to the ship, with the associated textures:

```
AnimSpriteComponent* asc = new AnimSpriteComponent(this);
std::vector<SDL_Texture*> anims = {
    game->GetTexture("Assets/Ship01.png"),
    game->GetTexture("Assets/Ship02.png"),
    game->GetTexture("Assets/Ship03.png"),
    game->GetTexture("Assets/Ship04.png"),
};
asc->SetAnimTextures(anims);
```

The keyboard input directly affects the speed of the ship. The game uses the W and S keys to move the ship up and down and the A and D keys to move the ship left and right. The ProcessKeyboard function takes in these inputs and updates mRightSpeed and mDownSpeed as appropriate.

The Ship::UpdateActor function implements the ship's movement, using techniques similar to those shown in Chapter 1:

```
void Ship::UpdateActor(float deltaTime)
{
    Actor::UpdateActor(deltaTime);
    // Update position based on speeds and delta time
    Vector2 pos = GetPosition();
    pos.x += mRightSpeed * deltaTime;
    pos.y += mDownSpeed * deltaTime;
    // Restrict position to left half of screen
    // ...
    SetPosition(pos);
}
```

Movement is such a common feature for games that it makes a lot of sense to implement it as a component, as opposed to in the `UpdateActor` function. Chapter 3, "Vectors and Basics Physics," discusses how to create a `MoveComponent` class.

Figure 2.6 Side-scroller project in action

The background is a generic `Actor` (not a subclass) that has two `BGSpriteComponents`. The different scroll speeds of these two backgrounds create a parallax effect. All these actors, including the ship, are created in the `Game::LoadData` function.

Summary

There are many ways to represent game objects. The simplest approach is to use a monolithic hierarchy with one base class that every game object inherits from, but this can quickly grow out of hand. With a component-based model, you can instead define the functionality of a game object in terms of the components it contains. This book uses a hybrid approach that has a shallow hierarchy of game objects but components that implement some behaviors, such as drawing and movement.

The very first games used 2D graphics. Although many games today are in 3D, 2D games still are very popular. Sprites are the primary visual building block of any 2D game, whether animated or not. SDL supports loading and drawing textures via a simple interface.

Many 2D games implement flipbook animation, drawing different images in rapid succession to make the sprite appear to animate. You can use other techniques to implement a scrolling background layer, and you can use the parallax effect to create the illusion of depth.

Additional Reading

Jason Gregory dedicates several pages to different types of game object models, including the model used at Naughty Dog. Michael Dickheiser's book contains an article on implementing a pure component model.

Dickheiser, Michael, Ed. *Game Programming Gems 6*. Boston: Charles River Media, 2006.

Gregory, Jason. *Game Engine Architecture, 2nd edition*. Boca Raton: CRC Press, 2014.

Exercises

The first exercise of this chapter is a thought experiment on the different types of game object models. In the second exercise you add functionality to the `AnimSpriteComponent` class. The final exercise involves adding support for **tile maps**, a technique for generating 2D scenes from tiles.

Exercise 2.1

Consider an animal safari game where the player can drive around in different vehicles to observe animals in the wild. Think about the different types of creatures, plants, and vehicles that might exist in such a game. How might you implement these objects in a monolithic class hierarchy object model?

Now consider the same game but implemented with a component game object model. How might you implement this? Which of these two approaches seems more beneficial for this game?

Exercise 2.2

The `AnimSpriteComponent` class currently supports only a single animation, composed of all the sprites in the vector. Modify the class to support several different animations. Define each animation as a range of textures in the vector. Use the `CharacterXX.png` files in the `Chapter02/Assets` directory for testing.

Now add support for non-looping animations. When defining an animation as a range of textures, also allow specification of looping or non-looping. When a non-looping animation finishes, it should not wrap back to the initial texture.

Exercise 2.3

One approach to generate a 2D scene is via a tile map. In this approach, an image file (called a **tile set**) contains a series of uniformly sized tiles. Many of these tiles combine to form a 2D scene. Tiled (http://www.mapeditor.org), which is a great program for generating tile sets and tile maps, generated the tile maps for this exercise. Figure 2.7 illustrates what a portion of the tile set looks like.

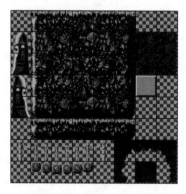

Figure 2.7 A portion of the tile set used in Exercise 2.3

In this case, the tile maps are in CSV files. Use the `MapLayerX.csv` files in `Chapter02/Assets`, where there are three different layers (Layer 1 being the closest and Layer 3 the farthest). `Tiles.png` contains the tile set. Each row in the CSV file contains a series of numbers, like this:

```
-1,0,5,5,5,5
```

`-1` means there is no image for that tile (so you should render nothing for that tile). Every other number references a specific tile from the tile set. The numbering goes left to right and then up to down. So, in this tile set, tile `8` is the leftmost tile on the second row.

Create a new component called `TileMapComponent` that inherits from `SpriteComponent`. This class needs a function to load and read in a tile map CSV file. Then override `Draw` to draw each tile from the tile set texture. In order to draw only part of a texture, instead of the entire texture, use the `srcrect` parameter of `SDL_RenderCopyEx`. This can then draw only a single tile square from the tile set texture rather than the entire tile set.

CHAPTER 3

VECTORS AND BASIC PHYSICS

Vectors are a fundamental mathematical concept that game programmers use every day. This chapter first explores all the different ways vectors can be used to solve problems in games. Next, it shows how to implement basic movement through a `MoveComponent` and control it with the keyboard via an `InputComponent`. This chapter then briefly explores the basics of Newtonian physics before ending with a discussion of how to detect collisions between objects. This chapter's game project uses some of these techniques to implement a version of the classic game *Asteroids*.

Vectors

A mathematical **vector** (not to be confused with `std::vector`) represents both a magnitude and direction in an *n*-dimensional space, with one component per dimension. This means that a two-dimensional (2D) vector has x and y components. To a game programmer, a vector is one of the most important mathematical tools. You can use vectors to solve many different problems in games, and understanding vectors is especially important when you're working with 3D games. This section covers both the properties of vectors and how to use them in games.

This book uses an arrow above a variable name to denote that the variable is a vector. This book also denotes each component of a vector with a subscript for each dimension. For example, this is the notation for the 2D vector $\vec{v}$:

$$\vec{v} = \langle v_x, v_y \rangle$$

A vector has no concept of a position. This seems confusing, given that Chapters 1, "Game Programming Overview," and 2, "Game Objects and 2D Graphics," use a `Vector2` variable to represent positions. (You'll learn why this is the case in a moment.)

If vectors have no position, this means that two vectors are equivalent if they have the same magnitude (or **length**) and point in the same direction. Figure 3.1 shows many vectors in a vector field. Even though the diagram shows many vectors drawn in different locations, because all the vectors have the same magnitude and direction, they are equivalent.

Figure 3.1 A vector field in which all vectors are equivalent

Even though where you draw a vector doesn't change its value, it often simplifies solving vector problems to draw the vector such that its start, or **tail**, is at the origin. You can then think of the arrow part of the vector (the **head**) as "pointing at" a specific point in space. When drawn in this manner, the position that the vector "points at" has the same components as the vector. For example, if you draw the 2D vector <1, 2> such that it starts at the origin, its head points at (1, 2), as shown in Figure 3.2.

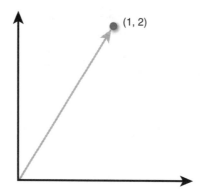

Figure 3.2 The 2D vector <1, 2> drawn with its tail at the origin and its head "pointing at" (1, 2)

Because a vector can represent a direction, you often use vectors in games to describe the orientation of an object. The **forward vector** of an object is the vector that represents the "straight ahead" direction for the object. For example, an object facing straight down the x-axis has a forward vector of <1, 0>.

You can compute many different vector operations. In general, game programmers use a library to perform all these different computations. Because of this, it's better to know *which* vector computations solve which problems than to simply memorize the equations. The remainder of this section explores some of the basic vector use cases.

This book's source code uses a custom-written vector library in the provided Math.h header file, included in the code for each game project from this chapter onward. The Math.h header file declares Vector2 and Vector3 classes, as well as implementations of many operators and member functions. Note that the x and y components are public variables, so you can write code like this:

```
Vector2 myVector;
myVector.x = 5;
myVector.y = 10;
```

Although the diagrams and examples in this section almost universally use 2D vectors, almost every operation outlined also works for 3D vectors; there is simply one more component in 3D.

Getting a Vector between Two Points: Subtraction

With vector subtraction, you subtract each component of one vector from the corresponding component of the other vector, which yields a new vector. For example, in 2D you subtract the x components of the vector separately from the y components:

$$\vec{c} = \vec{b} - \vec{a} = \left\langle b_x - a_x,\ b_y - a_y \right\rangle$$

To visualize the subtraction of two vectors, draw the vectors such that their tails start from the same position, as in Figure 3.3(a). Then construct a vector from the head of one vector to the head of the other. Because subtraction isn't commutative (that is, a − b is not the same as b − a), the order is significant. A mnemonic that helps remember the correct order is that a vector *from* $\vec{a}$ to $\vec{b}$ is $\vec{b} - \vec{a}$.

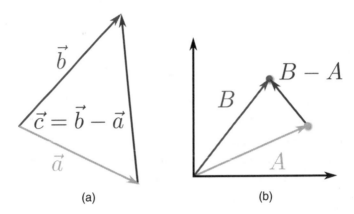

(a)   (b)

Figure 3.3 Vector subtraction (a) and subtraction between two points represented as vectors (b)

You can use subtraction to construct a vector between two points. For example, suppose that a space game allows a ship to fire a laser at a target. You can represent the position of the ship with point s and the position of the target with point t. Suppose that $s = (5,2)$ and $t = (3,5)$.

What if you instead thought of these points as the vectors $\vec{s}$ and $\vec{t}$, drawn with their tails at the origin and their heads "pointing at" their respective points? As previously discussed, the value of the x and y components of these vectors are identical to the points. However, if they are vectors, you can construct a vector between the two by using subtraction, as in Figure 3.8(b). Because the laser should point from the ship to the target, this is the subtraction:

$$\vec{t} - \vec{s} = \langle 3,5 \rangle - \langle 5,2 \rangle = \langle -2,3 \rangle.$$

In the provided `Math.h` library, the − operator subtracts two vectors:

```
Vector2 a, b;
Vector2 result = a - b;
```

Scaling a Vector: Scalar Multiplication

You can multiply a vector by a scalar (a single value). To do so, simply multiply each component of the vector by the scalar:

$$s \cdot \vec{a} = \langle s \cdot a_x, s \cdot a_y \rangle$$

Multiplying a vector by a positive scalar only changes the magnitude of the vector, while multiplying by a negative scalar also inverts the direction of the vector (meaning the head becomes the tail and vice versa). Figure 3.4 illustrates the result of multiplying the vector $\vec{a}$ by two different scalars.

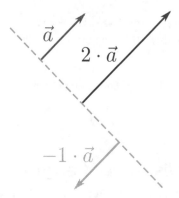

Figure 3.4 Scalar multiplication

In the provided `Math.h` library, the `*` operator performs scalar multiplication:

```
Vector2 a;
Vector2 result = 5.0f * a; // Scaled by 5
```

Combining Two Vectors: Addition

With vector addition, you add the components of two vectors, which yields a new vector:

$$\vec{c} = \vec{a} + \vec{b} = \langle a_x + b_x,\ a_y + b_y \rangle$$

To visualize addition, draw the vectors such that the head of one vector touches the tail of the other vector. The result of the addition is the vector from the tail of one vector to the head of the other, as shown in Figure 3.5.

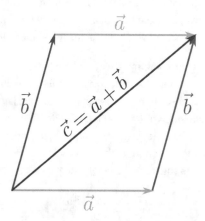

Figure 3.5 Vector addition

Note that the order of the addition doesn't change the result. This is because vector addition is commutative, just like addition between two real numbers:

$$\vec{a}+\vec{b}=\vec{b}+\vec{a}$$

You can use vector addition in a variety of ways. For example, suppose the player is at point p, and the player's forward vector is $\vec{f}$. The point that is 150 units "in front" of the player is then $\vec{p}+150\cdot\vec{f}$.

In the provided `Math.h` library, the + operator adds two vectors:

```
Vector2 a, b;
Vector2 result = a + b;
```

Determining a Distance: Length

As mentioned earlier in this chapter, a vector represents both a magnitude and direction. You use two vertical bars on either side of a vector variable to denote computing the magnitude (or length) of the vector. For example, you write the magnitude of $\vec{a}$ as $\|\vec{a}\|$. To calculate the length of a vector, take the square root of the sum of the squares of each component:

$$\|\vec{a}\|=\sqrt{a_x^2+a_y^2}$$

This may seem very similar to the Euclidean distance formula, and that's because it is just a simplification of the Euclidean distance formula! If you draw the vector such that it starts at the origin, the formula calculates the distance from the origin to the point the vector "points at."

You can use the magnitude to compute the distance between two arbitrary points. Given points p and q, treat them as vectors and perform vector subtraction. The magnitude of the result of the subtraction is equal to the distance between the two points:

$$distance=\|\vec{p}-\vec{q}\|$$

The square root in this length formula is a relatively expensive calculation. If you absolutely *must* know the length, there's no way to avoid this square root. However, in some cases, it may seem that you need to know the length, but you might actually be able to avoid the square root.

For example, suppose you want to determine whether the player is closer to object A or object B. You first construct a vector from object A to the player, or $\vec{p}-\vec{a}$. Similarly, you construct a vector from object B to the player, or $\vec{p}-\vec{b}$. It might seem natural to calculate the length of each vector and compare the two to figure out which object is closer. However, you can simplify the math somewhat. Assuming that you have no imaginary numbers, the length of a vector must be positive. In this case, comparing the length of these two vectors is logically equivalent to comparing the **length squared** (the square of the length) of each vector or, in other words:

$$\|\vec{a}\|<\|\vec{b}\|\equiv\|\vec{a}\|^2<\|\vec{b}\|^2$$

So for cases in which you merely need a relative comparison, you can use the length squared instead of the length:

$$\left\|\vec{a}\right\|^2 = a_x^2 + a_y^2$$

In the provided `Math.h` library, the `Length()` member function computes the length of a vector:

```
Vector2 a;
float length = a.Length();
```

Similarly, the `LengthSquared()` member function computes the length squared.

Determining Directions: Unit Vectors and Normalization

A **unit vector** is a vector with a length of one. The notation for unit vectors is to write a "hat" above the vector's symbol, such as $\hat{u}$. You can convert a vector with a non-unit length into a unit vector through **normalization**. To normalize a vector, divide each component by the length of the vector:

$$\hat{a} = \left\langle \frac{a_x}{\left\|\vec{a}\right\|}, \; \frac{a_y}{\left\|\vec{a}\right\|} \right\rangle$$

In some cases, using unit vectors simplifies calculations. However, normalizing a vector causes it to lose any of its original magnitude information. You must be careful, then, which vectors you normalize and when.

> ## warning
>
> **DIVIDE BY ZERO**   If a vector has zeros for all its components, the length of this vector is also zero. In this case, the normalization formula has a division by zero. For floating-point variables, dividing by zero yields the error value **NaN** (not a number). Once a calculation has NaNs, it's impossible to get rid of them because any operation on NaN also yields NaN.
>
> A common workaround for this is to make a "safe" normalize function that first tests whether the length of the vector if close to zero. If it is, then you simply don't perform the division, thus avoiding the division by zero.

A good rule of thumb is to always normalize vectors if you need only the direction. Some examples are the direction an arrow points or the forward vector of an actor. However, if the distance also matters, such as for a radar showing distances of objects, then normalizing would wipe away this information.

You usually normalize vectors such as the forward vector (which way is an object facing?) and the **up vector** (which way is up?). However, you may not want to normalize other vectors. For example, normalizing a gravity vector causes the loss of the magnitude of the gravity.

The `Math.h` library provides two different `Normalize()` functions. First, there's a member function that normalizes a given vector in place (overwriting its unnormalized version):

```
Vector2 a;
a.Normalize(); // a is now normalized
```

There also is a static function that normalizes a vector passed as a parameter and returns the normalized vector:

```
Vector2 a;
Vector2 result = Vector2::Normalize(a);
```

Converting from an Angle to a Forward Vector

Recall that the `Actor` class from Chapter 2 has a rotation represented by an angle in radians. This allows you to rotate the way an actor faces. Because the rotations are in 2D for now, the angle directly corresponds to an angle on the unit circle, as in Figure 3.6.

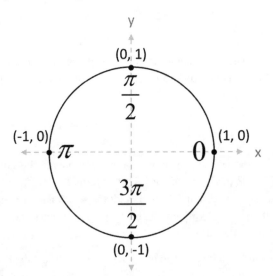

Figure 3.6 Unit circle

The equation of the unit circle in terms of an angle, theta, is:

$$x = \cos\theta$$
$$y = \sin\theta$$

You can directly use these equations to convert the actor's angle into a forward vector:

```
Vector3 Actor::GetForward() const
{
    return Vector2(Math::Cos(mRotation), Math::Sin(mRotation));
}
```

Here, the `Math::Cos` and `Math::Sin` functions are wrappers for the C++ standard library's sine and cosine functions. Notice that you don't explicitly normalize the vector. This is because the circle equation always returns a unit length vector because the unit circle has a radius of one.

Keep in mind that the unit circle has +y as up, whereas SDL 2D graphics use +y down. So for the correct forward vector in SDL, you must negate the y-component value:

```
Vector3 Actor::GetForward() const
{
    // Negate y-component for SDL
    return Vector2(Math::Cos(mRotation), -Math::Sin(mRotation));
}
```

Converting a Forward Vector to an Angle: Arctangent

Now suppose you have a problem opposite the problem described the previous section. Given a forward vector, you want to convert it into an angle. Recall that the tangent function takes in an angle and returns the ratio between the opposite and adjacent sides of a triangle.

Now imagine that you calculate a new "desired" forward vector for an actor, but you need to convert this to the angle for its rotation member variable. In this case, you can form a right triangle with this new forward vector $\vec{v}$ and the x-axis, as shown in Figure 3.7. For this triangle, the x component of the forward vector is the length of the adjacent side of the triangle, and the y component of the forward vector is the length of the opposite side of the triangle. Given this ratio, you can then use the arctangent function to calculate the angle θ.

In programming, the preferred arctangent function is the `atan2` function, which takes two parameters (the opposite length and the adjacent length) and returns an angle in the range $[-\pi, \pi]$. A positive angle means the triangle is in the first or second quadrant (a positive y value), and a negative angle means the triangle is in the third or fourth quadrant.

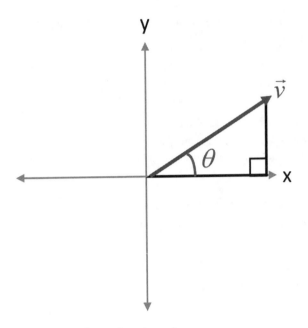

Figure 3.7 Right triangle between the x-axis and a vector

For example, suppose you want a ship to face toward an asteroid. You can first construct the vector from the ship to the asteroid and normalize this vector. Next, use atan2 to convert the new forward vector to an angle. Finally, set the ship actor's rotation to this new angle. Note that you must negate the y component to account for +y down in SDL's 2D coordinate system. This yields the following code:

```
// (ship and asteroid are Actors)
Vector2 shipToAsteroid = asteroid->GetPosition() - ship->GetPosition();
shipToAsteroid.Normalize();
// Convert new forward to angle with atan2 (negate y-component for SDL)
float angle = Math::Atan2(-shipToAsteroid.y, shipToAsteroid.x);
ship->SetRotation(angle);
```

This arctangent approach works very well for 2D games. However, it only works in this form for 2D games because all objects remain on the x-y plane. For 3D games, it's often preferable to use the dot product approach outlined in the next section.

Determining the Angle Between Two Vectors: Dot Product

The **dot product** between two vectors results in a single scalar value. One of the most common uses of the dot product in games is to find the angle between two vectors. The following equation calculates the dot product between vectors $\vec{a}$ and $\vec{b}$:

$$\vec{a} \cdot \vec{b} = a_x \cdot b_x + a_y \cdot b_y$$

The dot product also has a relationship to the cosine of an angle, and you can use the dot product to compute the angle between two vectors:

$$\vec{a} \cdot \vec{b} = \|\vec{a}\| \|\vec{b}\| \cos\theta$$

This formulation, illustrated in Figure 3.8, is based on the Law of Cosines. Given this formula, you can then solve for θ:

$$\theta = \arccos\left(\frac{\vec{a} \cdot \vec{b}}{\|\vec{a}\| \|\vec{b}\|}\right)$$

If the two vectors $\vec{a}$ and $\vec{b}$ are unit vectors, you can omit the division because the length of each vector is one:

$$\theta = \arccos\left(\hat{a} \cdot \hat{b}\right)$$

This is one reason it's helpful to normalize vectors in advance if only the direction matters.

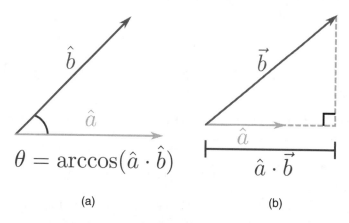

(a)   (b)

Figure 3.8 Computing the angle between two unit vectors

For example, consider a player at position p with a forward vector of $\hat{f}$. A new enemy appears at position e. Suppose you need the angle between the original forward vector and the vector from p to e. First, compute the vector from p to e, using the vector representations of the points:

$$\vec{v} = \vec{e} - \vec{p}$$

Next, because only the direction matters in this case, normalize $\vec{v}$:

$$\hat{v} = \left\langle \frac{v_x}{\|\vec{v}\|}, \frac{v_y}{\|\vec{v}\|} \right\rangle$$

Finally, use the dot product equations to determine the angle between $\hat{f}$ and $\hat{v}$:

$$\theta = \arccos\left(\hat{f} \cdot \hat{v}\right) = \arccos\left(f_x \cdot v_x + f_y \cdot v_y\right).$$

Because the dot product can calculate an angle between two vectors, a couple of special cases are important to remember. If the dot product between two unit vectors is 0, it means that they are perpendicular to each other because $\cos(\pi/2) = 0$. Furthermore, a dot product of 1 means the two vectors are parallel and face the same direction. Finally, a dot product of −1 means they are **antiparallel**, meaning the vectors are parallel and face in the opposite direction.

One drawback of using the dot product to calculate the angle is that the arccosine function returns an angle in the range $[0, \pi]$. This means that while the arccosine gives the minimum angle of rotation between the two vectors, it doesn't say whether this rotation is clockwise or counterclockwise.

As with multiplication between two real numbers, the dot product is commutative, distributive over addition, and associative:

$$\vec{a} \cdot \vec{b} = \vec{b} \cdot \vec{a}$$
$$\vec{a} \cdot \left(\vec{b} + \vec{c}\right) = \vec{a} \cdot \vec{b} + \vec{a} \cdot \vec{c}$$
$$\vec{a} \cdot \left(\vec{b} \cdot \vec{c}\right) = \left(\vec{a} \cdot \vec{b}\right) \cdot \vec{c}$$

Another useful tip is that the length squared calculation is equivalent to taking the dot product of a vector with itself:

$$\vec{v} \cdot \vec{v} = \left\|\vec{v}\right\|^2 = v_x^2 + v_y^2$$

The Math.h library defines a static Dot function for both Vector2 and Vector3. For example, to find the angle between origForward and newForward, you could use:

```
float dotResult = Vector2::Dot(origForward, newForward);
float angle = Math::Acos(dotResult);
```

Calculating a Normal: Cross Product

A **normal** is a vector perpendicular to a surface. Calculating the normal of a surface (such as a triangle) is a very useful calculation in 3D games. For example, the lighting models covered in Chapter 6, "3D Graphics," require calculating normal vectors.

Given two 3D vectors that are not parallel, there is a single plane that contains both vectors. The **cross product** finds a vector perpendicular to that plane, as in Figure 3.9.

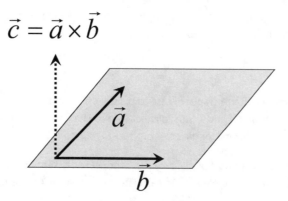

Figure 3.9 Cross product in a left-handed coordinate system

The cross product does not work with 2D vectors. However, to convert a 2D vector into a 3D vector, just add a z component of 0.

The × symbol denotes a cross product between two vectors:

$$\vec{c} = \vec{a} \times \vec{b}$$

Note that there's technically a second vector perpendicular to the plane in Figure 3.9: $-\vec{c}$. This illustrates an important property of the cross product. It's not commutative but instead **anticommutative**:

$$\vec{a} \times \vec{b} = -\vec{b} \times \vec{a}$$

Using the **left-hand rule** is a quick way to figure out the direction the cross product result faces. Take your left hand and point the index finger down $\vec{a}$ and then take your middle finger and point it down $\vec{b}$, rotating your wrist as needed. The natural position of your thumb points in the direction of $\vec{c}$. Here, you use the left hand because this book's coordinate system is left-handed. (You'll learn more about coordinate systems in Chapter 5, "OpenGL.") A right-handed coordinate system instead uses the right-hand rule.

The numeric calculation of the cross product is as follows:

$$\vec{c} = \vec{a} \times \vec{b} = \langle a_y b_z - a_z b_y,\ a_z b_x - a_x b_z,\ a_x b_y - a_y b_x \rangle$$

A popular mnemonic to remember the cross product calculation is "xyzzy." This mnemonic helps you remember the order of the subscripts for the x-component of the cross product result:

$$c_x = a_y b_z - a_z b_y$$

Then, the y and z components are the subscripts rotated in the order $x \rightarrow y \rightarrow z \rightarrow x$, yielding the next two components of the cross product result:

$$c_y = a_z b_x - a_x b_z$$
$$c_z = a_x b_y - a_y b_x$$

As with the dot product, there's a special case to consider. If the cross product returns the vector $\langle 0,0,0 \rangle$, this means that $\vec{a}$ and $\vec{b}$ are collinear. Two collinear vectors cannot form a plane, and therefore there's no normal for the cross product to return.

Because a triangle lies on a single plane, the cross product can determine the normal of the triangle. Figure 3.10 shows triangle ABC. To calculate the normal, first construct two vectors for edges of the triangle:

$$\vec{u} = B - A$$
$$\vec{v} = C - A$$

Then take the cross product between these two vectors and normalize the result. This yields the normal vector of the triangle:

$$\vec{n} = \vec{u} \times \vec{v}$$
$$\hat{n} = \frac{\vec{n}}{\|\vec{n}\|}$$

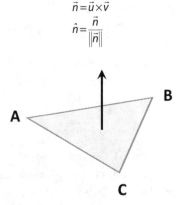

Figure 3.10 Normal to triangle ABC

The `Math.h` library provides a static `Cross` function. For example, the following calculates the cross product between vectors a and b:

```
Vector3 c = Vector3::Cross(a, b);
```

Basic Movement

Recall that Chapter 2's game project overrides the `UpdateActor` function for `Ship` (a subclass of `Actor`) to make the ship move. However, movement is such a common feature for a game that it makes sense to instead encapsulate this behavior in a component. This section first explores how to create a `MoveComponent` class that can move actors around the game world. You'll leverage this class to create asteroids that move around the screen. Next, this section shows how to create a subclass of `MoveComponent` called `InputComponent` that you can hook up directly to keyboard inputs.

Creating a Basic MoveComponent Class

At a basic level, MoveComponent should allow actors to move forward at a certain speed. To support this, you first need a function to calculate the forward vector for an actor, as implemented in the "Converting from an Angle to a Forward Vector" section, earlier in this chapter. Once you have the forward vector of the actor, you can move forward based on a speed (in units per second) and delta time, as in this pseudocode:

```
position += GetForward() * forwardSpeed * deltaTime;
```

You can use a similar mechanism to update the rotation (angle) of the actor, except in this case you don't need a forward vector. You just need angular speed (in rotations per second) and delta time:

```
rotation += angularSpeed * deltaTime;
```

This way, the actor can both move forward and rotate based on the respective speeds. To implement MoveComponent as a subclass of Component, you first declare the class as in Listing 3.1. It has separate speeds to implement both forward and rotational movement, as well as getter/setter functions for these speeds. It also overrides the Update function, which will contain the code that moves the actor. Note that the constructor of MoveComponent specifies a default update order of 10. Recall that the update order determines the order in which the actor updates its components. Because the default update order for other components is 100, MoveComponent will update before most other components do.

Listing 3.1 MoveComponent Declaration

```cpp
class MoveComponent : public Component
{
public:
    // Lower update order to update first
    MoveComponent(class Actor* owner, int updateOrder = 10);

    void Update(float deltaTime) override;

    float GetAngularSpeed() const { return mAngularSpeed; }
    float GetForwardSpeed() const { return mForwardSpeed; }
    void SetAngularSpeed(float speed) { mAngularSpeed = speed; }
    void SetForwardSpeed(float speed) { mForwardSpeed = speed; }
private:
    // Controls rotation (radians/second)
    float mAngularSpeed;
    // Controls forward movement (units/second)
    float mForwardSpeed;
};
```

The implementation of Update, shown in Listing 3.2, simply converts the movement pseudocode into actual code. Recall that a Component class can access its owning actor through the mOwner member variable. You use this mOwner pointer to then access the position, rotation, and forward of the owning actor. Also note the use of the Math::NearZero function here.

This function compares the absolute value of the parameter with some small epsilon amount to determine whether the value is "near" zero. In this specific case, you don't bother updating the rotation or position of the actor if the corresponding speed is near zero.

Listing 3.2 `MoveComponent::Update` Implementation

```cpp
void MoveComponent::Update(float deltaTime)
{
    if (!Math::NearZero(mAngularSpeed))
    {
        float rot = mOwner->GetRotation();
        rot += mAngularSpeed * deltaTime;
        mOwner->SetRotation(rot);
    }
    if (!Math::NearZero(mForwardSpeed))
    {
        Vector2 pos = mOwner->GetPosition();
        pos += mOwner->GetForward() * mForwardSpeed * deltaTime;
        mOwner->SetPosition(pos);
    }
}
```

Because this chapter's game project is a version of the classic *Asteroids* game, you also need code for screen wrapping. This means if an asteroid goes off the left side of the screen, it will teleport to the right side of the screen. (We omit this code here because it's not something desired for a generic `MoveComponent`. However, the source code for this chapter does include this modification for screen wrapping.)

With the basic `MoveComponent`, you can then declare `Asteroid` as a subclass of `Actor`. `Asteroid` doesn't need an overloaded `UpdateActor` function to move. Instead, you can simply construct a `MoveComponent` in its constructor, along with a `SpriteComponent` to display the asteroid image, as in Listing 3.3. The constructor also sets the speed of the asteroid to a fixed 150 units/second (which in this case, corresponds to 150 pixels/second).

Listing 3.3 `Asteroid` Constructor

```cpp
Asteroid::Asteroid(Game* game)
    :Actor(game)
{
    // Initialize to random position/orientation
    Vector2 randPos = Random::GetVector(Vector2::Zero,
        Vector2(1024.0f, 768.0f));
    SetPosition(randPos);
    SetRotation(Random::GetFloatRange(0.0f, Math::TwoPi));

    // Create a sprite component, and set texture
    SpriteComponent* sc = new SpriteComponent(this);
    sc->SetTexture(game->GetTexture("Assets/Asteroid.png"));
```

```
// Create a move component, and set a forward speed
MoveComponent* mc = new MoveComponent(this);
mc->SetForwardSpeed(150.0f);
}
```

One other new item in this `Asteroid` constructor is the use of the `Random` static functions. The implementation of these functions isn't particularly interesting: They simply wrap the built-in C++ random number generators to get a vector or float within a range of values. The `Random` functions here make sure that each asteroid gets a random position and orientation.

With this `Asteroid` class, you can then create several asteroids in the `Game::LoadData` function by using the following code:

```
const int numAsteroids = 20;
for (int i = 0; i < numAsteroids; i++)
{
    new Asteroid(this);
}
```

This results in several moving asteroids onscreen (see Figure 3.11).

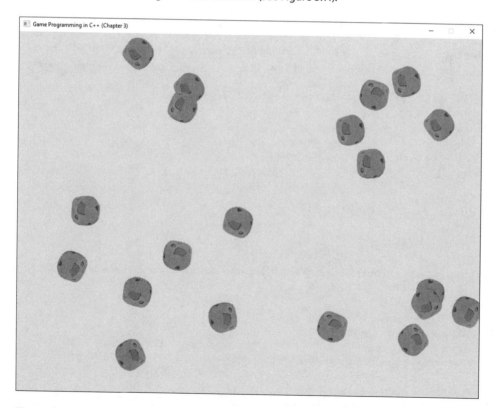

Figure 3.11 Asteroids moving with move components

Creating an `InputComponent` Class

The base `MoveComponent` is fantastic for objects like the asteroids that the player doesn't control. However, if you want a ship that the player can control with the keyboard, you have a dilemma. One idea is to create a custom function for input in the `Ship` class, as in the Chapter 2 game project. However, because hooking up input to an actor or a component is a common need, it's sensible to incorporate this into the game object model. In other words, you want overridable functions in both `Actor` and `Component` that subclasses can redefine for input as needed.

To support this, you first add a virtual `ProcessInput` function to `Component`, with an empty default implementation:

```
virtual void ProcessInput(const uint8_t* keyState) {}
```

Then in `Actor`, you declare two functions: a non-virtual `ProcessInput` and a virtual `ActorInput` function. The idea here is that actor subclasses that want custom input can override `ActorInput` but not `ProcessInput` (like how there are separate `Update` and `UpdateActor` functions):

```
// ProcessInput function called from Game (not overridable)
void ProcessInput(const uint8_t* keyState);
// Any actor-specific input code (overridable)
virtual void ActorInput(const uint8_t* keyState);
```

The `Actor::ProcessInput` function first checks if the actor's state is active. If it is, you first call `ProcessInput` on all components and then call `ActorInput` for any actor-overridable behavior:

```
void Actor::ProcessInput(const uint8_t* keyState)
{
    if (mState == EActive)
    {
        for (auto comp : mComponents)
        {
            comp->ProcessInput(keyState);
        }
        ActorInput(keyState);
    }
}
```

Finally, in `Game::ProcessInput`, you can loop over all actors and call `ProcessInput` on each one:

```
mUpdatingActors = true;
for (auto actor : mActors)
{
    actor->ProcessInput(keyState);
}
mUpdatingActors = false;
```

You set the `mUpdatingActors` bool to `true` before the loop to handle an actor or component trying to create another actor inside `ProcessInput`. In this case, you must add to the mPendingActors vector instead of mActors. This is the same technique used in Chapter 2 to ensure that you don't modify mActors while iterating over the vector.

With this glue code in place, you can then declare a subclass of MoveComponent called InputComponent, as in Listing 3.4. The main idea of InputComponent is that you can set up specific keys to control both forward/backward movement and rotation of the owning actor. In addition, because the overridden ProcessInput directly sets the forward/angular speeds of MoveComponent, you need to specify the "maximum" speeds to calculate the correct speed values based on the keyboard input.

Listing 3.4　InputComponent Declaration

```cpp
class InputComponent : public MoveComponent
{
public:
    InputComponent(class Actor* owner);

    void ProcessInput(const uint8_t* keyState) override;

    // Getters/setters for private variables
    // ...
private:
    // The maximum forward/angular speeds
    float mMaxForwardSpeed;
    float mMaxAngularSpeed;
    // Keys for forward/back movement
    int mForwardKey;
    int mBackKey;
    // Keys for angular movement
    int mClockwiseKey;
    int mCounterClockwiseKey;
};
```

Listing 3.5 shows the implementation of InputComponent::ProcessInput. You first set the forward speed to zero and then determine the correct forward speed based on the keys pressed. You then pass this speed into the inherited SetForwardSpeed function. Note that if the user presses both forward and back keys or neither of the keys, the forward speed becomes zero. You use similar code for setting the angular speed.

Listing 3.5　InputComponent::ProcessInput Implementation

```cpp
void InputComponent::ProcessInput(const uint8_t* keyState)
{
    // Calculate forward speed for MoveComponent
    float forwardSpeed = 0.0f;
    if (keyState[mForwardKey])
    {
        forwardSpeed += mMaxForwardSpeed;
    }
```

```
    if (keyState[mBackKey])
    {
        forwardSpeed -= mMaxForwardSpeed;
    }
    SetForwardSpeed(forwardSpeed);

    // Calculate angular speed for MoveComponent
    float angularSpeed = 0.0f;
    if (keyState[mClockwiseKey])
    {
        angularSpeed += mMaxAngularSpeed;
    }
    if (keyState[mCounterClockwiseKey])
    {
        angularSpeed -= mMaxAngularSpeed;
    }
    SetAngularSpeed(angularSpeed);
}
```

With this in place, you can then add keyboard-controlled movement to `Ship` by simply creating an `InputComponent` instance. (We omit the code for the `Ship` constructor here, but it essentially sets the various `InputComponent` member variables for the keys and maximum speed.) You also create a `SpriteComponent` and assign it a texture. This yields a user-controllable ship (see Figure 3.12).

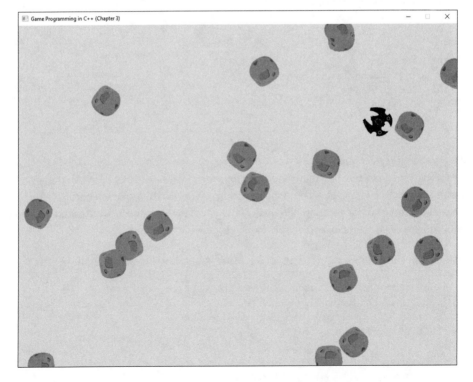

Figure 3.12 Ship controlled with the keyboard

This is an excellent first pass of a more flexible system for input. We explore input in much greater detail in Chapter 8, "Input Systems."

Newtonian Physics

Although the basic movement approach used so far in this chapter works for some games, for movement that more closely resembles the real world, you need a physically accurate approach. Luckily, Isaac Newton (among others) developed **Newtonian physics** (or classical mechanics) to describe laws of motion. Games commonly utilize Newtonian physics because its laws hold if objects are not moving near the speed of light and objects are larger than quantum particles. Because games typically don't feature objects in those edge cases, Newtonian physics works well.

There are several different aspects to Newtonian physics. This book considers only the most basic: movement without rotational forces, or **linear mechanics**. For deeper discussions of other components of Newtonian physics, consult either Ian Millington's book, listed in this chapter's "Additional Reading" section, or any college-level physics textbook.

Linear Mechanics Overview

The two cornerstones of linear mechanics are force and mass. **Force** is an influence that can cause an object to move. Because force has a magnitude and direction, it's natural to represent force with a vector. **Mass** is a scalar that represents the quantity of matter contained in an object. It's common to confuse mass with weight, but mass is independent of any gravity, whereas weight is not. The greater the mass of an object, the more difficult it is to change the movement of that object.

If you apply sufficient force to an object, it will start moving. **Newton's second law of motion** encapsulates this idea:

$$F = m \cdot a$$

In this equation, F is force, m is mass, and a is **acceleration**, or the rate at which the velocity of an object increases. Because force equals mass times acceleration, it's also true that acceleration is force divided by mass. This is the usual approach in games: An arbitrary object in the game has a mass, and you can apply forces to that object. From this, you can then compute the acceleration of the object.

In a physics course, the typical symbolic representation of linear mechanics is that position, velocity, and acceleration are functions over time. Then, with calculus, you can calculate the velocity function as the derivative of the position function and the acceleration function as the derivative of the velocity function.

However, this standard formulation in terms of symbolic equations and derivatives is not particularly applicable in a game. A game needs to apply a force to an object and, from that force, determine the acceleration over time. Once you have an object's acceleration, you can compute the change in the object's velocity. Finally, given a velocity, you can compute the change in the object's position. A game only needs to compute this in terms of the discrete time step of delta time. It doesn't need a symbolic equation. This requires using integration—but not symbolic integration. Instead, you must use **numeric integration**, which approximates the symbolic integral over a fixed time step. Although this sounds very complex, luckily, you can accomplish numeric integration with only a few lines of code.

Computing Positions with Euler Integration

Numeric integration allows a game to update the velocity based on the acceleration and then update the position based on the velocity. However, to compute the acceleration of an object, the game needs to know the mass of the object as well as the forces applied to the object.

There are multiple types of forces to consider. Some forces, such as gravity, are constant and should apply on every frame. Other forces may instead be **impulses**, or forces that apply only for a single frame.

For example, when a character jumps, an impulse force allows the player to get off the ground. However, the character will eventually return to the ground because of the constant force of gravity. Because multiple forces can act on an object simultaneously, and forces are vectors, adding up all the forces gives the total force applied to an object for that frame. Dividing the sum of forces by mass yields acceleration:

```
acceleration = sumOfForces / mass;
```

Next, you can use the **Euler integration** method of numeric integration to compute the velocity and the position:

```
// (Semi-Implicit) Euler Integration
// Update velocity
velocity += acceleration * deltaTime;
// Update position
position += velocity * deltaTime;
```

Note that force, acceleration, velocity, and position are all represented as vectors in these calculations. Because these calculation depend on the delta time, you can put them in the Update function of a component that simulates physics.

Issues with Variable Time Steps

For games that rely on physics simulation, variable frame times (or **time steps**) can cause problems. This is because the accuracy of numeric integration depends on the size of the time step. The smaller the time step, the more accurate the approximation.

If the frame rate varies from frame to frame, so does the accuracy of the numeric integration. The accuracy changing could affect the behavior in very noticeable ways. Imagine playing

Super Mario Bros., where the distance Mario can jump varies depending on the frame rate. The lower the frame rate, the further Mario can jump. This is because the error amount in numeric integration increases with a lower frame rate, which results in an exaggerated jump arc. This means that the game played on a slower machine allows Mario to jump farther than the game played on a fast machine. Figure 3.13 illustrates an example where the actual simulated arc diverges from the intended arc due to a large time step.

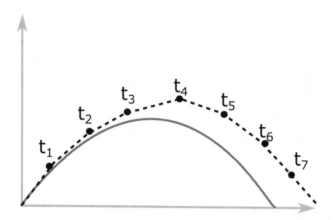

Figure 3.13 The actual jump arc diverges from an intended jump arc due to a large time step

For this reason, any game that uses physics to calculate the positions of objects should not use a variable frame rate—at least not for the physics simulation code. Instead, you can use the frame-limiting approach, as in Chapter 1, which works if the frame rate doesn't go below the target frame rate. A more complex alternative is to divide the larger time step into multiple fixed-size physics time steps.

Basic Collision Detection

Collision detection is how a game determines whether two objects in the game world touch each other. In Chapter 1, you implemented a form of collision detection to determine whether the ball collided with the wall or paddles. However, for the *Asteroids* game project in this chapter, you need slightly more complex calculations to decide whether the lasers the ship fires should collide with the asteroids in the game world.

A key concept in collision detection is simplification of the problem. For example, the asteroid image is circular but not exactly a circle. While it is more accurate to test collision against the actual contours of the asteroid, it's far more efficient to consider the asteroid as a circle for the purposes of collision detection. If you similarly simplify the laser into a circle, you then only need to determine whether these two circles collide.

Circle-Versus-Circle Intersection

Two circles intersect with each other if and only if the distance between their centers is less than or equal to the sum of their radii. Figure 3.14 demonstrates this between two circles. In the first case, the two circles are far enough apart that they do not intersect. In this case, the distance between their centers is greater than the sum of the radii. However, in the second case, where the circles do intersect, the distance between their centers is less than the sum of their radii.

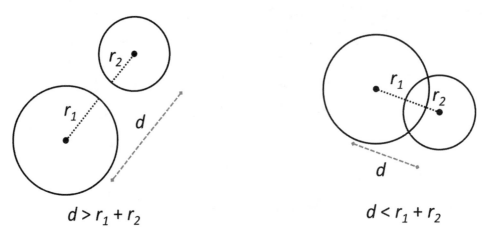

Figure 3.14 Testing intersection between two circles

You can perform this intersection test by first creating a vector between the two centers and calculating the magnitude of this vector. Then, compare this distance against the sum of the circle's radii:

$$\|A.center - B.center\| \le A.radius + B.radius$$

Recall the discussion earlier in the chapter regarding length versus length squared. In the case of circle intersection, all you need is a comparison between the distance and the sum of the radii. Because you know the distances and the radii cannot be negative, you can square both sides of the equation while preserving the inequality:

$$\|A.center - B.center\|^2 \le \left(A.radius + B.radius\right)^2$$

> **note**
>
> The approach covered in this section also works for spheres because the same principle applies.

Creating a `CircleComponent` Subclass

To support collision detection of actors, you can create a `CircleComponent` and a method to test for intersection between two circle components. You can then add a `CircleComponent` to any actor that needs collision.

First, declare `CircleComponent` as a subclass of `Component`, as in Listing 3.6. The only member data `CircleComponent` needs is a radius because the center of the circle is simply the position of the owning actor.

Listing 3.6 `CircleComponent` Declaration

```
class CircleComponent : public Component
{
public:
    CircleComponent(class Actor* owner);

    void SetRadius(float radius) { mRadius = radius; }
    float GetRadius() const;

    const Vector2& GetCenter() const;
private:
    float mRadius;
};
```

Next, declare a global `Intersect` function that takes in two circle components by reference and returns `true` if the two circles intersect with each other, as in Listing 3.7. Note that the implementation directly mirrors the equations from the previous section. You first calculate the distance squared between the two centers and then compare that to the sum of the radii squared.

Listing 3.7 `CircleComponent` Intersection

```
bool Intersect(const CircleComponent& a, const CircleComponent& b)
{
    // Calculate distance squared
    Vector2 diff = a.GetCenter() - b.GetCenter();
    float distSq = diff.LengthSq();

    // Calculate sum of radii squared
    float radiiSq = a.GetRadius() + b.GetRadius();
    radiiSq *= radiiSq;

    return distSq <= radiiSq;
}
```

You can then create a `CircleComponent` just like any other component. For example, the following two lines of code adds a `CircleComponent` to an `Asteroid` object (where `mCircle` is a member variable pointer to a `CircleComponent`):

```
mCircle = new CircleComponent(this);
mCircle->SetRadius(40.0f);
```

Because each laser fired by the ship needs to check for collision against all the asteroids, you can add a `std::vector` of `Asteroid` pointers to `Game`. Then, in `Laser::UpdateActor`, you can easily test for intersection against each of these asteroids:

```
void Laser::UpdateActor(float deltaTime)
{
    // Do you intersect with an asteroid?
    for (auto ast : GetGame()->GetAsteroids())
    {
        if (Intersect(*mCircle, *(ast->GetCircle())))
        {
            // If this laser intersects with an asteroid,
            // set ourselves and the asteroid to dead
            SetState(EDead);
            ast->SetState(EDead);
            break;
        }
    }
}
```

The `GetCircle` function that is called on each asteroid is simply a public function that returns the pointer to the asteroid's `CircleComponent`. Similarly, the `mCircle` variable is the laser's `CircleComponent`.

`CircleComponent` works well in the case of *Asteroids* because you can approximate the collision of all objects in the game with circles. However, circles don't work well for all types of objects, and certainly not in 3D. Chapter 10, "Collision Detection," dives into the topic of collision detection in much greater detail.

Game Project

This chapter's game project implements a basic version of the classic game *Asteroids*. The earlier sections of this chapter cover most of the new code used in the game project. The project implements movement with `MoveComponent` and `InputComponent`. The `CircleComponent` code tests if the ship's laser collides against asteroids. A notable feature that's missing in the game project is that the asteroids do not collide with the ship (though you will add that in Exercise 3.2). The game project also does not implement Newtonian physics (though you will add that in Exercise 3.3). The code is available in the book's GitHub repository, in the Chapter03 directory. Open Chapter03-windows.sln in Windows and Chapter03-mac.xcodeproj on Mac.

One game feature not covered earlier in the chapter is how to create lasers when the player presses the spacebar. Because detecting the spacebar input is unique to Ship, it follows that you should override the ActorInput function. However, if the player holds down the spacebar (or presses it rapidly), you don't want to create so many lasers that it trivializes the game. Instead, you want a cooldown where the ship can fire a laser only once every half second. To implement this, first create a float mLaserCooldown member variable in Ship and initialize it to 0.0f. Next, in ActorInput, check if the player presses the spacebar and mLaserCooldown is less than or equal to zero. If both conditions are met, you create the laser, set its position and rotation to the ship's (so it starts at the ship and faces the direction the ship faces), and set mLaserCooldown to 0.5f:

```
void Ship::ActorInput(const uint8_t* keyState)
{
    if (keyState[SDL_SCANCODE_SPACE] && mLaserCooldown <= 0.0f)
    {
        // Create a laser and set its position/rotation to mine
        Laser* laser = new Laser(GetGame());
        laser->SetPosition(GetPosition());
        laser->SetRotation(GetRotation());

        // Reset laser cooldown (half second)
        mLaserCooldown = 0.5f;
    }
}
```

Then, override UpdateActor to decrement mLaserCooldown by delta time:

```
void Ship::UpdateActor(float deltaTime)
{
    mLaserCooldown -= deltaTime;
}
```

This way, mLaserCooldown keeps track of the amount of time until the player can fire again. And because ActorInput doesn't create a laser if the timer hasn't run out, you make sure the player can't fire more often than desired. With lasers firing, you can then shoot and destroy asteroids with the previously covered collision code (see Figure 3.15).

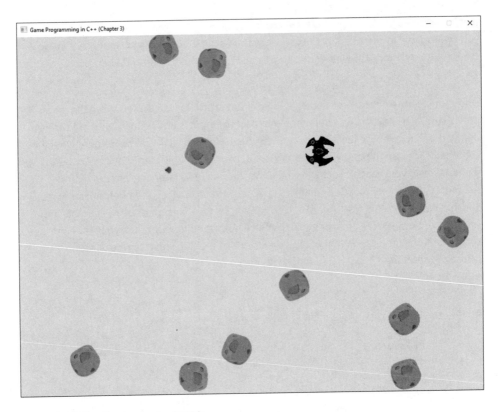

Figure 3.15 Shooting lasers at asteroids

You can use a similar float variable in `Laser` to force the laser to die (and be deleted from the game world) after one second, even if the laser doesn't collide with an asteroid.

Summary

A vector represents a magnitude and a direction. You can use vectors for many different computations, including creating a vector between two points (using subtraction), calculating the distance between two points (using subtraction and length), finding the angle between two vectors (using the dot product), and calculating a normal to a surface (with the cross product).

For basic movement, this chapter shows how to create a `MoveComponent` that allows actors to move in the forward direction as well as rotate. For forward movement, you multiply the forward vector of the actor by movement speed and delta time. Adding this to the current position of the actor yields the new position of the actor after the time step. In this chapter you also learned how to add support for overridable input behavior in actors and components, and how to leverage this to create an `InputComponent` that inherits from `MoveComponent`.

In Newtonian physics, the acceleration of an object is force applied to the object divided by the object's mass. You can use Euler integration to calculate the change in velocity and position on every frame.

Finally, collision detection is how a game decides if two objects touch each other. For some types of games, such as this chapter's game project, you can use circles to represent the collisions of objects. Two circles are considered to intersect if the distance between their centers is less than the sum of their radii. As an optimization, you can square both sides of this equation.

Additional Reading

Eric Lengyel provides an in-depth look at all the different mathematical concepts used in 3D game programming. Aspiring graphics programmers especially should review the more advanced material in his book. The *Gaffer on Games* site, maintained by Glenn Fielder, has several articles on the basics of physics in games, including articles on different forms of numeric integration and why fixing a time step is important. Finally, Ian Millington covers how to implement Newtonian physics in games in detail.

Fielder, Glenn. *Gaffer on Games*. Accessed July 18, 2016. http://gafferongames.com/.

Lengyel, Eric. *Mathematics for 3D Game Programming and Computer Graphics*, 3rd edition. Boston: Cengage, 2011.

Millington, Ian. *Game Physics Engine Development*, 2nd edition. Boca Raton: CRC Press, 2010.

Exercises

The first exercise for this chapter is a series of short problems that give you practice using the various vector techniques covered in this chapter. The next two exercises look at adding features to the chapter's game project.

Exercise 3.1

1. Given the vectors $\vec{a}=\langle 2,4 \rangle$ and $\vec{b}=\langle 3,5 \rangle$, and the scalar value $s=2$, calculate the following:

    (a) $\vec{a}+\vec{b}$

    (b) $s \cdot \vec{a}$

    (c) $\vec{a} \cdot \vec{b}$

2. Given the triangle in Figure 3.16 and the following points:

    $A=\langle -1,\ 1 \rangle$
    $B=\langle 2,\ 4 \rangle$
    $C=\langle 3,\ 3 \rangle$

    Calculate the θ using the vector operations discussed in this chapter.

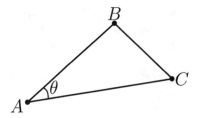

Figure 3.16 Triangle for problem 2 of Exercise 3.1

3. Suppose a 2D game features an arrow that points from the player to the next objective. When the game first begins, the arrow points down the x-axis $\langle 1,0 \rangle$.

   The player's initial position is at $(4,0)$.

   You create a new object at the position $(5,6)$.

   a. What is the *unit* vector *from* the player's initial position *to* the new waypoint?

   b. Calculate the *angle* of rotation between the initial arrow direction and the vector calculated in part (a).

   c. Calculate the vector perpendicular to the plane created by the initial arrow direction and the vector calculated in part (a).

Exercise 3.2

Currently, the ship does not collide against asteroids in the chapter game project. Add collision for the ship. To do so, you first need to create a `CollisionComponent` in `Ship` and specify a radius. Next, in `Ship::UpdateActor`, you need to test against the collision of all asteroids (much the way the laser does). If the ship collides with an asteroid, force it to reset in the center of the screen with a rotation of zero.

As an extra feature, make it so the ship disappears for a second or two after colliding with an asteroid. The ship should then reappear in the center after this delay.

Exercise 3.3

Modify `MoveComponent` so that it uses Newtonian physics. Specifically, change it to have a mass, a sum of forces, and a velocity as member variables. Then in `Update`, change the code for forward movement so it instead calculates an acceleration from the forces, a velocity from the acceleration, and a position from the velocity.

Then, you need some method to set forces on the component. One approach is to add an `AddForce` function that takes in a `Vector2` and adds that to the sum of forces variable. You can additionally clear the sum of forces on every frame after calculating acceleration. This way, for an impulse you just call `AddForce` once. And for a constant force, you simply call `AddForce` for that force on every frame.

Finally, change `InputComponent`, `Asteroid`, and `Ship` so that they work correctly with this new `MoveComponent` that supports Newtonian physics.

CHAPTER 4

ARTIFICIAL INTELLIGENCE

Artificial intelligence (AI) algorithms are used to determine the actions of computer-controlled entities in games. This chapter covers three useful game AI techniques: changing behaviors with state machines, computing paths for entities to move through the world (pathfinding), and making decisions in two-player turn-based games (minimax and game trees). The chapter shows you how to apply some of these AI techniques to create a tower defense game project.

State Machine Behaviors

For very simple games, the AI always has the same behavior. For instance, an AI for two-player *Pong* tracks the position of the ball as it moves. Because this behavior doesn't change throughout the game, it's stateless. But for more complex games, the AI behaves differently at different points in time. In *Pac-Man*, each ghost has three different behaviors: chasing the player, scattering away (where the ghost returns to a set "home area"), or running away from the player. One way to represent these changes in behaviors is with a **state machine**, where each behavior corresponds to a state.

Designing a State Machine

States by themselves only partially define a state machine. Equally important is how the state machine decides to change, or **transition** between, states. Furthermore, each state can have actions that occur on entry or exit of the state.

When implementing a state machine for a game character's AI, it's prudent to plan the different states and how they interconnect. Take the example of a basic guard character in a stealth game. By default, the guard patrols on a predefined path. If the guard detects the player while on patrol, it starts attacking the player. And, if at any point in time, the guard receives fatal damage, it dies. In this example, the guard AI has three different states: Patrol, Attack, and Death.

Next, you need to define the transitions for each state. The Death state transition is simple: When the guard takes fatal damage, it transitions to Death. This happens regardless of the current state. The guard enters the Attack state if, during the Patrol state, the guard spots the player. The state machine diagram in Figure 4.1 represents this combination of states and transitions.

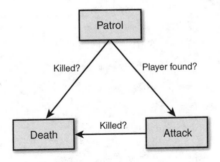

Figure 4.1 Basic stealth AI state machine

Although this AI is functional, AI characters in most stealth games are more complex. Suppose the guard hears a suspicious sound while in the Patrol state. The current state machine dictates that the guard continue patrolling. Ideally, the sound should startle the guard and cause the guard to search for the player. An Investigate state can represent this behavior.

Furthermore, in this state machine example, the guard always attacks when detecting the player. But for variety, maybe the guard occasionally triggers an alarm instead. An Alert state can represent this behavior. The Alert state randomly transitions out to either Attack or another new state, Alarm. Adding these refinements makes the state machine more complex, as shown in Figure 4.2.

From the Alert state you have two transitions: 75% and 25%. These transitions refer to the probability of the transition. So, there's a 75% chance that when in the Alert state, the AI will transition to the Attack state. In the Alarm state, the Complete transition means that after the AI finishes triggering the alarm (perhaps by interacting with some object in the game world), the AI transitions into the Attack state.

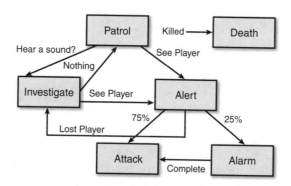

Figure 4.2 More complex stealth AI state machine

Further refinements to the state machine are possible. But the principles of designing an AI state machine are the same regardless of the number of states. In any event, after defining a state machine, the next step is to implement it in code.

Basic State Machine Implementation

There are several ways to implement a state machine. Minimally, the code must update the behavior of the AI based on the current state, and it must support enter and exit actions. An `AIComponent` class can encapsulate this state behavior.

If there are only two states, a simple Boolean check in `Update` would work, though it isn't very robust. A more flexible implementation is to use an enum to represent the different states. For the state machine in Figure 4.1, this is the enum declaration:

```
enum AIState
{
    Patrol,
    Death,
    Attack
};
```

Then, you create an `AIComponent` class that has an instance of `AIState` as member data. You also define separate update functions for each state: `UpdatePatrol`, `UpdateDeath`, and `UpdateAttack`. The `AIComponent::Update` function then has a switch on the `AIState` member variable and calls the update function that corresponds to the current state:

```
void AIComponent::Update(float deltaTime)
{
    switch (mState)
    {
    case Patrol:
        UpdatePatrol(deltaTime);
        break;
    case Death:
        UpdateDeath(deltaTime);
        break;
    case Attack:
        UpdateAttack(deltaTime);
        break;
    default:
        // Invalid
        break;
    }
}
```

You can handle the state machine transitions in a separate `ChangeState` function. This way, the various update functions can initiate a transition just by calling `ChangeState`. You can implement `ChangeState` as follows:

```
void AIComponent::ChangeState(State newState)
{
    // Exit current state
    // (Use switch to call corresponding Exit function)
    // ...

    mState = newState;

    // Enter current state
    // (Use switch to call corresponding Enter function)
    // ...
}
```

Although this implementation is simple, there are issues. First, it doesn't scale well; adding more states reduces the readability of both `Update` and `ChangeState`. Also, having so many separate `Update`, `Enter`, and `Exit` functions also makes the code harder to follow.

It's also not easy to mix and match functionality between multiple AIs. Two different AIs with different state machines need separate enums and, therefore, separate AI components. But many AI characters may share some functionality. Suppose two AIs have mostly different state machines, but both have a Patrol state. With this basic implementation, it isn't easy to share the Patrol code between both AI components.

States as Classes

An alternative approach to the one just described is to use classes to represent each state. First, define a base class for all states called `AIState`:

```
class AIState
{
public:
    AIState(class AIComponent* owner)
        :mOwner(owner)
    { }
    // State-specific behavior
    virtual void Update(float deltaTime) = 0;
    virtual void OnEnter() = 0;
    virtual void OnExit() = 0;
    // Getter for string name of state
    virtual const char* GetName() const = 0;
protected:
    class AIComponent* mOwner;
};
```

The base class includes several virtual functions to control the state: `Update` updates the state, `OnEnter` implements any entry transition code, and `OnExit` implements any exit transition code. The `GetName` function simply returns a human-readable name for the state. You also associate `AIState` with a specific `AIComponent` through the `mOwner` member variable.

Next, declare the `AIComponent` class, as follows:

```
class AIComponent : public Component
{
public:
    AIComponent(class Actor* owner);

    void Update(float deltaTime) override;
    void ChangeState(const std::string& name);

    // Add a new state to the map
    void RegisterState(class AIState* state);
private:
    // Maps name of state to AIState instance
    std::unordered_map<std::string, class AIState*> mStateMap;
    // Current state we're in
    class AIState* mCurrentState;
};
```

Notice how `AIComponent` has a hash map of state names to `AIState` instance pointers. It also has a pointer to the current `AIState`. The `RegisterState` function takes in a pointer to an `AIState` and adds the state to the map:

```
void AIComponent::RegisterState(AIState* state)
{
    mStateMap.emplace(state->GetName(), state);
}
```

The `AIComponent::Update` function is also straightforward. It simply calls `Update` on the current state, if it exists:

```
void AIComponent::Update(float deltaTime)
{
    if (mCurrentState)
    {
        mCurrentState->Update(deltaTime);
    }
}
```

However, the `ChangeState` function does several things, as shown in Listing 4.1. First, it calls `OnExit` on the current state. Next, it tries to find the state you're changing to in the map. If it finds this state, it changes `mCurrentState` to the new state and calls `OnEnter` on this new state. If it can't find the next state in the map, it outputs an error message and sets `mCurrentState` to `null`.

Listing 4.1 `AIComponent::ChangeState` Implementation

```
void AIComponent::ChangeState(const std::string& name)
{
    // First exit the current state
    if (mCurrentState)
    {
        mCurrentState->OnExit();
    }

    // Try to find the new state from the map
    auto iter = mStateMap.find(name);
    if (iter != mStateMap.end())
    {
        mCurrentState = iter->second;
        // We're entering the new state
        mCurrentState->OnEnter();
    }
    else
    {
        SDL_Log("Could not find AIState %s in state map", name.c_str());
        mCurrentState = nullptr;
    }
}
```

You can use this pattern by first declaring subclasses of `AIState`, like this `AIPatrol` class:

```cpp
class AIPatrol : public AIState
{
public:
   AIPatrol(class AIComponent* owner);

   // Override with behaviors for this state
   void Update(float deltaTime) override;
   void OnEnter() override;
   void OnExit() override;

   const char* GetName() const override
   { return "Patrol"; }
};
```

You then implement any special behaviors in `Update`, `OnEnter`, and `OnExit`. Suppose you want `AIPatrol` to change to the `AIDeath` state when the character dies. To initiate the transition, you need to call `ChangeState` on the owning component, passing in the name of the new state:

```cpp
void AIPatrol::Update(float deltaTime)
{
   // Do some other updating
   // ...
   bool dead = /* Figure out if I'm dead */;
   if (dead)
   {
      // Tell the ai component to change states
      mOwner->ChangeState("Death");
   }
}
```

On the `ChangeState` call, the `AIComponent` looks into its state map, and if it finds a state named Death, it transitions into this state. You can similarly declare `AIDeath` and `AIAttack` classes to complete the basic state machine from Figure 4.1.

To hook up the states into an `AIComponent`'s state map, first create an actor and its `AIComponent` and then call `Register` on any states you wish to add to the state machine:

```cpp
Actor* a = new Actor(this);
// Make an AIComponent
AIComponent* aic = new AIComponent(a);
// Register states with AIComponent
aic->RegisterState(new AIPatrol(aic));
aic->RegisterState(new AIDeath(aic));
aic->RegisterState(new AIAttack(aic));
```

To then set the `AIComponent` to an initial patrol state, you call `ChangeState`, as follows:

```
aic->ChangeState("Patrol");
```

Overall, this approach is useful because each state's implementation is in a separate subclass, which means the `AIComponent` remains simple. It also makes it significantly easier to reuse the same states for different AI characters. You simply need to register whichever states you want with the new actor's `AIComponent`.

Pathfinding

A **pathfinding** algorithm finds a path between two points, avoiding any obstacles in the way. The complexity of this problem stems from the fact that there might be a large set of paths between two points, but only a small number of these paths are the shortest. For example, Figure 4.3 shows two potential routes between points A and B. An AI traveling along the solid path is not particularly intelligent because the dashed path is shorter. Thus, you need a method to efficiently search through all the possible paths to find one with the shortest distance.

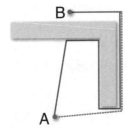

Figure 4.3 Two paths from A to B

Graphs

Before you can solve the pathfinding problem, you first need a way to represent the parts of the game world that the AI can path through. A popular choice is the **graph** data structure. A graph contains a set of **nodes** (also called vertices). These nodes connect to each other via **edges**. These edges can be **undirected**, meaning they are traversable in both directions, or **directed**, meaning they are traversable in only one direction. You might use a directed edge for a case where the AI can jump down from a platform but can't jump back up. You could represent this connection with a directed edge from the platform to the ground.

Optionally, edges may have **weights** associated with them, representing the cost of traversing the edge. In a game, the weight minimally accounts for the distance between the nodes. However, you might modify the weight based on the difficulty of traversing the edge.

For example, if an edge moves over quicksand in the game world, it should have a higher weight than an edge of the same length that moves over concrete. A graph without edge weights (an **unweighted graph**) effectively is a graph where the weight of every edge is a constant value. Figure 4.4 illustrates a simple undirected and unweighted graph.

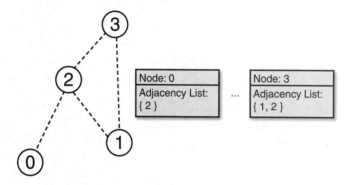

Figure 4.4 A sample graph

There are multiple ways to represent a graph in memory, but this book uses **adjacency lists**. In this representation, each node has a collection of adjacent nodes (using `std::vector`). For an unweighted graph, this adjacency list contains pointers to adjacent nodes. The graph is then just a collection of such nodes:

```
struct GraphNode
{
    // Each node has pointers to adjacent nodes
    std::vector<GraphNode*> mAdjacent;
};

struct Graph
{
    // A graph contains nodes
    std::vector<GraphNode*> mNodes;
};
```

For a weighted graph, instead of a list of connected nodes, each node stores its outgoing edges:

```
struct WeightedEdge
{
    // Which nodes are connected by this edge?
    struct WeightedGraphNode* mFrom;
    struct WeightedGraphNode* mTo;
    // Weight of this edge
    float mWeight;
};
```

```
struct WeightedGraphNode
{
    // Stores outgoing edges
    std::vector<WeightedEdge*> mEdges;
};
// (A WeightedGraph has WeightedGraphNodes)
```

By referencing both the "from" and "to" nodes in each edge, you can support a directed edge from node A to B by adding an edge to node A's mEdges vector but not to node B's. If you want an undirected edge, you simply add two directed edges, one in each direction (for example, from A to B *and* from B to A).

Different games represent the game world via graphs in different manners. Partitioning a world into a grid of squares (or hexes) is the simplest approach. This approach is very popular for turn-based strategy games such as *Civilization* or *XCOM*. However, for many other types of games, it isn't feasible to use this approach. For simplicity, most of this section sticks with a grid of squares. However, you will learn about other possible representations later in this chapter.

Breadth-First Search

Suppose a game takes place in a maze designed in a square grid. The game only allows movement in the four cardinal directions. Because each move in the maze is uniform in length, an unweighted graph can represent this maze. Figure 4.5 shows a sample maze and its corresponding graph.

Now imagine that a mouse AI character starts at some square in the maze (the **start node**) and wants to find the shortest path to a piece of cheese in the maze (the **goal node**). One approach is to first check all squares one move away from the start. If none of these squares contains the cheese, you then check all squares two moves away from the start. Repeat this process until either the cheese is found or there are no valid moves left. Because this algorithm only considers the further nodes once the closer nodes are exhausted, it won't miss the shortest path to the cheese. This describes what happens in a **breadth-first search** (**BFS**). The BFS algorithm guarantees to find the shortest path when either the edges are unweighted or every edge has the same positive weight.

With some minor bookkeeping during BFS, it's possible to reconstruct the path with the minimal number of moves. Once it's computed, AI characters can then follow along this path.

During BFS, each node needs to know the node visited immediately before it. That node, called the **parent** node, helps reconstruct the path after BFS completes. While you could add this data to the GraphNode struct, it's better to separate the data that doesn't change (the graph itself) from the parents. This is because the parents will change depending on the start and goal nodes selected. Separating these pieces of data also means that if you want to compute several paths simultaneously across multiple threads, the searches won't interfere with each other.

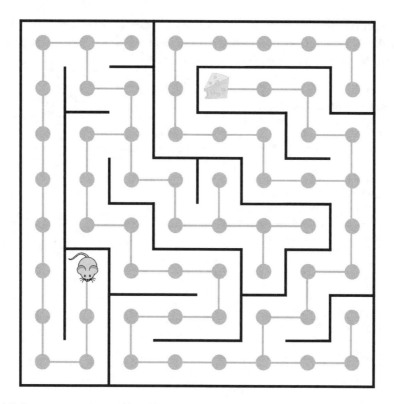

Figure 4.5 A maze on a square grid and its corresponding graph

To support this, first define a type of map called a `NodeToPointerMap`, which simply is an unordered map where both the key and value are `GraphNode` pointers (the pointers are `const` because you don't need to modify the graph nodes):

```
using NodeToParentMap =
    std::unordered_map<const GraphNode*, const GraphNode*>;
```

With this type of map, you can then implement BFS as in Listing 4.2. The simplest way to implement BFS is with a queue. Recall that a queue uses FIFO (first-in, first-out) behavior when adding and removing nodes. You can add a node to a queue via an enqueue operation and remove a node via dequeue. To begin, you enqueue the start node and enter a loop. In each iteration, you dequeue a node and enqueue its neighbors. You can avoid adding the same node multiple times to the queue by checking the parent map. A node's parent is null only if the node hasn't been enqueued before *or* it's the start node.

When you use the square brackets on the `outMap`, one of two things happens. If the key already exists in the map, you can just access its parent. Otherwise, if the key does not exist in the map, the map by default constructs a value for that key. In this case, if you access `outMap` and the node requested isn't in the map, you initialize that node's parent to `nullptr`.

Even if no path exists between the start and the goal, the loop will eventually terminate. This is because the algorithm checks all nodes that are reachable from start. Once all possibilities are exhausted, the queue becomes empty and the loop ends.

Listing 4.2 Breadth-First Search

```cpp
bool BFS(const Graph& graph, const GraphNode* start,
         const GraphNode* goal, NodeToParentMap& outMap)
{
    // Whether we found a path
    bool pathFound = false;
    // Nodes to consider
    std::queue<const GraphNode*> q;
    // Enqueue the first node
    q.emplace(start);

    while (!q.empty())
    {
        // Dequeue a node
        const GraphNode* current = q.front();
        q.pop();
        if (current == goal)
        {
            pathFound = true;
            break;
        }

        // Enqueue adjacent nodes that aren't already in the queue
        for (const GraphNode* node : current->mAdjacent)
        {
            // If the parent is null, it hasn't been enqueued
            // (except for the start node)
            const GraphNode* parent = outMap[node];
            if (parent == nullptr && node != start)
            {
                // Enqueue this node, setting its parent
                outMap[node] = current;
                q.emplace(node);
            }
        }
    }

    return pathFound;
}
```

Assuming that you have a `Graph g`, you can then run BFS between two `GraphNodes` in the graph with the following two lines:

```
NodeToParentMap map;
bool found = BFS(g, g.mNodes[0], g.mNodes[9], map);
```

If BFS succeeds, you can reconstruct the path by using the parent pointers in the `outMap`. This is because the goal's parent points to the preceding node on the path. Similarly, the parent of the node preceding the goal node is two moves away from the goal. Following this chain of parent pointers eventually leads back to the start node, yielding a path from goal to start.

Unfortunately, you want the path in the opposite direction: from start to goal. One solution is to reverse the path with a stack, but a more intelligent approach is to *reverse the search*. For example, instead of passing in the mouse node as start and the cheese node as goal, do the opposite. Then, following the parent pointers from the goal node yields the desired path.

BFS always finds a path between the start and goal nodes if one exists. But for weighted graphs, BFS doesn't guarantee to find the shortest path. This is because BFS doesn't look at the weight of the edges at all; every edge traversal is equivalent. In Figure 4.6, the dashed path has the shortest distance, but BFS returns the solid path as it requires only two moves.

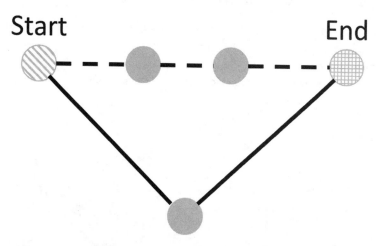

Figure 4.6 BFS finds the solid path even though the dashed path is shorter

Another issue with BFS is that it tests nodes even if they are in the opposite direction of the goal. By using a more complex algorithm, it's possible to reduce the number of nodes you test on the way to finding the optimal solution.

Most other pathfinding algorithms used in games have an overall structure like BFS. On every iteration, you pick one node to inspect next and add its neighbors to a data structure. What changes is that different pathfinding algorithms evaluate nodes in different orders.

Heuristics

Many search algorithms rely on a **heuristic**, which is a function that approximates an expected result. In pathfinding, the heuristic is the estimated cost from a given node to the goal node. A heuristic can help you more quickly find a path. For example, on each iteration of BFS, you dequeue the next node in the queue, even if that node sends you in a direction pointing away from the goal. With a heuristic, you can estimate how close you think a specific node is to the goal and then choose to look at the "closer" nodes first. This way, the pathfinding algorithm is likely to terminate with fewer iterations.

The notation **h(x)** denotes the heuristic, where x is a node in the graph. So, h(x) is the estimated cost from node x to the goal node.

A heuristic function is **admissible** if it is always less than or equal to the actual cost from node x to the goal. If the heuristic occasionally overestimates the actual cost, it's **inadmissible,** and you shouldn't use it. The A* algorithm, discussed later in this section, requires an admissible heuristic to guarantee the shortest path.

For a grid of squares, there are two common ways to compute the heuristic. For example, in Figure 4.7, the checkered node represents the goal and the solid node represents the start. The gray squares in this figure denote squares that are impassable.

The **Manhattan distance** heuristic, illustrated in Figure 4.7 (left), is akin to traveling along city blocks in a sprawling metropolis. A building might be "five blocks away," but there may be multiple routes five blocks in length. Manhattan distance assumes that diagonal movements are invalid. If diagonal movements are valid, Manhattan distance often overestimates the cost, making the heuristic inadmissible.

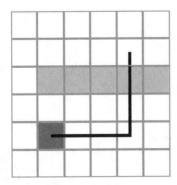

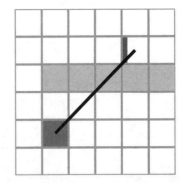

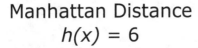

Manhattan Distance
h(x) = 6

Euclidean Distance
h(x) = 4.24

Figure 4.7 Manhattan heuristic (left) and Euclidean heuristic (right)

For a 2D grid, the following formula calculates Manhattan distance:

$$h(x) = |start.x - end.x| + |start.y - end.y|$$

A second type of heuristic is **Euclidean distance**, illustrated in Figure 4.7 (right). You use the standard distance formula to calculate this heuristic, which estimates an "as the crow flies" route. Unlike Manhattan distance, Euclidean distance can easily work for worlds more complex than a square grid. In 2D, the Euclidean distance equation is as follows:

$$h(x) = \sqrt{(start.x - end.x)^2 + (start.y - end.y)^2}$$

The Euclidean distance function is almost always admissible, even in cases where the Manhattan distance is inadmissible. This means that Euclidean distance is usually the recommended heuristic function. However, the Manhattan heuristic is more efficient to compute because it doesn't involve a square root.

The only case where a Euclidean distance heuristic overestimates the true cost is if the game allows non-Euclidean movement such as teleporting between two nodes across the level.

Notice that in Figure 4.7 both heuristic *h(x)* functions end up *underestimating* the actual cost of traveling from the start node to the goal node. This happens because the heuristic function knows nothing about the adjacency lists, so it doesn't know whether certain areas are impassable. This is fine because the heuristic is the lower bound of how close node *x* is to the goal node; the heuristic guarantees that node *x* is *at least* that distance away. This is more useful in a relative sense: The heuristic can help estimate whether node A or node B is closer to the goal node. And then you can use this estimate to help decide whether to explore node A or node B next.

The following section shows how to use the heuristic function to create a more complex pathfinding algorithm.

Greedy Best-First Search

BFS uses a queue to consider nodes in a FIFO manner. **Greedy best-first search (GBFS)** instead uses the *h(x)* heuristic function to decide which node to consider next. Although this seems like a reasonable pathfinding algorithm, GBFS *cannot guarantee a minimal path*. Figure 4.8 shows the resultant path from a sample GBFS search. Nodes in gray are impassible. Note that the path makes four additional moves from the start rather than going straight down.

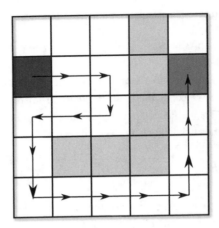

Figure 4.8 Greedy best-first path

> **note**
>
> Although GBFS does not guarantee optimality, it's useful to understand because it requires only a couple modifications to become A*. The A* algorithm *does* guarantee the shortest path if the heuristic is admissible. So before moving on to A*, it's important to understand the GBFS implementation.

Instead of using a single queue, GBFS uses two sets of nodes during the search. The **open set** contains the nodes that are under consideration. Once chosen for evaluation, a node moves into the **closed set**. When a node is in the closed set, GBFS need not investigate it further. There's no guarantee that a node in the open or closed set will ultimately be on the path; these sets just help prune nodes from consideration.

Selecting data structures for the open set and the closed set presents an interesting dilemma. For the open set, the two operations you need are removing the node with the lowest cost and testing for membership. The closed set only needs a membership test. To speed up the membership test, you can simply use Booleans in scratch data to track if a specific node is a member of the open set or the closed set. And because the closed set just needed this membership test, you don't use an actual collection for the closed set.

For the open set, one popular data structure is a priority queue. However, in the interest of simplicity, this chapter uses a vector for the open set. With a vector, you can just use a linear search to find the element in the open set with the lowest cost.

As with BFS, each node needs additional scratch data during the GBFS search. Because you now have multiple pieces of scratch data per node, it makes sense to define a struct to encapsulate it. To use a weighted graph, the parent is an incoming edge as opposed to a preceding node. In addition, each node tracks its heuristic value and its membership in the open and closed sets:

```
struct GBFSScratch
{
    const WeightedEdge* mParentEdge = nullptr;
    float mHeuristic = 0.0f;
    bool mInOpenSet = false;
    bool mInClosedSet = false;
};
```

Then, define a map where the key is a pointer to the node and the value is an instance of GBFSScratch:

```
using GBFSMap =
    std::unordered_map<const WeightedGraphNode*, GBFSScratch>;
```

Now you have the necessary components for a greedy best-first search. The GBFS function takes in a WeightedGraph, the start node, the goal node, and a reference to a GBFSMap:

```
bool GBFS(const WeightedGraph& g, const WeightedGraphNode* start,
        const WeightedGraphNode* goal, GBFSMap& outMap);
```

At the start of the GBFS function, you define a vector for the open set:

```
std::vector<const WeightedGraphNode*> closedSet;
```

Next, you need a variable to track the current node, which is the node under evaluation. This updates as the algorithm progresses. Initially, current is the start node, and you "add" it to the closed set by marking it as closed in the scratch map:

```
const WeightedGraphNode* current = start;
outMap[current].mInClosedSet = true;
```

Next, you enter the main loop of GBFS. This main loop does several things. First, it looks at all nodes adjacent to the current node. It only considers nodes that aren't already in the closed set. These nodes have their parent edge set to the edge incoming from the current node. For nodes not already in the open set, the code computes the heuristic (from the node to the goal) and adds the node to the open set:

```
do
{
    // Add adjacent nodes to open set
    for (const WeightedEdge* edge : current->mEdges)
    {
        // Get scratch data for this node
        GBFSScratch& data = outMap[edge->mTo];
```

```
    // Add it only if it's not in the closed set
    if (!data.mInClosedSet)
    {
        // Set the adjacent node's parent edge
        data.mParentEdge = edge;
        if (!data.mInOpenSet)
        {
            // Compute the heuristic for this node, and add to open set
            data.mHeuristic = ComputeHeuristic(edge->mTo, goal);
            data.mInOpenSet = true;
            openSet.emplace_back(edge->mTo);
        }
    }
}
```

The `ComputeHeuristic` function can use any heuristic *h(x)* function, such as Manhattan or Euclidean distance. In practice, this may require additional information stored in each node (such as the position of the node in the world).

After processing the nodes adjacent to the current node, you need to look at the open set. If it's empty, this means there are no nodes left to evaluate. This happens only if there is no path from start to goal:

```
if (openSet.empty())
{
    break; // Break out of outer loop
}
```

Alternatively, if there are still nodes in the open set, the algorithm continues. You need to find the node in the open set with the lowest heuristic cost and move it to the closed set. This node becomes the new current node:

```
// Find lowest cost node in open set
auto iter = std::min_element(openSet.begin(), openSet.end(),
    [&outMap](const WeightedGraphNode* a, const WeightedGraphNode* b)
{
        return outMap[a].mHeuristic < outMap[b].mHeuristic;
});
// Set to current and move from open to closed
current = *iter;
openSet.erase(iter);
outMap[current].mInOpenSet = false;
outMap[current].mInClosedSet = true;
```

To code to find the lowest element, uses the `std::min_element` function from the `<algorithm>` header. For its third parameter, `min_element` takes in a special type of function (called a *lambda expression*) to specify how to decide whether one element is less than another. The `min_element` function returns an iterator to the minimum element.

Finally, the main loop continues if the current node is not the goal node:

```
} while (current != goal);
```

The loop terminates either when the above `while` condition fails or when you hit the earlier break statement (for when the open set is empty). You can then figure out if GBFS found a path based on whether the current node equals the goal node:

```
return (current == goal) ? true : false;
```

Figure 4.9 shows the first two iterations of GBFS applied to a sample data set. In Figure 4.9(a), the start node (A2) is in the closed set, and its adjacent nodes are in the open set. To make the figure easy to read, it uses the Manhattan distance heuristic. The arrows point from children back to their parent node. The next step is to select the node with the lowest heuristic cost, which is the node with $h = 3$. This node becomes the new current node and moves into the closed set. Figure 4.9(b) shows the next iteration, where C2 is now the node with the lowest cost in the open set.

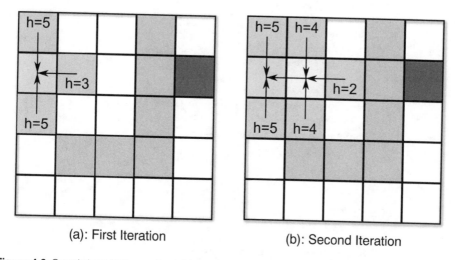

(a): First Iteration   (b): Second Iteration

Figure 4.9 Greedy best-first snapshots: (a) first iteration and (b) second iteration

Keep in mind that just because a node in the open set has the lowest heuristic cost doesn't mean it's on the optimal path. For example, in Figure 4.9(b), the node C2 is not on the optimal path. Unfortunately, the GBFS algorithm still selects C2 for its path. Clearly, you need to do some refinement to fix this issue.

Listing 4.3 shows the complete code for the greedy best-first search function.

Listing 4.3 Greedy Best-First Search

```cpp
bool GBFS(const WeightedGraph& g, const WeightedGraphNode* start,
          const WeightedGraphNode* goal, GBFSMap& outMap)
{
    std::vector<const WeightedGraphNode*> openSet;
    // Set current node to start, and mark in closed set
    const WeightedGraphNode* current = start;
    outMap[current].mInClosedSet = true;
    do
    {
        // Add adjacent nodes to open set
        for (const WeightedEdge* edge : current->mEdges)
        {
            // Get scratch data for this node
            GBFSScratch& data = outMap[edge->mTo];
            // Consider it only if it's not in the closed set
            if (!data.mInClosedSet)
            {
                // Set the adjacent node's parent edge
                data.mParentEdge = edge;
                if (!data.mInOpenSet)
                {
                    // Compute the heuristic for this node, and add to open set
                    data.mHeuristic = ComputeHeuristic(edge->mTo, goal);
                    data.mInOpenSet = true;
                    openSet.emplace_back(edge->mTo);
                }
            }
        }

        if (openSet.empty())
        { break; }

        // Find lowest cost node in open set
        auto iter = std::min_element(openSet.begin(), openSet.end(),
            [&outMap](const WeightedGraphNode* a, const WeightedGraphNode* b)
        {
            return outMap[a].mHeuristic < outMap[b].mHeuristic;
        });
        // Set to current and move from open to closed
        current = *iter;
        openSet.erase(iter);
        outMap[current].mInOpenSet = false;
        outMap[current].mInClosedSet = true;
    } while (current != goal);
```

```
    // Did you find a path?
    return (current == goal) ? true : false;
}
```

A* Search

The downside of GBFS is that it can't guarantee an optimal path. Luckily, with some modifications to GBFS, you can transform it into the **A* search** (pronounced "A-star"). A* adds a **path-cost** component, which is the *actual* cost from the start node to a given node. The notation *g(x)* denotes the path-cost of a node *x*. When selecting a new current node, A* selects the node with the lowest *f(x)* value, which is just the sum of the *g(x)* path-cost and the *h(x)* heuristic for that node:

$$f(x)=g(x)+h(x)$$

There are a few conditions for A* to find an optimal path. Of course, there must be some path between the start and goal. Furthermore, the heuristic must be admissible (so it can't overestimate the actual cost). Finally, all edge weights must be greater than or equal to zero.

To implement A*, you first define an `AStarScratch` struct, as you do for GBFS. The only difference is that the `AStarScratch` struct also has a float member `mActualFromStart` to store the *g(x)* value.

There are additional differences between the GBFS code and the A* code. When adding a node to the open set, A* must also compute the path-cost *g(x)*. And when selecting the minimum node, A* selects the node with the lowest *f(x)* cost. Finally, A* is pickier about which nodes become parents, using a process called **node adoption**.

In the GBFS algorithm, adjacent nodes always have their parents set to the current node. But in A*, the *g(x)* path-cost value of a node is dependent on the *g(x)* value of its parent. This is because the path-cost value for node *x* is simply its parent's path-cost value plus the cost of traversing the edge from the parent to node *x*. So before assigning a new parent to a node *x*, A* first makes sure the *g(x)* value will improve.

Figure 4.10(a) once again uses the Manhattan heuristic function. The current node (C3) checks its adjacent nodes. The node to its left has *g* = 2 and B2 as its parent. If that node instead had C3 as its parent, it would have *g* = 4, which is worse. So, A* will not change B2's parent in this case.

Figure 4.10(b) shows the final path as computed by A*, which clearly is superior to the GBFS solution.

Apart from node adoption, the code for A* ends up being very similar to the GBFS code. Listing 4.4 shows the loop over the adjacent nodes, which contains most of the code changes. The only other change not shown in the text is the code that selects the lowest-cost node in the open set based on *f(x)* instead of just *h(x)*. The game project for this chapter provides the code for the full A* implementation.

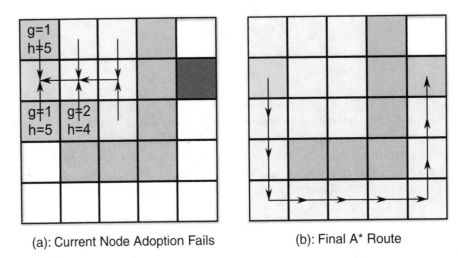

(a): Current Node Adoption Fails   (b): Final A* Route

Figure 4.10 (a) Current node adoption fails; (b) final A* path

Listing 4.4 Loop over the Adjacent Nodes in an A* Search

```cpp
for (const WeightedEdge* edge : current->mEdges)
{
    const WeightedGraphNode* neighbor = edge->mTo;
    // Get scratch data for this node
    AStarScratch& data = outMap[neighbor];
    // Only check nodes that aren't in the closed set
    if (!data.mInClosedSet)
    {
        if (!data.mInOpenSet)
        {
            // Not in the open set, so parent must be current
            data.mParentEdge = edge;
            data.mHeuristic = ComputeHeuristic(neighbor, goal);
            // Actual cost is the parent's plus cost of traversing edge
            data.mActualFromStart = outMap[current].mActualFromStart +
                edge->mWeight;
            data.mInOpenSet = true;
            openSet.emplace_back(neighbor);
        }
        else
        {
            // Compute what new actual cost is if current becomes parent
            float newG = outMap[current].mActualFromStart + edge->mWeight;
            if (newG < data.mActualFromStart)
            {
```

```
            // Current should adopt this node
            data.mParentEdge = edge;
            data.mActualFromStart = newG;
        }
    }
  }
}
```

> **note**
>
> Optimizing A* to run as efficiently as possible is a complex topic. One consideration is what happens if there are a lot of ties in the open set. This is bound to happen in a square grid, especially if you use the Manhattan heuristic. If there are too many ties, when it's time to select a node, you have a high probability of selecting one that doesn't end up on the path. This ultimately means you need to explore more nodes in the graph, which makes A* run more slowly.
>
> One way to help eliminate ties is to add a weight to the heuristic function, such as arbitrarily multiplying the heuristic by 0.75. This gives more weight to the path-cost $g(x)$ function over the heuristic $h(x)$ function, which means you're more likely to explore nodes further from the start node.
>
> From an efficiency standpoint, A* actually is a poor choice for grid-based pathfinding. Other pathfinding algorithms are far more efficient for grids. One of them is the JPS+ algorithm, outlined in Steve Rabin's *Game AI Pro 2* (see the "Additional Reading" section). However, A* works on any graph, whereas JPS+ works only on grids.

Dijkstra's Algorithm

Let's return to the maze example but now suppose that the maze has multiple pieces of cheese in it, and you want the mouse to move toward the closest cheese. A heuristic could approximate which cheese is closest, and A* could find a path to that cheese. But there's a chance that the cheese you select with the heuristic isn't actually the closest because the heuristic is only an estimate.

In **Dijkstra's algorithm**, there is a source node but no goal node. Instead, Dijkstra's computes the distance from the source node to every other reachable node in the graph. In the maze example, Dijkstra's would find the distance of all reachable nodes from the mouse, yielding the actual cost of travel to every piece of cheese and allowing the mouse to move to the closest one.

It's possible to convert the A* code from the previous section into Dijkstra's. First, you remove the $h(x)$ heuristic component. This is equivalent to a heuristic function of $h(x) = 0$, which is admissible because it's guaranteed to be less than or equal to the actual cost. Next, you remove the goal node and make the loop terminate only when the open set is empty. This then computes the *g(x)* path-cost for every node reachable from the start.

The original formulation of the algorithm by Edsger Dijkstra is slightly different. But the approach proposed in this section is functionally equivalent to the original. (AI textbooks sometimes call this approach **uniform cost search**). Interestingly, the invention of Dijkstra's algorithm predates GBFS and A*. However, games usually prefer heuristic-guided approaches such as A* because they generally search far fewer nodes than Dijkstra's.

Following a Path

Once the pathfinding algorithm generates a path, the AI needs to follow it. You can abstract the path as a sequence of points. The AI then just moves from point to point in this path. You can implement this in a subclass of MoveComponent called NavComponent. Because MoveComponent can already move an actor forward, NavComponent only needs to rotate the actor to face the correct direction as the actor moves along the path.

First, the TurnTo function in NavComponent rotates the actor to face a point:

```cpp
void NavComponent::TurnTo(const Vector2& pos)
{
    // Vector from me to pos
    Vector2 dir = pos - mOwner->GetPosition();
    // New angle is just atan2 of this dir vector
    // (Negate y because +y is down on screen)
    float angle = Math::Atan2(-dir.y, dir.x);
    mOwner->SetRotation(angle);
}
```

Next, NavComponent has a mNextPoint variable that tracks the next point in the path. The Update function tests whether the actor reaches mNextPoint:

```cpp
void NavComponent::Update(float deltaTime)
{
    // If you've reached the next point, advance along path
    Vector2 diff = mOwner->GetPosition() - mNextPoint;
    if (diff.Length() <= 2.0f)
    {
        mNextPoint = GetNextPoint();
        TurnTo(mNextPoint);
    }
    // This moves the actor forward
    MoveComponent::Update(deltaTime);
}
```

This assumes that the `GetNextPoint` function returns the next point on the path. Assuming that the actor starts at the first point on the path, initializing `mNextPoint` to the second point as well as setting a linear speed gets the actor moving along the path.

There's one issue with updating the movement along the path in this way: It assumes that the actor is not moving so fast that it jumps too far past a node in one step. If this happens, the distance between the two will never be close enough, and the actor will get lost.

Other Graph Representations

For a game with real-time action, non-player characters (NPCs) usually don't move from square to square on a grid. This makes it more complex to represent the world with a graph. This section discusses two alternative approaches: using path nodes and using navigation meshes.

Path nodes (also called *waypoint graphs*) became popular with the advent of first-person shooter (FPS) games in the early 1990s. With this approach, a designer places path nodes at locations in the game world that the AI can path to. These path nodes directly translate into nodes in the graph.

Typically, you generate the edges between path nodes automatically. The algorithm works as follows: For each path node, test whether there are obstructions between it and nearby nodes. Any paths without obstructions yield edges. A line segment cast or similar collision test can determine if there are obstructions. Chapter 10, "Collision Detection," covers how to implement line segment casts.

The primary drawback of using path nodes is that the AI can only move to locations on the nodes or edges. This is because even if path nodes form a triangle, there is no guarantee that the interior of the triangle is a valid location. There may be an obstruction in the way, so the pathfinding algorithm must assume that any location not on a node or an edge is invalid.

In practice, this means that either there's a lot of space in the world that's off-limits to AI or you need many path nodes. The first is undesirable because it results in less believable behavior from the AI, and the second is simply inefficient. The more nodes and more edges there are, the longer it takes a pathfinding algorithm to arrive at a solution. This presents a trade-off between performance and accuracy.

Other games use a **navigation mesh** (or *nav mesh*). In this approach, each node in the graph corresponds to a convex polygon. Adjacent nodes are any adjacent convex polygons. This means that a handful of convex polygons can represent entire regions in the game world. With a navigation mesh, the AI can safely travel to any location inside a convex polygon node. This means the AI has improved maneuverability. Figure 4.11 compares the path node and navigation mesh representations of a location in a game.

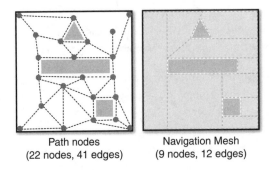

| Path nodes | Navigation Mesh |
| (22 nodes, 41 edges) | (9 nodes, 12 edges) |

Figure 4.11 Path node (a) and navigation mesh (b) representations of a room

Navigation meshes also better support characters of different sizes. Suppose a game has both cows and chickens walking around a farm. Given that chickens are smaller than cows, there are some areas that are accessible to chickens but not to cows. Therefore, a path node network designed for chickens won't work correctly for cows. This means that if the game uses path nodes, it needs two separate graphs: one for each type of creature. In contrast, each node in a navigation mesh is a convex polygon, so it's possible to calculate whether a character fits in a specific area. Therefore, the game can use a single navigation mesh for both chickens and cows.

Most games that use navigation meshes automatically generate them. This is useful because designers can change a level without worrying much about the effect on AI pathing. However, navigation mesh generation algorithms are complex. Luckily, there are open source libraries that implement nav mesh generation. The most popular, Recast, generates a navigation mesh given the triangle geometry of a 3D level. See the "Additional Reading" section at the end of this chapter for more information on Recast.

Game Trees

Games such as tic-tac-toe or chess are very different from most real-time games. First, the game has two players, and each player alternates taking a turn. Second, the game is **adversarial**, meaning that the two players are playing against each other. The AI needs for these types of games are very different from those of real-time games. These types of games require some representation of the overall game state, and this state informs the AI's decisions. One approach is to use a tree called a **game tree**. In a game tree, the root node represents the current state of the game. Each edge represents a move in the game and leads to a new game state.

Figure 4.12 shows a game tree for an in-progress game of tic-tac-toe. Starting at the root node, the current player (called the **max player**) can select from three different moves. After the max player makes a move, the game state transitions to a node in the first level of the tree. The opponent (called the **min player**) then selects a move leading to the second level of the tree. This process repeats until reaching a leaf node, which represents an end state of the game.

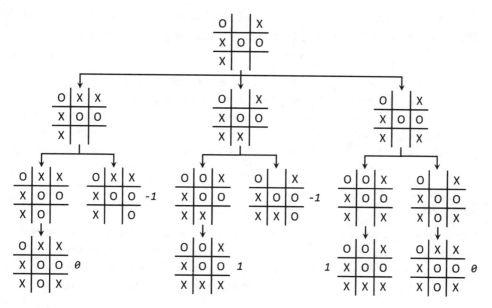

Figure 4.12 Partial game tree for tic-tac-toe

In tic-tac-toe, there are only three outcomes: win, lose, or draw. The numeric values assigned to the leaf nodes in Figure 4.12 reflect these outcomes. These values are scores from the perspective of the max player: 1 means the max player wins, −1 means the min player wins, and 0 means a tie.

Different games have different state representations. For tic-tac-toe, the state is simply a 2D array of the board:

```
struct GameState
{
    enum SquareState { Empty, X, O };
    SquareState mBoard[3][3];
};
```

A game tree node stores both a list of children as well as the game state at that node:

```
struct GTNode
{
    // Children nodes
    std::vector<GTNode*> mChildren;
    // State of game at this node
    GameState mState;
};
```

To generate a complete game tree, you set the root node to the current game state and create children for each possible first move. Then you repeat this process for each node in the first level and continue until all moves are exhausted.

The size of a game tree grows exponentially based on the number of potential moves. For tic-tac-toe, the upper bound of the game tree is *9!*, or 362,880 nodes. This means it's possible to generate and evaluate a complete game tree for tic-tac-toe. But for chess, a complete game tree would have 10^{120} nodes, which makes it impossible to fully evaluate (both in terms of time and space complexity). For now, let's assume we have a complete game tree. Later, we'll discuss how to manage an incomplete tree.

Minimax

The **minimax** algorithm evaluates a two-player game tree to determine the best move for the current player. Minimax assumes that each player will make the choice most beneficial to herself. Because scores are from the perspective of the max player, this means the max player tries to maximize her score, while the min player strives to minimize the score of the max player.

For example, in Figure 4.12 the max player (X in this case) has three possible moves. If max selects either top-mid or bottom-mid, the min player (O) can win with bottom-right. The min player would take this winning play when available. Thus, the max player selects bottom-right to maximize her potential final score.

If the max player selects bottom-right, the min player can select either top-mid or bottom-mid. The choice here is between a score of 1 or 0. Because the min player aims to minimize the max player's score, min selects bottom-mid. This means the game ends in a tie, which is the expected result of a game of tic-tac-toe where both players play optimally.

The implementation of minimax in Listing 4.5 uses a separate function for the min and max players' behavior. Both functions first test if the node is a leaf node, in which case the GetScore function computes the score. Next, both functions determine the best possible subtree using recursion. For the max player, the best subtree yields the highest value. Likewise, the min player finds the subtree with the lowest value.

Listing 4.5 `MaxPlayer` and `MinPlayer` Functions

```
float MaxPlayer(const GTNode* node)
{
    // If this is a leaf, return score
    if (node->mChildren.empty())
    {
        return GetScore(node->mState);
    }
    // Find the subtree with the maximum value
    float maxValue = -std::numeric_limits<float>::infinity();
```

```
    for (const GTNode* child : node->mChildren)
    {
        maxValue = std::max(maxValue, MinPlayer(child));
    }
    return maxValue;
}


float MinPlayer(const GTNode* node)
{
    // If this is a leaf, return score
    if (node->mChildren.empty())
    {
        return GetScore(node->mState);
    }
    // Find the subtree with the minimum value
    float minValue = std::numeric_limits<float>::infinity();
    for (const GTNode* child : node->mChildren)
    {
        minValue = std::min(minValue, MaxPlayer(child));
    }
    return minValue;
}
```

Calling `MaxPlayer` on the root node returns the best possible score for the max player. However, this doesn't specify which next move is optimal, which the AI player also wants to know. The code for determining the best move is in a separate `MinimaxDecide` function, given in Listing 4.6. `MinimaxDecide` resembles the `MaxPlayer` function, except it tracks which child yields the best value.

Listing 4.6 `MinimaxDecide` Implementation

```
const GTNode* MinimaxDecide(const GTNode* root)
{
    // Find the subtree with the maximum value, and save the choice
    const GTNode* choice = nullptr;
    float maxValue = -std::numeric_limits<float>::infinity();
    for (const GTNode* child : root->mChildren)
    {
        float v = MinPlayer(child);
        if (v > maxValue)
        {
            maxValue = v;
            choice = child;
        }
    }
    return choice;
}
```

Handling Incomplete Game Trees

As mentioned earlier in this chapter, it's not always viable to generate a complete game tree. Luckily, it's possible to modify the minimax code to account for incomplete game trees. First, the functions must operate on a game state as opposed to a node. Next, rather than iterate over child nodes, the code iterates over the next possible moves from a given state. These modifications mean the minimax algorithm generates the tree during execution rather than beforehand.

If the tree is too large, such as in chess, it's still not possible to generate the entire tree. Much as how an expert chess player can see only eight moves ahead, the AI needs to limit the depth of its game tree. This means the code treats some nodes as leaves even though they are not terminal states of the game.

To make informed decisions, minimax needs to know how good these nonterminal states are. But unlike with terminal states, it's impossible to know the exact score. Thus, the scoring function needs a heuristic component that approximates the quality of nonterminal states. This also means that scores are now ranges of values, unlike the {−1, 0, 1} ternary choice for tic-tac-toe.

Importantly, adding the heuristic component means minimax cannot guarantee to make the best decision. The heuristic tries to approximate the quality of a game state, but it's unknown how accurate this approximation is. With an incomplete game tree, it's possible that the move selected by minimax is suboptimal and eventually leads to a loss.

Listing 4.7 provides the `MaxPlayerLimit` function. (You would need to modify the other functions similarly.) This code assumes that `GameState` has three member functions: `IsTerminal`, `GetScore`, and `GetPossibleMoves`. `IsTerminal` returns `true` if the state is an end state. `GetScore` returns either the heuristic for nonterminal states or the score for terminal states. `GetPossibleMoves` returns a vector of the game states that are one move after the current state.

Listing 4.7 `MaxPlayerLimit` Implementation

```
float MaxPlayerLimit(const GameState* state, int depth)
{
    // If this is terminal or we've gone max depth
    if (depth == 0 || state->IsTerminal())
    {
        return state->GetScore();
    }
    // Find the subtree with the max value
    float maxValue = -std::numeric_limits<float>::infinity();
    for (const GameState* child : state->GetPossibleMoves())
    {
        maxValue = std::max(maxValue, MinPlayer(child, depth - 1));
    }
    return maxValue;
}
```

The heuristic function varies depending on the game. For example, a simple chess heuristic might count the number of pieces each player has, weighting the pieces by power. However, a drawback of such a simple heuristic is that sometimes sacrificing a piece in the short term is better for the long term. Other heuristics might look at control of the board's center, the safety of the king, or the mobility of the queen. Ultimately, several different factors affect the heuristic.

More complex heuristics require more calculations. Most games institute some sort of time limit for AI moves. For example, a chess game AI might have only 10 seconds to decide its next move. This makes it necessary to strike a balance between the depth explored and heuristic complexity.

Alpha-Beta Pruning

Alpha-beta pruning is an optimization of the minimax algorithm that, on average, reduces the number of nodes evaluated. In practice, this means it's possible to increase the maximum depth explored without increasing the computation time.

Figure 4.13 shows a game tree simplified by alpha-beta pruning. Assuming a left-to-right order of evaluation for siblings, the max player first inspects subtree B. The min player then sees the leaf with value 5, which means the min player has a choice between 5 and other values. If these other values are greater than 5, the min player obviously selects 5. This means that the upper bound of subtree B is 5, but the lower bound is negative infinity. The min player continues and sees the leaf with value 0 and selects this leaf because the min player wants the minimum possible score.

Control returns to the max player function, which now knows that subtree B has a value of 0. Next, the max player inspects subtree C. The min player first sees the leaf with value −3. As before, this means the upper bound of subtree C is −3. However, you already know that subtree B has a value of 0, which is better than −3. This means that there's no way subtree C can be better for the max player than subtree B. Alpha-beta pruning recognizes this and, as a result, does not inspect any other children of C.

Alpha-beta pruning adds two additional variables, called **alpha** and **beta**. **Alpha** is the best score guaranteed for the max player at the current level or higher. Conversely, **beta** is the best score guaranteed for the min player at the current level or higher. In other words, alpha and beta are the lower and upper bounds of the score.

Initially, alpha is negative infinity and beta is positive infinity—the worst possible values for both players. `AlphaBetaDecide`, in Listing 4.8, initializes alpha and beta to these values and then recurses by calling `AlphaBetaMin`.

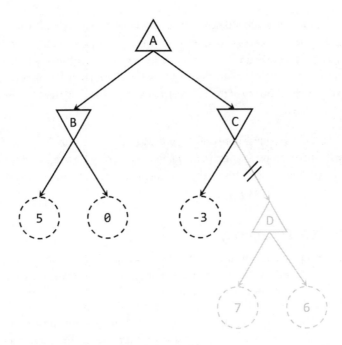

Figure 4.13 A game tree simplified by alpha-beta pruning

Listing 4.8 `AlphaBetaDecide` Implementation

```
const GameState* AlphaBetaDecide(const GameState* root, int maxDepth)
{
    const GameState* choice = nullptr;
    // Alpha starts at negative infinity, beta at positive infinity
    float maxValue = -std::numeric_limits<float>::infinity();
    float beta = std::numeric_limits<float>::infinity();
    for (const GameState* child : root->GetPossibleMoves())
    {
        float v = AlphaBetaMin(child, maxDepth - 1, maxValue, beta);
        if (v > maxValue)
        {
            maxValue = v;
            choice = child;
        }
    }
    return choice;
}
```

The implementation of `AlphaBetaMax`, shown in Listing 4.9, builds on `MaxPlayerLimit`. If
on any iteration the max value is greater than or equal to beta, it means the score can be no
better than the previous upper bound. This makes it unnecessary to test the remaining siblings,
and so the function returns. Otherwise, the code increases the alpha lower bound if the max
value is greater than alpha.

Listing 4.9 `AlphaBetaMax` Implementation

```cpp
float AlphaBetaMax(const GameState* node, int depth, float alpha,
                   float beta)
{
   if (depth == 0 || node->IsTerminal())
   {
      return node->GetScore();
   }
   float maxValue = -std::numeric_limits<float>::infinity();
   for (const GameState* child : node->GetPossibleMoves())
   {
      maxValue = std::max(maxValue,
         AlphaBetaMin(child, depth - 1, alpha, beta));
      if (maxValue >= beta)
      {
         return maxValue; // Beta prune
      }
      alpha = std::max(maxValue, alpha); // Increase lower bound
   }
   return maxValue;
}
```

Similarly, `AlphaBetaMin`, shown in Listing 4.10, checks whether the min value is less than or equal to alpha. In this case, the score can be no better than the lower bound, so the function returns. Then the code decreases the beta upper bound as necessary.

Listing 4.10 `AlphaBetaMin` Implementation

```cpp
float AlphaBetaMin(const GameState* node, int depth, float alpha,
                   float beta)
{
   if (depth == 0 || node->IsTerminal())
   {
      return node->GetScore();
   }
   float minValue = std::numeric_limits<float>::infinity();
   for (const GameState* child : node->GetPossibleMoves())
   {
      minValue = std::min(minValue,
         AlphaBetaMax(child, depth - 1, alpha, beta));
      if (minValue <= alpha)
      {
         return minValue; // Alpha prune
      }
      beta = std::min(minValue, beta); // Decrease upper bound
   }
   return minValue;
}
```

Note that the order of evaluation for children affects the number of nodes pruned. This means that even with a consistent depth limit, different starting states yield different execution times. This can be problematic if the AI has a fixed time limit; an incomplete search means the AI has no idea which move to take. One solution is **iterative deepening**, which runs the algorithm multiple times at increasing depth limits. For example, first run alpha-beta pruning with a depth limit of three, which yields some baseline move. Then run with a depth limit of four, then five, and so on, until time runs out. At this point, the code returns the move from the previous iteration. This guarantees that some move is always available, even when time runs out.

Game Project

This chapter's game project, shown in Figure 4.14, is a tower defense game. In this style of game, the enemies try to move from the start tile on the left to an end tile on the right. Initially, the enemies move in a straight line from left to right. However, the player can build towers on squares in the grid, even where the path is, which causes the path to redirect around these towers as needed. The code is available in the book's GitHub repository, in the `Chapter04` directory. Open `Chapter04-windows.sln` on Windows and `Chapter04-mac.xcodeproj` on Mac.

Use the mouse to click on and select tiles. After selecting a tile, use the `B` key to build a tower. The enemy airplanes path around the towers using the A* pathfinding algorithm. Each new tower built changes the path as necessary. To ensure that the player can't fully block in the enemies, when the player requests to build a tower, the code first ensures that a path would still exist for the enemies. If a tower would completely block the path, the game doesn't let the player build it.

As a simplification, the `Tile` class in the game project contains all the graph information, as well as the scratch data used by the A* search. The code that creates all the tiles and initializes the graph is in the constructor of the `Grid` class. The `Grid` class also contains the `FindPath` function that runs the actual A* search.

For completeness, the source code for this chapter also includes the versions of the search and minimax algorithms covered in the text in a separate `Search.cpp` file. It also includes the implementation of `AIState` and `AIComponent`, even though no actors in the game project use these features.

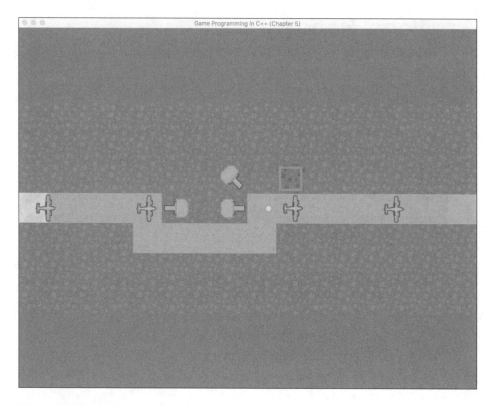

Figure 4.14 Chapter 4 game project

Summary

Artificial intelligence is a deep topic with many different sub-areas. Using state machines is an effective way to give behaviors to AI-controlled characters in a game. While a switch is the simplest implementation of a state machine, the state design pattern adds flexibility by making each state a separate class.

Pathfinding algorithms find the shortest path between two points in the game world. First, you formulate a graph representation for the game world. For a square grid, this is simple, but other games use path nodes or navigation meshes. For unweighted graphs, breadth-first search (BFS) guarantees to find the shortest path if one exists. But for weighted graphs, you need other algorithms, such as A* or Dijkstra's, to find the shortest path.

For two-player adversarial turn-based games such as checkers or chess, a game tree represents the sequence of possible moves from the current game state. The minimax algorithm assumes that the current player aims to maximize his or her score, and the opponent aims to minimize the current player's score. Alpha-beta pruning optimizes minimax, though for most games the tree must have a depth limit.

Additional Reading

Many resources cover AI techniques. Stuart Russell and Peter Norvig's book is a popular AI text that covers many techniques, though only some are applicable to games. Mat Buckland's book, although dated, covers many useful game AI topics. Steve Rabin's *Game AI Pro* series has many interesting articles written by different game AI developers.

For navigation meshes, Stephen Pratt's in-depth web article covers the steps to generate a navigation mesh from level geometry. The Recast project provides an open source implementation of both navigation mesh generation and pathfinding algorithms.

Buckland, Mat. *Programming Game AI by Example*. Plano: Wordware Publishing, 2005.

Mononen, Mikko. "Recast Navigation Mesh Toolkit." Accessed July 7, 2017. https://github.com/recastnavigation.

Pratt, Stephen. "Study: Navigation Mesh Generation." Accessed July 7, 2017. http://critterai.org/projects/nmgen_study/index.html.

Rabin, Steve, Ed. *Game AI Pro 3: Collected Wisdom of Game AI Professionals*. Boca Raton: CRC Press, 2017.

Russell, Stuart, and Peter Norvig. *Artificial Intelligence: A Modern Approach, 3rd edition*. Upper Saddle River: Pearson, 2009.

Exercises

The two exercises for this chapter implement techniques not used in this chapter's game project. The first looks at state machines, and the second uses alpha-beta pruning for a four-in-a-row game.

Exercise 4.1

Given this chapter's game project code, update either the `Enemy` or `Tower` class (or both!) to use an AI state machine. First, consider which behaviors the AI should have and design the state machine graph. Next, use the provided `AIComponent` and `AIState` base classes to implement these behaviors.

Exercise 4.2

In a four-in-a-row game, players have a vertical grid of six rows and seven columns. The two players take turns putting a piece at the top of a column, and then the piece slides down to the lowest free position in the column. The game continues until one player gets four in a row horizontally, vertically, or diagonally.

The starting code in `Exercises/4.2` allows the human player to click to make a move. In the starting code, the AI randomly selects a move from the set of valid moves. Modify the AI code to instead use alpha-beta pruning with a depth cutoff.

CHAPTER 5

OPENGL

This chapter provides an in-depth introduction on how to use OpenGL for graphics in games. It covers many topics, including initializing OpenGL, using triangles, writing shader programs, using matrices for transforms, and adding support for textures. The game project for this chapter converts the game project from Chapter 3, "Vectors and Basic Physics," to use OpenGL for all its graphics rendering.

Initializing OpenGL

Although the SDL renderer supports 2D graphics, it does not support 3D. Thus, to switch to 3D, which is used in every subsequent chapter in this book, you need to switch from SDL 2D graphics to a different library that supports both 2D and 3D graphics.

This book uses the OpenGL library. OpenGL is an industry-standard library for cross-platform 2D/3D graphics that's been around for 25 years. Unsurprisingly, the library has been around so long that it has evolved in many ways over the years. The set of functions the original version of OpenGL used is very different from the set in modern OpenGL. This book uses functions defined up to and including OpenGL 3.3.

> warning
>
> **OLDER VERSIONS OF OPENGL ARE VERY DIFFERENT**   Be careful when consulting any online OpenGL references, as many refer to older versions of OpenGL.

The goal of this chapter is to convert the game project from Chapter 3 from SDL graphics to OpenGL graphics. You need to take a lot of steps to get there. This section walks through the steps of configuring and initializing OpenGL and a helper library called GLEW.

Setting Up the OpenGL Window

To use OpenGL, you must drop usage of the `SDL_Renderer` from the earlier chapters. You therefore need to remove all references to `SDL_Renderer`, including the `mRenderer` variable in `Game`, the call to `SDL_CreateRenderer`, and any calls to the SDL functions in `GenerateOuput`. This also means that the `SpriteComponent` code (which relies on `SDL_Renderer`) won't work without changes. For now, all the code in `Game::GenerateOutput` is commented out until OpenGL is up and running.

In SDL, when you create a window, you can request a window for OpenGL usage by passing in the `SDL_WINDOW_OPENGL` flag as the final parameter of the `SDL_CreateWindow` call:

```
mWindow = SDL_CreateWindow("Game Programming in C++ (Chapter 5)", 100, 100,
    1024, 768, SDL_WINDOW_OPENGL);
```

Prior to creating the OpenGL window, you can request attributes such as the version of OpenGL, the color depth, and several other parameters. To configure these parameters, you use the `SDL_GL_SetAttribute` function:

```
// Set OpenGL window's attributes (use prior to creating the window)
// Returns 0 if successful, otherwise a negative value
SDL_GL_SetAttribute(
```

```
    SDL_GLattr attr,    // Attribute to set
    int value           // Value for this attribute
);
```

There are several different attributes in the SDL_GLattr enum, but this chapter uses only some of them. To set the attributes, you add the code in Listing 5.1 *prior* to the call of SDL_CreateWindow inside Game::Initialize. This code sets several attributes. First, it requests the core OpenGL profile.

> **note**
>
> There are three main profiles supported by OpenGL: core, compatibility, and ES. The core profile is the recommended default profile for a desktop environment. The only difference between the core and compatibility profiles is that the compatibility profile allows the program to call OpenGL functions that are **deprecated** (no longer intended for use). The OpenGL ES profile is for mobile development.

Listing 5.1 Requesting OpenGL Attributes

```
// Use the core OpenGL profile
SDL_GL_SetAttribute(SDL_GL_CONTEXT_PROFILE_MASK,
                    SDL_GL_CONTEXT_PROFILE_CORE);
// Specify version 3.3
SDL_GL_SetAttribute(SDL_GL_CONTEXT_MAJOR_VERSION, 3);
SDL_GL_SetAttribute(SDL_GL_CONTEXT_MINOR_VERSION, 3);
// Request a color buffer with 8-bits per RGBA channel
SDL_GL_SetAttribute(SDL_GL_RED_SIZE, 8);
SDL_GL_SetAttribute(SDL_GL_GREEN_SIZE, 8);
SDL_GL_SetAttribute(SDL_GL_BLUE_SIZE, 8);
SDL_GL_SetAttribute(SDL_GL_ALPHA_SIZE, 8);
// Enable double buffering
SDL_GL_SetAttribute(SDL_GL_DOUBLEBUFFER, 1);
// Force OpenGL to use hardware acceleration
SDL_GL_SetAttribute(SDL_GL_ACCELERATED_VISUAL, 1);
```

The next two attributes request OpenGL version 3.3. Although there are newer versions of OpenGL, the 3.3 version supports all the required features for this book and has a feature set closely aligned with the ES profile. Thus, most of the code in this book should also work on current mobile devices.

The next attributes specify the bit depth of each channel. In this case, the program requests 8 bits per RGBA channel, for a total of 32 bits per pixel. The second-to-last attribute asks to enable double buffering. The final attribute asks to run OpenGL with hardware acceleration. This means that the OpenGL rendering will run on graphics hardware (a GPU).

The OpenGL Context and Initializing GLEW

Once the OpenGL attributes are set and you've created the window, the next step is to create an OpenGL context. Think of a **context** as the "world" of OpenGL that contains every item that OpenGL knows about, such as the color buffer, any images or models loaded, and any other OpenGL objects. (While it is possible to have multiple contexts in one OpenGL program, this book sticks to one.)

To create the context, first add the following member variable to `Game`:

```
SDL_GLContext mContext;
```

Next, immediately after creating the SDL window with `SDL_CreateWindow`, add the following line of code, which creates an OpenGL context and saves it in the member variable:

```
mContext = SDL_GL_CreateContext(mWindow);
```

As with creating and deleting the window, you need to delete the OpenGL context in the destructor. To do this, add the following line of code to `Game::Shutdown`, right before the call to `SDL_DeleteWindow`:

```
SDL_GL_DeleteContext(mContext);
```

Although the program now creates an OpenGL context, there is one final hurdle you must pass to gain access to the full set of OpenGL 3.3 features. OpenGL supports backward compatibility with an extension system. Normally, you must query any extensions you want manually, which is tedious. To simplify this process, you can use an open source library called the OpenGL Extension Wrangler Library (GLEW). With one simple function call, GLEW automatically initializes all extension functions supported by the current OpenGL context's version. So in this case, GLEW initializes all extension functions supported by OpenGL 3.3 and earlier.

To initialize GLEW, you add the following code immediately after creating the OpenGL context:

```
// Initialize GLEW
glewExperimental = GL_TRUE;
if (glewInit() != GLEW_OK)
{
    SDL_Log("Failed to initialize GLEW.");
    return false;
}
// On some platforms, GLEW will emit a benign error code,
// so clear it
glGetError();
```

The `glewExperimental` line prevents an initialization error that may occur when using the core context on some platforms. Furthermore, because some platforms emit a benign error code when initializing GLEW, the call to `glGetError` clears this error code.

> **note**
>
> Some old PC machines with integrated graphics (from 2012 or earlier) may have issues running OpenGL version 3.3. In this case, you can try two things: updating to newer graphics drivers or requesting OpenGL version 3.1.

Rendering a Frame

You now need to convert the clear, draw scene, and swap buffers process in `Game::GenerateOutput` to use OpenGL functions:

```
// Set the clear color to gray
glClearColor(0.86f, 0.86f, 0.86f, 1.0f);
// Clear the color buffer
glClear(GL_COLOR_BUFFER_BIT);

// TODO: Draw the scene

// Swap the buffers, which also displays the scene
SDL_GL_SwapWindow(mWindow);
```

This code first sets the clear color to 86% red, 86% green, 86% blue, and 100% alpha, which yields a gray color. The `glClear` call with the `GL_COLOR_BUFFER_BIT` parameter clears the color buffer to the specified color. Finally, the `SDL_GL_SwapWindow` call swaps the front buffer and back buffer. At this point, running the game yields a gray screen because you aren't drawing the `SpriteComponent`s yet.

Triangle Basics

The graphical needs of 2D and 3D games couldn't seem more different. As discussed in Chapter 2, "Game Objects and 2D Graphics," most 2D games use sprites for their 2D characters. On the other hand, a 3D game features a simulated 3D environment that you somehow flatten into a 2D image that you show onscreen.

Early 2D games could simply copy sprite images into the desired locations of the color buffer. This process, called **blitting**, was efficient on sprite-based consoles such as the Nintendo Entertainment System (NES). However, modern graphical hardware is inefficient at blitting but is very efficient at polygonal rendering. Because of this, nearly all modern games, whether 2D or 3D, ultimately use polygons for their graphical needs.

Why Polygons?

There are many ways a computer could simulate a 3D environment. Polygons are popular in games for a multitude of reasons. Compared to other 3D graphics techniques, polygons do not require as many calculations at runtime. Furthermore, polygons are scalable: A game running on less-powerful hardware could simply use 3D models with fewer polygons. And, importantly, you can represent most 3D objects with polygons.

Triangles are the polygon of choice for most games. Triangles are the simplest polygon, and you need only three points (or **vertices**) to create a triangle. Furthermore, a triangle can only lie on a single plane. In other words, the three points of a triangle must be **coplanar**. Finally, triangles **tessellate** easily, meaning it's relatively simple to break any complex 3D object into many triangles. The remainder of this chapter talks about triangles, but the techniques discussed here also work for other polygons (such as quads), provided that they maintain the coplanar property.

2D games use triangles to represent sprites by drawing a rectangle and filling in the rectangle with colors from an image file. We discuss this in much greater detail later in the chapter.

Normalized Device Coordinates

To draw a triangle, you must specify the coordinates of its three vertices. Recall that in SDL, the top-left corner of the screen is (0, 0), positive x is to the right, and positive y is down. More generally, a **coordinate space** specifies where the origin is and in which direction its coordinates increase. The **basis vectors** of the coordinate space are the direction in which the coordinates increase.

An example of a coordinate space from basic geometry is a **Cartesian coordinate system** (see Figure 5.1). In a 2D Cartesian coordinate system, the origin (0, 0) has a specific point (usually the center), positive x is to the right, and positive y is up.

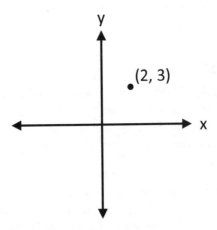

Figure 5.1 A point drawn at (2, 3) in a Cartesian coordinate system

Normalized device coordinates (**NDC**) is the default coordinate system used with OpenGL. Given an OpenGL window, the center of the window is the origin in normalized device coordinates. Furthermore, the bottom-left corner is (−1, −1), and the top-right corner is (1, 1).

This is regardless of the width and height of the window (hence *normalized* device coordinates). Internally, the graphics hardware then converts these NDC into the corresponding pixels in the window.

For example, to draw a square with sides of unit length in the center of the window, you need two triangles. The first triangle has the vertices (−0.5, 0.5), (0.5, 0.5), and (0.5, −0.5), and the second triangle has the vertices (0.5, −0.5), (−0.5, −0.5), and (−0.5, 0.5). Figure 5.2 illustrates this square. Keep in mind that if the length and width of the window are not uniform, a square in normalized device coordinates will not look like a square onscreen.

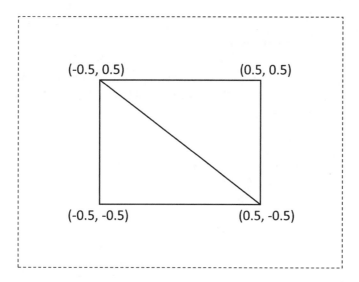

Figure 5.2 A square drawn in 2D normalized device coordinates

In 3D, the z component of normalized device coordinates also ranges from [−1, 1], with a positive z value going into the screen. For now, we stick with a z value of zero. We'll explore 3D in much greater detail in Chapter 6, "3D Graphics."

Vertex and Index Buffers

Suppose you have a 3D model comprised of many triangles. You need some way to store the vertices of these triangles in memory. The simplest approach is to directly store the coordinates of each triangle in a contiguous array or buffer. For example, assuming 3D coordinates, the following array contains the vertices of the two triangles shown in Figure 5.2:

```
float vertices[] = {
    -0.5f,  0.5f, 0.0f,
     0.5f,  0.5f, 0.0f,
     0.5f, -0.5f, 0.0f,
```

```
    0.5f, -0.5f, 0.0f,
   -0.5f, -0.5f, 0.0f,
   -0.5f,  0.5f, 0.0f,
};
```

Even in this simple example, the array of vertices has some duplicate data. Specifically, the coordinates (−0.5, 0.5, 0.0) and (0.5, −0.5, 0.0) appear twice. If there were a way to remove these duplicates, you would cut the number of values stored in the buffer by 33%. Rather than having 12 values, you would have only 8. Assuming single-precision floats that use 4 bytes each, you'd save 24 bytes of memory by removing the duplicates. This might seem insignificant, but imagine a much larger model with 20,000 triangles. In this case, the amount of memory wasted due to duplicate coordinates would be high.

The solution to this issue has two parts. First, you create a **vertex buffer** that contains only the *unique* coordinates used by the 3D geometry. Then, to specify the vertices of each triangle, you index into this vertex buffer (much like indexing into an array). The aptly named **index buffer** contains the indices for each individual triangle, in sets of three. For this example's sample square, you'd need the following vertex and index buffers:

```
float vertexBuffer[] = {
   -0.5f,  0.5f, 0.0f, // vertex 0
    0.5f,  0.5f, 0.0f, // vertex 1
    0.5f, -0.5f, 0.0f, // vertex 2
   -0.5f, -0.5f, 0.0f  // vertex 3
};
unsigned short indexBuffer[] = {
    0, 1, 2,
    2, 3, 0
};
```

For example, the first triangle has the vertices 0, 1, and 2, which corresponds to the coordinates (−0.5, 0.5, 0.0), (0.5, 0.5, 0.0), and (0.5, −0.5, 0.0). Keep in mind that the index is the vertex number, not the floating-point element (for example, vertex 1 instead of "index 2" of the array). Also note that this code uses an unsigned short (typically 16 bits) for the index buffer, which reduces the memory footprint of the index buffer. You can use smaller bit size integers to save memory in the index buffer.

In this example, the vertex/index buffer combination uses $12 \times 4 + 6 \times 2$, or 60 total bytes. On the other hand, if you just used the original vertices, you'd need 72 bytes. While the savings in this example is only 20%, a more complex model would save much more memory by using the vertex/index buffer combination.

To use the vertex and index buffers, you must let OpenGL know about them. OpenGL uses a **vertex array object** to encapsulate a vertex buffer, an index buffer, and the vertex layout. The **vertex layout** specifies what data you store for each vertex in the model. For now, assume the vertex layout is a 3D position (you can just use a z component of `0.0f` if you want something 2D). Later in this chapter you'll add other data to each vertex.

Because any model needs a vertex array object, it makes sense to encapsulate its behavior in a `VertexArray` class. Listing 5.2 shows the declaration of this class.

Listing 5.2 `VertexArray` Declaration

```
class VertexArray
{
public:
   VertexArray(const float* verts, unsigned int numVerts,
      const unsigned int* indices, unsigned int numIndices);
   ~VertexArray();

   // Activate this vertex array (so we can draw it)
   void SetActive();

   unsigned int GetNumIndices() const { return mNumIndices; }
   unsigned int GetNumVerts() const { return mNumVerts; }
private:
   // How many vertices in the vertex buffer?
   unsigned int mNumVerts;
   // How many indices in the index buffer
   unsigned int mNumIndices;
   // OpenGL ID of the vertex buffer
   unsigned int mVertexBuffer;
   // OpenGL ID of the index buffer
   unsigned int mIndexBuffer;
   // OpenGL ID of the vertex array object
   unsigned int mVertexArray;
};
```

The constructor for `VertexArray` takes in pointers to the vertex and index buffer arrays so that it can hand off the data to OpenGL (which will ultimately load the data on the graphics hardware). Note that the member data contains several unsigned integers for the vertex buffer, index buffer, and vertex array object. This is because OpenGL does not return pointers to objects that it creates. Instead, you merely get back an integral ID number. Keep in mind that the ID numbers are not unique across different types of objects. It's therefore very possible to have an ID of 1 for both the vertex and index buffers because OpenGL considers them different types of objects.

The implementation of the `VertexArray` constructor is complex. First, create the vertex array object and store its ID in the `mVertexArray` member variable:

```
glGenVertexArrays(1, &mVertexArray);
glBindVertexArray(mVertexArray);
```

Once you have a vertex array object, you can create a vertex buffer:

```
glGenBuffers(1, &mVertexBuffer);
glBindBuffer(GL_ARRAY_BUFFER, mVertexBuffer);
```

The `GL_ARRAY_BUFFER` parameter to `glBindBuffer` means that you intend to use the buffer as a vertex buffer.

Once you have a vertex buffer, you need to copy the `verts` data passed into the `VertexArray` constructor into this vertex buffer. To copy the data, use `glBufferData`, which takes several parameters:

```
glBufferData(
    GL_ARRAY_BUFFER,            // The active buffer type to write to
    numVerts * 3 * sizeof(float), // Number of bytes to copy
    verts,                      // Source to copy from (pointer)
    GL_STATIC_DRAW              // How will we use this data?
);
```

Note that you don't pass in the object ID to `glBufferData`; instead, you specify a currently bound buffer type to write to. In this case, `GL_ARRAY_BUFFER` means use the vertex buffer just created.

For the second parameter, you pass in the number of bytes, which is the amount of data for each vertex multiplied by the number of vertices. For now, you can assume that each vertex contains three floats for (x, y, z).

The usage parameter specifies how you want to use the buffer data. A `GL_STATIC_DRAW` usage means you only want to load the data once and use it frequently for drawing.

Next, create an index buffer. This is very similar to creating the vertex buffer, except you instead specify the `GL_ELEMENT_ARRAY_BUFFER` type, which corresponds to an index buffer:

```
glGenBuffers(1, &mIndexBuffer);
glBindBuffer(GL_ELEMENT_ARRAY_BUFFER, mIndexBuffer);
```

Then copy the `indices` data into the index buffer:

```
glBufferData(
    GL_ELEMENT_ARRAY_BUFFER,          // Index buffer
    numIndices * sizeof(unsigned int), // Size of data
    indices, GL_STATIC_DRAW);
```

Note that the type here is `GL_ELEMENT_ARRAY_BUFFER`, and the size is the number of indices multiplied by an unsigned int because that's the type used for indices here.

Finally, you must specify a vertex layout, also called the **vertex attributes**. As mentioned earlier, the current layout is a position with three float values.

To enable the first vertex attribute (attribute 0), use `glEnableVertexAttribArray`:

```
glEnableVertexAttribArray(0);
```

You then use `glVertexAttribPointer` to specify the size, type, and format of the attribute:

```
glVertexAttribPointer(
   0,                    // Attribute index (0 for first one)
   3,                    // Number of components (3 in this case)
   GL_FLOAT,             // Type of the components
   GL_FALSE,             // (Only used for integral types)
   sizeof(float) * 3,    // Stride (usually size of each vertex)
   0                     // Offset from start of vertex to this attribute
);
```

The first two parameters are 0 and 3 because the position is attribute 0 of the vertex, and there are three components (x, y, z). Because each component is a float, you specify the `GL_FLOAT` type. The fourth parameter is only relevant for integral types, so here you set it to `GL_FALSE`. Finally, the **stride** is the byte offset between consecutive vertices' attributes. But assuming you don't have padding in the vertex buffer (which you usually don't), the stride is just the size of the vertex. Finally, the offset is 0 because this is the only attribute. For additional attributes, you have to pass in a nonzero value for the offset.

The `VertexArray`'s destructor destroys the vertex buffer, index buffer, and vertex array object:

```
VertexArray::~VertexArray()
{
   glDeleteBuffers(1, &mVertexBuffer);
   glDeleteBuffers(1, &mIndexBuffer);
   glDeleteVertexArrays(1, &mVertexArray);
}
```

Finally, the `SetActive` function calls `glBindVertexArray`, which just specifies which vertex array you're currently using:.

```
void VertexArray::SetActive()
{
   glBindVertexArray(mVertexArray);
}
```

The following code in `Game::InitSpriteVerts` allocates an instance of `VertexArray` and saves it in a member variable of `Game` called `mSpriteVerts`:

```
mSpriteVerts = new VertexArray(vertexBuffer, 4, indexBuffer, 6);
```

The vertex and index buffer variables here are the arrays for the sprite quad. In this case, there are 4 vertices in the vertex buffer and 6 indices in the index buffer (corresponding to the 2 triangles in the quad). You will use this member variable later in this chapter to draw sprites, as all sprites will ultimately use the same vertices.

Shaders

In a modern graphics pipeline, you don't simply feed in the vertex/index buffers and have triangles draw. Instead, you specify how you want to draw the vertices. For example, should the triangles be a fixed color, or should they use a color from a texture? Do you want to perform lighting calculations for every pixel you draw?

Because there are many techniques you may want to use to display the scene, there is no truly one-size-fits-all method. To allow for more customization, graphics APIs including OpenGL support **shader programs**—small programs that execute on the graphics hardware to perform specific tasks. Importantly, shaders are *separate programs*, with their own separate main functions.

> ## note
>
> Shader programs do not use the C++ programming language. This book uses the GLSL programming language for shader programs. Although GLSL superficially looks like C, there are many semantics specific to GLSL. Rather than present all the details of GLSL at once, this book introduces the concepts as needed.

Because shaders are separate programs, you write them in separate files. Then in your C++ code, you need to tell OpenGL when to compile and load these shader programs and specify what you want OpenGL to use these shader programs for.

Although you can use several different types of shaders in games, this book focuses on the two most important ones: the vertex shader and the fragment (or pixel) shader.

Vertex Shaders

A **vertex shader** program runs once for every vertex of every triangle drawn. The vertex shader receives the vertex attribute data as an input. The vertex shader can then modify these vertex attributes as it sees fit. While it may seem unclear why you'd want to modify vertex attributes, it'll become more apparent as this chapter continues.

Given that triangles have three vertices, you can think of a vertex shader as running three times per triangle. However, if you use vertex and index buffers, then you will invoke the vertex shader less often because some triangles share vertices. This is an additional advantage of using a vertex and index buffer instead just a vertex buffer. Note that if you draw the same model multiple times per frame, the vertex shader calls for each time you draw it are independent of each other.

Fragment Shaders

After the vertices of a triangle have gone through the vertex shader, OpenGL must determine which pixels in the color buffer correspond to the triangle. This process of converting the triangle into pixels is **rasterization**. There are many different rasterization algorithms, but today's graphics hardware does rasterization for us.

The job of a **fragment shader** (or pixel shader) is to determine the color of each pixel, and so the fragment shader program executes at least once for every pixel. This color may take into account properties of the surface, such as textures, colors, and materials. If the scene has any lighting, the fragment shader might also do lighting calculations. Because there are so many potential calculations, the average 3D game has a lot more code in the fragment shader than in the vertex shader.

Writing Basic Shaders

Although you could load in the shader programs from hard-coded strings in C++ code, it's much better to put them in separate files. This book uses the `.vert` extension for vertex shader files and the `.frag` extension for fragment shader files.

Because these source files are in a different programming language, they are in the `Shaders` subdirectory for the chapter. For example, `Chapter05/Shaders` contains the source files for the shaders in this chapter.

The `Basic.vert` File

`Basic.vert` contains the vertex shader code. Remember that this code is *not C++ code*.

Every GLSL shader file first must specify the version of the GLSL programming language used. The following line represents the version of GLSL corresponding to OpenGL 3.3:

```
#version 330
```

Next, because this is a vertex shader, you must specify the vertex attributes for each vertex. These attributes should match the attributes of the vertex array object created earlier, and are the input to the vertex shader. However, in GLSL the `main` function does not receive any parameters. Instead, the shader inputs look like global variables, marked with a special `in` keyword.

For now, you only have one input variable—the 3D position. The following line declares this input variable:

```
in vec3 inPosition;
```

The type of `inPosition` variable is `vec3`, which corresponds to a vector of three floating-point values. This will contain the x, y, and z components corresponding to the vertex's position. You can access each component of the `vec3` via dot syntax; for example, `inPosition.x` accesses the x component of the vector.

As with a C/C++ program, a shader program has a `main` function as its entry point:

```
void main()
{
    // TODO: Shader code goes here
}
```

Note that the `main` function here returns `void`. GLSL also uses global variables to define the outputs of the shader. In this case, you'll use a built-in variable called `gl_Position` to store the vertex position output of the shader.

For now, the vertex shader directly copies the vertex position from `inPosition` to `gl_Position`. However, `gl_Position` expects four components: the normal (x, y, z) coordinates plus a fourth component called the **w component**. We'll look at what this w represents later in this chapter. For now, assume that w is always 1.0. To convert `inPosition` from `vec3` to `vec4`, you can use the following syntax:

```
gl_Position = vec4(inPosition, 1.0);
```

Listing 5.3 shows the complete `Basic.vert` code, which simply copies along the vertex position without any modification.

Listing 5.3 `Basic.vert` Code

```
// Request GLSL 3.3
#version 330

// Any vertex attributes go here
// For now, just a position.
in vec3 inPosition;

void main()
{
    // Directly pass along inPosition to gl_Position
    gl_Position = vec4(inPosition, 1.0);
}
```

The `Basic.frag` File

The job of the fragment shader is to compute an output color for the current pixel. For `Basic.frag`, you'll hard-code a blue output color for all pixels.

As with the vertex shader, the fragment shader always begin with a `#version` line. Next, you declare a global variable to store the output color, using the `out` variable specifier:

```
out vec4 outColor;
```

The `outColor` variable is a `vec4` corresponding to the four components of the RGBA color buffer.

Next, you declare the entry point of the fragment shader program. Inside this function, you set `outColor` to the desired color for the pixel. The RGBA value of blue is (0.0, 0.0, 1.0, 1.0), which means you use the following assignment:

```
outColor = vec4(0.0, 0.0, 1.0, 1.0);
```

Listing 5.4 gives the full source code for `Basic.frag`.

Listing 5.4 `Basic.frag` Code

```
// Request GLSL 3.3
#version 330

// This is output color to the color buffer
out vec4 outColor;

void main()
{
    // Set to blue
    outColor = vec4(0.0, 0.0, 1.0, 1.0);
}
```

Loading Shaders

Once you have the separate shader files written, you must load in these shaders in the game's C++ code to let OpenGL know about them. At a high level, you need to follow these steps:

1. Load and compile the vertex shader.
2. Load and compile the fragment shader.
3. Link the two shaders together into a "shader program."

There are many steps to loading a shader, so it is a good idea to declare a separate `Shader` class, as in Listing 5.5.

Listing 5.5   Initial `Shader` Declaration

```
class Shader
{
public:
    Shader();
    ~Shader();
    // Load the vertex/fragment shaders with the given names
    bool Load(const std::string& vertName,
              const std::string& fragName);
    // Set this as the active shader program
    void SetActive();
private:
    // Tries to compile the specified shader
    bool CompileShader(const std::string& fileName,
                       GLenum shaderType, GLuint& outShader);
    // Tests whether shader compiled successfully
    bool IsCompiled(GLuint shader);
    // Tests whether vertex/fragment programs link
    bool IsValidProgram();
    // Store the shader object IDs
    GLuint mVertexShader;
    GLuint mFragShader;
    GLuint mShaderProgram;
};
```

Note how the member variables here correspond to shader object IDs. They have object IDs much like the vertex and index buffers. (`GLuint` is simply OpenGL's version of `unsigned int`.)

You declare `CompileShader`, `IsCompiled`, and `IsValidProgram` in the `private` section because they are helper functions used by `Load`. This reduces the code duplication in `Load`.

The `CompileShader` Function

`CompileShader` takes three parameters: the name of the shader file to compile, the type of shader, and a reference parameter to store the ID of the shader. The return value is a `bool` that denotes whether `CompileShader` succeeded.

Listing 5.6 shows the implementation of `CompileShader`, which has several steps. First, create an `ifstream` to load in the file. Next, use a string stream to load the entire contents of the file into a single string, `contents`, and get the C-style string pointer with the `c_str` function.

Next, the `glCreateShader` function call creates an OpenGL shader object corresponding to the shader (and saves this ID in `outShader`). The `shaderType` parameter can be `GL_VERTEX_SHADER`, `GL_FRAGMENT_SHADER`, or a few other shader types.

The `glShaderSource` call specifies the string containing the shader source code, and `glCompileShader` compiles the code. You then use the `IsCompiled` helper function (implemented in a moment) to validate that the shader compiles.

In the event of any errors, including being unable to load the shader file or failing to compile it, `CompileShader` outputs an error message and returns `false`.

Listing 5.6 `Shader::CompileShader` Implementation

```
bool Shader::CompileShader(const std::string& fileName,
    GLenum shaderType,
    GLuint& outShader)
{
    // Open file
    std::ifstream shaderFile(fileName);
    if (shaderFile.is_open())
    {
        // Read all the text into a string
        std::stringstream sstream;
        sstream << shaderFile.rdbuf();
        std::string contents = sstream.str();
        const char* contentsChar = contents.c_str();

        // Create a shader of the specified type
        outShader = glCreateShader(shaderType);
        // Set the source characters and try to compile
        glShaderSource(outShader, 1, &(contentsChar), nullptr);
        glCompileShader(outShader);

        if (!IsCompiled(outShader))
        {
            SDL_Log("Failed to compile shader %s", fileName.c_str());
            return false;
        }
    }
    else
    {
        SDL_Log("Shader file not found: %s", fileName.c_str());
        return false;
    }
    return true;
}
```

The `IsCompiled` Function

The `IsCompiled` function, shown in Listing 5.7, validates whether a shader object compiled, and if it didn't, it outputs the compilation error message. This way, you can get some information about why a shader fails to compile.

Listing 5.7 `Shader::IsCompiled` Implementation

```cpp
bool Shader::IsCompiled(GLuint shader)
{
   GLint status;
   // Query the compile status
   glGetShaderiv(shader, GL_COMPILE_STATUS, &status);
   if (status != GL_TRUE)
   {
      char buffer[512];
      memset(buffer, 0, 512);
      glGetShaderInfoLog(shader, 511, nullptr, buffer);
      SDL_Log("GLSL Compile Failed:\n%s", buffer);
      return false;
   }
   return true;
}
```

The `glGetShaderiv` function queries the compilation status, which the function returns as an integral status code. If this status is not `GL_TRUE`, there was an error. In the event of an error, you can get a human-readable compile error message with `glGetShaderInfoLog`.

The `Load` Function

The `Load` function in Listing 5.8 takes in the filenames of both the vertex and fragment shaders and then tries to compile and link these shaders together.

As shown in Listing 5.8, you compile both the vertex and fragment shaders using `CompileShader` and then save their objects IDs in `mVertexShader` and `mFragShader`, respectively. If either of the `CompileShader` calls fail, `Load` returns `false`.

Listing 5.8 `Shader::Load` Implementation

```cpp
bool Shader::Load(const std::string& vertName,
                  const std::string& fragName)
{
   // Compile vertex and fragment shaders
   if (!CompileShader(vertName, GL_VERTEX_SHADER, mVertexShader) ||
      !CompileShader(fragName, GL_FRAGMENT_SHADER, mFragShader))
   {
      return false;
   }

   // Now create a shader program that
   // links together the vertex/frag shaders
```

```
mShaderProgram = glCreateProgram();
glAttachShader(mShaderProgram, mVertexShader);
glAttachShader(mShaderProgram, mFragShader);
glLinkProgram(mShaderProgram);

// Verify that the program linked successfully
if (!IsValidProgram())
{
    return false;
}
return true;
}
```

After you've compiled both the fragment and vertex shader, you link them together in a third object, called a shader program. When it's time to draw an object, OpenGL uses the currently active shader program to render the triangles.

You create a shader program with `glCreateProgram`, which returns the object ID to the new shader program. Next, use `glAttachShader` to add the vertex and fragment shaders to the combined shader program. Then use `glLinkProgram` to link together all attached shaders into the final shader program.

As with shader compilation, figuring out whether the link was successful requires additional function calls, which you can place in the `IsValidProgram` helper function.

The `IsValidProgram` Function

The code for `IsValidProgram` is very similar to the code for `IsCompiled`. There are only two differences. First, instead of calling `glGetShaderiv`, call `glGetProgramiv`:

```
glGetProgramiv(mShaderProgram, GL_LINK_STATUS, &status);
```

Next, instead of calling `glGetShaderInfoLog`, call `glGetProgramInfoLog`:

```
glGetProgramInfoLog(mShaderProgram, 511, nullptr, buffer);
```

The `SetActive` Function

The `SetActive` function sets a shader program as the active one:

```
void Shader::SetActive()
{
    glUseProgram(mShaderProgram);
}
```

OpenGL uses the active shader when drawing triangles.

The `Unload` Function

The `Unload` function simply deletes the shader program, the vertex shader, and the pixel shader:

```
void Shader::Unload()
{
   glDeleteProgram(mShaderProgram);
   glDeleteShader(mVertexShader);
   glDeleteShader(mFragShader);
}
```

Adding a Shader to the Game

With the `Shader` class, you can now add a `Shader` pointer as a member variable to `Game`:

```
class Shader* mSpriteShader;
```

This variable is called `mSpriteShader` because, ultimately, you'll use it to draw sprites. The `LoadShaders` function loads in the shader files and sets the shader as active:

```
bool Game::LoadShaders()
{
   mSpriteShader = new Shader();
   if (!mSpriteShader->Load("Shaders/Basic.vert", "Shaders/Basic.frag"))
   {
      return false;
   }
   mSpriteShader->SetActive();
}
```

You call `LoadShaders` in `Game::Initialize` immediately after finishing initialization of OpenGL and GLEW (and before you create the `mSpriteVerts` vertex array object).

After you've created simple vertex and pixel shaders and loaded in triangles, you can finally try to draw some triangles.

Drawing Triangles

As mentioned earlier, you can draw sprites with triangles by drawing rectangles onscreen. You've already loaded in the unit square vertices and a basic shader that can draw blue pixels. As before, you want to draw sprites in the `Draw` function in `SpriteComponent`.

First, you change the declaration of `SpriteComponent::Draw` so that it takes in `Shader*` instead of `SDL_Renderer*`. Next, draw a quad with a call to `glDrawElements`:

```
void SpriteComponent::Draw(Shader* shader)
{
   glDrawElements(
      GL_TRIANGLES,    // Type of polygon/primitive to draw
      6,               // Number of indices in index buffer
```

```
        GL_UNSIGNED_INT, // Type of each index
        nullptr          // Usually nullptr
    );
}
```

The first parameter to `glDrawElements` specifies the type of element you're drawing (in this case, triangles). The second parameter is the number of indices in the index buffer; in this case, because the index buffer for the unit square has six elements, you pass in 6 as the parameter. The third parameter is the type of each index, established earlier as `unsigned int`. The last parameter is `nullptr`.

The `glDrawElements` call requires both an active vertex array object and an active shader. On every frame, you need to activate both the sprite vertex array object and shader before drawing any `SpriteComponents`. You do this in the `Game::GenerateOutput` function, as shown in Listing 5.9. Once you've set the shader and vertex array as active, you call `Draw` once for each sprite in the scene.

Listing 5.9 `Game::GenerateOutput` Attempting to Draw Sprites

```
void Game::GenerateOutput()
{
    // Set the clear color to gray
    glClearColor(0.86f, 0.86f, 0.86f, 1.0f);
    // Clear the color buffer
    glClear(GL_COLOR_BUFFER_BIT);

    // Set sprite shader and vertex array objects active
    mSpriteShader->SetActive();
    mSpriteVerts->SetActive();

    // Draw all sprites
    for (auto sprite : mSprites)
    {
        sprite->Draw(mSpriteShader);
    }

    // Swap the buffers
    SDL_GL_SwapWindow(mWindow);
    return true;
}
```

What happens when you run this code now? Well, first, the fragment shader only writes out a blue color. So it's reasonable to expect that you'd see blue squares for each `SpriteComponent`. However, there's another issue: For every sprite, you use the same sprite verts. These sprite verts define a unit square in normalized device coordinates. This means that for every `SpriteComponent`, you merely draw the same unit square in NDC. Thus, if you run the game right now, you'll see only a gray background and a rectangle, as in Figure 5.3.

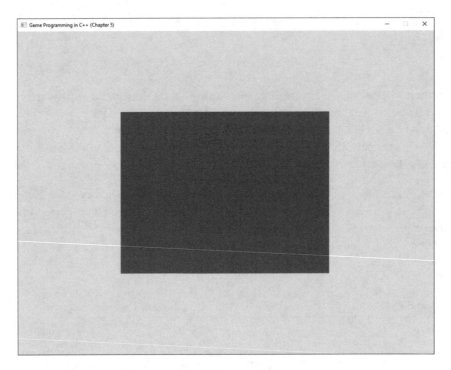

Figure 5.3 Drawing many NDC unit squares (even though it looks like one rectangle)

It may seem like the solution is to define different vertex arrays for each sprite. However, it turns out that with only this one vertex array, you can draw whichever sprites you want to. The key is to take advantage the vertex shader's ability to transform vertex attributes.

Transformation Basics

Suppose a game has 10 asteroids moving around. You could represent these 10 asteroids individually with different vertex array objects. However, you need these asteroids to show up in different locations onscreen. This means the triangles you draw for each asteroid need different normalized device coordinates.

A naïve idea is to create 10 different vertex buffers, 1 for each of the 10 asteroids, and recompute the vertex positions in these vertex buffers as needed. But this is wasteful both in terms of memory usage and in terms of computation. Changing vertices in vertex buffers and resubmitting them to OpenGL is not efficient. '

Instead, think of a sprite in an abstract sense. Every sprite is ultimately just a rectangle. Different sprites may have different locations on the screen, different sizes, or different rotations, but they're still rectangles.

Thinking of it this way, a more efficient solution is to have a single vertex buffer for the rectangle and just reuse it. Every time you draw the rectangle, you may have a position offset, scale, or rotation. But given the NDC unit square, you can change, or **transform**, it such that it is an arbitrary rectangle with an arbitrary position, scale, and/or orientation.

This same concept of reusing a single vertex buffer for a type of object also extends to 3D. For example, a game taking place in the forest might have hundreds of trees, many of which are only slight variations of each other. It's inefficient to have a separate vertex buffer for every single instance of the same tree. Instead, you could create a single tree vertex buffer, and the game could draw many instances of this same tree with some variation in position, scale, and orientation.

Object Space

When you create a 3D object (such as in a 3D modeling program), you generally don't express vertex positions in normalized device coordinates. Instead, the positions are relative to an arbitrary origin of the object itself. This origin is often in the center of the object, but it does not have to be. This coordinate space relative to the object itself is **object space,** or **model space**.

As discussed earlier in this chapter, defining a coordinate space requires knowing both the origin of the coordinate space and the direction in which the various components increase (the basis vectors). For example, some 3D modeling programs use +y as up, whereas others use +z as up. These different basis vectors define different object spaces for the objects. Figure 5.4 illustrates a 2D square where the center of the square is its object space origin, +y moves up, and +x moves right.

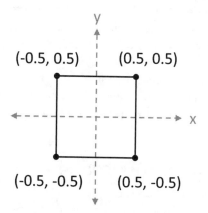

Figure 5.4 A quad relative to its object space origin

Now imagine a game that takes place in an office building. You'd need models for computer monitors, keyboards, desks, office chairs, and so on. You'd create each of these individual models in its own object space, which means each object's vertex positions are relative to that model's unique object space origin.

At runtime, you load each unique model into its own vertex array object (VAO). For example, you might have a VAO for the monitor, one for the keyboard, and so on. When it's time to render the scene, each vertex of each object you draw goes to the vertex shader. If you just directly passed along the vertex positions, as in `Basic.vert`, then you're saying that these vertex positions are in normalized device coordinates.

This is a problem because the coordinates for the models are not in NDC but instead are relative to each object's unique object space. Passing through the vertex positions as is would yield garbage output.

World Space

To solve the problem with different objects having different object space coordinates, you first define a coordinate space for the game world itself. This coordinate space, called **world space**, has its own origin and basis vectors. For the game in the office building, the origin of world space might be in the center of the building on the ground floor.

Much as an office planner might place the desks and chairs at different positions and orientations in the office, you can think of the objects in the game as having arbitrary positions, scales, or orientations relative to the world space origin. For example, if there are five instances of the same desk placed in the office, each of these instances needs information describing how the object appears in world space.

When you draw each instance of the desk, you use the same vertex array object for each desk. However, each instance now needs some additional information, specifying how you want to *transform* the object space coordinates into world space. You can send this extra data to the vertex shader when drawing an instance, which allows the vertex shader to adjust the vertex positions as needed. Of course, the graphics hardware ultimately needs the coordinates in NDC to draw them, so you still have an additional step after transforming the vertices into world space. For now, let's look at how to transform vertices from their object space into world space.

Transforming to World Space

When transforming between coordinate spaces, you need to know whether the basis vectors between the two coordinate spaces are the same. For example, consider the point (0, 5) in object space. If you define object space with +y as up, this means that the point (0, 5) is five units "above" the origin. However, if you choose to define world space such that +y is to the right, (0, 5) is instead five units to the right.

For now, assume that the basis vectors in object and world space are the same. Because the game currently is 2D, you can assume that +y is up and +x is to the right for both object space and world space.

> **note**
>
> The 2D coordinate system used here is different from the SDL coordinate system where +y is down! This means the code for `Actor::GetForward` no longer negates the y component. Furthermore, if you use `atan2` for any calculations, you no longer negate the first parameter.

Now consider a unit square centered around the object space origin, as in Figure 5.4. Assume that the world space origin is the center of the game window. The goal is to take the unit square centered around its object space origin and express it as a rectangle with an arbitrary position, scale, or orientation relative to the world space origin.

For example, suppose one instance of the rectangle should appear in world space such that it's double in size and is 50 units to the right of the world space origin. You can accomplish this by applying mathematical operations to each vertex of the rectangle.

One approach is to use algebra equations to compute the correct vertex positions. Although you ultimately won't approach it in this manner, this is a useful bridge to understanding the preferred solution. This chapter focuses on 2D coordinate systems, though the same method outlined here would also work in 3D (just with an additional z component).

Translation

Translation takes a point and **translates**, or moves, it by an offset. Given the point (x, y), you can translate it by the offset (a, b) by using the following equations:

$$x' = x + a$$
$$y' = y + b$$

For example, you could translate the point (1, 3) by the offset (20, 15) as follows:

$$x' = 1 + 20 = 21$$
$$y' = 3 + 15 = 18$$

If you apply the same translation to every vertex of a triangle, you translate the entire triangle.

Scale

When applied to each vertex in a triangle, scale increases or decreases the size of the triangle. In a **uniform scale**, you scale each component by the same scale factor, s:

$$x' = x \cdot s$$
$$y' = y \cdot s$$

So you can uniformly scale (1, 3) by 5 as follows:

$$x' = 1 \cdot 5 = 5$$
$$y' = 3 \cdot 5 = 15$$

Scaling each vertex in the triangle by 5 would quintuple the size of the triangle.

In a **non-uniform scale**, there are separate scale factors (s_x, s_y) for each component:

$$x' = x \cdot s_x$$
$$y' = y \cdot s_y$$

For the example of transforming a unit square, a non-uniform scale results in a rectangle instead of a square.

Rotation

Recall the discussion of the unit circle from Chapter 4, "Vectors and Basic Physics." The unit circle begins at the point (1, 0). A rotation of 90°, or $\frac{\pi}{2}$ radians, is counterclockwise to the point (0, 1), a rotation of 180°, or π radians, is the point (−1, 0), and so on. This is technically a rotation about the z-axis, even though you don't draw the z-axis in a typical unit circle diagram.

Using sine and cosine, you can rotate an arbitrary point (x, y) by the angle θ as follows:

$$x' = x \cos\theta - y \sin\theta$$
$$y' = x \sin\theta + y \cos\theta$$

Notice that both equations depend on the original x and y values. For example, rotating (5, 0) by 270° is as follows:

$$x' = 5 \cdot \cos(270°) - 0 \cdot \sin(270°) = 0$$
$$y' = 5 \cdot \sin(270°) + 0 \cdot \cos(270°) = -5.$$

As with the unit circle, the angle θ represents a counterclockwise rotation.

Keep in mind that this is a rotation *about the origin*. Given a triangle centered around the object space origin, rotating each vertex would rotate the triangle about the origin.

Combining Transformations

Although the preceding equations apply each transformation independently, it's common to require multiple transformations on the same vertex. For example, you might want to both translate *and* rotate a quad. It's important to combine these transformations in the correct order.

Suppose a triangle has the following points:

$$A = (-2, -1)$$
$$B = (0, 1)$$
$$C = (2, -1)$$

This original triangle points straight up, as in Figure 5.5(a). Now suppose you want to translate the triangle by (5, 0) and rotate it by 90°. If you rotate first and translate second, you get this:

$$A' = \left(-2\cos 90° + 1\sin 90° + 5, \ -2\sin 90° - 1\cos 90° + 0 \right) = \left(6, \ -2 \right)$$
$$B' = \left(-1\sin 90° + 5, \ 1\cos 90° + 0 \right) = \left(4, \ 0 \right)$$
$$C' = \left(2\cos 90° + 1\sin 90° + 5, \ 2\sin 90° - 1\cos 90° + 0 \right) = \left(6, \ 2 \right)$$

This results in the triangle rotated so that it points to the left and translated to the right, as in Figure 5.5(b).

If you reverse the order of the transformations so that you evaluate the translation first, you end up with this calculation:

$$A' = \left(\left(-2 + 5 \right)\cos 90° + 1\sin 90°, \ \left(-2 + 5 \right)\sin 90° - 1\cos 90° \right) = \left(1, \ 3 \right)$$
$$B' = \left(5\cos 90° - 1\sin 90°, \ 5\sin 90° + 1\cos 90° \right) = \left(-1, \ 5 \right)$$
$$C' = \left(\left(2 + 5 \right)\cos 90° + 1\sin 90°, \ \left(2 + 5 \right)\sin 90° - 1\cos 90° \right) = \left(1, \ 7 \right)$$

In the case of translation first, rotation second, you end up with a triangle still facing to the left but positioned several units above the origin, as in Figure 5.5(c). This happens because you first move the triangle to the right, and then you rotate about the origin. Usually, this behavior is undesirable.

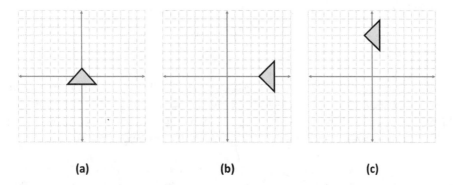

(a)   (b)   (c)

Figure 5.5 (a) Initial triangle, (b) rotating then translating, and (c) translating then rotating

Because the order of transformations matter, it's important to have a consistent order. For the transformation from object space to world space, always apply the transformations in the order scale, then rotation, then translation. Keeping this in mind, you could combine all three separate equations for scale, rotation, and translation into one set of equations to scale by (s_x, s_y), rotate by θ, and translate by (a, b):

$$x' = s_x \cdot x \cos\theta - s_y \cdot y \sin\theta + a$$
$$y' = s_x \cdot x \sin\theta + s_y \cdot y \cos\theta + b$$

Issues with Combining Equations

The combined equations derived in the previous section may seem like a solution to the problem: Take an arbitrary vertex in object space, apply the equations to each component, and you now have the vertex transformed into world space with an arbitrary scale, rotation, and position.

However, as alluded to earlier, this only transforms the vertices from object space to world space. Because world space is not normalized to device coordinates, you still have more transformations to apply in the vertex shader. These additional transformations typically do not have equations as simple as the equations covered thus far. This is especially because the basis vectors between these different coordinate spaces might be different. Combining these additional transformations into one equation would become unnecessarily complex.

The solution to these issues is to *not* use separate equations for each component. Instead, you use matrices to describe the different transformations, and you can easily combine these transformations with matrix multiplication.

Matrices and Transformations

A **matrix** is a grid of values, with *m* rows and *n* columns. For example, you could write a 2×2 matrix as follows, with *a* through *d* representing individual values in the matrix:

$$\begin{bmatrix} a & b \\ c & d \end{bmatrix}$$

You use matrices to represent transformations in computer graphics. All the transformations from the preceding section have corresponding matrix representations. If you are experienced in linear algebra, you might recall that matrices can be used to solve systems of linear equations. Thus, it's natural that you can represent the system of equations in the previous section as matrices.

This section explores some of the basic use cases of matrices in game programming. As with vectors, it's most important to understand how and when to use these matrices in code. This book's custom `Math.h` header file defines `Matrix3` and `Matrix4` classes, along with operators, member functions, and static functions that implement all the necessary features.

Matrix Multiplication

Much as with scalars, you can multiply two matrices together. Suppose you have the following matrices:

$$A = \begin{bmatrix} a & b \\ c & d \end{bmatrix} \quad B = \begin{bmatrix} e & f \\ g & h \end{bmatrix}$$

The result of the multiplication $C = AB$ is:

$$C = AB = \begin{bmatrix} a & b \\ c & d \end{bmatrix} \begin{bmatrix} e & f \\ g & h \end{bmatrix} = \begin{bmatrix} a \cdot e + b \cdot g & a \cdot f + b \cdot h \\ c \cdot e + d \cdot g & c \cdot f + d \cdot h \end{bmatrix}$$

In other words, the top-left element of C is the dot product of the first row of A with the first column of B.

Matrix multiplication does not require matrices to have identical dimensions, but the number of columns in the left matrix must be equal to the number of rows in the right matrix. For instance, the following multiplication is also valid:

$$\begin{bmatrix} a & b \end{bmatrix} \begin{bmatrix} c & d \\ e & f \end{bmatrix} = \begin{bmatrix} a \cdot c + b \cdot e & a \cdot d + b \cdot f \end{bmatrix}$$

Matrix multiplication is *not* commutative, though it is associative:

$$AB \neq BA$$
$$A(BC) = (AB)C$$

Transforming a Point by Using a Matrix

A key aspect of transformations is that you can represent an arbitrary point as a matrix. For example, you can represent the point $p = (x, y)$ as a single row (called a **row vector**):

$$p = \begin{bmatrix} x & y \end{bmatrix}$$

You can instead represent P as a single column (called a **column vector**):

$$p = \begin{bmatrix} x \\ y \end{bmatrix}$$

Either representation works, but it's important to consistently use one approach. This is because whether the point is a row or a column determines whether the point appears on the left- or right-hand side of the multiplication.

Suppose you have a transformation matrix T:

$$T = \begin{bmatrix} a & b \\ c & d \end{bmatrix}$$

With matrix multiplication, you can transform the point p by this matrix, yielding the transformed point (x', y'). However, whether p is a single row or a single column gives different results when multiplied by T.

If P is a row, the multiplication is as follows:

$$\begin{bmatrix} x' & y' \end{bmatrix} = pT = \begin{bmatrix} x & y \end{bmatrix} \begin{bmatrix} a & b \\ c & d \end{bmatrix}$$
$$x' = a \cdot x + c \cdot y$$
$$y' = b \cdot x + d \cdot y$$

But if P is a column, the multiplication would yield the following:

$$\begin{bmatrix} x' \\ y' \end{bmatrix} = Tp = \begin{bmatrix} a & b \\ c & d \end{bmatrix} \begin{bmatrix} x \\ y \end{bmatrix}$$
$$x' = a \cdot x + b \cdot y$$
$$y' = c \cdot x + d \cdot y$$

This gives two different values for x' and y', but only one is the correct answer—because the definition of a transform matrix relies on whether you're using row vectors or column vectors.

Whether to use row or column vectors is somewhat arbitrary. Most linear algebra textbooks use column vectors. However, in computer graphics there is a history of using either row or column vectors, depending on the resource and graphics API. *This book uses row vectors*, mainly because the transformations apply in a left-to-right order for a given point. For example, when using row vectors, the following equation transforms the point q by matrix T first and then by matrix R:

$$q' = qTR$$

You can switch between row and column vectors by taking the **transpose** of each transform matrix. The transpose of the matrix rotates the matrix such that the first row of the original matrix becomes the first column of the result:

$$\begin{bmatrix} a & b \\ c & d \end{bmatrix}^T = \begin{bmatrix} a & c \\ b & d \end{bmatrix}$$

If you wanted to switch the equation to transform q using column vectors, you would calculate as follows:

$$q' = R^T T^T q$$

The matrices in the remainder of this book assume that you are using row vectors. However, a simple transpose of these matrices converts them to work with column vectors.

Finally, the **identity matrix** is a special type of matrix represented by an uppercase I. An identity matrix always has an equal number of rows and columns. All values in the identity matrix are 0, except for the diagonal, which is all 1s. For example, the 3×3 identity matrix is as follows:

$$I_3 = \begin{bmatrix} 1 & 0 & 0 \\ 0 & 1 & 0 \\ 0 & 0 & 1 \end{bmatrix}$$

Any arbitrary matrix multiplied by the identity matrix does not change. In other words:

$$MI = M$$

Transforming to World Space, Revisited

You can represent the scale, rotation, and translation transformations with matrices. To combine the transformations, instead of deriving a combined equation, multiply the matrices together. Once you have a combined world transform matrix, you can transform every vertex of the object by this world transform matrix.

As before, let's focus on 2D transformations first.

Scale Matrix

You can use a 2×2 scale matrix to apply the scale transformation:

$$S(s_x, s_y) = \begin{bmatrix} s_x & 0 \\ 0 & s_y \end{bmatrix}$$

For example, this would scale $(1, 3)$ by $S(5, 2)$:

$$\begin{bmatrix} 1 & 3 \end{bmatrix} S(5,2) = \begin{bmatrix} 1 & 3 \end{bmatrix} \begin{bmatrix} 5 & 0 \\ 0 & 2 \end{bmatrix}$$
$$= \begin{bmatrix} 1 \cdot 5 + 3 \cdot 0 & 1 \cdot 0 + 3 \cdot 2 \end{bmatrix}$$
$$= \begin{bmatrix} 5 & 6 \end{bmatrix}$$

Rotation Matrix

A 2D rotation matrix represents a rotation (about the z-axis) by angle θ:

$$R(\theta) = \begin{bmatrix} \cos\theta & \sin\theta \\ -\sin\theta & \cos\theta \end{bmatrix}$$

So, you can rotate $(0,3)$ by $90°$ with the following:

$$\begin{bmatrix} 0 & 3 \end{bmatrix} R(90°) = \begin{bmatrix} 0 & 3 \end{bmatrix} \begin{bmatrix} \cos 90° & \sin 90° \\ -\sin 90° & \cos 90° \end{bmatrix}$$

$$= \begin{bmatrix} 0 & 3 \end{bmatrix} \begin{bmatrix} 0 & 1 \\ -1 & 0 \end{bmatrix}$$

$$= \begin{bmatrix} -3 & 0 \end{bmatrix}.$$

Translation Matrices

You can represent 2D scale and rotation matrices with 2×2 matrices. However, there's no way to write a generic 2D translation matrix of size 2×2. The only way to express the translation $T(a,b)$ is with a 3×3 matrix:

$$T(a,b) = \begin{bmatrix} 1 & 0 & 0 \\ 0 & 1 & 0 \\ a & b & 1 \end{bmatrix}$$

However, you can't multiply a 1×2 matrix representing a point by a 3×3 matrix because the 1×2 matrix doesn't have enough columns. The only way you can multiply these together is if you add an additional column to the row vector, making it a 1×3 matrix. This requires adding an extra component to the point. **Homogenous coordinates** use $n+1$ components to represent an n-dimensional space. So, for a 2D space, homogeneous coordinates use three components.

Although it might seem reasonable to call this third component the z component, it's a misnomer. That's because you're not representing a 3D space, and you want to reserve the z component for 3D spaces. Thus this special homogeneous coordinate is the **w component**. You use w for both 2D and 3D homogeneous coordinates. So, a 2D point represented in homogeneous coordinates is (x,y,w), while a 3D point represented in homogeneous coordinates is (x,y,z,w).

For now, you will only use a value of 1 for the w component. For example, you can represent the point $p=(x,y)$ with the homogeneous coordinate $(x,y,1)$. To understand how homogeneous coordinates work, suppose you wish to translate the point $(1,3)$ by $(20,15)$. First, you represent the point as a homogeneous coordinate with a w component of 1 and then you multiply the point by the translation matrix:

$$\begin{bmatrix} 1 & 3 & 1 \end{bmatrix} T(20,15) = \begin{bmatrix} 1 & 3 & 1 \end{bmatrix} \begin{bmatrix} 1 & 0 & 0 \\ 0 & 1 & 0 \\ 20 & 15 & 1 \end{bmatrix}$$

$$= \begin{bmatrix} 1 \cdot 1 + 3 \cdot 0 + 1 \cdot 20 & 1 \cdot 0 + 3 \cdot 1 + 1 \cdot 15 & 1 \cdot 0 + 3 \cdot 0 + 1 \cdot 1 \end{bmatrix}$$

$$= \begin{bmatrix} 21 & 18 & 1 \end{bmatrix}$$

Note that, in this calculation, the w component remains 1. However, you've translated the x and y components by the desired amount.

Combining Transformations

As mentioned earlier, you can combine multiple transform matrices by multiplying them together. However, you can't multiply a 2×2 matrix with a 3×3 matrix. Thus, you must represent the scale and rotation transforms with 3×3 matrices that work with homogeneous coordinates:

$$S(s_x, s_y) = \begin{bmatrix} s_x & 0 & 0 \\ 0 & s_y & 0 \\ 0 & 0 & 1 \end{bmatrix}$$

$$R(\theta) = \begin{bmatrix} \cos\theta & \sin\theta & 0 \\ -\sin\theta & \cos\theta & 0 \\ 0 & 0 & 1 \end{bmatrix}$$

Now that you've represented the scale, rotation, and translation matrices as 3×3 matrices, you can multiply them together into one combined transform matrix. This combined matrix that transforms from object space to world space is the **world transform matrix**. To compute the world transform matrix, multiply the scale, rotation, and translation matrices in the following order:

$$WorldTransform = S(s_x, s_y) \, R(\theta) \, T(a,b)$$

This order of multiplication corresponds to the order in which you wish to apply the transformations (scale, then rotate, then translate). You can then pass this world transform matrix to the vertex shader and use it to transform every vertex of an object by its world transform matrix.

Adding World Transforms to Actor

Recall that the declaration of the `Actor` class already has a `Vector2` for position, a float for scale, and a float for the angle rotation. You now must combine these different attributes into a world transform matrix.

First, add two member variables to `Actor`, a `Matrix4` and a `bool`:

```
Matrix4 mWorldTransform;
bool mRecomputeWorldTransform;
```

The `mWorldTransform` variable obviously stores the world transform matrix. The reason you use a `Matrix4` here instead of a `Matrix3` is because the vertex layout assumes that all vertices have a z component (even though in 2D, you don't actually need the z component). Since the homogenous coordinates for 3D are (x, y, z, w), you need a 4×4 matrix.

The Boolean tracks whether you need to recalculate the world transform matrix. The idea is that you want to recalculate the world transform only if the actor's position, scale, or rotation changes. In each of the setter functions for the position, scale, and rotation of the actor, you set mRecomputeWorldTransform to true. This way, whenever you change these component properties, you'll be sure to compute the world transform again.

You also initialize mRecomputeWorldTransform to true in the constructor, which guarantees to compute the world transform at least once for each actor.

Next, implement a CreateWorldTransform function, as follows:

```
void Actor::ComputeWorldTransform()
{
    if (mRecomputeWorldTransform)
    {
        mRecomputeWorldTransform = false;
        // Scale, then rotate, then translate
        mWorldTransform = Matrix4::CreateScale(mScale);
        mWorldTransform *= Matrix4::CreateRotationZ(mRotation);
        mWorldTransform *= Matrix4::CreateTranslation(
            Vector3(mPosition.x, mPosition.y, 0.0f));
    }
}
```

Note that you use various Matrix4 static functions to create the component matrices. CreateScale creates a uniform scale matrix, CreateRotationZ creates a rotation matrix about the z-axis, and CreateTranslation creates a translation matrix.

You call ComputeWorldTransform in Actor::Update, both before you update any components and after you call UpdateActor (in case it changes in the interim):

```
void Actor::Update(float deltaTime)
{
    if (mState == EActive)
    {
        ComputeWorldTransform();

        UpdateComponents(deltaTime);
        UpdateActor(deltaTime);

        ComputeWorldTransform();
    }
}
```

Next, add a call to ComputeWorldTransform in Game::Update to make sure any "pending" actors (actors created while updating other actors) have their world transform calculated in the same frame where they're created:

```
// In Game::Update (move any pending actors to mActors)
for (auto pending : mPendingActors)
{
    pending->ComputeWorldTransform();
    mActors.emplace_back(pending);
}
```

It would be nice to have a way to notify components when their owner's world transform gets updated. This way, the component can respond as needed. To support this, first add a virtual function declaration to the base Component class:

```
virtual void OnUpdateWorldTransform() { }
```

Next, call OnUpdateWorldTransform on each of the actor's components inside the ComputeWorldTransform function. Listing 5.10 shows the final version of ComputeWorldTransform.

Listing 5.10 `Actor::ComputeWorldTransform` Implementation

```
void Actor::ComputeWorldTransform()
{
    if (mRecomputeWorldTransform)
    {
        mRecomputeWorldTransform = false;
        // Scale, then rotate, then translate
        mWorldTransform = Matrix4::CreateScale(mScale);
        mWorldTransform *= Matrix4::CreateRotationZ(mRotation);
        mWorldTransform *= Matrix4::CreateTranslation(
            Vector3(mPosition.x, mPosition.y, 0.0f));

        // Inform components world transform updated
        for (auto comp : mComponents)
        {
            comp->OnUpdateWorldTransform();
        }
    }
}
```

For now, you won't implement OnUpdateWorldTransform for any components. However, you will use it for some components in subsequent chapters.

Although actors now have world transform matrices, you aren't using the matrices in the vertex shader yet. Therefore, running the game with the code as discussed so far would just yield the same visual output as in Figure 5.3. Before you can use the world transform matrices in the shader, we need to discuss one other transformation.

Transforming from World Space to Clip Space

With the world transform matrix, you can transform vertices into world space. The next step is to transform the vertices into clip space, which is the expected output for the vertex shader. **Clip space** is a close relative of normalized device coordinates. The only difference is that clip space also has a w component. This was why you created a vec4 to save the vertex position in the gl_Position variable.

The **view-projection matrix** transforms from world space to clip space. As might be apparent from the name, the view-projection matrix has two component matrices: the view and the projection. The **view** accounts for how a virtual camera sees the game world, and the **projection** specifies how to convert from the virtual camera's view to clip space. Chapter 6, "3D Graphics," talks about both matrices in much greater detail. For now, because the game is 2D, you can use a simple view-projection matrix.

Recall that in normalized device coordinates, the bottom-left corner of the screen is (−1, −1) and the top-right corner of the screen is (1, 1). Now consider a 2D game that does not have scrolling. A simple way to think of the game world is in terms of the window's resolution. For example, if the game window is 1024×768, why not make the game world that big, also?

In other words, consider a view of world space such that the center of the window is the world space origin, and there's a 1:1 ratio between a pixel and a unit in world space. In this case, moving up by 1 unit in world space is the same as moving up by 1 pixel in the window. Assuming a 1024×768 resolution, this means that the bottom-left corner of the window corresponds to (−512, −384) in world space, and the top-right corner of the window corresponds to (512, 384), as in Figure 5.6.

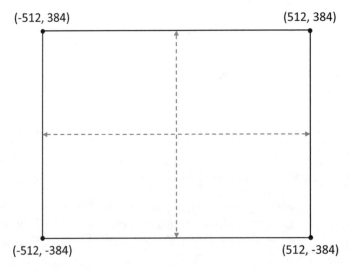

Figure 5.6 The view of a world where the screen resolution is 1024×768 and there's a 1:1 ratio between a pixel and a unit in world space

With this view of the world, it's not too difficult to convert from world space into clip space. Simply divide the x-coordinate by *width* / 2 and divide the y-coordinate by *height* / 2. In matrix form, assuming 2D homogeneous coordinates, this simple view projection matrix is as follows:

$$SimpleViewProjection = \begin{bmatrix} 2/width & 0 & 0 \\ 0 & 2/height & 0 \\ 0 & 0 & 1 \end{bmatrix}$$

For example, given the 1024×768 resolution and the point (256,192) in world space, if you multiply the point by *SimpleViewProjection*, you get this:

$$\begin{bmatrix} 256 & 192 & 1 \end{bmatrix} \begin{bmatrix} 2/1024 & 0 & 0 \\ 0 & 2/768 & 0 \\ 0 & 0 & 1 \end{bmatrix} = \begin{bmatrix} 512/1024 & 384/768 & 1 \end{bmatrix}$$
$$= \begin{bmatrix} 0.5 & 0.5 & 1 \end{bmatrix}$$

The reason this works is that you normalize the range [−512, 512] of the x-axis to [−1, 1], and the range of [−384, 384] on the y-axis [−1, 1], just as with normalized device coordinates!

Combining the *SimpleViewProjection* matrix with the world transform matrix, you can transform an arbitrary vertex *v* from its object space into clip space with this:

$$v' = v(WorldTransform)(SimpleViewProjection)$$

This is precisely what you will calculate in the vertex shader for every single vertex, at least until *SimpleViewProjection* has outlived its usefulness.

Updating Shaders to Use Transform Matrices

In this section, you'll create a new vertex shader file called `Transform.vert`. It starts initially as a copy of the `Basic.vert` shader from Listing 5.3. As a reminder, you write this shader code in GLSL, *not C++*.

First, you declare two new global variables in `Transform.vert` with the type specifier `uniform`. A **uniform** is a global variable that typically stays the same between numerous invocations of the shader program. This contrasts `in` and `out` variables, which will change every time the shader runs (for example, once per vertex or pixel). To declare a uniform variable, use the keyword `uniform`, followed by the type, followed by the variable name.

In this case, you need two uniforms for the two different matrices. You can declare these uniforms as follows:

```
uniform mat4 uWorldTransform;
uniform mat4 uViewProj;
```

Here, the `mat4` type corresponds to a 4×4 matrix, which is needed for a 3D space with homogeneous coordinates.

Then you change the code in the vertex shader's `main` function. First, convert the 3D `inPosition` into homogeneous coordinates:

```
vec4 pos = vec4(inPosition, 1.0);
```

Remember that this position is in object space. So you next multiply it by the world transform matrix to transform it into world space, and then multiply it by the view-projection matrix to transform it into clip space:

```
gl_Position = pos * uWorldTransform * uViewProj;
```

These changes yield the final version of `Transform.vert`, shown in Listing 5.11.

Listing 5.11   `Transform.vert` Vertex Shader

```
#version 330
// Uniforms for world transform and view-proj
uniform mat4 uWorldTransform;
uniform mat4 uViewProj;

// Vertex attributes
in vec3 inPosition;
void main()
{
    vec4 pos = vec4(inPosition, 1.0);
    gl_Position = pos * uWorldTransform * uViewProj;
}
```

You then change the code in `Game::LoadShaders` to use the `Transform.vert` vertex shader instead of `Basic.vert`:

```
if (!mSpriteShader->Load("Shaders/Transform.vert", "Shaders/Basic.frag"))
{
    return false;
}
```

Now that you have uniforms in the vertex shader for the world transform and view-projection matrices, you need a way to set these uniforms from C++ code. OpenGL provides functions to set uniform variables in the active shader program. It makes sense to add wrappers for these functions to the `Shader` class. For now, you can add a function called `SetMatrixUniform`, shown in Listing 5.12, to `Shader`.

Listing 5.12 `Shader::SetMatrixUniform` Implementation

```
void Shader::SetMatrixUniform(const char* name, const Matrix4& matrix)
{
    // Find the uniform by this name
    GLuint loc = glGetUniformLocation(mShaderProgram, name);
    // Send the matrix data to the uniform
    glUniformMatrix4fv(
        loc,       // Uniform ID
        1,         // Number of matrices (only 1 in this case)
        GL_TRUE,   // Set to TRUE if using row vectors
        matrix.GetAsFloatPtr() // Pointer to matrix data
    );
}
```

Notice that `SetMatrixUniform` takes in a name as a string literal, as well as a matrix. The name corresponds to the variable name in the shader file. So, for `uWorldTransform`, the parameter would be `"uWorldTransform"`. The second parameter is the matrix to send to the shader program for that uniform.

In the implementation of `SetMatrixUniform`, you get the location ID of the uniform with `glGetUniformLocation`. Technically, you don't have to query the ID every single time you update the same uniform because the ID doesn't change during execution. You could improve the performance of this code by caching the values of specific uniforms.

Next, the `glUniformMatrix4fv` function assigns a matrix to the uniform. The third parameter of this function must be set to `GL_TRUE` when using row vectors. The `GetAsFloatPtr` function is simply a helper function in `Matrix4` that returns a `float*` pointer to the underlying matrix.

> **note**
>
> OpenGL has a newer approach to setting uniforms, called **uniform buffer objects** (abbreviated **UBOs**). With UBOs, you can group together multiple uniforms in the shader and send them all at once. For shader programs with many uniforms, this generally is more efficient than individually setting each uniform's value.
>
> With uniform buffer objects, you can split up uniforms into multiple groups. For example, you may have a group for uniforms that update once per frame and uniforms that update once per object. The view-projection won't change more than once per frame, while every actor will have a different world transform matrix. This way, you can update all per-frame uniforms in just one function call at the start of the frame. Likewise, you can update all per-object uniforms separately for each object. To implement this, you must change how you declare uniforms in the shader and how you mirror that data in the C++ code.

> However, at this writing, some hardware still has spotty support for UBOs. Specifi-
> cally, the integrated graphics chips of some laptops don't fully support uniform
> buffer objects. On other hardware, UBOs may even run more slowly than uniforms
> set the old way. Because of this, this book does not use uniform buffer objects.
> However, the concept of buffer objects is prevalent in other graphics APIs, such as
> DirectX 11 and higher.

Now that you have a way to set the vertex shader's matrix uniforms, you need to set them.
Because the simple view-projection won't change throughout the course of the program, you
only need to set it once. However, you need to set the world transform matrix once for each
sprite component you draw because each sprite component draws with the world transform
matrix of its owning actor.

In `Game::LoadShaders`, add the following two lines to create and set the view-projection
matrix to the simple view projection, assuming a screen width of 1024×768:

```
Matrix4 viewProj = Matrix4::CreateSimpleViewProj(1024.f, 768.f);
mShader.SetMatrixUniform("uViewProj", viewProj);
```

The world transform matrix for `SpriteComponent` is a little more complex. The actor's
world transform matrix describes the position, scale, and orientation of the actor in the game
world. However, for a sprite, you also want to scale the size of the rectangle based on the size
of the texture. For example, if an actor has a scale of 1.0f, but the texture image corresponding to its sprite is 128×128, you need to scale up the unit square to 128×128. For now, assume
that you have a way to load in the textures (as you did in SDL) and that the sprite component
knows the dimensions of these textures via the `mTexWidth` and `mTexHeight` member
variables.

Listing 5.13 shows the implementation of `SpriteComponent::Draw` (for now). First, create a
scale matrix to scale by the width and height of the texture. You then multiply this by the owning actor's world transform matrix to create the desired world transform matrix for the sprite.
Next, call `SetMatrixUniform` to set the `uWorldTransform` in the vertex shader program.
Finally, you draw the triangles as before, with `glDrawElements`.

Listing 5.13   Current Implementation of `SpriteComponent::Draw`

```
void SpriteComponent::Draw(Shader* shader)
{
    // Scale the quad by the width/height of texture
    Matrix4 scaleMat = Matrix4::CreateScale(
        static_cast<float>(mTexWidth),
        static_cast<float>(mTexHeight),
        1.0f);
    Matrix4 world = scaleMat * mOwner->GetWorldTransform();
```

```
    // Set world transform
    shader->SetMatrixUniform("uWorldTransform", world);
    // Draw quad
    glDrawElements(GL_TRIANGLES, 6, GL_UNSIGNED_INT, nullptr);
}
```

With the world transform and view-projection matrices added to the shader, you now can see the individual sprite components in the world at arbitrary positions, scales, and rotations, as in Figure 5.7. Of course, all the rectangles are just a solid color for now because `Basic.frag` just outputs blue. This is the last thing to fix to achieve feature parity with the SDL 2D rendering from the previous chapters.

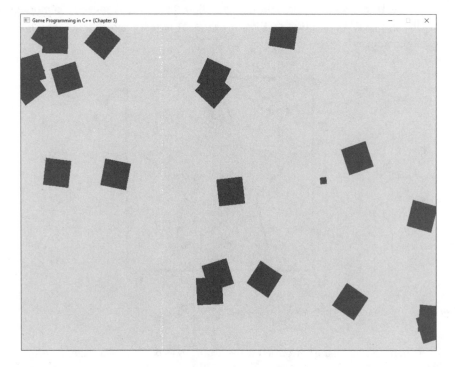

Figure 5.7 Drawing sprite components with different world transform matrices

Texture Mapping

Texture mapping is a technique for rendering a **texture** (image) on the face of a triangle. It allows you to use colors from a texture when drawing a triangle instead of using just a solid color.

To use texture mapping, you need an image file. Next, you need to decide how to apply textures to each triangle. If you have just the sprite rectangle, it makes sense that the top-left corner of the rectangle should correspond to the top-left corner of the texture. However, you can use texture mapping with arbitrary 3D objects in the game. For example, to correctly apply a texture to a character's face, you need to know which parts of the texture should correspond to which triangles.

To support this, you need an additional vertex attribute for every vertex in the vertex buffer. Previously, the vertex attributes only stored a 3D position in each vertex. For texture mapping, each vertex also needs a **texture coordinate** that specifies the location in the texture that corresponds to that vertex.

Texture coordinates typically are normalized coordinates. In OpenGL, the coordinates are such that the bottom-left corner of the texture is (0, 0) and the top-right corner is (1, 1), as shown in Figure 5.8. The **U component** defines the right direction of the texture, and the **V component** defines the up direction of the texture. Thus, many use the term **UV coordinates** as a synonym for texture coordinates.

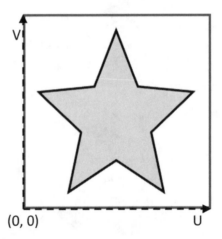

Figure 5.8 UV coordinates for a texture in OpenGL

Because OpenGL specifies the bottom left of the texture as its origin, it also expects the image pixel data format as one row at a time, starting at the bottom row. However, a big issue with this is that most image file formats store their data starting at the top row. Not accounting for this discrepancy results in textures that appear upside down. There are multiple ways to solve this problem: invert the V-component, load the image upside down, or store the image on disk upside down. This book simply inverts the V component—that is, assumes that the top-left corner is (0, 0). This corresponds to the texture coordinate system that DirectX uses.

Each vertex of a triangle has its own separate UV coordinates. Once you know the UV coordinates for each vertex of a triangle, you can fill in every pixel in the triangle by blending (or **interpolating**) the texture coordinate, based on the distance from each of the three vertices.

For example, a pixel exactly in the center of the triangle corresponds to a UV coordinate that's the average of the three vertices' UV coordinates, as in Figure 5.9.

Recall that a 2D image is just a grid of pixels with different colors. So, once you have a texture coordinate for a specific pixel, you need to convert this UV coordinate to correspond to a specific pixel in the texture. This "pixel in the texture" is a **texture pixel,** or **texel**. The graphics hardware uses a process called **sampling** to select a texel corresponding to a specific UV coordinate.

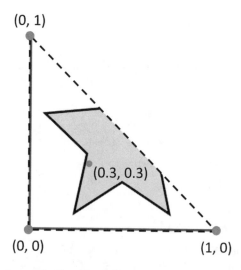

Figure 5.9 Texture mapping applied to a triangle

One complication of using normalized UV coordinates is that two slightly different UV coordinates may end up closest to the same texel in the image file. The idea of selecting the texel closest to a UV coordinate and using that for the color is called **nearest-neighbor filtering**.

However, nearest-neighbor filtering has some issues. Suppose you map a texture to a wall in a 3D world. As the player gets closer to the wall, the wall appears larger and larger onscreen. This looks like zooming in on an image file in a paint program, and the texture appears blocky or **pixelated** because each individual texel is very large onscreen.

To solve this pixelation, you can instead use **bilinear filtering**. With bilinear filtering, you select a color based on the blending of each texel neighboring the nearest neighbor. If you use bilinear filtering for the wall example, as the player gets closer, the wall seems to blur instead of appearing pixelated. Figure 5.10 shows a comparison between nearest-neighbor and bilinear filtering of part of the star texture.

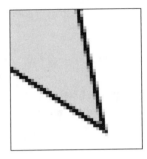 

Figure 5.10 Nearest-neighbor filtering (left) and bilinear filtering (right)

We explore the idea of improving the quality of textures further in Chapter 13, "Intermediate Graphics." For now, let's enable bilinear filtering for all textures.

To use texture mapping in OpenGL, there are three things you need to do:

- Load image files (textures) and create OpenGL texture objects.
- Update the vertex format to include texture coordinates.
- Update the shaders to use the textures.

Loading the Texture

Although you can use the SDL Image library to load images for OpenGL, the Simple OpenGL Image Library (SOIL) is a little easier to use. SOIL can read in several file formats, including PNG, BMP, JPG, TGA, and DDS. As it's designed to work with OpenGL, it slots in easily with the other OpenGL code needed for creating a texture object.

Listing 5.14 gives the declaration of a `Texture` class that encapsulates loading in a texture file and using it with OpenGL. The names of the functions and member variables are mostly self-explanatory; for example, `Load` loads the texture from the file. For member variables, you have a width and height of the texture and an OpenGL texture ID.

Listing 5.14 `Texture` Declaration

```
class Texture
{
public:
    Texture();
    ~Texture();

    bool Load(const std::string& fileName);
    void Unload();

    void SetActive();
```

```
    int GetWidth() const { return mWidth; }
    int GetHeight() const { return mHeight; }
private:
    // OpenGL ID of this texture
    unsigned int mTextureID;
    // Width/height of the texture
    int mWidth;
    int mHeight;
};
```

The implementation of Load contains the bulk of the Texture class code. You first declare a local variable to store the number of channels and then call SOIL_load_image to load in the texture:

```
int channels = 0;
unsigned char* image = SOIL_load_image(
    fileName.c_str(), // Name of file
    &mWidth,          // Stores width
    &mHeight,         // Stores height
    &channels,        // Stores number of channels
    SOIL_LOAD_AUTO    // Type of image file, or auto for any
);
```

If SOIL fails to load the image file, SOIL_load_image returns nullptr. Therefore, you should add a check to make sure the image loaded.

Then you need to determine whether the image is RGB or RGBA. You can assume that this is based on the number of channels (three means RGB, four means RGBA):

```
int format = GL_RGB;
if (channels == 4)
{
    format = GL_RGBA;
}
```

Next, use glGenTextures to create an OpenGL texture object (saving the ID in mTextureID) and glBindTexture to set the texture as active:

```
glGenTextures(1, &mTextureID);
glBindTexture(GL_TEXTURE_2D, mTextureID);
```

The GL_TEXTURE_2D target passed to glBindTexture is by far the most common texture target, but there are other choices for advanced types of textures.

Once you have an OpenGL texture object, the next step is to copy the raw image data into it with the glTexImage2D function, which takes quite a few parameters:

```
glTexImage2D(
    GL_TEXTURE_2D,    // Texture target
    0,                // Level of detail (for now, assume 0)
```

```
format,           // Color format OpenGL should use
mWidth,           // Width of texture
mHeight,          // Height of texture
0,                // Border - "this value must be 0"
format,           // Color format of input data
GL_UNSIGNED_BYTE, // Bit depth of input data
                  // Unsigned byte specifies 8-bit channels
image             // Pointer to image data
);
```

Once you've copied the image data to OpenGL, you can tell SOIL to free the image from memory:

```
SOIL_free_image_data(image);
```

Finally, use the `glTexParameteri` function to enable bilinear filtering:

```
glTexParameteri(GL_TEXTURE_2D, GL_TEXTURE_MIN_FILTER, GL_LINEAR);
glTexParameteri(GL_TEXTURE_2D, GL_TEXTURE_MAG_FILTER, GL_LINEAR);
```

For now, don't worry about the parameters passed to `glTexParameteri`. (They are discussed further in Chapter 13, "Intermediate Graphics.")

Listing 5.15 shows the final version of `Texture::Load`.

Listing 5.15 `Texture::Load` Implementation

```
bool Texture::Load(const std::string& fileName)
{
    int channels = 0;
    unsigned char* image = SOIL_load_image(fileName.c_str(),
        &mWidth, &mHeight, &channels, SOIL_LOAD_AUTO);

    if (image == nullptr)
    {
        SDL_Log("SOIL failed to load image %s: %s",
            fileName.c_str(), SOIL_last_result());
        return false;
    }
    int format = GL_RGB;
    if (channels == 4)
    {
        format = GL_RGBA;
    }

    glGenTextures(1, &mTextureID);
    glBindTexture(GL_TEXTURE_2D, mTextureID);
    glTexImage2D(GL_TEXTURE_2D, 0, format, mWidth, mHeight, 0, format,
            GL_UNSIGNED_BYTE, image);
    SOIL_free_image_data(image);
```

```
    // Enable bilinear filtering
    glTexParameteri(GL_TEXTURE_2D, GL_TEXTURE_MIN_FILTER, GL_LINEAR);
    glTexParameteri(GL_TEXTURE_2D, GL_TEXTURE_MAG_FILTER, GL_LINEAR);

    return true;
}
```

The `Texture::Unload` and `Texture::SetActive` functions are each just a single line.
`Unload` deletes the texture object, and `SetActive` calls `glBindTexture`:

```
void Texture::Unload()
{
    glDeleteTextures(1, &mTextureID);
}

void Texture::SetActive()
{
    glBindTexture(GL_TEXTURE_2D, mTextureID);
}
```

You can then load textures into a map in `Game`, much as you did for `SDL_Texture` previously.
The `Game::GetTexture` function then returns a `Texture*` for the requested texture. Next,
`SpriteComponent` needs a `Texture*` member variable instead of `SDL_Texture*`.

Finally, in `SpriteComponent::Draw`, add a call to `SetActive` on `mTexture`, right before
drawing the vertices. This means you can now set a different active texture for each sprite
component you draw:

```
// In SpriteComponent::Draw...
// Set current texture
mTexture->SetActive();
// Draw quad
glDrawElements(GL_TRIANGLES, 6,
    GL_UNSIGNED_INT, nullptr);
```

Updating the Vertex Format

To use texture mapping, the vertices need to have texture coordinates, so you need to update
the sprite `VertexArray`:

```
float vertices[] = {
    -0.5f,  0.5f, 0.f, 0.f, 0.f, // top left
     0.5f,  0.5f, 0.f, 1.f, 0.f, // top right
     0.5f, -0.5f, 0.f, 1.f, 1.f, // bottom right
    -0.5f, -0.5f, 0.f, 0.f, 1.f  // bottom left
};
```

Remember that the V texture coordinate is flipped to account for OpenGL's idiosyncrasy with how it expects the image data.

For each vertex, the first three floating-point values are the position and the next two floating-point values are the texture coordinates. Figure 5.11 shows the memory layout of this new vertex format.

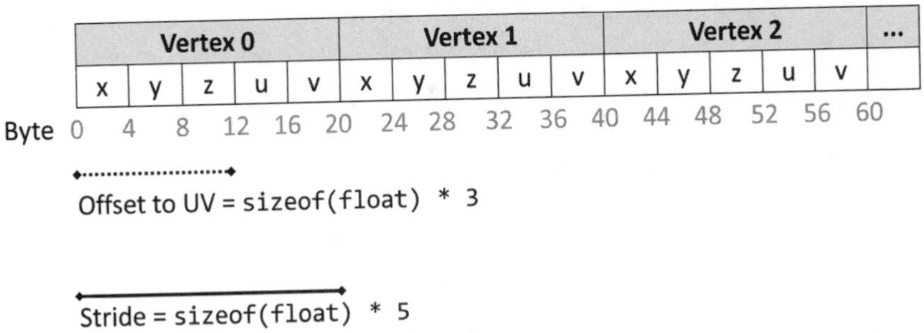

Figure 5.11 Vertex memory layout with position and texture coordinates

Because you're changing the vertex layout, you must change code in the `VertexArray` constructor. For simplicity, assume that all vertices must have a 3D position and 2D texture coordinates. (You'll change this in subsequent chapters.)

Because the size of each vertex has changed, you need to update the `glBufferData` call to specify that each vertex now has five floats per vertex:

```
glBufferData(GL_ARRAY_BUFFER, numVerts * 5 * sizeof(float),
    verts, GL_STATIC_DRAW);
```

Because the index buffer is still the same, the `glBufferData` call for that doesn't change. However, you must change vertex attribute 0 to specify that the stride of the vertex is now five floats:

```
glEnableVertexAttribArray(0);
glVertexAttribPointer(0, 3, GL_FLOAT, GL_FALSE,
    sizeof(float) * 5, // The stride is now 5 floats
    0);                // Vertex position is still offset 0
```

This only fixes the position vertex attribute. However, because you now have a second vertex attribute for the texture coordinate, you must enable vertex attribute 1 and specify its format:

```
glEnableVertexAttribArray(1);
glVertexAttribPointer(
    1,                 // Vertex attribute index
    2,                 // Number of components (2 because UV)
    GL_FLOAT,          // Type of each component
```

```
GL_FALSE,            // Not used for GL_FLOAT
sizeof(float) * 5, // Stride (usually size of each vertex)
reinterpret_cast<void*>(sizeof(float) * 3) // Offset pointer
);
```

The last parameter to this `glVertexAttribPointer` call is rather ugly. OpenGL needs to know the number of bytes from the start of a vertex to this attribute. That's where the `sizeof(float) * 3` comes from. However, OpenGL wants this as an offset pointer. Thus, you must use `reinterpret_cast` to coerce the type into a `void*` pointer.

> **tip**
>
> If you use a struct in C++ code to represent the format of the vertices, you can use the `offsetof` macro to determine the offsets to a vertex attribute rather than manually computing them. This is especially helpful if there is padding between vertex elements.

Updating the Shaders

Because the vertex format now uses texture coordinates, you should create two new shaders: `Sprite.vert` (initially a copy of `Transform.vert`) and `Sprite.frag` (initially a copy of `Basic.frag`).

The `Sprite.vert` Shader

There previously was only one vertex attribute, so you could just declare position as an `in` variable, and GLSL knew which vertex attribute it corresponded to. However, now that there are multiple vertex attributes, you must specify which attribute slot corresponds to which `in` variable. This changes the variable declarations to the following:

```
layout(location=0) in vec3 inPosition;
layout(location=1) in vec2 inTexCoord;
```

The `layout` directive specifies which attribute slot corresponds to which `in` variable. Here, you specify that there's a 3D vector of floats for vertex attribute slot 0 and a 2D vector of floats for vertex attribute slot 1. This corresponds to the slot numbers in the `glVertexAttribPointer` calls.

Next, although the texture coordinates are an input to the vertex shader (because it's in the vertex layout), the fragment shader also needs to know the texture coordinates. This is because the fragment shader needs to know the texture coordinates to determine the color at the pixel. Luckily, you can pass data from the vertex shader to the fragment shader by declaring a global `out` variable in the vertex shader:

```
out vec2 fragTexCoord;
```

Then, inside the vertex shader's `main` function, add the following line, which copies the texture coordinates directly from the vertex input variable to the output variable:

```
fragTexCoord = inTexCoord;
```

The reason this ultimately works is that OpenGL automatically interpolates vertex shader outputs across the face of the triangle. Therefore, even though a triangle has only three vertices, any arbitrary pixel on the face of a triangle will know its corresponding texture coordinates in the fragment shader.

For completeness, Listing 5.16 gives the full source code for `Sprite.vert`.

Listing 5.16　`Sprite.vert` Implementation

```
#version 330
// Uniforms for world transform and view-proj
uniform mat4 uWorldTransform;
uniform mat4 uViewProj;

// Attribute 0 is position, 1 is tex coords.
layout(location = 0) in vec3 inPosition;
layout(location = 1) in vec2 inTexCoord;

// Add texture coordinate as output
out vec2 fragTexCoord;

void main()
{
    // Convert position to homogeneous coordinates
    vec4 pos = vec4(inPosition, 1.0);
    // Transform position to world space, then clip space
    gl_Position = pos * uWorldTransform * uViewProj;
    // Pass along the texture coordinate to frag shader
    fragTexCoord = inTexCoord;
}
```

The `Sprite.frag` Shader

As a rule, any `out` variables in the vertex shader should have a corresponding `in` in the fragment shader. The name and type of the `in` variable in the fragment shader must have the same name and type as the corresponding `out` variable in the vertex shader:

```
in vec4 fragTexCoord;
```

Next, you need to add a uniform for a texture sampler (that can get the color from a texture given a texture coordinate):

```
uniform sampler2D uTexture;
```

The `sampler2D` type is a special type that can sample 2D textures. Unlike with the world transform and view-projection uniforms in the vertex shader, you currently don't need any code in C++ to bind this sampler uniform. This is because you currently bind only one texture at a time, so OpenGL automatically knows that the only texture sampler in the shader corresponds to the active texture.

Finally, replace the `outColor` assignment in the `main` function with the following:

```
outColor = texture(uTexture, fragTexCoord);
```

This samples the color from the texture, using the texture coordinates received from the vertex shader (after the coordinates interpolate across the face of the triangle).

Listing 5.17 shows the full source code for `Sprite.frag`.

Listing 5.17 `Sprite.frag` Implementation

```
#version 330
// Tex coord input from vertex shader
in vec2 fragTexCoord;
// Output color
out vec4 outColor;
// For texture sampling
uniform sampler2D uTexture;

void main()
{
    // Sample color from texture
    outColor = texture(uTexture, fragTexCoord);
}
```

You then change the code in `Game:LoadShaders` to now load `Sprite.vert` and `Sprite.frag`. The previous code inside the various actors that set textures on `SpriteComponent`s now also successfully loads the textures with SOIL. With this code, you can now draw sprites with texture mapping, as shown in Figure 5.12. Unfortunately, there's still one last issue to fix. Right now, the code is drawing black for pixels that should be transparent.

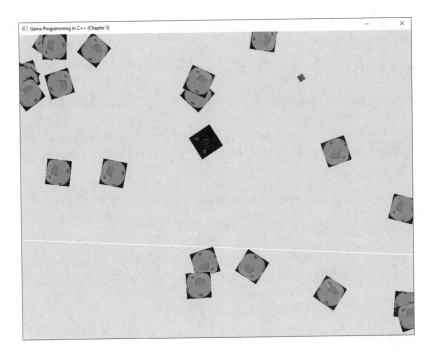

Figure 5.12 Texture-mapped sprites

Alpha Blending

Alpha blending determines how to blend pixels with transparency (an alpha channel less than 1). Alpha blending uses an equation in the following form to calculate the pixel color:

$$outputColor = srcFactor \cdot sourceColor + dstFactor \cdot destinationColor$$

In this equation, the **source color** is the color for the new source you're drawing (from the fragment shader), and the destination color is the color that's already in the color buffer. You can customize the alpha blending function by specifying the factor parameters.

To get the desired alpha blending result for transparency, you set the source factor to the alpha of the pixel you're drawing (the source alpha) and the destination factor to one minus source alpha:

$$outputColor = srcAlpha \cdot sourceColor + (1 - srcAlpha) \cdot destinationColor$$

For example, suppose you have 8 bits per color, and the color buffer at some pixel is red. In this case, this is the destination color:

$$destinationColor = (255, \ 0, \ 0)$$

Next, say that you want to draw a pixel that's blue; this is the source color:

$$sourceColor = (0, \ 0, \ 255)$$

Now suppose the source alpha is zero, meaning the pixel is completely transparent. In this case, our equation evaluates to the following:

$$outputColor = 0 \cdot (0, 0, \ 255) + (1-0) \cdot (255, \ 0, \ 0)$$
$$outputColor = (255, \ 0, \ 0)$$

This is the result you want for a fully transparent pixel. You completely ignore the source color if the alpha is zero and just use whatever color is already in the color buffer.

To enable this in code, add the following to `Game::GenerateOuput`, right before drawing all the sprites:

```
glEnable(GL_BLEND);
glBlendFunc(
    GL_SRC_ALPHA,           // srcFactor is srcAlpha
    GL_ONE_MINUS_SRC_ALPHA // dstFactor is 1 - srcAlpha
);
```

The `glEnable` call says to turn on color buffer blending (which is disabled by default). Then you use `glBlendFunc` to specify the `srcFactor` and `dstFactor` that you want.

With alpha blending in place, the sprites now look correct, as shown in Figure 5.13. The 2D OpenGL rendering code now has feature parity with the previous use of SDL 2D rendering. It took a lot of work to get here, but the advantage is that the game code now has the foundations for 3D graphics support, which is the topic of Chapter 6.

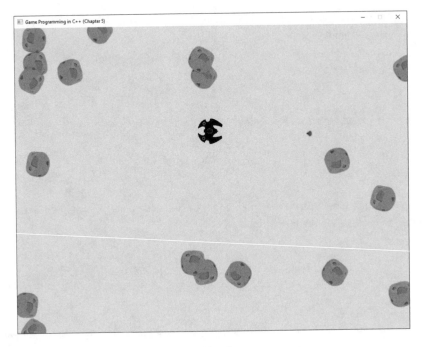

Figure 5.13 Texture-mapped sprites, with alpha blending

Game Project

This chapter's game project demonstrates all the code to convert the game code from SDL graphics to OpenGL. It converts the *Asteroids* game project from Chapter 3 to instead use OpenGL. The controls are the same as in Chapter 3: `WASD` to move the ship and spacebar to fire lasers. The code is available in the book's GitHub repository, in the `Chapter05` directory. Open `Chapter05-windows.sln` on Windows and `Chapter05-mac.xcodeproj` on Mac.

Summary

Because graphics hardware is optimized for polygons, 2D and 3D games internally use polygons (usually triangles) to represent all graphical objects in the world. Even a 2D sprite that you might think of as an image is a rectangle with a texture mapped to it. To send triangles to the graphics hardware, you must declare the attributes of each vertex and create a vertex and an index buffer.

All modern graphics APIs expect a programmer to use vertex and fragment (pixel) shaders to specify how polygons should render. You write these shaders as separate programs in a shader programming language (not C++). The vertex shader minimally outputs the vertex position in clip space, while the fragment shader determines the final color at a pixel.

Transformations allow you to draw several instances of the same object without needing separate vertex and index buffers for each instance. Object space is the coordinate space relative to the origin of an object, while world space is the coordinate space relative to the game world.

Games use matrices to represent transformations, and there are several different matrices for transformations, such as scale, rotation, and translation. Combining these transformations in the order scale, rotate, and translate yields a world transform matrix that can transform from object space to world space. To convert from world space to clip space, you use the view-projection matrix. For 2D games, you can simplify this by making 1 unit in world space equivalent to 1 pixel in the window.

Texture mapping applies part of a texture to the face of a triangle. To implement this, you need texture (UV) coordinates as a vertex attribute. In the fragment shader, you sample the texture color from the UV coordinate. This can either be based on the color of the texture pixel (texel) nearest to the UV coordinate, or it can be based on a bilinear filtering that considers nearby texels.

Finally, even though the task seems trivial, displaying sprites in OpenGL requires a lot of code. First, you must initialize OpenGL and GLEW. Next, to render any triangles, you must create a vertex array object, specify a vertex layout, write a vertex and pixel shader, and write code to load these shader programs. To transform the vertices from object space to clip space, you have to use uniforms to specify the world transform and view-projection matrices. To add texture mapping, you have to load an image, change the vertex layout to include UV coordinates, and update the shaders to sample from the texture.

Additional Reading

There are many excellent online references for aspiring OpenGL developers. The official OpenGL reference pages are useful for finding out what the parameters for each function do. Of all the OpenGL tutorial sites, one of the best is *Learn OpenGL*. For an extensive look at the graphical techniques used in game development, *Real-Time Rendering* by Thomas Akenine-Moller et al. is a definitive reference.

Akenine-Moller, Thomas, Eric Haines, and Naty Hoffman. *Real-Time Rendering,* 3rd edition. Natick: A K Peters, 2008.

Learn OpenGL. Accessed November 24, 2017. http://learnopengl.com/.

OpenGL Reference Pages. Accessed November 24, 2017. https://www.opengl.org/sdk/docs/man/.

Exercises

The exercises for this chapter involve making some modifications to this chapter's game project to gain more experience using various OpenGL functions.

Exercise 5.1

Modify the background clear color so that it smoothly changes between colors. For example, starting from black, smoothly change over several seconds to blue. Then select another color (such as red) and smoothly change over several seconds to this other color. Think about how you can use `deltaTime` in `Game::Update` to facilitate this smooth transition.

Exercise 5.2

Modify the sprite vertices so that each vertex also has an RGB color associated with it. This is known as a **vertex color**. Update the vertex shader to take the vertex color as an input and pass it to the fragment shader. Then change the fragment shader so that rather than simply drawing the color sampled from the texture, it averages the color between the vertex color and texture color.

CHAPTER 6

3D GRAPHICS

This chapter covers how to switch from a 2D environment to a full 3D game, which requires several changes. The `Actor` transform, including 3D rotations, becomes more complex. In addition, you need to load and draw 3D models. Finally, most 3D games have some type of lighting applied to the scene. The game project for this chapter demonstrates all these 3D techniques.

The Actor Transform in 3D

The representation of the `Actor` transform you have used so far in this book works for 2D graphics. However, supporting a fully 3D world requires some modification. Most obviously, the position `Vector2` becomes `Vector3`. But this brings up an important question: Which directions are x, y, and z in the world? Most 2D games use a coordinate system where x is the horizontal direction and y is the vertical direction. But even in 2D, +y might be up or down, depending on the implementation. Adding a third component increases the possible representations. It's an arbitrary decision, but it should be consistent. In this book, +x is forward, +y is to the right, and +z is up. Figure 6.1 illustrates this coordinate system.

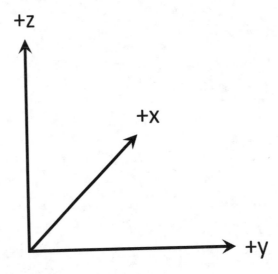

Figure 6.1 3D coordinate system used in this book

If you take your left hand and pretend that the thumb is up, the index finger is forward, and the middle finger is right, you see that it matches the coordinate system in Figure 6.1 perfectly. Thus, this type of coordinate system is a **left-handed coordinate system**. It would be right-handed if +y were instead to the left.

Transform Matrices for 3D

Using 3D coordinates means that the homogenous coordinates are now (x,y,z,w). Recall that you need the w component for translation matrices to work. With 3D coordinates, the translation matrices become 4×4 matrices. This modification is simple for translation and scale.

A 4×4 translation matrix translates by the offset (a,b,c) :

$$T(a,b,c) = \begin{bmatrix} 1 & 0 & 0 & 0 \\ 0 & 1 & 0 & 0 \\ 0 & 0 & 1 & 0 \\ a & b & c & 1 \end{bmatrix}$$

Similarly, the scale matrix can scale by up to three factors:

$$S(s_x, s_y, s_z) = \begin{bmatrix} s_x & 0 & 0 & 0 \\ 0 & s_y & 0 & 0 \\ 0 & 0 & s_z & 0 \\ 0 & 0 & 0 & 1 \end{bmatrix}$$

However, rotations in 3D are not as simple.

Euler Angles

Representing rotations in 3D is more complex than in 2D. Previously, an actor only needed one float for rotation. This represented a rotation about the z-axis because that's the only rotation possible in 2D. But in 3D, it's valid to rotate about any of the three coordinate axes. One approach for 3D rotations is **Euler angles**, where there are three angles (yaw, pitch, and roll) representing rotation about each axis. The names yaw, pitch, and roll come from airplane terminology. **Yaw** is a rotation about the up axis, **pitch** is a rotation about the side axis, and **roll** is a rotation about the forward axis. In the coordinate from Figure 6.1, yaw is rotation about +z, pitch is rotation about +y, and roll is rotation about +x.

When you have three different rotation angles, you can combine them by creating a separate rotation matrix for each Euler angle. You then multiply these three matrices, and the order of multiplication affects the final rotation of the object. One common approach is roll, then pitch, then yaw:

$$FinalRot = (RollMatrix)(PitchMatrix)(YawMatrix)$$

However, there isn't any one "correct" order to apply these Euler angles. You simply must pick one order and stick with it.

With Euler angles, it's difficult to derive an arbitrary rotation. Suppose a spaceship faces down the +x (forward) axis in object space. You want to rotate the ship so it points toward an arbitrary object at position P. Achieving this new orientation may require some combination of yaw, pitch, and roll, and computing these separate angles is not straightforward.

Furthermore, suppose you have an object with an initial Euler angle orientation, and you also have a target Euler angle orientation. You want to smoothly transition, or **interpolate** between, these two orientations over some period. You can interpolate Euler angles by interpolating each angle separately. However, in various situations, this interpolation will not look correct because when you interpolate each component separately, you may encounter singularities where the interpolation appears at odd orientations.

Although it is possible to use Euler angles in a game, for arbitrary rotations there's another choice that tends to work better.

Quaternions

Many games use **quaternions** instead of Euler angles. The formal mathematical definition of a quaternion is complex. For the purposes of this book, think of a quaternion as a method to represent a rotation about an arbitrary axis (not just x, y, or z).

Basic Definition

3D graphics use **unit quaternions**, which are quaternions with a magnitude of one. A quaternion has both a vector and a scalar component. This book uses the following notation to represent a quaternion as its vector and scalar components:

$$q = [q_v, q_s]$$

The calculation of the vector and scalar components depends on the normalized axis of rotation, $\hat{a}$, and the angle of rotation, θ:

$$q_v = \hat{a}\sin\frac{\theta}{2}$$

$$q_s = \cos\frac{\theta}{2}$$

This equation works only with a normalized axis of rotation. An unnormalized axis yields a non-unit quaternion and causes shearing (non-uniform stretching) of objects in the game.

To crystalize the use of quaternions, consider the earlier problem of rotating a ship to face an arbitrary object. Remember that with Euler angles, it's difficult to calculate the exact yaw, pitch, and roll angles. However, quaternions make this problem easier. Initially, the ship is at position S with an initial facing down the x-axis. Say that you want to rotate the ship to instead face an arbitrary point P. First, compute the vector from the ship to the new point and normalize this vector:

$$NewFacing = \frac{P - S}{\|P - S\|}$$

Next, compute the axis of rotation between the original facing and the new facing, using the cross product, and normalize this vector:

$$\hat{a} = \frac{\langle 1,0,0 \rangle \times NewFacing}{\|\langle 1,0,0 \rangle \times NewFacing\|}$$

Then compute the angle of rotation using the dot product and arccosine:

$$\theta = \arccos\left(\langle 1,0,0 \rangle \cdot NewFacing\right)$$

Finally, plug in this axis and angle to create the quaternion representing the rotation of the ship such that it faces point P. This works wherever P is in the 3D world.

One edge case is that if *NewFacing* is parallel to the original facing, the cross product yields a vector of all zeros. This vector has a length of zero, and so dividing by zero to normalize the vector corrupts the axis of rotation. Thus, any code doing such calculations needs to verify that *NewFacing* is not parallel to the original facing. If they are parallel, this means the object already faces in the *NewFacing* direction. In this case, the quaternion is just the identity quaternion, which applies no rotation. If the vectors are antiparallel, then you must rotate by π radians about up.

Combining Rotations

Another common operation is applying an additional rotation to an existing quaternion. Given two quaternions, p and q, the **Grassmann product** is the rotation of q followed by p:

$$\left(pq\right)_v = p_s q_v + q_s p_v + p_v \times q_v$$
$$\left(pq\right)_s = p_s q_s - p_v \cdot q_v$$

Note that even though the multiplication has p to the left of q, the rotation applies in a right-to-left order. Also, because the Grassmann product uses a cross product, it isn't commutative. So, swapping p and q will reverse the order of rotation.

Much like a matrix, a quaternion has an inverse. For unit quaternions, the inverse of a quaternion is the negation of its vector component:

$$q^{-1} = \left[-q_v,\ q_s\right]$$

Because there's an inverse, there is also an identity quaternion, defined as follows:

$$i_v = \langle 0,\ 0,\ 0 \rangle$$
$$i_s = 1$$

Rotating a Vector by a Quaternion

To rotate a 3D vector, *v*, by a quaternion, first represent *v* as the following quaternion, *r*:

$$r = \begin{bmatrix} \vec{v}, & 0 \end{bmatrix}$$

Next, compute *r'* with two Grassmann products:

$$r' = (qr)q^{-1}$$

The rotated vector is then simply the vector component of *r'*:

$$\vec{v}' = r'_v$$

Spherical Linear Interpolation

Quaternions support a more accurate form of interpolation called **spherical linear interpolation** (Slerp). The Slerp equation takes in two quaternions, *a* and *b*, as well as the fractional value in the range [0, 1] from *a* to *b*. For example, the following yields a quaternion rotation 25% of the way from *a* to *b*:

$$Slerp(a,b,0.25)$$

In the interest of brevity, this section omits the calculations for Slerp.

Quaternion-to-Rotation Matrix

Because you ultimately still need a world transform matrix, you need to eventually convert the quaternion rotation into a matrix. The conversion of a quaternion into a matrix has quite a few terms:

$$q_v = \langle q_x, q_y, q_z \rangle$$
$$q_s = q_w$$

$$Rotate(q) = \begin{bmatrix} 1-2q_y^2-2q_z^2 & 2q_xq_y+2q_wq_z & 2q_xq_z-2q_wq_y & 0 \\ 2q_xq_y-2q_wq_z & 1-2q_x^2-2q_z^2 & 2q_yq_z+2q_wq_x & 0 \\ 2q_xq_z+2q_wq_y & 2q_yq_z-2q_wq_x & 1-2q_x^2-2q_y^2 & 0 \\ 0 & 0 & 0 & 1 \end{bmatrix}$$

Quaternions in Code

As with vectors and matrices, for quaternions the custom Math.h header file has a Quaternion class. Listing 6.1 shows the most useful functions. Because the order of multiplication of quaternions often confuses game programmers (for example, to rotate *p* followed by *q*, you multiply *q* by *p*), instead of using the multiplication operator, the Math.h library declares a Concatenate function.

This function simply takes in the quaternions in the order many expect—so the rotation "*p* followed by *q*" is as follows:

```
Quaternion result = Quaternion::Concatenate(q, p);
```

Listing 6.1 Quaternion Functions of Note

```
class Quaternion
{
public:
   // Functions/data omitted
   // ...

   // Construct the quaternion from an axis and angle
   explicit Quaternion(const Vector3& axis, float angle);
   // Spherical Linear Interpolation
   static Quaternion Slerp(const Quaternion& a, const Quaternion& b,
float f);
    // Concatenate (rotate by q FOLLOWED BY p, uses Grassmann product pq)
   static Quaternion Concatenate(const Quaternion& q, const Quaternion&
p);
   // v = (0, 0, 0); s = 1
   static const Quaternion Identity;
};

// In Matrix4...
// Create Matrix4 from Quaternion
static Matrix4 CreateFromQuaternion(const class Quaternion& q);
// In Vector3...
// Transform a Vector3 by a Quaternion
static Vector3 Transform(const Vector3& v, const class Quaternion& q);
```

New `Actor` Transform in Action

With the rotation question settled, the `Actor` class transformation now has a `Vector3` for position, a `Quaternion` for rotation, and a `float` for scale:

```
Vector3 mPosition;
Quaternion mRotation;
float mScale;
```

With this new transform representation, the code for calculating the world transform matrix in `ComputeWorldTransform` changes to this:

```
// Scale, then rotate, then translate
mWorldTransform = Matrix4::CreateScale(mScale);
mWorldTransform *= Matrix4::CreateFromQuaternion(mRotation);
mWorldTransform *= Matrix4::CreateTranslation(mPosition);
```

Getting the forward vector of an actor now requires transforming the initial forward vector (+x) by the rotation quaternion:

```
Vector3 GetForward() const
{
    return Vector3::Transform(Vector3::UnitX, mRotation);
}
```

You then need to fix any code that applied rotations using a single angle, such as `MoveComponent::Update`. To keep things simple for now, `MoveComponent` only rotates about the +z axis (yaw). This updated code is in Listing 6.2, which first gets the existing quaternion rotation of the owning actor. It next creates a new quaternion representing the additional rotation to apply. Finally, it concatenates the original rotation with the new quaternion to get the final rotation quaternion.

Listing 6.2 `MoveComponent::Update` Implementation with Quaternions

```
void MoveComponent::Update(float deltaTime)
{
    if (!Math::NearZero(mAngularSpeed))
    {
        Quaternion rot = mOwner->GetRotation();
        float angle = mAngularSpeed * deltaTime;
        // Create quaternion for incremental rotation
        // (Rotate about up axis)
        Quaternion inc(Vector3::UnitZ, angle);
        // Concatenate old and new quaternion
        rot = Quaternion::Concatenate(rot, inc);
        mOwner->SetRotation(rot);
    }

    // Updating position based on forward speed stays the same
    // ...
}
```

Loading 3D Models

For sprite-based games, every sprite draws with a single quad, which means it's okay to hard-code the vertex and index buffers. However, for a full 3D game, there are a lot of other triangular meshes. For example, a first-person shooter has enemy meshes, weapon meshes, character meshes, meshes for the environment, and so on. An artist creates these models in a 3D modeling program such as Blender or Autodesk Maya. The game then needs code to load these models into vertex and index buffers.

Choosing a Model Format

Before you can use 3D models, you need to decide how to store the models in files. One idea is to choose a modeling program and add support for loading that program's proprietary file format. However, doing so has several drawbacks. First, the feature set of a 3D modeling program is significantly higher than that of a game. Modeling programs support many other types of geometry, including NURBS, quads, and n-gons. Modeling programs also support complex lighting and rendering techniques, including ray-tracing. No game will replicate all these features.

Furthermore, most modeling files have a great deal of data that's unnecessary at runtime. For example, the file format might store the undo history of the model. Clearly, the game doesn't need access to this when running. All this extra information means that a modeling file format is large, and loading it at runtime is a performance hit.

Furthermore, modeling file formats are opaque and, depending on the format, may not have any documentation. So outside of reverse-engineering the file format, it might not even be possible to load it into the game.

Finally, choosing one modeling format ties the game directly to one specific modeling program. What if a new artist wants to use an entirely different modeling program? Using a proprietary format makes this difficult if there's no easy conversion process.

Exchange formats aim to work across several modeling programs. Among the most popular formats are FBX and COLLADA, which many different modeling programs support. Even though SDKs exist for loading these formats, the formats still suffer from having way more data than needed for a game at runtime.

It's useful to consider how a commercial engine such as Unity or Epic's Unreal Engine works. While both engines support importing file formats such as FBX into their editors, the runtime doesn't use these formats. Instead, on import there's a conversion process into an internal engine format. The game runtime then loads models in this internal format.

Other engines provide exporter plugins for popular modeling programs. The exporter plugin converts the modeling program's format into a custom format designed for the game runtime's consumption.

In the spirit of independence, this book uses a custom file format. While a binary file format is more efficient (and what most real games use), for simplicity, this book's model file format is a JSON (JavaScript Object Notation) text format. This makes it very easy to manually edit a model file and validate that the model file loads properly. You will eventually explore how to use a binary format in Chapter 14, "Level Files and Binary Data."

Listing 6.3 shows the representation of a cube in the gpmesh file format this book uses. The first entry specifies the version, which currently is 1. The next line specifies the vertex format for the model. Recall that in Chapter 5, "OpenGL," you used three floats for position and two floats for texture coordinates as the vertex format. The `PosNormTex` format specified here adds three floats for the vertex normal in between the position and texture coordinates. For now, don't worry about what a vertex normal is; we revisit this topic in the lighting discussion later in this chapter.

Listing 6.3 `Cube.gpmesh`

```
{
    "version":1,
    "vertexformat":"PosNormTex",
    "shader":"BasicMesh",
    "textures":[
        "Assets/Cube.png"
    ],
    "vertices":[
        [1.0,1.0,-1.0,0.57,0.57,-0.57,0.66,0.33],
        [1.0,-1.0,-1.0,0.57,-0.57,-0.57,0.66,0.0],
        [-1.0,-1.0,-1.0,-0.57,-0.57,-0.57,1.0,0.33],
        [-1.0,1.0,-1.0,-0.57,0.57,-0.57,0.66,0.66],
        [1.0,0.99,1.0,0.57,0.57,0.57,0.33,0.33],
        [0.99,-1.0,1.0,0.57,-0.57,0.57,0.0,0.0],
        [-1.0,-1.0,1.0,-0.57,-0.57,0.57,0.66,0.33],
        [-1.0,1.0,1.0,-0.57,0.57,0.57,0.33,0.66]
    ],
    "indices":[
        [1,3,0],
        [7,5,4],
        [4,1,0],
        [5,2,1],
        [2,7,3],
        [0,7,4],
        [1,2,3],
        [7,6,5],
        [4,5,1],
        [5,6,2],
        [2,6,7],
        [0,3,7]
    ]
}
```

The shader entry specifies which shader program you should use for drawing the model. (You'll define the `BasicMesh` shader program later in this chapter.) Next, the textures array specifies a list of textures associated with the model.

The final two elements, `vertices` and `indices`, specify the vertex and index buffers for the model. Each row in `vertices` is one individual vertex, while each row in `indices` is one triangle.

Of course, a model file format isn't particularly useful if there's no way to create a model of that format in a modeling program. To solve this, the GitHub code repository provides two exporters in the `Exporter` directory. One is an export script for the Blender modeling program, and it supports the basic style of mesh used throughout most of this book. The other is an exporter plug-in for Epic Unreal Engine, which can export not only meshes but also the animation data used in Chapter 12, "Skeletal Animation." The code for these exporters is very specific to Blender and Unreal, respectively, so we omit the discussion here. However, interested readers can peruse the code in the repository. Each exporter also includes a text file with instructions on how to use each exporter with its respective program.

Updating the Vertex Attributes

Because the gpmesh file uses three vertex attributes (position, normal, and texture coordinates) for each vertex, let's assume that all meshes use this format for now. This means even the quad mesh will need normals. Figure 6.2 shows this new vertex layout.

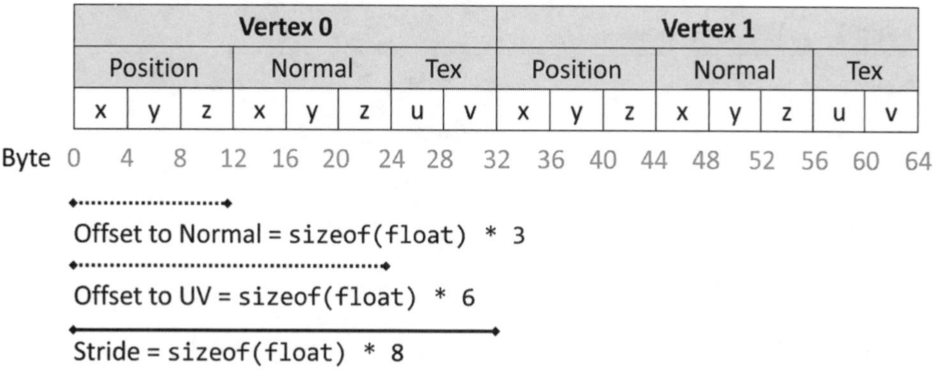

Figure 6.2 Vertex layout with a position, normal, and texture coordinates

Every vertex array will use the new vertex layout, so the constructor for `VertexArray` changes to specify this new layout. Most notably, the size of each vertex is now eight floats, and you add an attribute for the normal:

```
// Position is 3 floats
glEnableVertexAttribArray(0);
glVertexAttribPointer(0, 3, GL_FLOAT, GL_FALSE, 8 * sizeof(float), 0);
// Normal is 3 floats
glEnableVertexAttribArray(1);
glVertexAttribPointer(1, 3, GL_FLOAT, GL_FALSE, 8 * sizeof(float),
   reinterpret_cast<void*>(sizeof(float) * 3));
// Texture coordinates is 2 floats
glEnableVertexAttribArray(2);
glVertexAttribPointer(2, 2, GL_FLOAT, GL_FALSE, 8 * sizeof(float),
   reinterpret_cast<void*>(sizeof(float) * 6));
```

Next, you change the `Sprite.vert` to also reference the new vertex layout:

```
// Attribute 0 is position, 1 is normal, 2 is tex coords
layout(location = 0) in vec3 inPosition;
layout(location = 1) in vec3 inNormal;
layout(location = 2) in vec2 inTexCoord;
```

Finally, the quad created in `Game::CreateSpriteVerts` adds three additional floats for the normals. (They can be zero because they aren't used by the sprite shader program.) With these changes, sprites still draw correctly with the new vertex layout.

Loading a gpmesh File

Because the gpmesh format is in JSON, there are many libraries you can use to parse the JSON. This book uses RapidJSON (http://rapidjson.org), which supports efficient reading of JSON files. As with textures in Chapter 5, here you encapsulate mesh loading in a `Mesh` class. Listing 6.4 shows the declaration of `Mesh`.

Listing 6.4 Mesh Declaration

```
class Mesh
{
public:
    Mesh();
    ~Mesh();
    // Load/unload mesh
    bool Load(const std::string& fileName, class Game* game);
    void Unload();
    // Get the vertex array associated with this mesh
    class VertexArray* GetVertexArray() { return mVertexArray; }
    // Get a texture from specified index
    class Texture* GetTexture(size_t index);
    // Get name of shader
    const std::string& GetShaderName() const { return mShaderName; }
    // Get object space bounding sphere radius
    float GetRadius() const { return mRadius; }
private:
    // Textures associated with this mesh
    std::vector<class Texture*> mTextures;
    // Vertex array associated with this mesh
    class VertexArray* mVertexArray;
    // Name of shader specified by mesh
    std:string mShaderName;
    // Stores object space bounding sphere radius
    float mRadius;
};
```

As before, there are a constructor and a destructor as well as Load and Unload. However, notice that Load also takes in a pointer to Game. This is so that Mesh can access any textures associated with the meshes because the game has a map of the loaded textures.

The member data of Mesh contains a vector of texture pointers (one for each texture specified in the gpmesh file), a VertexArray pointer (for the vertex/index buffer), and a radius for the object space bounding sphere. This bounding sphere radius computes as the mesh file loads. The radius is simply the distance between the object space origin and the point farthest away from the origin. Computing this on load means that later, any collision components that require an object space radius have access to the data. Chapter 10, "Collision Detection," covers collision in detail. As a performance improvement, you could instead compute this radius in the gpmesh exporter.

The implementation of Mesh::Load is lengthy but not especially interesting. It constructs two temporary vectors: one for all the vertices and one for all the indices. When it's finished reading in all the values through the RapidJSON library, it constructs a VertexArray object. To see the full implementation of Mesh::Load, open this chapter's game project in the Chapter06 directory on GitHub.

You also create a map of loaded meshes and a GetMesh function in Game. As with textures, GetMesh determines whether a mesh is already in the map or you need to load it from disk.

Drawing 3D Meshes

Once 3D meshes are loading, the next step is to draw them. However, there are a lot of topics to touch on before the 3D meshes start showing up.

Before we dive into these topics, it's time for some housekeeping. The amount of rendering-specific code in Game has grown to the point that it's difficult to separate out what's related to rendering and what isn't. Adding 3D mesh drawing is only going to compound the issue. To solve this, it makes sense to now create a separate Renderer class that encapsulates all rendering code. This is the same code that was previously in Game, just moved into a separate class. Listing 6.5 provides an abbreviated declaration of Renderer.

Listing 6.5 Abbreviated Renderer Declaration

```
class Renderer
{
public:
    Renderer();
    ~Renderer();
    // Initialize and shutdown renderer
    bool Initialize(float screenWidth, float screenHeight);
    void Shutdown();
    // Unload all textures/meshes
    void UnloadData();
```

```
    // Draw the frame
    void Draw();

    void AddSprite(class SpriteComponent* sprite);
    void RemoveSprite(class SpriteComponent* sprite);
    class Texture* GetTexture(const std::string& fileName);
    class Mesh* GetMesh(const std::string& fileName);
private:
    bool LoadShaders();
    void CreateSpriteVerts();
    // Member data omitted
    // ...
};
```

The Game class then constructs and initializes an instance of Renderer in Game::Initialize. Note that the Initialize function takes in the width/height of the screen and saves these parameters in member variables. Next, Game::GenerateOutput calls Draw on the renderer instance. The map of loaded textures, map of loaded meshes, and vector of SpriteComponents also move over to Renderer. This requires some changes throughout the codebase. However, none of this code is new; it's just moved. From this point forward, all rendering-related code will go in Renderer instead of Game.

Transforming to Clip Space, Revisited

Recall that with the OpenGL 2D rendering implemented in Chapter 5, the simple view-projection matrix scales down world space coordinates into clip-space coordinates. For a 3D game, this type of view-projection matrix is insufficient. Instead, you need to decompose the view-projection matrix into separate view and projection matrices.

View Matrix

The **view matrix** represents the position and orientation of the camera, or "eye" in the world. Chapter 9, "Cameras," covers several different implementations of cameras, but for now let's keep it simple. At a minimum, a **look-at matrix** represents the position and orientation of the camera.

In the typical construction of a look-at matrix, there are three parameters: the position of the eye, the target position the eye "looks at," and the up direction. Given these parameters, you first compute four different vectors:

$$\hat{k} = \frac{target - eye}{\|target - eye\|}$$

$$\hat{i} = \frac{up \times \hat{k}}{\|up \times \hat{k}\|}$$

$$\hat{j} = \frac{\hat{k} \times \hat{i}}{\|\hat{k} \times \hat{i}\|}$$

$$\vec{t} = \left\langle -\hat{i} \cdot eye, -\hat{j} \cdot eye, -\hat{k} \cdot eye \right\rangle$$

These vectors then define the elements of the look-at matrix as follows:

$$
LookAt = \begin{bmatrix} i_x & j_x & k_x & 0 \\ i_y & j_y & k_y & 0 \\ i_z & j_z & k_z & 0 \\ t_x & t_y & t_z & 1 \end{bmatrix}
$$

A quick way to make the camera move is to create an actor for the camera. The position of this actor represents the eye position. The target position is then some point in front of the camera actor. For the up direction, +z works if the actor can't flip upside down (which currently is the case). Pass in these parameters to `Matrix4::CreateLookAt`, and you have a valid view matrix.

For example, if the camera actor is `mCameraActor`, the following code constructs a view matrix:

```
// Location of camera
Vector3 eye = mCameraActor->GetPosition();
// Point 10 units in front of camera
Vector3 target = mCameraActor->GetPosition() +
   mCameraActor->GetForward() * 10.0f;
Matrix4 view = Matrix4::CreateLookAt(eye, target, Vector3::UnitZ);
```

Projection Matrix

The **projection matrix** determines how the 3D world flattens into the 2D world drawn onscreen. Two types of projection matrices are common in 3D games: orthographic and perspective.

In an **orthographic projection**, objects farther away from the camera are the same size as objects closer to the camera. This means that players will not be able to perceive whether objects are closer or farther away from the camera. Most 2D games use an orthographic projection. Figure 6.3 illustrates a scene rendered with an orthographic projection.

In a **perspective projection**, objects farther away from the camera are smaller than closer ones. Thus, players perceive that there's depth in the scene. Most 3D games use this sort of projection, and you'll use it for the game project in this chapter. Figure 6.4 shows the same 3D scene as Figure 6.3, except this time using a perspective projection.

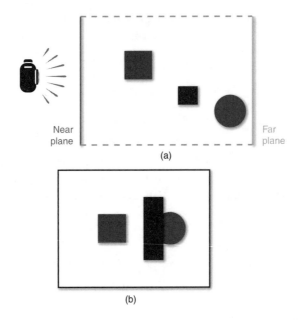

Figure 6.3 (a) Top-down view of an orthographic projection and (b) the resulting 2D image onscreen

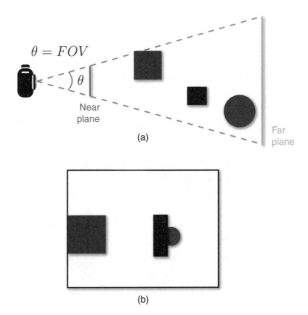

Figure 6.4 (a) Top-down view of a perspective projection and (b) the resulting 2D image onscreen

Each of these projections has a near plane and a far plane. The near plane is typically very close to the camera. Anything between the camera and the near plane is not visible onscreen. This is why games have objects partially disappear if the camera gets too close to them. Similarly, the far plane is far away from the camera, and anything past it is not visible. Games sometimes allow the player to reduce the "draw distance" to improve performance. This is often just a matter of pulling in the far plane.

The orthographic projection matrix has four parameters: the width of the view, the height of the view, the distance to the near plane, and the distance to the far plane. Given these parameters, this is the orthographic projection matrix:

$$Orthographic = \begin{bmatrix} \dfrac{2}{width} & 0 & 0 & 0 \\ 0 & \dfrac{2}{height} & 0 & 0 \\ 0 & 0 & \dfrac{1}{far-near} & 0 \\ 0 & 0 & \dfrac{near}{near-far} & 1 \end{bmatrix}$$

Note that this orthographic projection matrix is like the *SimpleViewProjection* matrix in Chapter 5, except there are additional terms accounting for the near and far planes.

The perspective projection has an additional parameter called the **horizontal field of view** (**FOV**). This is the horizontal angle around the camera that's visible in the projection. Changing the field of view determines how much of the 3D world is visible. This is the perspective matrix:

$$yScale = \cot\left(\frac{fov}{2}\right)$$

$$xScale = yScale \cdot \frac{height}{width}$$

$$Perspective = \begin{bmatrix} xScale & 0 & 0 & 0 \\ 0 & yScale & 0 & 0 \\ 0 & 0 & \dfrac{far}{far-near} & 1 \\ 0 & 0 & \dfrac{-near \cdot far}{far-near} & 0 \end{bmatrix}$$

Note that the perspective matrix changes the w component of the homogeneous coordinate. The **perspective divide** divides each component of the transformed vertex by the w component, so that the w component becomes 1 again. This is what reduces the size of objects as they get farther from the camera. OpenGL automatically does a perspective divide behind the scenes.

> **note**
>
> We omit the derivation of the orthographic and perspective matrices here.

Both types of protection matrices have helper functions in the `Math.h` library. You can use `Matrix4::CreateOrtho` for an orthographic matrix and `Matrix4::CreatePerspectiveFOV` for a perspective matrix.

Calculating the View-Projection

The view-projection matrix is just the product of the separate view and projection matrices:

$$ViewProjection = (View)(Projection)$$

The vertex shader then uses this view-projection matrix to transform vertex positions from world space into clip space.

Out with the Painter's Algorithm, in with Z-Buffering

Chapter 2, "Game Objects and 2D Graphics," introduces the painter's algorithm. Recall that the painter's algorithm draws objects from back to front. While this is great for 2D games, it faces complications in 3D.

Painter's Algorithm Blues

A major problem with the painter's algorithm for 3D games is that the back-to-front ordering is not static. As the camera moves and rotates through the scene, which object is in front or behind changes. To use the painter's algorithm in a 3D scene, you must sort all the triangles in the scene from back to front, potentially every frame. For even a slightly complex scene, this perpetual sorting is a performance bottleneck.

It gets even worse for a split-screen game. If player A and player B face each other, the back-to-front ordering is different for each player. To solve this, you must sort on a per-view basis.

Another issue is that the painter's algorithm can result in a massive amount of **overdraw**, or writing the color of a single pixel more than once per frame. This happens all the time in the painter's algorithm, as objects in the back of the scene have pixels overwritten by closer objects. In a modern 3D game, the process of calculating the final color of a pixel is one of the most expensive parts of the rendering pipeline. This is because the fragment shader contains code for texturing, lighting, and many other advanced techniques. Every pixel overdrawn is an execution of the fragment shader wasted. Thus, 3D games aim to eliminate as much overdraw as possible.

Finally, there's an issue with overlapping triangles. Look at the three triangles in Figure 6.5. Which one is the farthest back? The answer is that no one triangle is the farthest back. In this case, the only way the painter's algorithm can draw these triangles correctly is by splitting one triangle in half, which isn't ideal. For these reasons, 3D games do not use the painter's algorithm for most objects.

Figure 6.5 Overlapping triangles painter's algorithm failure case

Z-Buffering

Z-buffering (or depth buffering) uses an additional memory buffer during the rendering process. This buffer, known as the **z-buffer** (or **depth buffer**), stores data for each pixel in the scene, much like the color buffer. But while the color buffer stores color information, the z-buffer stores the distance from the camera, or **depth**, at each pixel. Collectively, the set of buffers that graphically represent the frame (including the color buffer, z-buffer, and others) is the **frame buffer**.

At the start of a frame, you need to clear the z-buffer (much like the color buffer). Instead of clearing to a color, you clear each pixel to the maximum depth value in normalized device coordinates, which is 1.0. During rendering, before drawing a pixel, z-buffering computes the depth at the pixel. If the depth at the pixel is less than the current depth value stored in the z-buffer (meaning it's closer), that pixel draws to the color buffer. The z-buffer then updates the depth value for that pixel.

Figure 6.6 shows a visualization of the z-buffer for a scene. Because the sphere is closer than the cube, its z-buffer values are closer to zero (and thus closer to black). The first object drawn in a frame will always have all its pixels' color and depth information written into the color and z-buffers, respectively. But when drawing the second object, only pixels with depths closer than the values in the z-buffer draw. Listing 6.6 gives pseudocode for the z-buffer algorithm.

Listing 6.6   Z-Buffering Pseudocode

```
// zBuffer[x][y] grabs depth at that pixel
foreach MeshComponent m in scene
    foreach Pixel p in m
        float depth = p.Depth()
        if zBuffer[p.x][p.y] < depth
            p.draw
        endif
    endfor
endfor
```

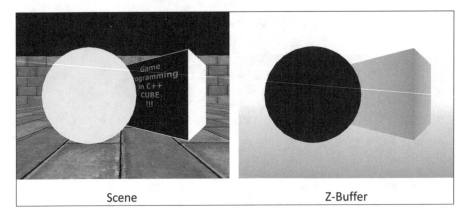

Scene   Z-Buffer

Figure 6.6 A sample scene (left) and its corresponding z-buffer (right)

With z-buffering, drawing the scene in any arbitrary order will look correct if there are no objects with transparency. This is not to say that the order is irrelevant. For example, drawing a scene back-to-front yields the same amount of overdraw as the painter's algorithm. Conversely, drawing a scene front-to-back yields zero overdraw. But the gain of z-buffering is that any arbitrary order works. And because z-buffering is on a per-pixel basis, not a per-object or per-triangle basis, it will work even for the overlapping triangles in Figure 6.5.

Luckily, z-buffering is not something a graphics programmer implements anymore; you merely need to enable it. OpenGL supports depth buffering with minimal effort. (OpenGL uses the term *depth buffer* instead of *z-buffer*.) First, prior to creating the OpenGL context, you need to request a depth buffer (24-bit is a typical size):

```
SDL_GL_SetAttribute(SDL_GL_DEPTH_SIZE, 24);
```

Then, the following call enables depth buffering:

```
glEnable(GL_DEPTH_TEST);
```

The `glClear` function handles clearing the depth buffer. One call can clear both the color and depth buffers:

```
glClear(GL_COLOR_BUFFER_BIT | GL_DEPTH_BUFFER_BIT);
```

Although z-buffering works well, there are some issues. For one, transparent objects don't work with z-buffering as specified. Suppose a game has semi-transparent water, and under this water is a rock. In z-buffering, drawing the water first writes to the z-buffer and prevents the rock from drawing, since the rock has a higher depth.

The solution to this dilemma is to render opaque objects first, using z-buffering. Then disable depth buffer writes and render transparent objects back-to-front. As the pixels render, you should test the depth at each pixel to ensure that transparent pixels behind opaque objects don't draw. Although this means the transparent objects render with the painter's algorithm, the number of transparent objects is hopefully very small.

Although you don't need to use transparent 3D objects in this book, remember that sprite rendering uses alpha blending to support textures with transparency. Because this doesn't play nicely with z-buffering, you must disable alpha blending for 3D objects and then reenable it for sprites. Likewise, sprites must render with z-buffering disabled.

This naturally leads to rendering in two phases: First, render all 3D objects with alpha blending disabled and z-buffering enabled. Then render all sprites with alpha blending enabled and z-buffering disabled. When you do this, all 2D sprites appear on top of the 3D scene. This is okay because a 3D game uses 2D sprites only for UI or HUD elements.

The `BasicMesh` Shader

Recall that earlier in this chapter, you modified the `Sprite.vert` shader file to include support for vertex normals in the vertex layout. It turns out that this modified code for the sprite vertex shader and the original code for the `Sprite.frag` shader file from Chapter 5 also works for full 3D meshes. You set the view-projection matrix uniform to a different value for 3D meshes, but the actual vertex/fragment shader code is fine as is. So for now, the `BasicMesh.vert`/ `BasicMesh.frag` shader files are just copies of the `Sprite.vert`/`Sprite.frag` shader files.

Next, add a `Shader*` member variable for the mesh shader to `Renderer`, as well as separate `Matrix4` variables for the view and projection matrices. `Renderer::InitShaders` then loads the `BasicMesh` shader (with code very similar to code for loading the sprite shader) and initializes the view and projection matrices. You initialize the view matrix to a look-at matrix facing down the x-axis and the projection matrix to a perspective matrix:

```
mMeshShader->SetActive();
// Set the view-projection matrix
mView = Matrix4::CreateLookAt(
    Vector3::Zero,  // Camera position
    Vector3::UnitX, // Target position
    Vector3::UnitZ  // Up
);
mProjection = Matrix4::CreatePerspectiveFOV(
    Math::ToRadians(70.0f), // Horizontal FOV
    mScreenWidth,           // Width of view
```

```
    mScreenHeight,              // Height of view
    25.0f,                      // Near plane distance
    10000.0f                    // Far plane distance
);
mMeshShader->SetMatrixUniform("uViewProj", mView * mProjection);
```

For simplicity, we assume here that all meshes use the same shader (ignoring the shader property stored in the gpmesh file). In Exercise 6.1 you add support for different mesh shaders.

In any event, now that there's a shader for meshes, the next step is to create a MeshComponent class to draw 3D meshes.

The MeshComponent Class

Recall that all the code for transforming vertices from object space into clip space is in the vertex shader. The code for filling in the color of each pixel is in the fragment shader. This means that the MeshComponent class doesn't need to do much for drawing.

Listing 6.7 provides the declaration of MeshComponent. Note that unlike SpriteComponent, MeshComponent does not have a draw order variable. This is because the order doesn't matter because 3D meshes use z-buffering. The only member data is a pointer to the associated mesh and a texture index. Because a gpmesh can have multiple associated textures, the index determines which texture to use when drawing the MeshComponent.

Listing 6.7 MeshComponent Declaration

```
class MeshComponent : public Component
{
public:
    MeshComponent(class Actor* owner);
    ~MeshComponent();
    // Draw this mesh component with provided shader
    virtual void Draw(class Shader* shader);
    // Set the mesh/texture index used by mesh component
    virtual void SetMesh(class Mesh* mesh);
    void SetTextureIndex(size_t index);
protected:
    class Mesh* mMesh;
    size_t mTextureIndex;
};
```

The Renderer then has a vector of MeshComponent pointers and functions to add and remove these components. The constructor and destructor of MeshComponent call these add/remove functions.

The `Draw` function, shown in Listing 6.8, first sets the world transform matrix uniform. `MeshComponent` directly uses the owning actor's world transform matrix because there's no extra scale needed, as there is in `SpriteComponent`. Next, the code activates the texture and vertex array associated with the mesh. Finally, `glDrawElements` draws the triangles. The index buffer size isn't hard-coded here because different meshes have different numbers of indices.

Listing 6.8 `MeshComponent::Draw` Implementation

```
void MeshComponent::Draw(Shader* shader)
{
    if (mMesh)
    {
        // Set the world transform
        shader->SetMatrixUniform("uWorldTransform",
            mOwner->GetWorldTransform());
        // Set the active texture
        Texture* t = mMesh->GetTexture(mTextureIndex);
        if (t) { t->SetActive(); }
        // Set the mesh's vertex array as active
        VertexArray* va = mMesh->GetVertexArray();
        va->SetActive();
        // Draw
        glDrawElements(GL_TRIANGLES, va->GetNumIndices(),
            GL_UNSIGNED_INT, nullptr);
    }
}
```

Finally, the `Renderer` needs code that draws all the mesh components. After clearing the frame buffer, the `Renderer` first draws all meshes with depth buffering enabled and alpha blending disabled. It next draws all sprites in the same manner as before. After drawing everything, the `Renderer` swaps the front and back buffers. Listing 6.9 shows only the new code for rendering meshes. The code recalculates the view-projection matrix every frame to account for a moving camera.

Listing 6.9 Drawing `MeshComponent`s in `Renderer::Draw`

```
// Enable depth buffering/disable alpha blend
glEnable(GL_DEPTH_TEST);
glDisable(GL_BLEND);
// Set the basic mesh shader active
mMeshShader->SetActive();
// Update view-projection matrix
mMeshShader->SetMatrixUniform("uViewProj", mView * mProjection);
for (auto mc : mMeshComps)
{
    mc->Draw(mMeshShader);
}
```

Because `MeshComponent` is just like any other component, you can attach it to an arbitrary actor and draw meshes for the actor. Figure 6.7 shows `MeshComponent` in action, drawing a sphere and a cube mesh.

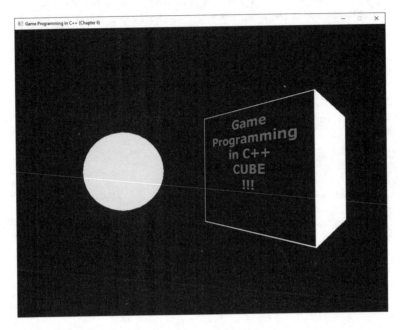

Figure 6.7 Drawing a simple scene with `MeshComponent`

Lighting

So far, the mesh fragment shader directly uses the texture color as the final color for a pixel. However, without any contrast, the scene looks dull. To approximate concepts such as the sun or light bulbs or simply to add variety to the scene, you need lighting.

Revisiting Vertex Attributes

Lighting meshes require more vertex attributes than just the vertex position and UV (texture) coordinates. They also need vertex normals. You added this vertex attribute earlier in this chapter. However, the concept of a **vertex normal** requires further explanation. It seems almost nonsensical because a normal is a vector perpendicular to a surface, but a single point is not a surface, so how can there be a normal to a point?

You can compute a vertex normal by averaging the normals of the triangles that contain that vertex, as in Figure 6.8(a). This works well for smooth models but doesn't quite work for hard edges. For example, rendering a cube with averaged vertex normals yields rounded corners. To solve this, the artist creates multiple vertices for the corners of the cube, and each vertex on the corner has a different normal. Figure 6.8(b) shows a cube authored in this manner.

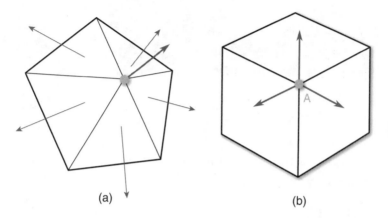

(a)   (b)

Figure 6.8 (a) Averaged vertex normals. (b) Vertex A on the cube uses one of three different normals, depending on the face

Remember that all vertex attributes interpolate across the triangle when sent to the fragment shader. This means that any arbitrary pixel on the face of a triangle has a normal value that's the interpolation between the triangle's three vertex normals.

Types of Lights

While there are many potential choices, a handful of light types consistently see use in 3D games. Some lights globally affect the entire scene, whereas other lights affect only the area around the light.

Ambient Light

Ambient light is a uniform amount of light applied to every single object in a scene. The amount of ambient light might differ for different levels in a game, depending on the time of day. A level set at night will have a much darker and cooler ambient light than a level set in the daytime, which will be brighter and warmer.

Because it provides an even amount of lighting, ambient light does not light different sides of objects differently. It is a global amount of light uniformly applied to every part of every object in a scene. This is akin to the sun on a cloudy day in nature, as in Figure 6.9(a).

(a)   (b)

Figure 6.9 Examples in nature of ambient light (a) and directional light (b)

In code, the simplest representation of ambient light is an RGB color value that represents both the color and intensity of the light. For example, (0.2, 0.2, 0.2) is darker than (0.5, 0.5, 0.5).

Directional Light

A **directional light** is a light emitted from a specific direction. Like ambient light, directional light affects an entire scene. However, because a directional light comes from a specific direction, it illuminates one side of objects while leaving the other side in darkness. An example of a directional light is the sun on a sunny day. The direction of the light depends on where the sun is at that time of day. The side facing the sun is bright, while the other side is dark. Figure 6.9(b) shows a directional light at Yellowstone National Park. (Note that in a game, shadowing is not a property of a directional light itself. Instead, computing shadows requires additional calculations.)

Games that use directional lights often have only one directional light for the entire level, representing either the sun or the moon. But this isn't always the case. For example, an approximation of the lighting of a sports stadium at night could use multiple directional lights.

In code, a directional light needs both an RGB color value (as with ambient light) and a normalized vector for the direction of the light.

Point Light

A **point light** exists at a specific point and emanates in all directions from that point. Because it starts at a specific point, a point light also illuminates only one side of an object. Usually, a point light also has a radius of influence. For example, think of a light bulb in a dark room, as in Figure 6.10(a). There's visible light in the area immediately around the light, but it slowly dissipates until it no longer adds light. The point light doesn't go on infinitely.

In code, a point light should have an RGB color, a position of the light, and a **falloff radius** that determines how much the light value decreases as the distance from the light increases.

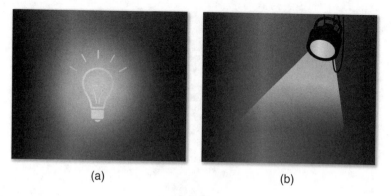

(a)

(b)

Figure 6.10 A light build point light (a) and (b) a spotlight

Spotlight

A **spotlight** is much like a point light, except that instead of traveling in all directions, it's focused in a cone. To simulate a spotlight, you need all the parameters of a point light and additionally the angle of the cone. A classic example of a spotlight is a theater spotlight, but another example is a flashlight in the dark. Figure 6.10(b) illustrates a spotlight.

Phong Reflection Model

To simulate lights, not only do you need their associated data, you also need to calculate how the lights affect the objects in the scene. A tried-and-true method for approximating light is a **bidirectional reflectance distribution function** (**BRDF**), which is a function that approximates how light bounces off surfaces. There are many different types of BRDFs, but a classic one is the **Phong reflection model**.

The Phong model is a **local lighting model** because it doesn't calculate secondary reflections of light. In other words, the reflection model lights each object as if it's the only object in the entire scene. In the real world, shining a red light on a white wall will fill the rest of the room with a reddish color. However, this does not happen in the Phong model.

The Phong model divides light into three distinct components: ambient, diffuse, and specular. Figure 6.11 illustrates these components. All three components consider the color of the surface as well as the color of the light affecting the surface.

The **ambient component** is the overall illumination of the scene. Thus, it makes sense to directly tie the ambient component to the ambient light. Because ambient light applies evenly to the entire scene, the ambient component is independent of any other lights and the camera.

Figure 6.11 Phong reflection model

The **diffuse component** is the primary reflection of light off the surface. Any directional lights, point lights, or spotlights affecting the object affect the diffuse component. The diffuse component calculation uses both the normal of the surface and a vector from the surface to the light. The position of the camera does not affect the diffuse component.

The final component in the Phong model is the **specular component**. This approximates shiny reflections off a surface. An object with a high degree of specularity, such as a polished metal object, has stronger highlights than an object painted in matte black. As with the diffuse component, the specular component depends on both the light vector and the normal of the surface. However, specularity also depends on the position of the camera. This is because looking at a shiny object from different angles changes the perceived reflections.

Figure 6.12 shows the Phong reflection from a side view. Computing Phong reflection requires a series of calculations that include several variables:

- $\hat{n}$—Normalized surface normal
- $\hat{l}$—Normalized vector from the surface to the light
- $\hat{v}$—Normalized vector from the surface to the camera (eye) position
- $\hat{r}$—Normalized reflection of $-\hat{l}$ about $\hat{n}$
- α—Specular power (which determines the shininess of the object)

In addition, there are colors for the lights:

- k_a—Ambient color
- k_d—Diffuse color
- k_s—Specular color

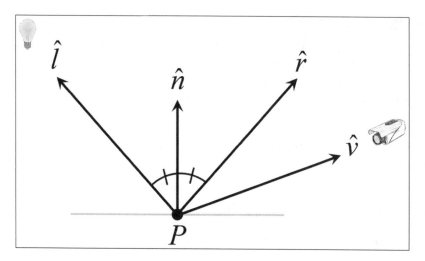

Figure 6.12 Diagram of Phong reflection calculations (vectors not to scale)

In the Phong reflection model, you calculate the light applied to a surface as follows:

$$Ambient = k_a$$
$$Diffuse = k_d \left(\hat{n} \cdot \hat{l} \right)$$
$$Specular = k_s \left(\hat{r} \cdot \hat{v} \right)^{\alpha}$$
$$Phong = Ambient + \sum_{\forall lights} \begin{cases} Specular + Diffuse & \text{if } \hat{n} \cdot \hat{l} > 0 \\ 0 & \text{otherwise} \end{cases}$$

Note that the diffuse and specular component computes for all lights in the scene, but there's only one ambient component. The $\hat{n} \cdot \hat{l}$ test ensures that the light affects only surfaces facing the light.

In any event, the Phong equation as described here yields a color for all lights in the scene. The final color of the surface is the light color multiplied by the color of the surface. Because both the light and surface color are RGB values, you use component-wise multiplication.

A more complex implementation separates the surface color into separate ambient, diffuse, and specular colors. In this implementation, the equations change to multiply each separate color by each component rather than only one multiplication at the end.

One remaining question is how frequently to compute the BRDF. There are three common options: once per surface (**flat shading**), once per vertex (**Gouraud shading**), or once per pixel (**Phong shading**). Although per-pixel lighting is more computationally expensive, modern graphics hardware can easily handle it. It's conceivable that some games might choose other types of shading for aesthetic reasons, but this chapter sticks to per-pixel lighting.

Implementing Lighting

This section covers how to add ambient and directional lights to the game. Implementing this requires changes to both the vertex and fragment shaders. The `BasicMesh.vert/.frag` shaders are a starting point for the new `Phong.vert/.frag` shaders. (Remember that this shader code is in GLSL, not C++.) You'll then change it so all meshes use this new Phong shader.

Because the lighting is per pixel, the Phong fragment shader needs several additional uniforms: a camera position, an ambient light color, and several variables for a directional light (see Listing 6.10).

Listing 6.10   `Phong.frag` Lighting Uniforms

```
// Create a struct for directional light
struct DirectionalLight
{
    // Direction of light
    vec3 mDirection;
    // Diffuse color
    vec3 mDiffuseColor;
    // Specular color
    vec3 mSpecColor;
};

// Uniforms for lighting
// Camera position (in world space)
uniform vec3 uCameraPos;
// Ambient light level
uniform vec3 uAmbientLight;
// Specular power for this surface
uniform float uSpecPower;
// Directional Light (only one for now)
uniform DirectionalLight uDirLight;
```

Note the declaration of a `DirectionalLight` struct. GLSL supports struct declarations, much like those in C/C++. Next, you declare a corresponding `DirectionalLight` struct in the C++ code and add two member variables to `Renderer` for the ambient light and directional light.

Back in C++, the `glUniform3fv` and `glUniform1f` functions set 3D vector and float uniforms, respectively. You create two new functions in `Shader`, `SetVectorUniform` and `SetFloatUniform`, to call these functions. The implementation of both these functions is like that of the `SetMatrixUniform` function in Chapter 5.

A new function in `Renderer` called `SetLightUniforms` handles setting the new uniform values:

```
void Renderer::SetLightUniforms(Shader* shader)
{
   // Camera position is from inverted view
   Matrix4 invView = mView;
   invView.Invert();
   shader->SetVectorUniform("uCameraPos", invView.GetTranslation());
   // Ambient light
   shader->SetVectorUniform("uAmbientLight", mAmbientLight);
   // Directional light
   shader->SetVectorUniform("uDirLight.mDirection", mDirLight.mDirection);
   shader->SetVectorUniform("uDirLight.mDiffuseColor",
      mDirLight.mDiffuseColor);
   shader->SetVectorUniform("uDirLight.mSpecColor", mDirLight.mSpecColor);
}
```

Note that this function uses dot notation to reference specific members of the `uDirLight` struct.

Extracting the camera position from the view matrix requires inverting the view matrix. After inverting the view matrix, the first three components of the fourth row (returned by the `GetTranslation` member function) correspond to the world space position of the camera.

Next, you update the gpmesh file format so that you can specify the specular power of a mesh's surface with the `specularPower` property. You then update the `Mesh::Load` code to read in this property, and set the `uSpecPower` uniform in `MeshComponent::Draw` right before drawing the mesh.

Back in GLSL, you must make some changes to the vertex shader in `Phong.vert`. Both the camera position and the directional light's direction are in world space. However, the `gl_Position` computed in the vertex shader is in clip space. Getting the correct vector from the surface to the camera requires a position in world space. Furthermore, the input vertex normals are in object space, but they also need to be in world space. This means the vertex shader must compute both the world space normal and the world space position and send these to the fragment shader via `out` variables:

```
// Normal (in world space)
out vec3 fragNormal;
// Position (in world space)
out vec3 fragWorldPos;
```

Similarly, you declare `fragNormal` and `fragWorldPos` as in variables in the fragment shader. Next, the main function of the vertex shader, in Listing 6.11, computes both `fragNormal` and `fragWorldPos`. The `.xyz` syntax, known as a **swizzle**, is a shorthand for extracting the x, y, and z components from a 4D vector and creating a new 3D vector with those values. This effectively converts between a `vec4` and `vec3`.

The code also converts the normal into homogenous coordinates so that multiplication by the world transform matrix works. However, the w component here is 0 instead of 1. This is because the normal is not a position, so translating the normal makes no sense. Setting the w component to 0 means the translation component of the world transform matrix zeros out in the multiplication.

Listing 6.11   `Phong.vert` Main Function

```
void main()
{
    // Convert position to homogeneous coordinates
    vec4 pos = vec4(inPosition, 1.0);
    // Transform position to world space
    pos = pos * uWorldTransform;
    // Save world position
    fragWorldPos = pos.xyz;
    // Transform to clip space
    gl_Position = pos * uViewProj;

    // Transform normal into world space (w = 0)
    fragNormal = (vec4(inNormal, 0.0f) * uWorldTransform).xyz;

    // Pass along the texture coordinate to frag shader
    fragTexCoord = inTexCoord;
}
```

The fragment shader, in Listing 6.12, computes the Phong reflection model as outlined in the equations in the previous section. Note that you must normalize `fragNormal` because OpenGL interpolates the vertex normal across the face of the triangle. Interpolating two normalized vectors does not guarantee a normalized vector at each step of the interpolation, so you must renormalize it.

Because the directional light emits from a direction, the vector from the surface to the light is just the negation of the light's direction vector. The fragment shader uses a handful of new GLSL functions. The `dot` function computes a dot product, `reflect` computes a reflection vector, `max` selects the maximum of two values, and `pow` computes a power. The `clamp` function restricts the value of each component of the passed in vector to the range specified. In this case, the valid light values are from 0.0 (no light) to 1.0 (maximum light of that color). The final color is the texture color multiplied by the Phong light.

One edge case occurs when the dot product between R and V is negative. In this case, the specular component might end up negative, or effectively remove light from the scene. The max function call prevents this because if the dot product is negative, max selects 0.

Listing 6.12 Phong.frag Main Function

```
void main()
{
    // Surface normal
    vec3 N = normalize(fragNormal);
    // Vector from surface to light
    vec3 L = normalize(-uDirLight.mDirection);
    // Vector from surface to camera
    vec3 V = normalize(uCameraPos - fragWorldPos);
    // Reflection of -L about N
    vec3 R = normalize(reflect(-L, N));

    // Compute phong reflection
    vec3 Phong = uAmbientLight;
    float NdotL = dot(N, L);
    if (NdotL > 0)
    {
        vec3 Diffuse = uDirLight.mDiffuseColor * NdotL;
        vec3 Specular = uDirLight.mSpecColor *
            pow(max(0.0, dot(R, V)), uSpecPower);
        Phong += Diffuse + Specular;
    }

    // Final color is texture color times phong light (alpha = 1)
    outColor = texture(uTexture, fragTexCoord) * vec4(Phong, 1.0f);
}
```

Figure 6.13 shows the Phong shader in action, lighting the sphere and cube from Figure 6.10. This figure uses the following light values:

- **Ambient light**—Dark gray (0.2, 0.2, 0.2)
- **Directional direction**—Down and to the left (0, −0.7, −0.7)
- **Directional diffuse color**—Green (0, 1, 0)
- **Directional specular color**—Bright green (0.5, 1, 0.5)

In Figure 6.13, the specular power of the sphere is 10.0 and the specular power of the cube is 100.0f to make the sphere shinier than the cube.

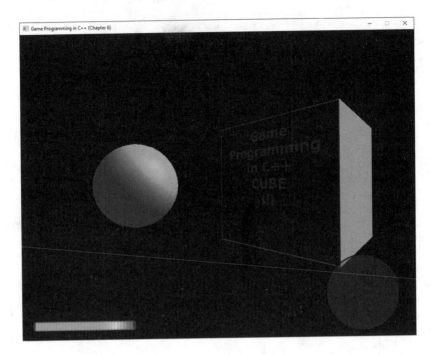

Figure 6.13 Phong shader in action

Game Project

This chapter's game project implements most of the topics covered: mesh loading, a `MeshComponent`, and the Phong shader. Figure 6.14 shows the final version of this chapter's game project. The code is available in the book's GitHub repository, in the `Chapter06` directory. Open `Chapter06-windows.sln` on Windows and `Chapter06-mac.xcodeproj` on Mac.

The `LoadData` function in `Game` instantiates several different actors for the objects in the world. A simple `CameraActor` allows the camera to move through the world. Use the `W` and `S` keys to move forward and back and the `A` and `D` keys to yaw the camera. (Chapter 9 discusses more complex cameras. The current camera is a simple version of a first-person camera.)

The sprite elements on the screen, such as health and radar, don't do anything yet. They are onscreen just to demonstrate that sprite rendering still works. Chapter 11, "User Interfaces," shows how to implement some UI features.

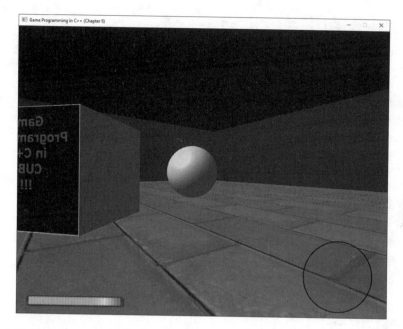

Figure 6.14 Chapter 6 game project

Summary

This chapter covers the process of transitioning from a 2D game world to a 3D game world. Actors now have a transform with a 3D position and a quaternion for rotations about an arbitrary axis.

A 3D scene also needs a more complex view-projection matrix. Using a look-at matrix is a preferred method to create a view matrix. A projection matrix can be either orthographic or perspective, but only a perspective projection gives the scene depth. 3D games also shy away from using the painter's algorithm and instead use z-buffering to determine which pixels are visible.

The simple gpmesh file format contains enough information to create vertex and index buffers for 3D models at runtime—without including the extraneous data of a complex file format. The MeshComponent class can attach to any actor and implements 3D mesh rendering (through the shaders).

A game might use many types of lights. Ambient and directional lights affect the entire scene, while point and spotlights affect only certain areas. One method to approximate how light affects the scene is the Phong reflection model. The Phong model has three components: ambient, diffuse, and specular.

Additional Reading

Rendering is a highly specialized area of game programming, and excelling in rendering requires a strong foundation in mathematics. There are many excellent resources available. Thomas Akenine-Moller's book, although somewhat dated, is a popular reference for rendering programmers—and an updated fourth edition is forthcoming. Although this book uses OpenGL, there are alternative graphics APIs. For PC and Xbox, the DirectX API dominates. Frank Luna's book covers how to use DirectX 11. Finally, Matt Pharr's text is an excellent overview of a realistic lighting technique called physically based rendering.

Akenine-Moller, Thomas, Eric Haines, and Naty Hoffman. *Real-Time Rendering*, 3rd edition. Natick: A K Peters, 2008.

Luna, Frank. *Introduction to 3D Game Programming with DirectX 11*. Dulles: Mercury Learning and Information, 2012.

Pharr, Matt, Wenzel Jakob, and Greg Humphreys. *Physically Based Rendering: From Theory to Implementation,* 3rd edition. Cambridge: Elsevier, 2017.

Exercises

This chapter's exercises involve adding improvements to the game project. In the first exercise you add support for different meshes rendering with different shaders. In the second exercise you add point lights, which provide a great deal of flexibility in the lighting of the game.

Exercise 6.1

Modify the mesh rendering code so that it's possible to draw different meshes with different shaders. This means storing the different mesh shaders in a map and ensuring that each shader has its uniforms set properly.

However, constantly switching between shaders is inefficient. To solve this, group mesh components by their corresponding shader. For example, if there are 10 meshes drawn with the BasicMesh shader and 5 drawn with the Phong shader, the code shouldn't alternate between the two shaders repeatedly. Instead, draw all meshes that use BasicMesh first and then draw all meshes that use Phong.

To test this, modify the gpmesh files so that some draw with BasicMesh and others draw with Phong. Remember that because the gpmesh files are JSON, you can use any text editor to edit them.

Exercise 6.2

Because a point light affects a limited radius, these lights can add a lot to a scene. Modify the Phong shader so that it also supports a maximum of four point lights in the scene. Create a struct for point lights much like the struct for directional lights. This struct needs a position of the light, diffuse color, specular color, specular power, and a radius of influence. Then create an array of point lights as a uniform. (Arrays work in GLSL just like in C/C++.)

The Phong equations are the same, except the code now needs to consider all lights for specular and diffuse. In addition, a point light should affect a pixel only if the pixel is within that light's radius. To test this, create different point lights at different positions and with different colors.

CHAPTER 7

AUDIO

Though sometimes overlooked, audio is an important part of games. Whether it's to provide audio cues for gameplay situations or enhance the overall atmosphere, quality sound adds a lot to games.

Leveraging the powerful FMOD API, this chapter covers how to bootstrap an audio system that goes well beyond simply playing sound files. Covered topics include using sound events, adding positional 3D audio, mixing sounds, and adding effects.

Bootstrapping Audio

A rudimentary game audio system loads and plays back standalone sound files (such as WAV or OGG files) as needed. Although this approach is functional—and might be perfectly acceptable for a simple 2D game—it has limitations. In many cases, a single game action does not correspond to a single sound file. Suppose a game features a character that runs around. Every time the character's foot hits the ground, a footstep sound should play. If there were only a single footstep sound file played repeatedly, it would quickly become repetitive.

At the very least, rather than having a single footstep sound file, you might want 10 different sound files for variety. Each time the player takes a step, the game might want to randomly pick one of these 10 footstep sound files. Or maybe the player can walk on different surfaces, and a footstep on grass sounds different than a footstep on concrete. In this case, the game needs a way to choose from the correct set of footstep sounds based on the surface the player is walking on.

Another consideration is that the game can only play a limited number of sounds simultaneously. You use sound **channels** to track the sounds that are playing, and there is some limit on the number of channels. Imagine a game where there are several enemies onscreen at any one time. If each enemy individually plays footstep sounds, it not only overwhelms the ear of the player but may also take up all available channels. Certain sounds, such as the player character attacking the enemy, are far more important than an enemy's footstep. Different sounds might therefore need different priorities.

Now consider a 3D game with a fireplace. Imagine that as the player character moves through the game world, the fireplace sound plays at the same volume level from all speakers. It doesn't matter if the player stands right next to the fireplace or is hundreds of feet away; the sound plays at the same level. Not only is this annoying, but it's unrealistic. The game needs to account for the distance between the player and the fireplace and calculate a volume based on this distance.

So even though games need sound files to play audio, they also need additional information to play these sounds correctly. Ideally, the decision-making power of what sounds "correct" shouldn't be the audio programmer's. Much like how a 3D artist creates models in a specialized modeling program, ideally sound designers construct dynamic sounds using external tools designed for their skill sets.

FMOD

Designed by Firelight Technologies, FMOD (https://fmod.com) is a popular sound engine for video games. FMOD supports any realistic game platform, including Windows, Mac, Linux, iOS, Android, HTML5, and every modern console. The current version of FMOD has two distinct components: FMOD Studio, which is an external authoring tool for sound designers, and the FMOD API (application programming interface), which integrates into games that use FMOD.

The FMOD Studio tool grants a lot of power to sound designers and can implement many of the features discussed earlier. A **sound event** can correspond to one or more sound files, and these events can have **parameters** that dynamically drive the behavior of the sound events. FMOD Studio also allows designers to control how the different sounds mix together. For example, the designer can place music and sound effects on separate tracks and then adjust the volume of the tracks separately.

> **note**
>
> This chapter doesn't cover how to use FMOD Studio, but there are excellent references available on the official FMOD website, among other places. For interested readers, the FMOD Studio project file used for the audio content in this chapter is in the GitHub repository, in the `FMODStudio/Chapter07` directory.

The FMOD API has two parts. The FMOD Low Level API is the foundation for FMOD. It contains functionality to load and play sounds, manage channels, update sounds in a 3D environment, add digital effects to sound, and more. It's possible to use the Low Level API by itself, but then any events created in FMOD Studio are not usable. Supporting FMOD Studio requires the FMOD Studio API, which builds on the Low Level API. However, using the FMOD Studio API does not preclude an audio programmer from accessing the Low Level API if needed. For the most part, this chapter uses the FMOD Studio API.

Installing FMOD

Because of FMOD's licensing terms, the book's source code on GitHub does not include the FMOD library and header files. Luckily, FMOD is free to download and has very favorable licensing terms for commercial projects. (See the FMOD site for details.) To download the FMOD library, go to the FMOD site (https://fmod.com) and create an account.

Once you have an account on the FMOD website, click the Download link. From here, find the downloads for the FMOD Studio API. Make sure you select the version 1.09.09 from the Version dropdown. (Version 1.10.x or newer may not work with this chapter's code.) Next, select Windows if you're developing on Windows or Mac if you're developing on Mac.

On Windows, run the installer and choose the default installation directories. Choosing a different directory doesn't work out of the box because the Visual Studio project file points directly to the default directories. However, if you really want to install the FMOD API to another directory, you can change the project file (which means changing the include directories, the library directories, and the post-build step that copies DLL files to the executable directory).

On Mac, the FMOD API download is a DMG package file. Open this package file and copy all its contents into the `External/FMOD` directory in your copy of the book's source code. You should end up with an `External/FMOD/FMOD Programmers API` directory after copying.

To make sure the installation worked properly, try opening the `Chapter07/Chapter07-Windows.sln` file on a PC or `Chapter07-mac.xcodeproj` on a Mac and make sure you can compile and run the code.

> ### note
>
> With the exception of Chapter 8, "Input Systems," every chapter after this one also uses the audio code from this chapter. Therefore, it's important to ensure that you install FMOD properly, or none of the subsequent chapters' projects will run.

Creating an Audio System

Much as the `Renderer` class is separate from the `Game`, it's sensible to create a new `AudioSystem` class that handles audio. This helps ensure that the FMOD API calls aren't all over the codebase.

Listing 7.1 shows the initial declaration of `AudioSystem`. The declarations of the `Initialize`, `Shutdown`, and `Update` functions are standard at this point. The member variables include pointers to the FMOD Studio system as well as the Low Level API system. You'll mostly use the `mSystem` pointer, but this listing includes a `mLowLevelSystem` pointer as well.

Listing 7.1   Initial `AudioSystem` Declaration

```cpp
class AudioSystem
{
public:
    AudioSystem(class Game* game);
    ~AudioSystem();

    bool Initialize();
    void Shutdown();
    void Update(float deltaTime);
private:
    class Game* mGame;
    // FMOD studio system
    FMOD::Studio::System* mSystem;
    // FMOD Low-level system (in case needed)
    FMOD::System* mLowLevelSystem;
};
```

The header `fmod_studio.hpp` defines the FMOD Studio API types. However, to avoid this include, `AudioSystem.h` instead creates forward declarations of the FMOD types. This way, you only need to include the FMOD header in `AudioSystem.cpp`.

Initializing FMOD, which is handled in `AudioSystem::Initialize`, involves several steps. First, call `Debug_Initialize` to set up error logging:

```
FMOD::Debug_Initialize(
   FMOD_DEBUG_LEVEL_ERROR, // Log only errors
   FMOD_DEBUG_MODE_TTY // Output to stdout
);
```

The first parameter to `Debug_Initialize` controls the verbosity of the logging messages. (The default is quite verbose.) The second parameter specifies where to write log messages. In this case, log messages write to `stdout`. For games that have custom debug code, it's also possible to declare a custom callback function for all FMOD log messages.

> ### note
>
> Initializing debug logging is relevant only if you're using the logging build of FMOD, as is the case in this chapter. Enabling error logging is extremely useful during development, but a shipped version of a game shouldn't include logging.

Next, construct an instance of an FMOD Studio system with this code:

```
FMOD_RESULT result;
result = FMOD::Studio::System::create(&mSystem);
if (result != FMOD_OK)
{
   SDL_Log("Failed to create FMOD system: %s",
      FMOD_ErrorString(result));
   return false;
}
```

Note that the function call returns an `FMOD_RESULT`. An FMOD function always returns a result value to let the caller know if everything went okay. The `FMOD_ErrorString` function converts the error code into a human-readable message. In this case, if the system fails to create, `AudioSystem::Initialize` returns `false`.

After constructing the system, the next step is to call `initialize` on the FMOD system:

```
result = mSystem->initialize(
   512,                     // Max number of concurrent sounds
   FMOD_STUDIO_INIT_NORMAL, // Use default settings
   FMOD_INIT_NORMAL,        // Use default settings
   nullptr                  // Usually null
);
// Validate result == FMOD_OK...
```

The first parameter here specifies the maximum number of channels. The next two parameters can adjust the behavior of both the FMOD Studio and FMOD Low Level APIs. For now, stick to the default parameters. You use the last parameter if you want to use extra driver data, but because you usually don't, this parameter usually is `nullptr`.

> **note**
>
> FMOD uses a naming convention in which member functions begin with a lowercase letter. This is different from this book's naming convention, which uses an uppercase letter for the first letter of a member function.

Finally, you grab and save the Low Level system pointer to complete initialization:

```
mSystem->getLowLevelSystem(&mLowLevelSystem);
```

For now, `AudioSystem`'s `Shutdown` and `Update` functions each make a single function call. `Shutdown` calls `mSystem->release()`, while `Update` calls `mSystem->update()`. FMOD requires calling the `update` function once per frame. This function performs actions such as updating 3D audio calculations.

As with `Renderer`, you then add an `AudioSystem` pointer as a member variable to `Game`:

```
class AudioSystem* mAudioSystem;
```

`Game::Initialize` then creates and calls `mAudioSystem->Initialize()`, `UpdateGame` calls `mAudioSystem->Update(deltTime)`, and `Shutdown` calls `mAudioSystem->Shutdown`.

For convenience, a `Game::GetAudioSystem` function returns the `AudioSystem` pointer.

With these functions, FMOD now initializes and updates. Of course, no sounds are playing yet.

Banks and Events

In FMOD Studio, **events** correspond to sounds played in the game. An event can have multiple associated sound files, parameters, information about the event's timing, and so on. Rather than play back sound files directly, the game plays these events.

A **bank** is a container for events, sample data, and streaming data. **Sample data** is the raw audio data that events reference. This data comes from the sound files that the sound designer imports into FMOD Studio (such as WAV or OGG files). At runtime, sample data is either preloaded or loaded on demand. However, an event cannot play until its associated sample data is in memory. Most in-game sound effects use sample data. **Streaming data** is sample data that streams into memory in small pieces at a time. Events using streaming data can start playing without preloading the data. Music and dialogue files typically use streaming data.

A sound designer creates one or more banks in FMOD Studio. Then the game runtime needs to load in these banks. After it loads the banks, the events contained within are accessible.

There are two different classes associated with events in FMOD. **EventDescription** contains information about an event, such as its associated sample data, volume settings, parameters, and so on. **EventInstance** is an active instance of an event, and it is what plays the event. In other words, EventDescription is like a type of event, while EventInstance is an instance of that type. For example, if there's an explosion event, it will globally have one EventDescription, but it can have any number of EventInstances based on the number of active explosion instances.

To track loaded banks and events, you add two maps to the private data in AudioSystem:

```
// Map of loaded banks
std::unordered_map<std::string, FMOD::Studio::Bank*> mBanks;
// Map of event name to EventDescription
std::unordered_map<std::string, FMOD::Studio::EventDescription*> mEvents;
```

Both maps have strings for their keys. The string in mBanks is the filename of the bank, while the string in mEvents is the name assigned by FMOD for the event. FMOD events have names in the form of a path—for example, event:/Explosion2D.

Loading/Unloading Banks

Loading a bank minimally requires calling the loadBank function on the mSystem object. However, this does not load the sample data and does not give easy access to the event descriptions. It makes sense to create a new function in AudioSystem called LoadBank, as shown in Listing 7.2, that does a bit more than the minimum loadBank call. Once the bank loads, you add the bank to the mBanks map. You then load the sample data for the bank. Then use getEventCount and getEventList to get the list of all event descriptions in the bank. Finally, you add each of these event descriptions to the mEvents map so they are easily accessible.

Listing 7.2 `AudioSystem::LoadBank` Implementation

```
void AudioSystem::LoadBank(const std::string& name)
{
    // Prevent double-loading
    if (mBanks.find(name) != mBanks.end())
    {
        return;
    }
```

```
// Try to load bank
FMOD::Studio::Bank* bank = nullptr;
FMOD_RESULT result = mSystem->loadBankFile(
    name.c_str(), // File name of bank
    FMOD_STUDIO_LOAD_BANK_NORMAL, // Normal loading
    &bank // Save pointer to bank
);

const int maxPathLength = 512;
if (result == FMOD_OK)
{
    // Add bank to map
    mBanks.emplace(name, bank);
    // Load all non-streaming sample data
    bank->loadSampleData();
    // Get the number of events in this bank
    int numEvents = 0;
    bank->getEventCount(&numEvents);
    if (numEvents > 0)
    {
        // Get list of event descriptions in this bank
        std::vector<FMOD::Studio::EventDescription*> events(numEvents);
        bank->getEventList(events.data(), numEvents, &numEvents);
        char eventName[maxPathLength];
        for (int i = 0; i < numEvents; i++)
        {
            FMOD::Studio::EventDescription* e = events[i];
            // Get the path of this event (like event:/Explosion2D)
            e->getPath(eventName, maxPathLength, nullptr);
            // Add to event map
            mEvents.emplace(eventName, e);
        }
    }
}
}
```

Similarly, you create an `AudioSystem::UnloadBank` function. This function first removes all the bank's events from the `mEvents` banks, unloads the sample data, unloads the bank, and removes the bank from the `mBanks` map.

For easy cleanup, you also create an `AudioSystem::UnloadAllBanks` function. This function just unloads all banks and clears out `mEvents` and `mBanks`.

Every FMOD Studio project has two default bank files named `"Master Bank.bank"` and `"Master Bank.strings.bank"`. The FMOD Studio runtime does not have access to any other banks or events unless it loads in the two master banks first. Because the master banks always exist, you load them in `AudioSystem::Initialize` with the following code:

```
// Load the master banks (strings first)
LoadBank("Assets/Master Bank.strings.bank");
LoadBank("Assets/Master Bank.bank");
```

Note how the code loads the master strings bank first. The master strings bank is a special bank that contains the human-readable names of all events and other data in the FMOD Studio project. If you don't load this bank, the names are inaccessible in code. Without the names, the code needs to use **GUID**s (globally unique IDs) to access all the FMOD Studio data. This means that, technically, loading the master strings bank is optional, but loading the strings makes the `AudioSystem` easier to implement.

Creating and Playing Event Instances

Given an FMOD `EventDescription`, the `createInstance` member function creates an FMOD `EventInstance` for that event. Once you have an `EventInstance`, the `start` function begins playing it. So, a first pass of a `PlayEvent` function in `AudioSystem` might look like this:

```
void AudioSystem::PlayEvent(const std::string& name)
{
    // Make sure event exists
    auto iter = mEvents.find(name);
    if (iter != mEvents.end())
    {
        // Create instance of event
        FMOD::Studio::EventInstance* event = nullptr;
        iter->second->createInstance(&event);
        if (event)
        {
            // Start the event instance
            event->start();
            // Release schedules destruction of the event
            // instance when it stops.
            // (Non-looping events automatically stop.)
            event->release();
        }
    }
}
```

Although this version of `PlayEvent` is simple to use, it does not expose much FMOD functionality. For example, if the event is a looping event, there's no way to stop the event. There's also no way to set any event parameters, change the volume of the event, and so on.

It might be tempting to return the `EventInstance` pointer directly from `PlayEvent`. Then, the caller can access all the FMOD member functions. However, this is not ideal because it exposes FMOD API calls outside the audio system. This means that any programmer who wants to simply play and stop sounds would need some knowledge of the FMOD API.

Exposing the raw pointer also might be dangerous because of the way FMOD cleans up memory for event instances. After calling the `release` function, FMOD destroys the event sometime after the event stops. If a caller has access to the `EventInstance` pointer, dereferencing it after destruction might cause a memory access violation. Skipping the `release` call is also not a great idea because then the system will leak memory over time. Therefore, you need a more robust solution.

The SoundEvent Class

Rather than directly return an `EventInstance` pointer from `PlayEvent`, you can track each active event instance via an integer ID. Next, you can create a new class called `SoundEvent` that allows manipulation of the active events, using the integer IDs to reference events. `PlayEvent` then returns an instance of `SoundEvent`.

To track event instances, `AudioSystem` needs a new map of unsigned integers to event instances:

```
std::unordered_map<unsigned int,
    FMOD::Studio::EventInstance*> mEventInstances;
```

You also add a static `sNextID` variable that's initialized to 0. Each time `PlayEvent` creates an event instance, it increments `sNextID` and adds the event instance to the map with that new ID. Then `PlayEvent` returns a `SoundEvent` with the associated ID, as in Listing 7.3. (The declaration of `SoundEvent` is forthcoming.)

Listing 7.3 `AudioSystem::PlayEvent` Implementation with Event IDs

```
SoundEvent AudioSystem::PlayEvent(const std::string& name)
{
    unsigned int retID = 0;
    auto iter = mEvents.find(name);
    if (iter != mEvents.end())
    {
        // Create instance of event
        FMOD::Studio::EventInstance* event = nullptr;
        iter->second->createInstance(&event);
        if (event)
        {
            // Start the event instance
            event->start();
            // Get the next id, and add to map
```

```
            sNextID++;
            retID = sNextID;
            mEventInstances.emplace(retID, event);
        }
    }
    return SoundEvent(this, retID);
}
```

Because `sNextID` is an `unsigned int`, IDs start repeating after more than 4 billion calls to `PlayEvent`. This should not be an issue, but it's something to keep in mind.

Note that `PlayEvent` no longer calls `release` on the event instance. Instead, `AudioSystem::Update` now handles cleaning up event instances that are no longer needed. Every frame, `Update` checks the playback state of each event instance in the map by using `getPlayBackState`. It releases any event instances in the stopped state and then removes them from the map. This assumes that stopping an event means freeing it is okay. A caller who wants to keep an event around can pause it instead of stopping it. Listing 7.4 shows the implementation of `Update`.

Listing 7.4 `AudioSystem::Update` Implementation with Event IDs

```
void AudioSystem::Update(float deltaTime)
{
    // Find any stopped event instances
    std::vector<unsigned int> done;
    for (auto& iter : mEventInstances)
    {
        FMOD::Studio::EventInstance* e = iter.second;
        // Get the state of this event
        FMOD_STUDIO_PLAYBACK_STATE state;
        e->getPlaybackState(&state);
        if (state == FMOD_STUDIO_PLAYBACK_STOPPED)
        {
            // Release the event and add id to done
            e->release();
            done.emplace_back(iter.first);
        }
    }
    // Remove done event instances from map
    for (auto id : done)
    {
        mEventInstances.erase(id);
    }
    // Update FMOD
    mSystem->update();
}
```

Next, you add a `GetEventInstance` helper function to `AudioSystem` that takes in an ID. If the ID exists in the map, this function returns the corresponding `EventInstance` pointer. Otherwise, `GetEventInstance` returns `nullptr`. To prevent every class from accessing event instances, `GetEventInstance` is in the protected section of `AudioSystem`. But because `SoundEvent` needs access to this function, `SoundEvent` is declared as a friend of `AudioSystem`.

Listing 7.5 gives the declaration of `SoundEvent`. Most notably, its member data includes a pointer to the `AudioSystem` and the ID. Note that while the default constructor is public, the constructor with parameters is protected. Because `AudioSystem` is a friend of `SoundEvent`, only `AudioSystem` has access to this constructor. This ensures that only `AudioSystem` can assign IDs to `SoundEvents`. The rest of the functions in `SoundEvent` are wrappers for various event instance functionality, such as pausing sound events, changing their volume, and setting event parameters.

Listing 7.5 `SoundEvent` Declaration

```
class SoundEvent
{
public:
    SoundEvent();
    // Returns true if associated FMOD event instance exists
    bool IsValid();
    // Restart event from beginning
    void Restart();
    // Stop this event
    void Stop(bool allowFadeOut = true);
    // Setters
    void SetPaused(bool pause);
    void SetVolume(float value);
    void SetPitch(float value);
    void SetParameter(const std::string& name, float value);
    // Getters
    bool GetPaused() const;
    float GetVolume() const;
    float GetPitch() const;
    float GetParameter(const std::string& name);
protected:
    // Make this constructor protected and AudioSystem a friend
    // so that only AudioSystem can access this constructor.
    friend class AudioSystem;
    SoundEvent(class AudioSystem* system, unsigned int id);
private:
    class AudioSystem* mSystem;
    unsigned int mID;
};
```

The implementations for most of the `SoundEvent` member functions have very similar syntax. They call `GetEventInstance` to get an `EventInstance` pointer and then call some function on the `EventInstance`. For example, the implementation of `SoundEvent::SetPaused` is as follows:

```
void SoundEvent::SetPaused(bool pause)
{
    auto event = mSystem ?
        mSystem->GetEventInstance(mID) : nullptr;
    if (event)
    {
        event->setPaused(pause);
    }
}
```

Note how the code validates that both the `mSystem` and event pointer are non-null. This ensures that even if the ID is not in the map, the function will not crash. Similarly, the `SoundEvent::IsValid` function returns `true` only if `mSystem` is non-null and the ID is in the event instance map in `AudioSystem`.

With this code hooked up, it's now possible to control events after they start playing. For example, the following starts playing an event called `Music` and saves the `SoundEvent` in `mMusicEvent`:

```
mMusicEvent = mAudioSystem->PlayEvent("event:/Music");
```

Elsewhere, you can toggle the pause state of the music event with this:

```
mMusicEvent.SetPaused(!mMusicEvent.GetPaused());
```

With the addition of `SoundEvent`, you now have a reasonable integration of FMOD for 2D audio.

3D Positional Audio

For 3D games, most sound effects are **positional**. This means that an object in the world, such as a fireplace, **emits** a sound. The game has a **listener**, or a virtual microphone, that picks up this sound. For example, if the listener faces the fireplace, it should sound like the fireplace is in front. Similarly, if the listener has his or her back to the fireplace, the fireplace should sound like it's behind.

Positional audio also means that as the listener gets farther away from a sound, the volume of the sound decreases, or **attenuates**. A **falloff function** describes how the volume of the sound attenuates as the listener gets farther away. In FMOD Studio, 3D sound events can have user-configurable falloff functions.

The effect of positional audio is most apparent in a **surround sound** configuration where there are more than two speakers as output devices. For example, the common **5.1** configuration (see Figure 7.1) features front-left, front-center, front-right, back-left, and back-right speakers as well as a subwoofer (or LFE) for low frequency sounds. For the example of the in-game fireplace, if the player faces the fireplace on screen, he or she expects the sound to come out of the front speakers.

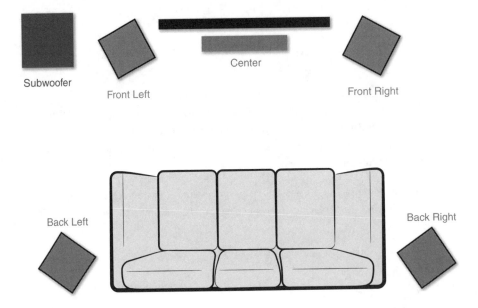

Figure 7.1 A 5.1 surround sound configuration

Luckily, FMOD has built-in support for positional audio. To integrate this into a game, you must provide position and orientation data for both the listener and any active 3D event instances. There are three parts to this: setting up the listener, adding positional functionality to `SoundEvent`, and creating an `AudioComponent` to associate actors with sound events.

Setting Up a Basic Listener

A common approach is to use the camera as the listener. In this case, the position of the listener is the position of the camera in the world, and the orientation of the listener is the orientation of the camera. This approach works great for games with a first-person camera, such as this chapter's game project. However, third-person cameras have additional issues to consider, as discussed later in this section.

A trap to watch out for when using any 3D positional audio library (not just FMOD) is that the library may use a different coordinate system than the game. For example, FMOD uses a left-handed coordinate system with +z forward, +x right, and +y up. However, our game uses a left-handed coordinate system with +x forward, +y right, +z up. So, when passing position and directions from the game to FMOD, you must convert the coordinates. This just involves switching around some components when converting between a `Vector3` and FMOD's vector type, `FMOD_VECTOR`. To help with this, declare a `VecToFMOD` helper function:

```
FMOD_VECTOR VecToFMOD(const Vector3& in)
{
    // Convert from our coordinates (+x forward, +y right, +z up)
    // to FMOD (+z forward, +x right, +y up)
    FMOD_VECTOR v;
    v.x = in.y;
    v.y = in.z;
    v.z = in.x;
    return v;
}
```

Next, you add a function called `SetListener` to `AudioSystem`. This function, as shown in Listing 7.6, takes in the view matrix and sets the listener's position, forward, and up vectors from the view. This means the same code that sets the renderer's view matrix can also call `SetListener`. This process involves a little bit of math. Recall that the view matrix transforms from world space to view space. However, the listener requires a world space position and orientation.

Extracting this information from the view matrix requires several steps. First, you invert the view matrix. Given this inverted view matrix, the first three components of the fourth row (returned by `GetTranslation`) correspond to the world space position of the camera. The first three components of the third row (returned by `GetZAxis`) correspond to the forward vector, and the first three components of the second row (returned by `GetYAxis`) correspond to the up vector. You use `VecToFMOD` on all three of these vectors to convert them to the FMOD coordinate system.

Listing 7.6 `AudioSystem::SetListener` Implementation

```
void AudioSystem::SetListener(const Matrix4& viewMatrix)
{
    // Invert the view matrix to get the correct vectors
    Matrix4 invView = viewMatrix;
    invView.Invert();
    FMOD_3D_ATTRIBUTES listener;
    // Set position, forward, up
    listener.position = VecToFMOD(invView.GetTranslation());
    // In the inverted view, third row is forward
    listener.forward = VecToFMOD(invView.GetZAxis());
    // In the inverted view, second row is up
    listener.up = VecToFMOD(invView.GetYAxis());
```

```
    // Set velocity to zero (fix if using Doppler effect)
    listener.velocity = {0.0f, 0.0f, 0.0f};
    // Send to FMOD (0 = only one listener)
    mSystem->setListenerAttributes(0, &listener);
}
```

Note that `SetListener` currently sets the `velocity` parameter of `FMOD_3D_ATTRIBUTES` to all zeros. The velocity parameter matters only when enabling the Doppler effect on sound events, as discussed later in this section.

Adding Positional Functionality to `SoundEvent`

Each `EventInstance` has 3D attributes that describe its world position and orientation. It makes sense to integrate this into the existing `SoundEvent` class with two new functions, `Is3D` and `Set3DAttributes`, both in Listing 7.7.

When you create a sound event in FMOD Studio, the event can be 2D or 3D. The `Is3D` function returns `true` if the event is 3D, and it returns `false` otherwise.

The `Set3DAttributes` function takes in a world transform matrix and converts it into FMOD's 3D attributes. This makes it simple to pass in the world transform matrix of an `Actor` to update the position and orientation of the event. Note that this function *does not* need to invert the matrix because the matrix is already in world space. However, it's still necessary to convert between the game and FMOD coordinate systems.

Listing 7.7 `SoundEvent`'s `Is3D` and `Set3DAttributes` Implementation

```cpp
bool SoundEvent::Is3D() const
{
    bool retVal = false;
    auto event = mSystem ? mSystem->GetEventInstance(mID) : nullptr;
    if (event)
    {
        // Get the event description
        FMOD::Studio::EventDescription* ed = nullptr;
        event->getDescription(&ed);
        if (ed)
        {
            ed->is3D(&retVal); // Is this 3D?
        }
    }
    return retVal;
}
```

```
void SoundEvent::Set3DAttributes(const Matrix4& worldTrans)
{
    auto event = mSystem ? mSystem->GetEventInstance(mID) : nullptr;
    if (event)
    {
        FMOD_3D_ATTRIBUTES attr;
        // Set position, forward, up
        attr.position = VecToFMOD(worldTrans.GetTranslation());
        // In world transform, first row is forward
        attr.forward = VecToFMOD(worldTrans.GetXAxis());
        // Third row is up
        attr.up = VecToFMOD(worldTrans.GetZAxis());
        // Set velocity to zero (fix if using Doppler effect)
        attr.velocity = { 0.0f, 0.0f, 0.0f };
        event->set3DAttributes(&attr);
    }
}
```

Creating an `AudioComponent` to Associate Actors with Sound Events

The premise behind an `AudioComponent` class is to associate sound events with specific actors. This way, when the actor moves, `AudioComponent` can update the associated event's 3D attributes. Furthermore, if an actor dies, any sound events associated with the actor can stop.

Listing 7.8 gives the declaration of `AudioComponent`. Note that it has two different `std::vector` collections: one for 2D events and one for 3D events. The only member functions not inherited from `Component` are `PlayEvent` and `StopAllEvents`.

Listing 7.8 `AudioComponent` Declaration

```
class AudioComponent : public Component
    AudioComponent(class Actor* owner, int updateOrder = 200);
    ~AudioComponent();

    void Update(float deltaTime) override;
    void OnUpdateWorldTransform() override;

    SoundEvent PlayEvent(const std::string& name);
    void StopAllEvents();
private:
    std::vector<SoundEvent> mEvents2D;
    std::vector<SoundEvent> mEvents3D;
};
```

The `AudioComponent::PlayEvent` function first calls `PlayEvent` on the `AudioSystem`. You then check whether the event is 3D to determine which of the two vectors should store the `SoundEvent`. Finally, if the event is 3D, call `Set3DAttributes` on it:

```
SoundEvent AudioComponent::PlayEvent(const std::string& name)
{
    SoundEvent e = mOwner->GetGame()->GetAudioSystem()->PlayEvent(name);
    // Is this 2D or 3D?
    if (e.Is3D())
    {
        mEvents3D.emplace_back(e);
        // Set initial 3D attributes
        e.Set3DAttributes(mOwner->GetWorldTransform());
    }
    else
    {
        mEvents2D.emplace_back(e);
    }
    return e;
}
```

The `AudioComponent::Update` function (omitted here) removes any of the events in `mEvents2D` or `mEvents3D` that are no longer valid. (`IsValid` returns `false`.)

Next, you add an override of `OnUpdateWorldTransform`. Recall that every time the owning actor computes its world transform matrix, it notifies each component by calling this function. For the `AudioComponent`, it needs to update the 3D attributes of any 3D events in `mEvents3D` every time the world transform changes:

```
void AudioComponent::OnUpdateWorldTransform()
{
    Matrix4 world = mOwner->GetWorldTransform();
    for (auto& event : mEvents3D)
    {
        if (event.IsValid())
        {
            event.Set3DAttributes(world);
        }
    }
}
```

Finally, `AudioComponent::StopAllEvents` (also omitted here) simply calls stop on every event in both vectors and clears out the vectors. The destructor of `AudioComponent` calls this function, but there may be other situations in which a game wants to just stop the sound events for an actor.

With these additions, you can attach an `AudioComponent` to an actor and play sound events on the audio component. The `AudioComponent` then automatically updates the 3D attributes of the associated events as needed.

The Listener in a Third-Person Game

The listener directly using the camera position and orientation works great for first-person games where the camera is from the perspective of the player's character. However, things are not quite as simple for a third-person game where the camera follows the player character. Figure 7.2 illustrates the side view of a third-person game. The player character is at position *P*, and the camera is at position *C*. Position *A* represents a sound effect right next to the player character. Position *B* is a sound effect close to the camera.

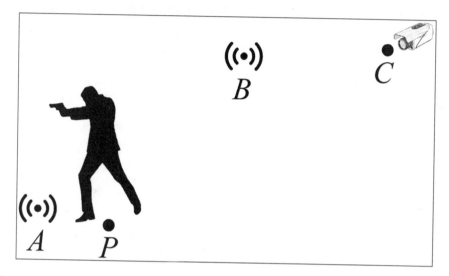

Figure 7.2 Sound effects in a third-person game

Now suppose the listener uses the camera position and orientation, as in the preceding code. In this case, both sounds *A* and *B* will sound like they're in front. This is good because both sound effects are visible onscreen, so you as the player should perceive the sounds in front. However, sound *B* will sound closer than sound *A*. This seems weird because you expect sounds right next to the player to be louder. And even if there were no sound *B*, any sounds right next to (or even *on*) the player will always have some attenuation applied to them, which may be frustrating for the sound designer.

If instead the listener uses the player position and orientation, then sound *A* will be louder than sound *B*. However, sound *B* then sounds like it's behind because it's positioned behind the player. This is very weird because the sound is onscreen, so you expect it to sound like it's in front.

What you effectively want is an attenuation based on the player position but an orientation based on the camera. Guy Somberg describes a great solution to this problem (his book is listed in the "Additional Reading" section at the end of the chapter), which involves just a little bit of vector math. Given the player at position P, the camera at position C, and a sound at position S, first compute two vectors—one vector from camera to sound and the other vector from player to sound:

$$PlayerToSound = S - P$$
$$CameraToSound = S - C$$

The length of the *PlayerToSound* vector is the desired distance for attenuation. The normalized *CameraToSound* vector is the correct heading. Scalar multiplying the normalized *CameraToSound* vector by the length of *PlayerToSound* yields a virtual position for the sound:

$$VirtualPos = \|PlayerToSound\| \frac{CameraToSound}{\|CameraToSound\|}$$

This virtual position, illustrated in Figure 7.3, yields both the correct attenuation *and* the correct orientation of the sound. The listener itself then directly uses the camera, as before.

Note that this approach may be untenable if true world positions of sounds are necessary for other calculations (such as for occlusion, discussed later in this chapter).

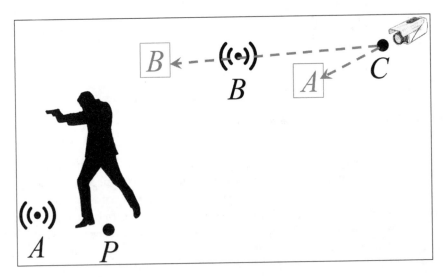

Figure 7.3 Sound effects in a third-person game with virtual positions

The Doppler Effect

Imagine standing on a street corner. While the police car is approaching, the pitch of the siren sound is increased. Conversely, after the police car passes, the pitch of the sound decreases. This is the Doppler effect in action, and it is illustrated in Figure 7.4.

The **Doppler effect** (or Doppler shift) occurs because sound waves take time to travel through the air. As the police car gets closer, each sound wave starts closer, which means the waves arrive closer together. This causes a perceived increase in frequency, leading to the heightened pitch. The true pitch of the sound is audible when the car is right next to the listener. Finally, as the car travels off, the opposite effect occurs: The sound waves arrive farther apart, yielding a lower pitch. The Doppler effect applies to all types of waves, but sound waves are the most easily observable.

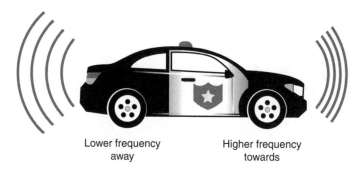

Lower frequency
away

Higher frequency
towards

Figure 7.4 Doppler effect

In a game, the Doppler effect can create more realistic sounds for objects such as vehicles. FMOD can automatically calculate Doppler pitch shifts; it just requires passing in the correct velocities both in `setListenerAttributes` and `set3DAttributes`. This means the game likely needs a more correct physics-based movement approach with forces, as briefly discussed in Chapter 3, "Vectors and Basic Physics."

There also are some additional Doppler parameters accessible through the Low Level API. The `set3DSettings` function sets these parameters:

```
mLowLevelSystem->set3DSettings(
    1.0f,  // Doppler scale, 1 = normal, higher exaggerates effect
    50.0f, // How many game units = 1 meter (our game is ~50)
    1.0f   // (Not for Doppler, leave at 1)
);
```

Mixing and Effects

One of the advantages of digitized sounds is that manipulation during playback is easy. You've already manipulated sounds as they play to account for the sound's position relative to the listener. The term **digital signal processing** (**DSP**) refers to computational manipulation of a signal. For audio, adjusting the volume or pitch of the signal is a type of DSP.

Two other common DSP effects in games are reverb and equalization. **Reverb** simulates sound bouncing in an enclosed area. For example, sound effects while inside a cave have an echo because of waves bouncing off the walls. **Equalization**, on the other hand, tries to normalize the volume levels of sounds into a set range.

FMOD Studio allows configuration of chains of DSP effects. In other words, a sound can pass through multiple stages that modify the signal prior to output. Although each sound event can have its own DSP chain, a more common approach is to group sounds into types. Then, different groups can have different effects applied to them.

Buses

In FMOD Studio, a **bus** is a grouping of sounds. For example, you might have a bus for sound effects, a bus for music, and a bus for dialogue. Each bus can individually have different DSP effects attached to it, and at runtime you can adjust buses. For instance, many games offer separate volume sliders for different categories of sound. This is straightforward to implement with buses.

By default, every project has a master bus, specified by the root path `bus:/`. However, a sound designer can add any number of additional buses. So, much as with loading in event descriptions on bank load, you can load in buses at the same time. First, you add a map of buses to `AudioSystem`:

```
std::unordered_map<std::string, FMOD::Studio::Bus*> mBuses;
```

Then, when loading in a bank, call `getBusCount` and `getBusList` on the bank to get the list of buses to add to `mBuses`. (This is very similar to the code for event descriptions, so this chapter omits that code.)

Next, add functions to `AudioSystem` to control the buses:

```
float GetBusVolume(const std::string& name) const;
bool GetBusPaused(const std::string& name) const;
void SetBusVolume(const std::string& name, float volume);
void SetBusPaused(const std::string& name, bool pause);
```

The implementations of these functions are similar—and aren't surprising. For example, `SetVolume` is as follows:

```
void AudioSystem::SetBusVolume(const std::string& name, float volume)
{
    auto iter = mBuses.find(name);
    if (iter != mBuses.end())
    {
        iter->second->setVolume(volume);
    }
}
```

In this chapter's game project, there are three buses in all: master, SFX, and music. The sound effects, including footsteps, the fire loop, and the explosion sound, go through the SFX bus, while the background music goes through the music bus.

Snapshots

In FMOD, **snapshots** are special types of events that control buses. Because they're just events, they use the same event interface that already exists, and the existing `PlayEvent` function works with them. The only difference is that their paths begin with `snapshot:/` instead of `event:/`.

Note that the game project in this chapter uses a snapshot to enable reverb on the SFX bus. Use the R key to enable or disable reverb.

Occlusion

Imagine living in a small apartment when there's a party next door. The music at the party is very loud and travels through your wall. You've heard the song before, but it sounds different when listening through the wall. The bass is more dominant, and it's tough to hear the high-frequency parts. This is **sound occlusion**, as illustrated in Figure 7.5(a).

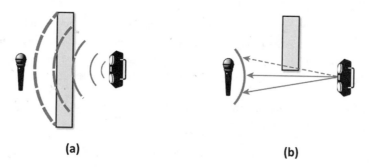

(a)   **(b)**

Figure 7.5 Sound occlusion (a) and testing for occlusion (b)

Sound occlusion occurs when a sound does not have a direct path from emitter to listener. Instead, the sound must travel through some material to reach the listener. The predominant result of sound occlusion is a **low-pass filter**, which means a reduction in volume of higher-frequency sounds.

Implementing occlusion involves two separate tasks: detection of occlusion and modification of occluded sounds. One approach for detection is to draw line segments between the emitter and an arc around the listener, as in Figure 7.5(b). If all line segments can reach the listener without hitting any objects, there is no occlusion. If only some line segments reach, there's partial occlusion, and if none reach, there's full occlusion. This style of detection requires the collision calculations covered in Chapter 10, "Collision Detection."

Modifying occluded sounds in FMOD is simple. However, it requires calls into the Low Level API. First, when initializing FMOD, you enable software low-pass filtering:

```
result = mSystem->initialize(
    512, // Max number of concurrent sounds
    FMOD_STUDIO_INIT_NORMAL, // Use default settings
    FMOD_INIT_CHANNEL_LOWPASS, // Initialize low-pass filter
    nullptr // Usually null
);
```

Next, each event instance affected by occlusion needs to set occlusion parameters. For example, the following code enables occlusion for event:

```
// Flush commands to ensure channel group is available
mSystem->flushCommands();
// Get channel group from event
FMOD::ChannelGroup* cg = nullptr;
event->getChannelGroup(&cg);
// Set occlusion factor - occFactor ranges
// from 0.0 (no occlusion) to 1.0 (full occlusion)
cg->set3DOcclusion(occFactor, occFactor);
```

Game Project

This chapter's game project demonstrates most of the audio features covered in this chapter. The code is available in the book's GitHub repository, in the Chapter07 directory. Open Chapter07-windows.sln on Windows and Chapter07-mac.xcodeproj on Mac. The FMOD Studio project corresponding to this chapter's content is in FMODStudio/Chapter07.

A music track plays in the background. As the player walks around, a footstep event triggers. The sphere emits a positional fire loop sound.

As before, use WASD to move around. The following keys provide additional behavior:

- E—Play the explosion (2D) sound
- M—Pause/unpause the music event
- R—Enable/disable reverb on the SFX bus (via a snapshot)
- 1—Set footstep parameter to default
- 2—Set footstep parameter to grass
- -—Reduce master bus volume
- +—Increase master bus volume

All the corresponding function calls for these behaviors are in `Game::HandleKeyPress`.

The sound files used in this chapter come from https://opengameart.org and http://freesound.org, both great websites for finding quality sounds for games.

Summary

Most games require audio systems that go beyond simply playing sound files. Using the FMOD API, this chapter shows how to implement a production-quality sound system into the game. The audio system loads in banks and plays back events. The `SoundEvent` class tracks outstanding event instances and allows manipulation of these instances.

Positional audio simulates sounds in a 3D environment. By setting the properties of the listener and every 3D event instance, the audio behaves as it would in a real 3D environment. While a first-person game can directly use the camera orientation and position for the listener, a third-person game is more complex. For fast-moving objects, the Doppler effect shifts the pitch of the sound as it approaches or leaves.

Mixing adds more control to the sound environment. Buses group different sounds into independently controllable categories. Snapshots can also dynamically change the buses at runtime, such as enabling DSP effects like reverb. Finally, occlusion simulates sounds traveling through surfaces.

Additional Reading

Until recently, it was difficult to find references for aspiring game audio programmers. However, Guy Somberg's excellent book has articles from many experienced developers. This book provides the most complete coverage of game audio currently available.

Somberg, Guy, Ed. *Game Audio Programming: Principles and Practices*. Boca Raton: CRC Press, 2016.

Exercises

This chapter's exercises build on the audio features implemented in the chapter. In the first exercise you add support for the Doppler effect, while in the second exercise you implement virtual positions for a third-person listener.

Exercise 7.1

Adjust the listener and event instance attribute code so that it correctly sets the velocity parameters. Then make the sphere actor (created in `Game::LoadData`) move quickly back and forth to test the Doppler effect. Use `set3DSettings` to adjust the intensity of the effect as needed. The Doppler effect should be perceptible for the fire loop audio sound once it's working correctly.

Exercise 7.2

Implement virtual positions for event instances as per the third-person listener formulas in this chapter. Replace the `CameraActor` class in the Chapter 7 game project with the `CameraActor` class in `Exercise/7.2` on GitHub. This version of the `CameraActor` implements a basic third-person camera for testing purposes.

CHAPTER 8

INPUT SYSTEMS

This chapter takes an in-depth look at a wide variety of input devices for games, including the keyboard, mouse, and controller. It explores how to integrate these devices into a cohesive system that all actors and components in the game can interact with for their input needs.

Input Devices

Without input, games would be a static form of entertainment, much like film or television. The fact that a game responds to the keyboard, mouse, controller, or another input device is what enables interactivity. You query these input devices for their current state during the "process input" phase of the game loop, and this affects the game world during the "update game world" phase of the game loop.

Some input devices yield only Boolean values. For example, for the keyboard you can check the state of each key, and this state is true or false, depending on whether the key is down or up. There's no way for us to discern whether a key is "half pressed" because the input device simply doesn't detect this.

Other input devices give a range of values. For example, most joysticks yield a range of values in two axes that you can use to determine how far the user has moved the joystick in a specific direction.

Many of the devices used in games are **composite**, meaning they combine multiple types of inputs into one. For example, a typical controller might have two joysticks and triggers that yield a range of values, as well as other buttons that yield only Boolean values. Similarly, the movement of the mouse or scroll wheel might be some range, but the mouse buttons may be Boolean.

Polling

Earlier in this book, you used the SDL_GetKeyboardState function to get the Boolean state of every key on the keyboard. With the additions in Chapter 3, "Vectors and Basic Physics," you then passed this keyboard state to every actor's ProcessInput function, which in turn passes it to every component's ProcessInput function. Then, in these functions you can query the state of a specific key to decide whether to perform an action, such as moving the player character forward when pressing the W key. Because you're checking the value of a specific key on every frame, this approach is considered **polling** the state of the key.

Input systems designed around polling are conceptually simple to understand, and for this reason many game developers prefer to use a polling approach. It works especially well for things like character movement because you need to know the state of some input device on every frame and update the character movement based on that. And, in fact, you will stick to this basic polling approach for most of the input needs in the code for this book.

Positive and Negative Edges

Consider a game where pressing the spacebar causes a character to jump. On every frame, you check the state of the spacebar. Suppose the spacebar is up for the first three frames, and then the player presses the spacebar prior to frame 4. The player continues to hold the spacebar down until prior to frame 6 and then releases it. You can draw this as a graph, as in Figure 8.1, where the x-axis corresponds to the time at each frame and the y-axis corresponds to the binary value for that frame. On frame 4, the spacebar changes from 0 to 1, and on frame 6, the spacebar changes back from 1 to 0. The frame where the input changes from 0 to 1 is a **positive edge** (or rising edge), and the frame where the input changes from 1 to 0 is a **negative edge** (or falling edge).

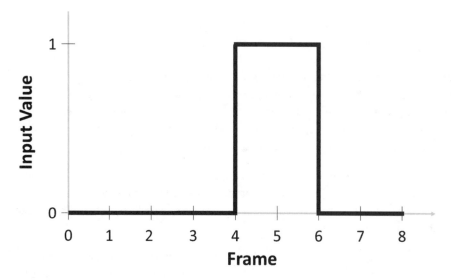

Figure 8.1 Graph of the spacebar polled over nine frames

Now consider what would happen if the process input for the character simply said the following (in pseudocode):

```
if (spacebar == 1)
    character.jump()
```

For the sample input in Figure 8.1, this code would call the `character.jump()` function twice: once on frame 4 and once on frame 5. And if the player held the button for 10 frames instead of 2, then you'd call `character.jump()` 10 times. Clearly, you don't want the character to jump every frame when the `spacebar` value is 1. Instead, you should only call `character.jump()` on the frame where the spacebar has a positive edge. For the input graph in Figure 8.1, this is on frame 4. This way, for every press of the spacebar, regardless of how long the player holds the spacebar, the character jumps only once. In this case, you want pseudocode like this:

```
if (spacebar has positive edge)
    character.jump()
```

The "has positive edge" term in the pseudocode means that on the last frame the key was 0, and on this frame the key is 1. But with the current method of using `SDL_GeyKeyboardState` to get the state of the keyboard on the current frame, it might not be apparent how to implement this. If you add a variable called `spacebarLast` that you initialize to 0, you can use this variable to track the value in the last frame. Then you initiate the jump only if the value in the last frame is 0 and the value in this frame is 1:

```
if (spacebar == 1 and spacebarLast == 0)
    character.jump()

spacebarLast = spacebar
```

Consider what happens in the case of the example in Figure 8.1. On frame 3, you set `spacebarLast` to the current value of `spacebar`, or 0. Then, on frame 4, `spacebar` is 1 while `spacebarLast` is 0, so you trigger `character.jump()`. After this, `spacebarLast` becomes the current value of `spacebar`, or 1. Then on frame 5, both spacebar and `spacebarLast` are 1, so the character doesn't jump.

You could use this pattern throughout the code. However, it would be nice to have a system that tracks values of keys on the previous frame automatically. That way, you could easily ask the system whether a key has a positive edge or negative edge, which might reduce the burden for other programmers on the team.

If you generalize the approach of storing the value of the input last frame and comparing it to the value this frame, there are four possible results, as shown in Table 8.1. If both values are 0, the button state is `None`. Similarly, if both values are 1, this means the player holds the key for consecutive frames, or the button state is `Held`. Finally, if the values are different, it's either a positive edge or negative edge, which you denote with the button states `Pressed` and `Released`, respectively.

Table 8.1 Four Possible Input States, Given the Value in the Last Frame and in the Current Frame

Last Frame	Current Frame	Button State
0	0	None
0	1	Pressed
1	0	Released
1	1	Held

Consider how you might use this for a game where the player can hold a key to charge up an attack. On the frame on which you detect the `Pressed` state of the key, you begin charging the attack. Then as long as the key's state on subsequent frames remains `Held`, you continue to charge the attack. Finally, when the key's state becomes `Released`, it means the player let go of the key, and you can now execute the attack with the appropriate charge level.

But for actions such as just moving forward if W is 1, you'd rather just use the old approach, where you check the value of the input on that frame. In this chapter's input system, you will give the option of either querying this basic value or querying for the different input states.

Events

Recall from Chapter 1, "Game Programming Overview," that SDL generates different events that the program can optionally respond to. Currently, you respond to the SDL_Quit event, which occurs when the player tries to close the window. Game::ProcessInput checks every frame if there are events in the queue and can selectively choose to respond to them.

SDL also generates events for input devices. For example, every time the player presses a key on the keyboard, SDL generates an SDL_KEYDOWN event (corresponding to the Pressed button state). Conversely, every time the player releases a key, it generates an SDL_KEYUP event (corresponding to the Released state). If you only care about positive and negative edges, then this is a very quick way to set up code to respond to these actions.

However, for the case of pressing W to move forward, this means you need extra code to track whether W is held because you only get the negative and positive edges from the SDL events. Although you can certainly design an input system entirely based around events, this chapter uses SDL events only when required (such as for mouse wheel scrolling).

There is one subtle relationship between SDL events and the various polling functions. The keyboard state you get from SDL_GetKeyboardState updates only *after* calling SDL_PollEvents in the message pump loop. This means you can delineate when the state data changes between frames because you know where the code calls SDL_PollEvents. This comes in handy when implementing an input system that saves the data for the previous frame.

Basic InputSystem Architecture

Before diving into each of the different input devices, let's consider a structure for an input system. Currently you let actors and components know about the current keyboard state via ProcessInput. However, this mechanism means that ProcessInput currently cannot access the mouse or controller without directly calling SDL functions. While this works for a simple game (and it's the approach largely used outside this chapter), it's better if the programmers writing the code for actors and components do not need much specific knowledge of SDL functions. Furthermore, some SDL input functions return the difference in state between calls of the function. If you call those functions more than once during one frame, you'll get values of zero after the first call.

To solve this problem, you can have the InputSystem class populate data in a helper class called InputState. You can then pass this InputState by const reference to actors/components via their `ProcessInput` function. You can also add several helper functions to `InputState` to make it easy to query whatever state the actor/component cares about.

Listing 8.1 shows the initial declaration of the relevant pieces. First, declare a `ButtonState` enum to correspond to the four different states outlined in Table 8.1. Next, declare an `InputState` struct (which currently has no members). Finally, you declare `InputSystem`, which contains `Initialize/Shutdown` functions (much like `Game`). It also has a `PrepareForUpdate` function that is called before `SDL_PollEvents`, and then an `Update` function that is called after polling events. The `GetState` function returns a `const` reference to the `InputState` it holds as member data.

Listing 8.1 Basic `InputSystem` Declarations

```
enum ButtonState
{
    ENone,
    EPressed,
    EReleased,
    EHeld
};

// Wrapper that contains current state of input
struct InputState
{
    KeyboardState Keyboard;
};

class InputSystem
{
public:
    bool Initialize();
    void Shutdown();

    // Called right before SDL_PollEvents loop
    void PrepareForUpdate();
    // Called right after SDL_PollEvents loop
    void Update();

    const InputState& GetState() const { return mState; }
private:
    InputState mState;
};
```

To integrate this code into the game, you add an `InputSystem` pointer to the member data of `Game` called `mInputSystem`. `Game::Initialize` allocates and initializes `InputSystem` and `Game::Shutdown` shuts down and deletes it.

Next, you change the declaration of `ProcessInput` in both `Actor` and `Component` to the following:

```
void ProcessInput(const InputState& state);
```

Recall that in `Actor`, `ProcessInput` is not overridable because it calls `ProcessInput` on all the attached components. However, actors also have an overridable `ActorInput` function for any input specific to that actor. So, you similarly change the declaration of `ActorInput` to take in a constant `InputState` reference.

Finally, the implementation of `Game::ProcessInput` changes to the following outline of steps:

```
void Game::ProcessInput()
{
    mInputSystem->PrepareForUpdate();

    // SDL_PollEvent loop...

    mInputSystem->Update();
    const InputState& state = mInputSystem->GetState();

    // Process any keys here as desired...

    // Send state to all actor's ProcessInput...
}
```

With the `InputSystem` in place, you now have the basics needed to add support for several input devices. For each of these devices, you need to add a new class to encapsulate the state and add an instance of this class to the `InputState` struct.

Keyboard Input

Recall that the `SDL_GetKeyboardState` function returns a pointer to the keyboard state. Notably, the return value of `SDL_GetKeyboardState` does not change throughout the lifetime of the application, as it points to internal SDL data. Therefore, to track the current state of the keyboard, you merely need a single pointer that you initialize once. However, because SDL overwrites the current keyboard state when you call `SDL_PollEvents`, you need a separate array to save the previous frame state.

This leads naturally to the member data in the declaration of `KeyboardState`, shown in Listing 8.2. You have a pointer that points to the current state and an array for the previous state. The size of the array corresponds to the size of the buffer that SDL uses for keyboard scan codes. For the member functions of `KeyboardState`, you provide both a method to get the basic current value of a key (`GetKeyValue`) and one that returns one of the four button states (`GetKeyState`). Finally, you make `InputSystem` a friend of `KeyboardState`. This makes it easy for `InputSystem` to directly manipulate the member data of `KeyboardState`.

Listing 8.2 `KeyboardState` Declaration

```
class KeyboardState
{
public:
    // Friend so InputSystem can easily update it
    friend class InputSystem;

    // Get just the boolean true/false value of key
    bool GetKeyValue(SDL_Scancod keyCode) const;

    // Get a state based on current and previous frame
    ButtonState GetKeyState(SDL_Scancode keyCode) const;
private:
    // Current state
    const Uint8* mCurrState;
    // State previous frame
    Uint8 mPrevState[SDL_NUM_SCANCODES];
};
```

Next, you add a `KeyboardState` instance called `Keyboard` to the member data of `InputState`:

```
struct InputState
{
    KeyboardState Keyboard;
};
```

Next, you need to add code to both `Initialize` and `PrepareForUpdate` within `InputSystem`. In `Initialize`, you need to first set the `mCurrState` pointer and then also zero out the memory of `mPrevState` (because before the game starts, the keys have no previous state). You get the current state pointer from `SDL_GetKeyboardState`, and you can clear the memory with `memset`:

```
// (In InputSystem::Initialize...)
// Assign current state pointer
mState.Keyboard.mCurrState = SDL_GetKeyboardState(NULL);
```

```
// Clear previous state memory
memset(mState.Keyboard.mPrevState, 0,
   SDL_NUM_SCANCODES);
```

Then in `PrepareForUpdate`, you need to copy all the "current" data to the previous buffer. Remember that when you call `PrepareForUpdate`, the "current" data is stale from the previous frame. This is because you call `PrepareForUpdate` when you're on a new frame *but* haven't called `SDL_PollEvents` yet. This is critical because `SDL_PollEvents` is what updates the internal SDL keyboard state data (which you're pointing to with `mCurrState`). So, before SDL overwrites the current state, use `memcpy` to copy from the current buffer to the previous buffer:

```
// (In InputSystem::PrepareForUpdate...)
memcpy(mState.Keyboard.mPrevState,
   mState.Keyboard.mCurrState,
   SDL_NUM_SCANCODES);
```

Next, you need to implement the member functions in `KeyboardState`. `GetKeyValue` is straightforward. It simply indexes into the `mCurrState` buffer and returns `true` if the value is 1 and `false` if the value is 0.

The `GetKeyState` function, shown in Listing 8.3, is slightly more complex. It uses both the current frame's and previous frame's key state to determine which of the four button states to return. This simply maps the entries in Table 8.1 into source code.

Listing 8.3 `KeyboardState::GetKeyState` Implementation

```
ButtonState KeyboardState::GetKeyState(SDL_Scancode keyCode) const
{
    if (mPrevState[keyCode] == 0)
    {
        if (mCurrState[keyCode] == 0)
        { return ENone; }
        else
        { return EPressed; }
    }
    else // Prev state must be 1
    {
        if (mCurrState[keyCode] == 0)
        { return EReleased; }
        else
        { return EHeld; }
    }
}
```

With this `KeyboardState` code, you can still access the value of a key with the `GetKeyValue` function. For example, the following checks if the current value of the spacebar is `true`:

```
if (state.Keyboard.GetKeyValue(SDL_SCANCODE_SPACE))
```

However, the advantage of the `InputState` object is that you can also query the button state of a key. For example, the following code in `Game::ProcessInput` detects if the button state of the Escape key is `EReleased`, and it exits only at that point:

```
if (state.Keyboard.GetKeyState(SDL_SCANCODE_ESCAPE)
    == EReleased)
{
   mIsRunning = false;
}
```

This means that initially pressing Escape does not immediately quit the game, but releasing the key causes the game to quit.

Mouse Input

For mouse input, there are three main types of input to focus on: button input, movement of the mouse, and movement of the scroll wheel. The button input code is like the keyboard code except that the number of buttons is significantly smaller. The movement input is a little more complex because there are two modes of input (absolute and relative). Ultimately, you can still poll the mouse input with a single function call per frame. However, for the scroll wheel, SDL only reports the data via an event, so you must add some code to `InputSystem` to also process certain SDL events.

By default, SDL shows the system's mouse cursor (at least on platforms that have a system mouse cursor). However, you can enable or disable the cursor by using `SDL_ShowCursor`, passing in `SDL_TRUE` to enable it and `SDL_FALSE` to disable it. For example, this disables the cursor:

```
SDL_ShowCursor(SDL_FALSE);
```

Buttons and Position

For querying both the position of the mouse and the state of its buttons, you use a single call to `SDL_GetMouseState`. The return value of this function is a bitmask of the button state, and you pass in two integers by address to get the x/y coordinates of the mouse, like this:

```
int x = 0, y = 0;
Uint32 buttons = SDL_GetMouseState(&x, &y);
```

> **note**
>
> For the position of the mouse, SDL uses the SDL 2D coordinate system. This means that the top-left corner is (0, 0), positive x is to the right, and positive y is down. However, you can easily convert these coordinates to whichever other system you prefer.
>
> For example, to convert to the simple view-projection coordinate system from Chapter 5, "OpenGL," you can use the following two lines of code:
>
> ```
> x = x - screenWidth/2;
> y = screenHeight/2 - y;
> ```

Because the return value of `SDL_GetMouseState` is a bitmask, you need to use a bitwise-AND along with the correct bit value to find out if a specific button is up or down. For example, given the `buttons` variable populated from `SDL_GetMouseState`, the following statement is `true` if the left mouse button is down:

```
bool leftIsDown = (buttons & SDL_BUTTON(SDL_BUTTON_LEFT)) == 1;
```

The `SDL_BUTTON` macro shifts a bit based on the requested button, and the bitwise-AND returns `1` if the button is down and `0` if it's up. Table 8.2 shows the button constants corresponding to the five different mouse buttons that SDL supports.

Table 8.2 SDL Mouse Button Constants

Button	Constant
Left	SDL_BUTTON_LEFT
Right	SDL_BUTTON_RIGHT
Middle	SDL_BUTTON_MIDDLE
Mouse button 4	SDL_BUTTON_X1
Mouse button 5	SDL_BUTTON_X2

You now have enough knowledge to create the initial declaration of `MouseState`, which is shown in Listing 8.4. You save a 32-bit unsigned integer for both the previous and current buttons' bitmasks and a `Vector2` for the current mouse position. Listing 8.4 omits the implementations of the button functions because they are almost identical to the functions for the keyboard keys. The only difference is that these functions use the bitmask as outlined earlier.

Listing 8.4 Initial `MouseState` Declaration

```
class MouseState
{
public:
    friend class InputSystem;

    // For mouse position
    const Vector2& GetPosition() const { return mMousePos; }

    // For buttons
    bool GetButtonValue(int button) const;
    ButtonState GetButtonState(int button) const;
private:
    // Store mouse position
    Vector2 mMousePos;
    // Store button data
    Uint32 mCurrButtons;
    Uint32 mPrevButtons;
};
```

Next, you add a `MouseState` instance called `Mouse` to `InputState`. Then, in `InputSystem`, add the following to `PrepareForUpdate`, which copies the current button state to the previous state:

```
mState.Mouse.mPrevButtons = mState.Mouse.mCurrButtons;
```

In `Update`, you call `SDL_GetMouseState` to update all the `MouseState` members:

```
int x = 0, y = 0;
mState.Mouse.mCurrButtons = SDL_GetMouseState(&x, &y);
mState.Mouse.mMousePos.x = static_cast<float>(x);
mState.Mouse.mMousePos.y = static_cast<float>(y);
```

With these changes, you can now access basic mouse information from `InputState`. For example, to determine if the left mouse button is in state `EPressed`, you use the following:

```
if (state.Mouse.GetButtonState(SDL_BUTTON_LEFT) == EPressed)
```

Relative Motion

SDL supports two different modes for detecting mouse movement. In the default mode, SDL reports the current coordinates of the mouse. However, sometimes you instead want to know the relative change of the mouse between frames. For example, in many first-person games on PC, you can use the mouse to rotate the camera. The speed of the camera's rotation depends on how fast the player moves the mouse. In this case, exact coordinates of the mouse aren't useful, but the relative movement between frames is.

You could approximate the relative movement between frames by saving the position of the mouse on the previous frame. However, SDL supports a **relative** mouse mode that instead reports the relative movement between calls to the `SDL_GetRelativeMouseState` function. The big advantage of SDL's relative mouse mode is that it hides the mouse, locks the mouse to the window, and centers the mouse on every frame. This way, it's not possible for the player to accidentally move the mouse cursor out of the window.

To enable relative mouse mode, call the following:

```
SDL_SetRelativeMouseMode(SDL_TRUE);
```

Similarly, to disable relative mouse mode, pass in `SDL_FALSE` as the parameter.

Once you've enabled relative mouse mode, instead of using `SDL_GetMouseState`, you use `SDL_GetRelativeMouseState`.

To support this in `InputSystem`, you first add a function that can enable or disable relative mouse mode:

```
void InputSystem::SetRelativeMouseMode(bool value)
{
   SDL_bool set = value ? SDL_TRUE : SDL_FALSE;
   SDL_SetRelativeMouseMode(set);

   mState.Mouse.mIsRelative = value;
}
```

You save the state of the relative mouse mode in a Boolean variable in `MouseState` that you initialize to `false`.

Next, change the code in `InputSystem::Update` so that if you're in relative mouse mode, you use the correct function to grab the position and buttons of the mouse:

```
int x = 0, y = 0;
if (mState.Mouse.mIsRelative)
{
   mState.Mouse.mCurrButtons = SDL_GetRelativeMouseState(&x, &y);
}
else
{
   mState.Mouse.mCurrButtons = SDL_GetMouseState(&x, &y);
}
mState.Mouse.mMousePos.x = static_cast<float>(x);
mState.Mouse.mMousePos.y = static_cast<float>(y);
```

With this code, you can now enable relative mouse mode and access the relative mouse position via `MouseState`.

Scroll Wheel

For the scroll wheel, SDL does not provide a function to poll the current state of the wheel. Instead, SDL generates the `SDL_MOUSEWHEEL` event. To support this in the input system, then, you must first add support for passing SDL events to `InputSystem`. You can do this via a `ProcessEvent` function, and then you update the event polling loop in `Game::ProcessInput` to pass the mouse wheel event to the input system:

```
SDL_Event event;
while (SDL_PollEvent(&event))
{
   switch (event.type)
   {
      case SDL_MOUSEWHEEL:
         mInputSystem->ProcessEvent(event);
         break;
      // Other cases omitted ...
   }
}
```

Next, in `MouseState` add the following member variable:

```
Vector2 mScrollWheel;
```

You use a `Vector2` object because SDL reports scrolling in both the vertical and horizontal directions, as many mouse wheels support scrolling in both directions.

You then need to make changes to `InputSystem`. First, implement `ProcessEvent` to read in the scroll wheel's x/y values from the `event.wheel` struct, as in Listing 8.5.

Listing 8.5 `InputSystem::ProcessEvent` Implementation for the Scroll Wheel

```
void InputSystem::ProcessEvent(SDL_Event& event)
{
   switch (event.type)
   {
   case SDL_MOUSEWHEEL:
      mState.Mouse.mScrollWheel = Vector2(
         static_cast<float>(event.wheel.x),
         static_cast<float>(event.wheel.y));
      break;
   default:
      break;
   }
}
```

Next, because the mouse wheel event only triggers on frames where the scroll wheel moves, you need to make sure to reset the `mScrollWheel` variable during `PrepareForUpdate`:

```
mState.Mouse.mScrollWheel = Vector2::Zero;
```

This ensures that if the scroll wheel moves on frame 1 but doesn't move on frame 2, you don't erroneously report the same scroll value on frame 2.

With this code, you can now access the scroll wheel state every frame with the following:

```
Vector2 scroll = state.Mouse.GetScrollWheel();
```

Controller Input

For numerous reasons, detecting controller input in SDL is more complex than for the keyboard and mouse. First, a controller has a much greater variety of sensors than a keyboard or mouse. For example, a standard Microsoft Xbox controller has two analog joysticks, a directional pad, four standard face buttons, three special face buttons, two bumper buttons, and two triggers—which is a lot of different sensors to get data from.

Furthermore, while PC/Mac users have only a single keyboard or mouse, it's possible to have multiple controllers connected. Finally, controllers support **hot swapping**, which means it's possible to plug and unplug controllers while a program is running. Combined, these elements add complexity to handling controller input.

> note
>
> Depending on the controller and your platform, you may need to first install a driver for your controller in order for SDL to detect it.

Before you can use a controller, you must first initialize the SDL subsystem that handles controllers. To enable it, simply add the `SDL_INIT_GAMECONTROLLER` flag to the `SDL_Init` call in `Game::Initialize`:

```
SDL_Init(SDL_INIT_VIDEO | SDL_INIT_AUDIO | SDL_INIT_GAMECONTROLLER);
```

Enabling a Single Controller

For now, assume that you're using only a single controller and that this controller is plugged in when the game starts. To initialize the controller, you need to use the `SDL_GameControllerOpen` function. This function returns a pointer to an `SDL_Controller` struct upon successful initialization or `nullptr` if it fails. You can then use the `SDL_Controller*` variable to query the state of the controller.

For this single controller, you first add an `SDL_Controller*` pointer called `mController` to the `InputState` member data. Then, add the following call to open controller 0:

```
mController = SDL_GameControllerOpen(0);
```

To disable a controller, you can call `SDL_GameControllerClose`, which takes the `SDL_GameController` pointer as its parameter.

> ### tip
>
> By default, SDL supports a handful of common controllers, such as the Microsoft Xbox controller. You can find controller mappings that specify the button layouts of many other controllers. The `SDL_GameControllerAddMappingsFromFile` function can load controller mappings from a supplied file. A community-maintained mapping file is available on GitHub at https://github.com/gabomdq/SDL_GameControllerDB.

Because you do not want to assume that the player has a controller, you must be vigilant to null check `mController` wherever you might want to access it in code.

Buttons

Game controllers in SDL support many different buttons. SDL uses a naming convention that mirrors the button names of a Microsoft Xbox controller. For example, the names of the face buttons are A, B, X, and Y. Table 8.3 lists the different button constants defined by SDL, where * is a wildcard that denotes multiple possible values.

Table 8.3 SDL Controller Button Constants

Button	Constant
A, B, X, or Y	`SDL_CONTROLLER_BUTTON_*` (replace * with A, B, X, or Y)
Back	`SDL_CONTROLLER_BACK`
Start	`SDL_CONTROLLER_START`
Pressing left/right stick	`SDL_CONTROLLER_BUTTON_*STICK` (replace * with LEFT or RIGHT)
Left/right shoulder	`SDL_CONTROLLER_BUTTON_*SHOULDER` (replace * with LEFT or RIGHT)
Directional pad	`SDL_CONTROLLER_BUTTON_DPAD_*` (replace * with UP, DOWN, LEFT, or RIGHT)

Note that the left and right stick buttons are for when the user physically presses in the left/right stick. Some games use pressing in the right stick for sprinting, for example.

SDL does not have a mechanism to query the state of all controller buttons simultaneously. Instead, you must individually query each button via the `SDL_GameControllerGetButton` function.

However, you can take advantage of the fact that the enum for the controller button names defines an `SDL_CONTROLLER_BUTTON_MAX` member that is the number of buttons the controller has. Thus, the first pass of the `ControllerState` class, shown in Listing 8.6, contains arrays for both the current and previous button states. The code also has a Boolean so the game code can determine whether there's a controller connected. Finally, the class has declarations for the now-standard button value/state functions.

Listing 8.6 Initial `ControllerState` Declaration

```
class ControllerState
{
public:
    friend class InputSystem;

    // For buttons
    bool GetButtonValue(SDL_GameControllerButton button) const;
    ButtonState GetButtonState(SDL_GameControllerButton button)
        const;

    bool GetIsConnected() const { return mIsConnected; }
private:
    // Current/previous buttons
    Uint8 mCurrButtons[SDL_CONTROLLER_BUTTON_MAX];
    Uint8 mPrevButtons[SDL_CONTROLLER_BUTTON_MAX];
    // Is this controlled connected?
    bool mIsConnected;
};
```

Then add an instance of `ControllerState` to `InputState`:

```
ControllerState Controller;
```

Next, back in `InputSystem::Initialize`, after you try to open controller 0, set the `mIsConnected` variable based on whether the `mController` pointer is non-null. You also clear out the memory for both `mCurrButtons` and `mPrevButtons`:

```
mState.Controller.mIsConnected = (mController != nullptr);
memset(mState.Controller.mCurrButtons, 0,
    SDL_CONTROLLER_BUTTON_MAX);
memset(mState.Controller.mPrevButtons, 0,
    SDL_CONTROLLER_BUTTON_MAX);
```

As with the keyboard, the code in `PrepareForUpdate` then copies the button states from current to previous:

```
memcpy(mState.Controller.mPrevButtons,
    mState.Controller.mCurrButtons,
    SDL_CONTROLLER_BUTTON_MAX);
```

Finally, in `Update`, loop over the `mCurrButtons` array and set the value of each element to the result of the `SDL_GameControllerGetButton` call that queries the state of that button:

```
for (int i = 0; i < SDL_CONTROLLER_BUTTON_MAX; i++)
{
    mState.Controller.mCurrButtons[i] =
        SDL_GameControllerGetButton(mController,
            SDL_GameControllerButton(i));
}
```

With this code, you can then query the state of a specific game controller button, using a pattern like the keyboard and mouse buttons. For example, this code checks if the A button on the controller has a positive edge this frame:

```
if (state.Controller.GetButtonState(SDL_CONTROLLER_BUTTON_A) == EPressed)
```

Analog Sticks and Triggers

SDL supports a total of six axes. Each analog stick has two axes: one in the x direction and one in the y direction. Furthermore, each of the triggers has a single axis. Table 8.4 shows the list of axes. (Once again, * denotes a wildcard.)

Table 8.4   SDL Controller Axis Constants

Button	Constant
Left analog stick	SDL_CONTROLLER_AXIS_LEFT* (replace * with X or Y)
Right analog stick	SDL_CONTROLLER_AXIS_RIGHT* (replace * with X or Y)
Left/right triggers	SDL_CONTROLLER_AXIS_TRIGGER* (replace * with LEFT or RIGHT)

For triggers, the value ranges from 0 to 32,767, with 0 meaning there is no pressure on the trigger. For the analog stick axes, the value ranges from -32,768 to 32,767, with 0 representing centered. A positive y-axis value corresponds to down on the analog stick, and a positive x-axis value corresponds to right.

However, an issue with continuous input such as these axes is that the ranges specified by the API are *theoretical*. Each individual device has its own imprecisions. You can observe this behavior by releasing one of the analog sticks, which returns the stick to its center. You might reasonably expect that because the stick is at rest, the values reported for the stick's x- and y-axes are zero. However, in practice the values will be *around* zero but rarely *precisely* zero. Conversely, if the player slams the stick all the way to the right, the value reported by the stick's x-axis will be *near* the maximum value but rarely *precisely* the maximum value.

This is problematic for games for two reasons. First, it may cause **phantom inputs,** where the player isn't touching an input axis but the game reports that something is happening. For example, suppose the player completely puts the controller down on a table. The player should rightfully expect that his or her character in game will not move around. However, if the issue isn't handled, the game will detect some value of input to the axis and move the character.

Furthermore, many games have the character move based on how far the analog stick is moved in one direction—so that slightly moving the stick might cause the character to slowly walk, whereas moving the stick all the way in a direction might cause the character to sprint. However, if you only make the player sprint when the axis reports the maximum value, the player will never sprint.

To solve this issue, code that processes the input from an axis should **filter** the value. Specifically, you want to interpret values *close* to zero as zero and values *close* to the minimum or maximum as the minimum or maximum. Furthermore, it's convenient for users of the input system if you convert the integral ranges into a normalized floating-point range. For the axes that yield both positive and negative values, this means a range between –1.0 and 1.0.

Figure 8.2 shows an example of such a filter for a single axis. The numbers above the line are the integral values before filtering, and the numbers below the line are the floating-point values after filtering. The area near zero that you interpreted as 0.0 is called a **dead zone**.

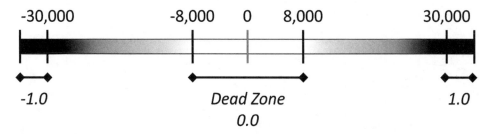

Figure 8.2 A sample filter for an axis, with the input values above and the output values below

Listing 8.7 shows the implementation the `InputSystem::Filter1D` function, which the input system uses to filter one-dimensional axes such as the triggers. First, you declare two constants for the dead zone and maximum value. Note that `deadZone` here is `250`—which is less than in Figure 8.2 because this value works better for the triggers (but you could make the constants parameters or user configurable, if desired).

Next, the code takes the absolute value of the input by using a ternary operator. If this value is less than the dead zone constant, you simply return 0.0f. Otherwise, you convert the input to a fractional value representing where it lands in between the dead zone and the maximum value. For example, an input halfway between deadZone and maxValue is 0.5f.

Then you ensure that the sign of this fractional value matches the sign of the original input. Finally, you clamp the value to the range of -1.0 to 1.0 to account for the cases where the input is greater than the maximum value constant. The implementation Math::Clamp is in the custom Math.h header file.

Listing 8.7   `Filter1D` Implementation

```
float InputSystem::Filter1D(int input)
{
    // A value < dead zone is interpreted as 0%
    const int deadZone = 250;
    // A value > max value is interpreted as 100%
    const int maxValue = 30000;

    float retVal = 0.0f;

    // Take absolute value of input
    int absValue = input > 0 ? input : -input;
    // Ignore input within dead zone
    if (absValue > deadZone)
    {
        // Compute fractional value between dead zone and max value
        retVal = static_cast<float>(absValue - deadZone) /
            (maxValue - deadZone);

        // Make sure sign matches original value
        retVal = input > 0 ? retVal : -1.0f * retVal;

        // Clamp between -1.0f and 1.0f
        retVal = Math::Clamp(retVal, -1.0f, 1.0f);
    }

    return retVal;
}
```

Using the Filter1D function, an input value of 5000 returns 0.0f, and a value of -19000 returns -0.5f.

The `Filter1D` function works well when you only need a single axis, such as for one of the triggers. However, because the analog sticks really are two different axes in concert, it's usually preferable to instead filter them in two dimensions, as discussed in the next section.

For now, you can add two floats to `ControllerState` for the left and right triggers:

```
float mLeftTrigger;
float mRightTrigger;
```

Next, in `InputSystem::Update` use the `SDL_GameControllerGetAxis` function to read in the values of both triggers and call the `Filter1D` function on this value to convert it to a range of 0.0 to 1.0 (because triggers cannot be negative). For example, the following sets the `mLeftTrigger` member:

```
mState.Controller.mLeftTrigger =
   Filter1D(SDL_GameControllerGetAxis(mController,
      SDL_CONTROLLER_AXIS_TRIGGERLEFT));
```

You then add `GetLeftTrigger()` and `GetRightTrigger()` functions to access these. For example, the following code gets the value of the left trigger:

```
float left = state.Controller.GetLeftTrigger();
```

Filtering Analog Sticks in Two Dimensions

A common control scheme for an analog stick is that the orientation of the stick corresponds to the direction in which the player's character moves. For example, pressing the stick up and to the left would cause the character onscreen to also move in that direction. To implement this, you should interpret the x- and y-axes together.

Although it is tempting to apply the `Filter1D` function to the x- and y-axes independently, doing so can cause an interesting issue. If the player moves the stick all the way up, interpreting it as a normalized vector yields <0.0, 1.0>. On the other hand, if the player moves the stick all the way up and to the right, the normalized vector is <1.0, 1.0>. The length of these two vectors is different, which is a problem if you use the length to dictate the speed at which the character moves: The character could move faster diagonally than straight in one direction!

Although you could just normalize vectors with a length greater than one, interpreting each axis independently still ultimately means you're interpreting the dead zone and maximum values as a square. A better approach is to interpret them as concentric circles, as shown in Figure 8.3. The square border represents the raw input values, the inner circle represents the dead zone, and the outer circle represents the maximum values.

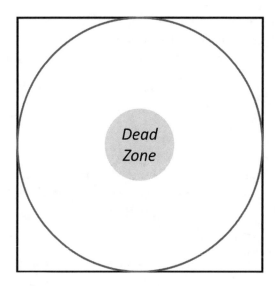

Figure 8.3 Filtering in two dimensions

Listing 8.8 gives the code for `Filter2D`, which takes in both the x- and y-axes for the analog stick and filters in two dimensions. You first create a 2D vector and then determine the length of that vector. Lengths less than the dead zone result in `Vector2::Zero`. For lengths greater than the dead zone, you determine the fractional value between the dead zone and max and set the length of the vector to this fractional value.

Listing 8.8 `InputSystem::Filter2D` Implementation

```
Vector2 InputSystem::Filter2D(int inputX, int inputY)
{
   const float deadZone = 8000.0f;
   const float maxValue = 30000.0f;

   // Make into 2D vector
   Vector2 dir;
   dir.x = static_cast<float>(inputX);
   dir.y = static_cast<float>(inputY);

   float length = dir.Length();

   // If length < deadZone, should be no input
   if (length < deadZone)
   {
      dir = Vector2::Zero;
   }
   else
```

```
{
    // Calculate fractional value between
    // dead zone and max value circles
    float f = (length - deadZone) / (maxValue - deadZone);
    // Clamp f between 0.0f and 1.0f
    f = Math::Clamp(f, 0.0f, 1.0f);
    // Normalize the vector, and then scale it to the
    // fractional value
    dir *= f / length;
}

return dir;
}
```

Next, add two `Vector2s` to `ControllerState` for the left and right sticks, respectively. You can then add code in `InputSystem::Update` to grab the values of the two axes for each stick and then run `Filter2D` to get the final analog stick value. For example, the following code filters the left stick and saves the result in the controller state:

```
x = SDL_GameControllerGetAxis(mController,
    SDL_CONTROLLER_AXIS_LEFTX);
y = -SDL_GameControllerGetAxis(mController,
    SDL_CONTROLLER_AXIS_LEFTY);
mState.Controller.mLeftStick = Filter2D(x, y);
```

Note that this code negates the y-axis value. This is because SDL reports the y-axis in the SDL coordinate system where +y is down. Thus, to get the expected values in the game's coordinate system, you must negate the value.

You can then access the value of the left stick via `InputState` with code like this:

```
Vector2 leftStick = state.Controller.GetLeftStick();
```

Supporting Multiple Controllers

Supporting multiple local controllers is more complex than supporting one. This section briefly touches on the different pieces of code needed to support it, though it does not fully implement this code. First, to initialize *all* connected controllers at startup, you need to rewrite the controller detection code to loop over all joysticks and see which ones are controllers. You can then open each one individually, with code roughly like this:

```
for (int i = 0; i < SDL_NumJoysticks(); ++i)
{
    // Is this joystick a controller?
```

```
    if (SDL_IsGameController(i))
    {
        // Open this controller for use
        SDL_GameController* controller = SDL_GameControllerOpen(i);
        // Add to vector of SDL_GameController* pointers
    }
}
```

Next, you change `InputState` to contain several `ControllerStates` instead of just one. You also update all the functions in `InputSystem` to support each of these different controllers.

To support hot swapping (adding/removing controllers while the game is running), SDL generates two different events for adding and removing controllers: `SDL_CONTROLLERDEVICEADDED` and `SDL_CONTROLLERDEVICEREMOVED`. Consult the SDL documentation for further information about these events (see https://wiki.libsdl.org/SDL_ControllerDeviceEvent).

Input Mappings

The way you currently use the data from `InputState`, the code assumes that specific input devices and keys map directly to actions. For example, if you want the player character to jump on the positive edge of a spacebar, you add code like this to `ProcessInput`:

```
bool shouldJump = state.Keyboard.GetKeyState(SDL_SCANCODE_SPACE)
                == Pressed;
```

Although this works, ideally you'd like to instead define an abstract "Jump" action. Then, you want some mechanism that allows the game code to specify that "Jump" corresponds to the spacebar key. To support this, you want a map between these abstract actions and the {device, button} pair corresponding to this abstract action. (You will actually work on implementing this in Exercise 8.2.)

You could further enhance this system by allowing for multiple bindings to the same abstract action. This means you could bind both the spacebar and the A button on the controller to "Jump."

Another advantage of defining such abstract actions is that doing so makes it easier for AI-controlled characters to perform the same action. Rather than needing some separate code path for the AI, you could update the AI character such that it generates a "Jump" action when the AI wants to jump.

Another improvement to this system allows for the definition of a movement along an axis, such as a "ForwardAxis" action that corresponds to the W and S keys *or* one of the controller axes. You can then use this action to specify movement of characters in the game.

Finally, with these types of mappings, you can add a mechanism to load mappings from a file. This makes it easy for designers or users to configure the mappings without modifying the code.

Game Project

This chapter's game project adds a full implementation of the `InputSystem` from this chapter to the game project from Chapter 5. This includes all the code for the keyboard, mouse, and controller. Recall that the Chapter 5 project uses 2D movement (so position is a `Vector2`). The code is available in the book's GitHub repository, in the `Chapter08` directory. Open `Chapter08-windows.sln` on Windows and `Chapter08-mac.xcodeproj` on Mac.

In this chapter's project, the game controller moves the spaceship. The left stick affects the direction in which the ship travels, and the right stick rotates the direction the ship faces. The right trigger fires a laser. This is a control scheme popularized by "twin stick shooter" games.

With the input system already returning 2D axes for the left/right stick, implementing the twin stick–style controls does not require too much code. First, in `Ship::ActorInput`, you add the following lines of code to grab both the left and right sticks and save them in member variables:

```
if (state.Controller.GetIsConnected())
{
    mVelocityDir = state.Controller.GetLeftStick();
    if (!Math::NearZero(state.Controller.GetRightStick().Length()))
    {
        mRotationDir = state.Controller.GetRightStick();
    }
}
```

You add the `NearZero` check for the right stick to make sure that if the player releases the right stick completely, the ship doesn't snap back to an initial angle of zero.

Next, in `Ship::UpdateActor`, add the following code to move the actor based on the direction of the velocity, a speed, and delta time:

```
Vector2 pos = GetPosition();
pos += mVelocityDir * mSpeed * deltaTime;
SetPosition(pos);
```

Note that this code reduces the speed based on how far you move the left stick in a direction because `mVelocityDir` can have a length less than one in this case.

Finally, you add the following code (also in `UpdateActor`) to rotate the actor based on the `mRotationDir`, using the `atan2` approach:

```
float angle = Math::Atan2(mRotationDir.y, mRotationDir.x);
SetRotation(angle);
```

Again, this code compiles because the `Actor` class in this chapter's project harkens back to the 2D actor class that used a single float for the angle, as opposed to the quaternion rotation used in 3D.

Figure 8.4 shows what the game looks like with the ship moving around.

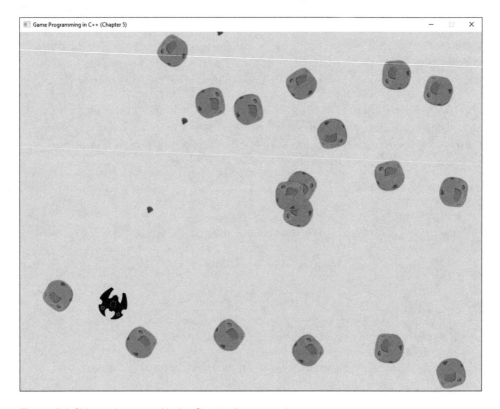

Figure 8.4 Ship moving around in the Chapter 8 game project

Summary

Many different input devices are used for games. A device might report either a single Boolean value or a range of inputs. For a key/button that reports a simple on/off state, it's useful to consider the difference between the value in this frame and the value in the last frame. This way, you can detect the positive or negative edge of the input, corresponding to a "pressed" or "released" state.

SDL provides support for the most common input devices including the keyboard, mouse, and controller. For each of these devices, you add data in an `InputState` struct that you then pass to each actor's `ProcessInput` function. This way, actors can query the input state for not only the current values of inputs but also negative and positive edges.

For devices that give a range of values, such as the triggers or analog sticks, you typically need to filter this data. This is because even when the device is at rest, the device may give spurious signals. The filtering implemented in this chapter ensures that input less than some dead zone is ignored and also ensures that you detect the maximum input even when the input is only "almost" the maximum.

This chapter's game project takes advantage of the new controller input functionality to add support for twin-stick shooter–style movement.

Additional Reading

Bruce Dawson covers how to record input and then play it back, which is very useful for testing. The Oculus SDK documentation covers how to interface with Oculus VR touch controllers. Finally, Mick West explores how to measure **input lag**, which is the amount of time it takes a game to detect inputs from controllers. Input lag is generally not the fault of the input code, but West's material is interesting nonetheless.

Dawson, Bruce. "Game Input Recording and Playback." *Game Programming Gems 2*, edited by Mark DeLoura. Cengage Learning, 2001.

Oculus PC SDK. Accessed November 29, 2017. https://developer.oculus.com/documentation/pcsdk/latest/.

West, Mick. "Programming Responsiveness." Gamasutra. Accessed November 29, 2017. http://www.gamasutra.com/view/feature/1942/programming_responsiveness.php?print=1.

Exercises

In this chapter's exercises you will improve the input system. In the first exercise you add support for multiple controllers. In the second exercise you add input mappings.

Exercise 8.1

Recall that to support multiple controllers, you need to have multiple `ControllerState` instances in the `InputState` struct. Add code to support a maximum of four controllers simultaneously. On initialization, change the code to detect any connected controllers and enable them individually. Then change the `Update` code so that it updates up to all four controllers instead of just a single one.

Finally, investigate the events that SDL sends when the user connects/disconnects controllers and add support to dynamically add and remove controllers.

Exercise 8.2

Add support for basic input mappings for actions. To do this, create a text file format that maps actions to both a device and a button/key on that device. For example, an entry in this text file to specify that the "Fire" action corresponds to the A button on the controller might look like this:

```
Fire,Controller,A
```

Then parse this data in the `InputSystem` and save it into a map. Next, add a generic `GetMappedButtonState` function to `InputState` that takes in the action name and returns the `ButtonState` from the correct device. The signature of this function is roughly the following:

```
ButtonState GetMappedButtonState(const std::string& actionName);
```

CHAPTER 9

CAMERAS

The camera determines the player's point of view in a 3D game world, and there are many different types of cameras. This chapter covers the implementation of four cameras: a first-person camera, a follow camera, an orbit camera, and a spline camera that follows paths. And because the camera often dictates the movement of the player character, this chapter also covers how to update movement code for different types of cameras.

First-Person Camera

A **first-person camera** shows the game world from the perspective of a character moving through the world. This type of camera is popular in first-person shooters such as *Overwatch* but also sees use in some role-playing games like *Skyrim* or narrative-based games such as *Gone Home*. Some designers feel that a first-person camera is the most immersive type of camera for a video game.

Even though it's tempting to think of a camera as just a view, the camera also informs the player how the player character moves around the world. This means the camera and movement system implementations depend on each other. The typical controls for a first-person shooter on PC use both the keyboard and mouse. The W/S keys move forward and backward, while the A/D keys **strafe** the character (that is, move left and right). Moving the mouse left and right rotates the character about the up axis, but moving the mouse up and down pitches only the view, *not* the character.

Basic First-Person Movement

Implementing movement is easier than working with the view, so this is a good starting point. You create a new actor called FPSActor that implements first-person movement. The forward/back movement in MoveComponent already works in the 3D world, based on the changes made in Chapter 6, "3D Graphics." Implementing strafing requires just a few updates. First, you create a GetRight function in Actor, which is like GetForward (just using the y-axis instead):

```
Vector3 Actor::GetRight() const
{
   // Rotate right axis using quaternion rotation
   return Vector3::Transform(Vector3::UnitY, mRotation);
}
```

Next, you add a new variable in MoveComponent called mStrafeSpeed that affects the speed at which the character strafes. In Update, you simply use the right vector of the actor to adjust the position based on the strafe speed:

```
if (!Math::NearZero(mForwardSpeed) || !Math::NearZero(mStrafeSpeed))
{
   Vector3 pos = mOwner->GetPosition();
   pos += mOwner->GetForward() * mForwardSpeed * deltaTime;
   // Update position based on strafe
   pos += mOwner->GetRight() * mStrafeSpeed * deltaTime;
   mOwner->SetPosition(pos);
}
```

Then in `FPSActor::ActorInput`, you can detect the `A/D` keys and adjust the strafe speed as needed. Now the character can move with standard first-person `WASD` controls.

The left/right rotation also already exists in `MoveComponent` via the angular speed. So, the next task is to convert mouse left/right movements to angular speed. First, the game needs to enable relative mouse mode via `SDL_RelativeMouseMode`. Recall from Chapter 8, "Input Systems," that relative mouse mode reports the change in (x, y) values per frame, as opposed to absolute (x, y) coordinates. (Note that in this chapter, you will directly use SDL input functions rather than the input system created in Chapter 8.)

Converting the relative x movement into an angular speed only requires a few calculations, shown in Listing 9.1. First, `SDL_GetRelativeMouseState` retrieves the (x, y) motion. The `maxMouseSpeed` constant is an expected maximum amount of relative motion possible per frame, though this might be an in-game setting. Similarly, `maxAngularSpeed` converts the motion into a rotation per second. You then take the reported x value, divide by `maxMouseSpeed`, and multiply by `maxAngularSpeed`. This yields an angular speed that's sent to the `MoveComponent`.

Listing 9.1 FPS Angular Speed Calculation from the Mouse

```
// Get relative movement from SDL
int x, y;
Uint32 buttons = SDL_GetRelativeMouseState(&x, &y);
// Assume mouse movement is usually between -500 and +500
const int maxMouseSpeed = 500;
// Rotation/sec at maximum speed
const float maxAngularSpeed = Math::Pi * 8;
float angularSpeed = 0.0f;
if (x != 0)
{
   // Convert to approximately [-1.0, 1.0]
   angularSpeed = static_cast<float>(x) / maxMouseSpeed;
   // Multiply by rotation/sec
   angularSpeed *= maxAngularSpeed;
}
mMoveComp->SetAngularSpeed(angularSpeed);
```

Camera (Without Pitch)

The first step to implement a camera is to create a subclass of `Component` called `CameraComponent`. All the different types of cameras in this chapter will subclass from `CameraComponent`, so any common camera functionality can go in this new component. The declaration of `CameraComponent` is like that of any other component subclass.

For now, the only new function is a protected function called `SetViewMatrix`, which simply forwards the view matrix to the renderer and audio system:

```
void CameraComponent::SetViewMatrix(const Matrix4& view)
{
   // Pass view matrix to renderer and audio system
   Game* game = mOwner->GetGame();
   game->GetRenderer()->SetViewMatrix(view);
   game->GetAudioSystem()->SetListener(view);
}
```

For the FPS camera specifically, you create a subclass of `CameraComponent` called `FPSCamera`, which has an overridden `Update` function. Listing 9.2 shows the code for `Update`. For now, `Update` uses the same logic as the basic camera actor introduced in Chapter 6. The camera position is the owning actor's position, the target point is an arbitrary point in the forward direction of the owning actor, and the up vector is the z-axis. Finally, `Matrix4::CreateLookAt` creates the view matrix.

Listing 9.2   `FPSCamera::Update` Implementation (Without Pitch)

```
void FPSCamera::Update(float deltaTime)
{
   // Camera position is owner position
   Vector3 cameraPos = mOwner->GetPosition();
   // Target position 100 units in front of owner
   Vector3 target = cameraPos + mOwner->GetForward() * 100.0f;
   // Up is just unit z
   Vector3 up = Vector3::UnitZ;
   // Create look at matrix, set as view
   Matrix4 view = Matrix4::CreateLookAt(cameraPos, target, up);
   SetViewMatrix(view);
}
```

Adding Pitch

Recall from Chapter 6 that yaw is rotation about the up axis and pitch is rotation about the side axis (in this case, the right axis). Incorporating pitch into the FPS camera requires a few changes. The camera still starts with the forward vector from the owner, but you apply an additional rotation to account for the pitch. Then, you derive a target from this view forward. To implement this, you add three new member variables to `FPSCamera`:

```
// Rotation/sec speed of pitch
float mPitchSpeed;
// Maximum pitch deviation from forward
float mMaxPitch;
// Current pitch
float mPitch;
```

The `mPitch` variable represents the current (absolute) pitch of the camera, while `mPitchSpeed` is the current rotation/second in the pitch direction. Finally, the `mMaxPitch` variable is the maximum the pitch can deviate from the forward vector in either direction. Most first-person games limit the total amount the player can pitch the view up or down. The reason for this limitation is that the controls seem odd if the player faces straight up. In this case, you can use 60° (converted to radians) as the default maximum pitch value.

Next, you modify `FPSCamera::Update` to take into account the pitch, as in Listing 9.3. First, the current pitch value updates based on the pitch speed and delta time. Second, you clamp the pitch to make sure it does not exceed +/– the maximum pitch. Recall from Chapter 6 that a quaternion can represent an arbitrary rotation. Thus, you can construct a quaternion representing this pitch. Note that this rotation is about the owner's right axis. (It's not just the y-axis because the pitch axis changes depending on the owner's yaw.)

The view forward is then the owner's forward vector, transformed by the pitch quaternion. You use this view forward to determine the target position that's "in front" of the camera. You also rotate the up vector by the pitch quaternion. Then you construct the look-at matrix from these vectors. The camera position is still the owner's position.

Listing 9.3 `FPSCamera::Update` Implementation (with Pitch Added)

```
void FPSCamera::Update(float deltaTime)
{
    // Call parent update (doesn't do anything right now)
    CameraComponent::Update(deltaTime);
    // Camera position is owner position
    Vector3 cameraPos = mOwner->GetPosition();

    // Update pitch based on pitch speed
    mPitch += mPitchSpeed * deltaTime;
    // Clamp pitch to [-max, +max]
    mPitch = Math::Clamp(mPitch, -mMaxPitch, mMaxPitch);
    // Make a quaternion representing pitch rotation,
    // which is about owner's right vector
    Quaternion q(mOwner->GetRight(), mPitch);

    // Rotate owner forward by pitch quaternion
    Vector3 viewForward = Vector3::Transform(
        mOwner->GetForward(), q);
    // Target position 100 units in front of view forward
    Vector3 target = cameraPos + viewForward * 100.0f;
    // Also rotate up by pitch quaternion
    Vector3 up = Vector3::Transform(Vector3::UnitZ, q);

    // Create look at matrix, set as view
    Matrix4 view = Matrix4::CreateLookAt(cameraPos, target, up);
    SetViewMatrix(view);
}
```

Finally, `FPSActor` updates the pitch speed based on the relative y motion of the mouse. This requires code in ProcessInput that is almost identical to the code you use to update the angular speed based on the x motion from Listing 9.1. With this in place, the first-person camera now pitches without adjusting the pitch of the owning actor.

First-Person Model

Although it's not strictly part of the camera, most first-person games also incorporate a first-person model. This model may have parts of an animated character, such as arms, feet, and so on. If the player carries a weapon, then when the player pitches up, the weapon appears to also aim up. You want the weapon model to pitch up even though the player character remains flat with the ground.

You can implement this with a separate actor for the first-person model. Then every frame, `FPSActor` updates the first-person model position and rotation. The position of the first-person model is the position of the `FPSActor` with an offset. This offset places the first-person model a little to the right of the actor. The rotation of the model starts with the rotation of the `FPSActor` but then has an additional rotation applied for the view pitch. Listing 9.4 shows the code for this.

Listing 9.4 Updating Position and Rotation of the First-Person Model

```
// Update position of FPS model relative to actor position
const Vector3 modelOffset(Vector3(10.0f, 10.0f, -10.0f));
Vector3 modelPos = GetPosition();
modelPos += GetForward() * modelOffset.x;
modelPos += GetRight() * modelOffset.y;
modelPos.z += modelOffset.z;
mFPSModel->SetPosition(modelPos);

// Initialize rotation to actor rotation
Quaternion q = GetRotation();

// Rotate by pitch from camera
q = Quaternion::Concatenate(q,
    Quaternion(GetRight(), mCameraComp->GetPitch()));
mFPSModel->SetRotation(q);
```

Figure 9.1 demonstrates the first-person camera with a first-person model. The aiming reticule is just a `SpriteComponent` positioned in the center of the screen.

Figure 9.1 First-person camera with first-person model

Follow Camera

A **follow camera** is a camera that follows behind a target object. This type of camera is popular in many games, including racing games where the camera follows behind a car and third-person action/adventure games such as *Horizon Zero Dawn*. Because follow cameras see use in many different types of games, there is a great deal of variety in their implementation. This section focuses on a follow camera tracking a car.

As was the case with the first-person character, you'll create a new actor called `FollowActor` to correspond to the different style of movement when the game uses a follow camera. The movement controls are W/S to move the car forward and A/D to rotate the car left/right. The normal `MoveComponent` supports both types of movements, so it doesn't require any changes here.

Basic Follow Camera

With a basic follow camera, the camera always follows a set distance behind and above the owning actor. Figure 9.2 gives the side view of this basic follow camera. The camera is a set horizontal distance *HDist* behind the car and a set vertical distance *VDist* above the car.

The target point of the camera is not the car itself but a point *TargetDist* in front of the car. This causes the camera to look at a point a little in front of the car rather than directly at the car itself.

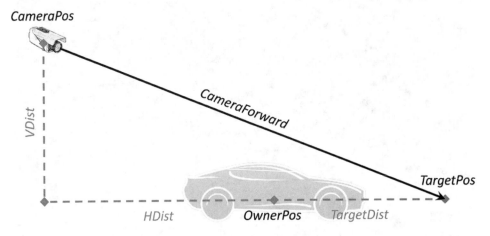

Figure 9.2 Basic follow camera tracking a car

To compute the camera position, you use vector addition and scalar multiplication. The camera position is *HDist* units behind the owner and *VDist* units above the owner, yielding the following equation:

$$CameraPos = OwnerPos - OwnerForward \cdot HDist + OwnerUp \cdot VDist$$

OwnerForward and *OwnerUp* in this equation are the owner's forward and up vectors, respectively.

Similarly, *TargetPos* is just a point *TargetDist* units in front of the owner:

$$TargetPos = OwnerPos + OwnerForward \cdot TargetDist$$

In code, you declare a new subclass of `CameraComponent` called `FollowCamera`. It has member variables for the horizontal distance (`mHorzDist`), vertical distance (`mVertDist`), and target distance (`mTargetDist`). First, you create a function to compute the camera position (using the previous equation):

```
Vector3 FollowCamera::ComputeCameraPos() const
{
    // Set camera position behind and above owner
    Vector3 cameraPos = mOwner->GetPosition();
    cameraPos -= mOwner->GetForward() * mHorzDist;
    cameraPos += Vector3::UnitZ * mVertDist;
    return cameraPos;
}
```

Next, the `FollowCamera::Update` function uses this camera position as well as a computed target position to create the view matrix:

```cpp
void FollowCamera::Update(float deltaTime)
{
    CameraComponent::Update(deltaTime);
    // Target is target dist in front of owning actor
    Vector3 target = mOwner->GetPosition() +
        mOwner->GetForward() * mTargetDist;
    // (Up is just UnitZ since we don't flip the camera)
    Matrix4 view = Matrix4::CreateLookAt(GetCameraPos(), target,
        Vector3::UnitZ);
    SetViewMatrix(view);
}
```

Although this basic follow camera successfully tracks the car as it moves through the game world, it appears very rigid. Because the camera is always a set distance from the target, it's difficult to get a sense of speed. Furthermore, when the car turns, it almost seems like the world—not the car—is turning. So even though the basic follow camera is a good starting point, it's not a very polished solution.

One simple change that improves the sense of speed is to make the horizontal follow distance a function of the speed of the owner. Perhaps at rest the horizontal distance is 350 units, but when moving at max speed it increases to 500. This makes it easier to perceive the speed of the car, but the camera still seems stiff when the car is turning. To solve the rigidity of the basic follow camera, you can add springiness to the camera.

Adding a Spring

Rather than having the camera position instantly changing to the position as per the equation, you can have the camera adjust to this position over the course of several frames. To accomplish this, you can separate the camera position into an "ideal" camera position and an "actual" camera position. The ideal camera position is the position derived from the basic follow camera equations, while the actual camera position is what the view matrix uses.

Now, imagine that there's a spring connecting the ideal camera and the actual camera. Initially, both cameras are at the same location. As the ideal camera moves, the spring stretches and the actual camera also starts to move—but at a slower rate. Eventually, the spring stretches completely, and the actual camera moves just as quickly as the ideal camera. Then, when the ideal camera stops, the spring eventually compresses back to its steady state. At this point, the ideal camera and actual camera are at the same point again. Figure 9.3 visualizes this idea of a spring connecting the ideal and actual cameras.

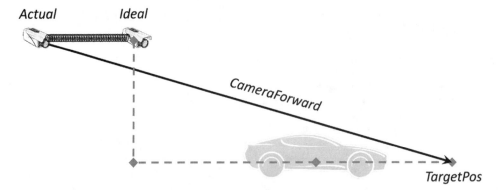

Figure 9.3 A spring connecting the ideal and actual cameras

Implementing a spring requires a few more member variables in `FollowCamera`. A spring constant (`mSpringConstant`) represents the stiffness of the spring, with a higher value being stiffer. You also must track the actual position (`mActualPos`) and the velocity (`mVelocity`) of the camera from frame to frame, so you add two vector member variables for these.

Listing 9.5 gives the code for `FollowCamera::Update` with a spring. First, you compute a spring dampening based on the spring constant. Next, the ideal position is simply the position from the previously implemented `ComputeCameraPos` function. You then compute the difference between the actual and ideal positions and compute an acceleration of the camera based on this distance and a dampening of the old velocity. Next, you compute the velocity and acceleration of the camera by using the Euler integration technique introduced in Chapter 3, "Vectors and Basic Physics." Finally, the target position calculation remains the same, and the `CreateLookAt` function now uses the actual position as opposed to the ideal one.

Listing 9.5   `FollowCamera::Update` Implementation (with Spring)

```
void FollowCamera::Update(float deltaTime)
{
    CameraComponent::Update(deltaTime);

    // Compute dampening from spring constant
    float dampening = 2.0f * Math::Sqrt(mSpringConstant);

    // Compute ideal position
    Vector3 idealPos = ComputeCameraPos();

    // Compute difference between actual and ideal
```

```
   Vector3 diff = mActualPos - idealPos;
   // Compute acceleration of spring
   Vector3 acel = -mSpringConstant * diff -
      dampening * mVelocity;

   // Update velocity
   mVelocity += acel * deltaTime;
   // Update actual camera position
   mActualPos += mVelocity * deltaTime;

   // Target is target dist in front of owning actor
   Vector3 target = mOwner->GetPosition() +
      mOwner->GetForward() * mTargetDist;

   // Use actual position here, not ideal
   Matrix4 view = Matrix4::CreateLookAt(mActualPos, target,
      Vector3::UnitZ);
   SetViewMatrix(view);
}
```

A big advantage of using a spring camera is that when the owning object turns, the camera takes a moment to catch up to the turn. This means that the side of the owning object is visible as it turns. This gives a much better sense that the object, not the world, is turning. Figure 9.4 shows the spring follow camera in action.

The red sports car model used here is "Racing Car" by Willy Decarpentrie, licensed under CC Attribution and downloaded from https://sketchfab.com.

Finally, to make sure the camera starts out correctly at the beginning of the game, you create a SnapToIdeal function that's called when the FollowActor first initializes:

```
void FollowCamera::SnapToIdeal()
{
   // Set actual position to ideal
   mActualPos = ComputeCameraPos();
   // Zero velocity
   mVelocity = Vector3::Zero;
   // Compute target and view
   Vector3 target = mOwner->GetPosition() +
      mOwner->GetForward() * mTargetDist;
   Matrix4 view = Matrix4::CreateLookAt(mActualPos, target,
      Vector3::UnitZ);
   SetViewMatrix(view);
}
```

Figure 9.4 Spring follow camera following a car as it turns

Orbit Camera

An **orbit camera** focuses on a target object and orbits around it. This type of camera might be used in a builder game such as *Planet Coaster*, as it allows the player to easily see the area around an object. The simplest implementation of an orbit camera stores the camera's position as an *offset* from the target rather than as an absolute world space position. This takes advantage of the fact that rotations always rotate about the origin. So, if the camera position is an offset from the target object, any rotations are effectively about the target object.

In this section, you'll create an `OrbitActor` as well as an `OrbitCamera` class. A typical control scheme uses the mouse for both yaw and pitch around the object. The input code that converts relative mouse movement into rotation values is like the code covered in the "First-Person Camera" section, earlier in this chapter. However, you add a restriction that the camera rotates only when the player is holding down the right mouse button (since this is a typical control scheme). Recall that the `SDL_GetRelativeMouseState` function returns the state of the buttons. The following conditional tests whether the player is holding the right mouse button:

```
if (buttons & SDL_BUTTON(SDL_BUTTON_RIGHT))
```

The `OrbitCamera` class requires the following member variables:

```
// Offset from target
Vector3 mOffset;
// Up vector of camera
Vector3 mUp;
// Rotation/sec speed of pitch
float mPitchSpeed;
// Rotation/sec speed of yaw
float mYawSpeed;
```

The pitch speed (`mPitchSpeed`) and yaw speed (`mYawSpeed`) simply track the current rotations per second of the camera for each type of rotation. The owning actor can update these speeds as needed, based on the mouse rotation. In addition, the `OrbitCamera` needs to track the offset of the camera (`mOffset`), as well as the up vector of the camera (`mUp`). The up vector is needed because the orbit camera allows full 360-degree rotations in both yaw and pitch. This means the camera could flip upside down, so you can't universally pass in (0, 0, 1) as up. Instead, you must update the up vector as the camera rotates.

The constructor for `OrbitCamera` initializes `mPitchSpeed` and `mYawSpeed` both to zero. The `mOffset` vector can initialize to any value, but here you initialize it to 400 units behind the object (−400, 0, 0). The `mUp` vector initializes to world up (0, 0, 1).

Listing 9.6 shows the implementation of `OrbitCamera::Update`. First, you create a quaternion representing the amount of yaw to apply this frame, which is about the world up vector. You use this quaternion to transform both the camera offset and up. Next, you compute the camera forward vector from the new offset. The cross product between the camera forward and camera yields the camera right vector. You then use this camera right vector to compute the pitch quaternion and transform both the camera offset and up by this quaternion, as well.

Listing 9.6 `OrbitCamera::Update` Implementation

```
void OrbitCamera::Update(float deltaTime)
{
    CameraComponent::Update(deltaTime);
    // Create a quaternion for yaw about world up
    Quaternion yaw(Vector3::UnitZ, mYawSpeed * deltaTime);
    // Transform offset and up by yaw
    mOffset = Vector3::Transform(mOffset, yaw);
    mUp = Vector3::Transform(mUp, yaw);

    // Compute camera forward/right from these vectors
    // Forward owner.position - (owner.position + offset)
    // = -offset
    Vector3 forward = -1.0f * mOffset;
    forward.Normalize();
    Vector3 right = Vector3::Cross(mUp, forward);
    right.Normalize();
```

```
    // Create quaternion for pitch about camera right
    Quaternion pitch(right, mPitchSpeed * deltaTime);
    // Transform camera offset and up by pitch
    mOffset = Vector3::Transform(mOffset, pitch);
    mUp = Vector3::Transform(mUp, pitch);

    // Compute transform matrix
    Vector3 target = mOwner->GetPosition();
    Vector3 cameraPos = target + mOffset;
    Matrix4 view = Matrix4::CreateLookAt(cameraPos, target, mUp);
    SetViewMatrix(view);
}
```

For the look-at matrix, the target position of the camera is simply the owner's position, the camera position is the owner's position plus the offset, and the up is the camera up. This yields the final orbited camera. Figure 9.5 demonstrates the orbit camera with the car as the target.

Figure 9.5 Orbit camera focused on the car

Spline Camera

A **spline** is a mathematical representation of a curve specified by a series of points on the curve. Splines are popular in games because they enable an object to smoothly move along a curve over some period. This can be very useful for a cutscene camera because the camera can follow a predefined spline path. This type of camera also sees use in games like *God of War*, where the camera follows along a set path as the player progresses through the world.

The **Catmull-Rom** spline is a type of spline that's relatively simple to compute, and it is therefore used frequently in games and computer graphics. This type of spline minimally requires four control points, named P_0 through P_3. The actual curve runs from P_1 to P_2, while P_0 is a control point prior to the curve and P_3 is a control point after the curve. For best results, you can space these control points roughly evenly along the curve—and you can approximate this with Euclidean distance. Figure 9.6 illustrates a Catmull-Rom spline with four control points.

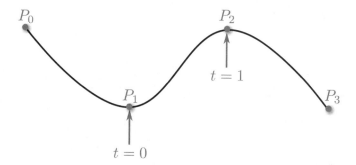

Figure 9.6 Catmull-Rom spline

Given these four control points, you can express the position between P_1 and P_2 as the following parametric equation, where $t = 0$ is at P_1 and $t = 1$ is at P_2:

$$p(t)=0.5\cdot\left(2P_1+\left(-P_0+P_2\right)t+\left(2P_0-5P_1+4P_2-P_3\right)t^2+\left(-P_0+3P_1-3P_2+P_3\right)t^3\right)$$

Although the Catmull-Rom spline equation has only four control points, you can extend the spline to any arbitrary number of control points. This works provided that there still is one point before the path and one point after the path because those control points are not part of the path. In other words, you need $n + 2$ points to represent a curve of n points. You can then take any sequence of four neighboring points and substitute them into the spline equation.

To implement a camera that follows a spline path, you first create a struct to define a spline. The only member data `Spline` needs is a vector of the control points:

```
struct Spline
{
    // Control points for spline
    // (Requires n+2 points where n is number
```

```
    // of points in segment)
    std::vector<Vector3> mControlPoints;
    // Given spline segment where startIdx = P1,
    // compute position based on t value
    Vector3 Compute(size_t startIdx, float t) const;
    size_t GetNumPoints() const { return mControlPoints.size(); }
};
```

The `Spline::Compute` function applies the spline equation given a start index corresponding to P_1 and a *t* value in the range [0.0, 1.0]. It also performs boundary checks to make sure `startIdx` is a valid index, as shown in Listing 9.7.

Listing 9.7 `Spline::Compute` Implementation

```
Vector3 Spline::Compute(size_t startIdx, float t) const
{
    // Check if startIdx is out of bounds
    if (startIdx >= mControlPoints.size())
    { return mControlPoints.back(); }
    else if (startIdx == 0)
    { return mControlPoints[startIdx]; }
    else if (startIdx + 2 >= mControlPoints.size())
    { return mControlPoints[startIdx]; }

    // Get p0 through p3
    Vector3 p0 = mControlPoints[startIdx - 1];
    Vector3 p1 = mControlPoints[startIdx];
    Vector3 p2 = mControlPoints[startIdx + 1];
    Vector3 p3 = mControlPoints[startIdx + 2];

    // Compute position according to Catmull-Rom equation
    Vector3 position = 0.5f * ((2.0f * p1) + (-1.0f * p0 + p2) * t +
        (2.0f * p0 - 5.0f * p1 + 4.0f * p2 - p3) * t * t +
        (-1.0f * p0 + 3.0f * p1 - 3.0f * p2 + p3) * t * t * t);
    return position;
}
```

The `SplineCamera` class then needs a `Spline` in its member data. In addition, it tracks the current index corresponding to P_1, the current *t* value, a speed, and whether the camera should move along the path:

```
// Spline path camera follows
Spline mPath;
// Current control point index and t
size_t mIndex;
float mT;
```

```
// Amount t changes/sec
float mSpeed;
// Whether to move the camera along the path
bool mPaused;
```

The spline camera updates by first increasing the *t* value as a function of speed and delta time. If the *t* value is greater than or equal to 1.0, P_1 advances to the next point on the path (assuming that there are enough points on the path). Advancing P_1 also means you must subtract 1 from the *t* value. If the spline has no more points, the spline camera pauses.

For the camera calculations, the position of the camera is simply the point computed from the spline. To compute the target point, you increase *t* by a small delta to determine the direction the spline camera is moving. Finally, the up vector stays at (0, 0, 1), which assumes that you do not want the spline to flip upside down. Listing 9.8 gives the code for `SplineCamera::Update`, and Figure 9.7 shows the spline camera in action.

Listing 9.8 `SplineCamera::Update` Implementation

```
void SplineCamera::Update(float deltaTime)
{
   CameraComponent::Update(deltaTime);
   // Update t value
   if (!mPaused)
   {
      mT += mSpeed * deltaTime;
      // Advance to the next control point if needed.
      // This assumes speed isn't so fast that you jump past
      // multiple control points in one frame.
      if (mT >= 1.0f)
      {
         // Make sure we have enough points to advance the path
         if (mIndex < mPath.GetNumPoints() - 3)
         {
            mIndex++;
            mT = mT - 1.0f;
         }
         else
         {
            // Path's done, so pause
            mPaused = true;
         }
      }
   }

   // Camera position is the spline at the current t/index
   Vector3 cameraPos = mPath.Compute(mIndex, mT);
   // Target point is just a small delta ahead on the spline
   Vector3 target = mPath.Compute(mIndex, mT + 0.01f);
```

```
// Assume spline doesn't flip upside-down
   const Vector3 up = Vector3::UnitZ;
   Matrix4 view = Matrix4::CreateLookAt(cameraPos, target, up);
   SetViewMatrix(view);
}
```

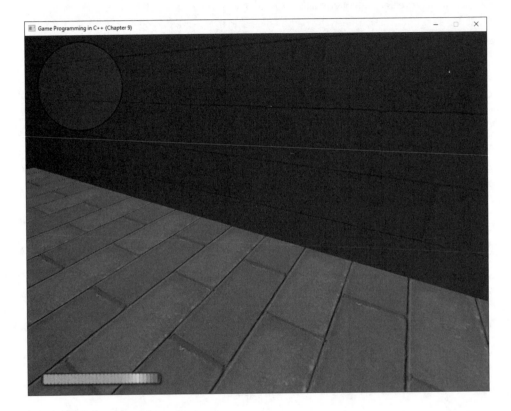

Figure 9.7 Spline camera in a game

Unprojection

Given a point in world space, to transform it into clip space, you first multiply by the view matrix followed by the projection matrix. Imagine that the player in a first-person shooter wants to fire a projectile based on the screen position of the aiming reticule. In this case, the aiming reticule position is a coordinate in screen space, but to correctly fire the projectile, you need a position in world space. An **unprojection** is a calculation that takes in a screen space coordinate and converts it into a world space coordinate.

Assuming the screen space coordinate system described in Chapter 5, "OpenGL," the center of the screen is (0, 0), the top-left corner is (−512, 384), and the bottom-right corner is (512, −384).

The first step to calculating an unprojection is converting a screen space coordinate into a normalized device coordinate with a range of [−1, 1] for both the x and y components:

$$ndcX = screenX / 512$$

$$ndcY = screenY / 384$$

However, the issue is that any single (x, y) coordinate can correspond to any z coordinate in the range [0, 1], where 0 is a point on the near plane (right in front of the camera), and 1 is a point on the far plane (the maximum distance you can see from the camera). So, to correctly perform the unprojection, you also need a z component in the range [0, 1]. You then represent this as a homogenous coordinate:

$$ndc = (ndcX, ndcY, z, 1)$$

Now you construct an unprojection matrix, which is simply the inverse of the view-projection matrix:

$$Unprojection = \left((View)(Projection) \right)^{-1}$$

When multiplying the NDC point by the unprojection matrix, the w component changes. However, you need to renormalize the w component (setting it back to 1) by dividing each component by w. This yields the following calculation for the point in world space:

$$temp = (ndc)(Unprojection)$$

$$worldPos = \frac{temp}{temp_w}$$

You add a function for an unprojection into the `Renderer` class because it's the only class with access to both the view and projection matrices. Listing 9.9 provides the implementation for `Unproject`. In this code, the `TransformWithPerspDiv` function does the w component renormalization.

Listing 9.9 `Renderer::Unproject` Implementation

```
Vector3 Renderer::Unproject(const Vector3& screenPoint) const
{
    // Convert screenPoint to device coordinates (between -1 and +1)
    Vector3 deviceCoord = screenPoint;
    deviceCoord.x /= (mScreenWidth) * 0.5f;
    deviceCoord.y /= (mScreenHeight) * 0.5f;

    // Transform vector by unprojection matrix
    Matrix4 unprojection = mView * mProjection;
    unprojection.Invert();
    return Vector3::TransformWithPerspDiv(deviceCoord, unprojection);
}
```

You can use Unproject to calculate a single world space position. However, it some cases, it's more useful to construct a vector in the direction of the screen space point, as it gives opportunities for other useful features. One such feature is **picking**, which is the capability to click to select an object in the 3D world. Figure 9.8 illustrates picking with a mouse cursor.

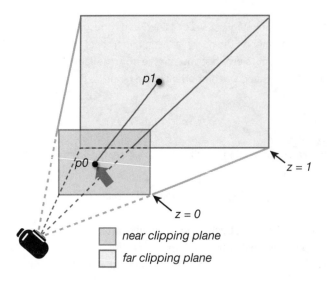

Figure 9.8 Picking with a vector in the direction of the screen space coordinate of the mouse

To construct a direction vector, you use Unproject twice, once for a start point and once for the end point. Then simply use vector subtraction and normalize this vector, as in the implementation of Renderer::GetScreenDirection in Listing 9.10. Note how the function computes both the start point of the vector in world space and the direction.

Listing 9.10 Renderer::GetScreenDirection Implementation

```
void Renderer::GetScreenDirection(Vector3& outStart,
   Vector3& outDir) const
{
   // Get start point (in center of screen on near plane)
   Vector3 screenPoint(0.0f, 0.0f, 0.0f);
   outStart = Unproject(screenPoint);

   // Get end point (in center of screen, between near and far)
   screenPoint.z = 0.9f;
   Vector3 end = Unproject(screenPoint);

   // Get direction vector
   outDir = end - outStart;
   outDir.Normalize();
}
```

Game Project

This chapter's game project demonstrates all the different cameras discussed in the chapter, as well as the unprojection code. The code is available in the book's GitHub repository, in the Chapter09 directory. Open `Chapter09-windows.sln` on Windows and `Chapter09-mac.xcodeproj` on Mac.

The camera starts out in first-person mode. To switch between the different cameras, use the 1 through 4 keys:

- 1—Enable first-person camera mode
- 2—Enable follow camera mode
- 3—Enable orbit camera mode
- 4—Enable spline camera mode and restart the spline path

Depending on the camera mode, the character has different controls, summarized below:

- First-person—Use W/S to move forward and back, A/D to strafe, and the mouse to rotate
- Follow—Use W/S to move forward and back and use A/D to rotate (yaw)
- Orbit camera mode—Hold down the right mouse button and move the mouse to rotate
- Spline camera mode—No controls (moves automatically)

In addition, in any camera mode, you can left-click to compute the unprojection. This positions two spheres—one at the "start" position of the vector and one at the "end" position.

Summary

This chapter shows how to implement many different types of cameras. The first-person camera presents the world from the perspective of a character moving through it. A typical first-person control scheme uses the WASD keys for movement and the mouse for rotation. Moving the mouse left and right rotates the character, while moving the mouse up and down pitches the view. You can additionally use the first-person view pitch to orient a first-person model.

A basic follow camera follows rigidly behind an object. However, this camera does not look polished when rotating because it's difficult to discern if the character or the world is rotating. An improvement is to incorporate a spring between "ideal" and "actual" camera positions. This adds smoothness to the camera that's especially noticeable when turning.

An orbit camera rotates around an object, typically with mouse or joystick control. To implement orbiting, you represent the camera as an offset from the target object. Then, you can apply both yaw and pitch rotations by using quaternions and some vector math to yield the final view.

A spline is a curve defined by points on the curve. Splines are popular for cutscene cameras. The Catmull-Rom spline requires a minimum of $n + 2$ points to represent a curve of n points. By applying the Catmull-Rom spline equations, you can create a camera that follows along this spline path.

Finally, an unprojection has many uses, such as selecting or picking objects with the mouse. To compute an unprojection, you first transform a screen space point into normalized device coordinates. You then multiply by the unprojection matrix, which is simply the inverse of the view-projection matrix.

Additional Reading

There are not many books dedicated to the topic of game cameras. However, Mark Haigh-Hutchinson, the primary programmer for the *Metroid Prime* camera system, provides an overview of many different techniques relevant for game cameras.

Haigh-Hutchinson, Mark. *Real-Time Cameras*. Burlington: Morgan Kaufmann, 2009.

Exercises

In this chapter's exercises, you will add features to some of the cameras. In the first exercise, you add mouse support to the follow camera, and in the second exercise, you add features to the spline camera.

Exercise 9.1

Many follow cameras have support for user-controlled rotation of the camera. For this exercise, add code to the follow camera implementation that allows the user to rotate the camera. When the player holds down the right mouse button, apply an additional pitch and yaw rotation to the camera. When the player releases the right mouse button, set the pitch/yaw rotation back to zero.

The code for the rotation is like the rotation code for the orbit camera. Furthermore, as with the orbit camera, the code can no longer assume that the z-axis is up. When the player releases the mouse button, the camera won't immediately snap back to the original orientation because of the spring. However, this is aesthetically pleasing, so there's no reason to change this behavior!

Exercise 9.2

Currently, the spline camera goes in only one direction on the path and stops upon reaching the end. Modify the code so that when the spline hits the end of the path, it starts moving backward.

CHAPTER 10

COLLISION DETECTION

You use collision detection to determine whether objects in the game world intersect with each other. While earlier chapters discuss some basic ways to check for collisions, this chapter takes a deeper look at the topic. This chapter first introduces the basic geometric types commonly used in games and then covers the calculation of intersection between these types. It concludes with a discussion of how to incorporate collisions into game behavior.

Geometric Types

Collision detection for games utilizes several different concepts from geometry and linear algebra. This section covers some fundamental geometric types commonly used in games, such as line segments, planes, and boxes. Each geometric type discussed here has a corresponding declaration in the `Collision.h` header file included in this chapter's game project.

Line Segments

A **line segment** comprises start and end points:

```
struct LineSegment
{
    Vector3 mStart;
    Vector3 mEnd;
};
```

To calculate any arbitrary point on a line segment, you can use the following parametric equation, where *Start* and *End* are the start and end points, and *t* is the parameter:

$$L(t) = Start + (End - Start)t \quad \text{where } 0 \le t \le 1$$

For convenience, you can add a member function to `LineSegment` that returns a point on the line segment given a *t* value:

```
Vector3 LineSegment::PointOnSegment(float t) const
{
    return mStart + (mEnd - mStart) * t;
}
```

The parametric representation of a line segment easily expands to define a ray or a line. A ray follows the above equation, but the bounds for *t* are as follows:

$$0 \le t \le \infty$$

Similarly, a line has an unbounded *t*:

$$-\infty \le t \le \infty$$

Line segments and rays are versatile primitives for many different types of collision detection in games. For example, firing a bullet in a straight line or testing for landing on a ground can use a line segment. You can also use line segments for aiming reticules (as in Chapter 11, "User Interfaces"), sound occlusion tests (as in Chapter 7, "Audio"), or mouse picking (as in Chapter 9, "Cameras").

Another useful operation is finding the minimal distance between a line segment and an arbitrary point. Imagine that a line segment starts at point *A* and ends at point *B*. Given an arbitrary point C, you want to find the minimal distance between the segment and point C. There are three different cases to consider, shown in Figure 10.1.

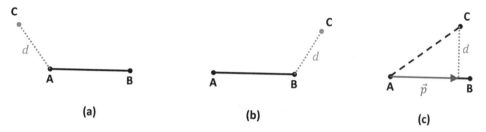

Figure 10.1 Three cases for minimal distance between a point and a line segment

In the first case, shown in Figure 10.1(a), the angle between AB and AC is greater than 90°. You can test this by using the dot product because a negative dot product between two vectors means they form an obtuse angle. If this is true, the minimal distance between C and the line segment is the length of the vector AC.

In the second case, shown in Figure 10.1(b), the angle between BA and BC is greater than 90°. As in the first case, you can test this with a dot product. If this is true, the minimal distance is the length of BC.

In the final case, shown in Figure 10.1(c), you draw a new line segment from AB to C that's perpendicular to AB. The distance of this new line segment is the minimal distance between C and AB. To figure out this line segment, you first need to compute the vector p.

You already know the direction of p, as it's in the same direction as the normalized AB. To figure out the distance of p, you apply a property of the dot product called the **scalar projection**. Given a unit vector and a non-unit vector, extend (or contract) the unit vector such that a right triangle forms with the non-unit vector. The dot product then returns the length of this extended unit vector.

In this example, the length of p is the dot product between AC and a normalized AB:

$$\|\vec{p}\| = \overline{AC} \cdot \frac{\overline{AB}}{\|\overline{AB}\|}$$

The vector p is then the scalar multiplication between the length of p and the normalized AB:

$$\vec{p} = \|\vec{p}\| \frac{\overline{AB}}{\|\overline{AB}\|}$$

Using some algebraic manipulation—and remembering that the length squared of a vector is the same as a dot product with itself—you can simplify p as follows:

$$\vec{p} = \left(\overrightarrow{AC} \cdot \frac{\overrightarrow{AB}}{\|\overrightarrow{AB}\|} \right) \frac{\overrightarrow{AB}}{\|\overrightarrow{AB}\|} = \frac{\overrightarrow{AC} \cdot \overrightarrow{AB}}{\|\overrightarrow{AB}\|} \frac{\overrightarrow{AB}}{\|\overrightarrow{AB}\|} = \frac{\overrightarrow{AC} \cdot \overrightarrow{AB}}{\|\overrightarrow{AB}\|^2} \overrightarrow{AB}$$

$$= \frac{\overrightarrow{AC} \cdot \overrightarrow{AB}}{\overrightarrow{AB} \cdot \overrightarrow{AB}} \overrightarrow{AB}$$

Finally, you construct the vector from p to AC, and the length of this vector is the minimum distance from AB to C:

$$d = \left\| \overrightarrow{AC} - \vec{p} \right\|$$

Remember that because the distance must be positive in this case, you can square both sides of the equation to instead get the minimal distance squared from AB to C:

$$d^2 = \left\| \overrightarrow{AC} - \vec{p} \right\|^2$$

This way you avoid the expensive square root operation. For the most part, you will calculate the distance squared instead of distance throughout this chapter. Listing 10.1 gives the code for this `MinDistSq` function.

Listing 10.1 `LineSegment::MinDistSq` Implementation

```
float LineSegment::MinDistSq(const Vector3& point) const
{
    // Construct vectors
    Vector3 ab = mEnd - mStart;
    Vector3 ba = -1.0f * ab;
    Vector3 ac = point - mStart;
    Vector3 bc = point - mEnd;
    // Case 1: C projects prior to A
    if (Vector3::Dot(ab, ac) < 0.0f)
    {
        return ac.LengthSq();
    }
    // Case 2: C projects after B
    else if (Vector3::Dot(ba, bc) < 0.0f)
    {
        return bc.LengthSq();
    }
    // Case 3: C projects onto line
    else
    {
        // Compute p
        float scalar = Vector3::Dot(ac, ab)
```

```
              / Vector3::Dot(ab, ab);
       Vector3 p = scalar * ab;
       // Compute length squared of ac - p
       return (ac - p).LengthSq();
   }
}
```

Planes

A **plane** is a flat, two-dimensional surface that extends infinitely, much as a line is a one-dimensional object that extends infinitely. In a game, you may use a plane as an abstraction for the ground or walls. The equation of a plane is as follows:

$$P \cdot \hat{n} + d = 0$$

where P an arbitrary point on the plane, n is the normal to the plane, and d is the signed minimal distance between the plane and the origin.

In code, a typical test is whether a point lies on the plane (and thus satisfies the plane equation). Because of this, the definition of the `Plane` struct only stores the normal and d:

```
struct Plane
{
   Vector3 mNormal;
   float mD;
};
```

By definition, a triangle lies on a single plane. So, given a triangle, you can derive the equation of that plane. You compute the normal to the triangle with the cross product, which corresponds to the normal of the plane. You already know an arbitrary point on the plane, as well, because all three of the vertices of the triangle are on the plane. Given this normal and point, you can then solve for d, as in Listing 10.2.

Listing 10.2 Constructing a Plane from Three Points

```
Plane::Plane(const Vector3& a, const Vector3& b, const Vector3& c)
{
   // Compute vectors from a to b and a to c
   Vector3 ab = b - a;
   Vector3 ac = c - a;
   // Cross product and normalize to get normal
   mNormal = Vector3::Cross(ab, ac);
   mNormal.Normalize();
   // d = -P dot n
   mD = -Vector3::Dot(a, mNormal);
}
```

Finding the minimum distance between an arbitrary point C and the plane is simpler than for a line segment, though it also uses the scalar projection property of the dot product. Figure 10.2 illustrates the calculation, showing the plane from a side view.

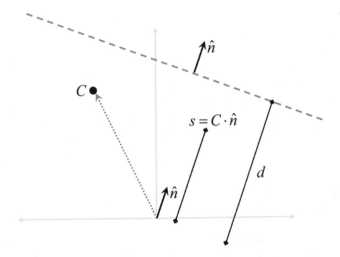

Figure 10.2 Calculations for minimum distance between point C and a plane

You already know the normal of the plane n and the minimal distance d between the origin and the plane. You need to calculate the scalar projection of C onto the normal n, which is simply the dot product:

$$s = C \cdot \hat{n}$$

Then, the difference between d and this scalar projection yields a signed distance between C and the plane:

$$SignedDist = s - d = C \cdot \hat{n} - d$$

A negative value means C is below the plane (facing away from the normal), while a positive value means C is above. The signed distance calculation translates to the following code:

```
float Plane::SignedDist(const Vector3& point) const
{
    return Vector3::Dot(point, mNormal) - mD;
}
```

Bounding Volumes

Modern 3D games have characters and objects drawn with thousands of triangles. When determining whether two objects collide, it's not efficient to test all the triangles comprising the object. For this reason, games use simplified **bounding volumes**, such as boxes or spheres.

When deciding whether two objects intersect, the game uses the simplified collision for calculations. This yields greatly improved efficiency.

Spheres

The simplest representation of the bounds of a 3D object is a sphere. The definition of a sphere only requires the position of the center of the sphere and a radius:

```
struct Sphere
{
    Vector3 mCenter;
    float mRadius;
};
```

As illustrated in Figure 10.3, bounding spheres fit around some objects better than others. For example, a sphere around a humanoid character has a lot of empty space between the character and the bounds of the sphere. Having loose bounds for an object increases the number of **false positive** collisions, meaning the bounding volumes for two objects intersect but the objects themselves do not. For instance, if a first-person shooter used bounding spheres for humanoids, players could shoot way to the left or right of a character, and the game would count that as a hit.

However, the advantage of using bounding spheres is that intersection calculations are extremely efficient. Furthermore, rotation has no effect on a sphere, so a bounding sphere works regardless of the rotation of the underlying 3D object. And for some objects, like balls, spheres perfectly express the bounds.

Figure 10.3 Bounding spheres for different objects

Axis-Aligned Bounding Boxes

In 2D, an **axis-aligned bounding box** (**AABB**) is a rectangle where the edges are parallel to either the x-axis or y-axis. Similarly, in 3D, an AABB is a rectangular prism where every face of the prism is parallel to one of the coordinate axis planes.

You can define an AABB by two points: a minimum point and a maximum point. In 2D, the minimum point corresponds to the bottom-left point, while the maximum corresponds to the top-right point. In other words, the minimum point has the minimal x and y values for the box, and the maximum point has the maximal x and y values for the box. This carries over directly to 3D, where the minimum point has the minimal x, y, and z values, and the maximum is likewise the maximal x, y, and z values. This translates to the following struct:

```
struct AABB
{
    Vector3 mMin;
    Vector3 mMax;
};
```

One useful operation with an AABB is constructing it from a series of points. For example, when loading in a model, you have a sequence of vertices, and you can use this sequence of vertices to define an AABB for the model. To do this, you can create a new function called `UpdateMinMax` that takes in a point and updates min and max, accounting for this point:

```
void AABB::UpdateMinMax(const Vector3& point)
{
    // Update each component separately
    mMin.x = Math::Min(mMin.x, point.x);
    mMin.y = Math::Min(mMin.y, point.y);
    mMin.z = Math::Min(mMin.z, point.z);
    mMax.x = Math::Max(mMax.x, point.x);
    mMax.y = Math::Max(mMax.y, point.y);
    mMax.z = Math::Max(mMax.z, point.z);
}
```

Because you do not know where the new point is in relation to all the other points, you must test every component independently to decide which components of min and max should update.

Then, given a container of points, you first initialize min and max of the AABB to the first point in the container. For each remaining point, you simply call `UpdateMinMax`:

```
// Assume points is a std::vector<Vector3>
AABB box(points[0], points[0]);
for (size_t i = 1; i < points.size(); i++)
{
    box.UpdateMinMax(points[i]);
}
```

Because an AABB must keep its sides parallel to the coordinate planes, rotating an object does not rotate the AABB. Instead, it changes the dimensions of the AABB, as in Figure 10.4. In some cases, it may be desirable not to compute AABB rotations. For example, most humanoid characters in games only rotate about the up axis. If you make the AABB for the character wide enough, rotating the character does not change the AABB enough to warrant rotating the

AABB (though watch out for animations that move the character too much). However, for other objects, it is necessary to compute a rotated AABB.

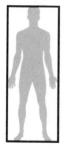  

Figure 10.4 AABBs for different orientations of a character

One way to compute an AABB after rotation is to first construct the eight points representing the corners of the AABB. These points are simply all possible permutations of the min and max x, y, and z components. Then you rotate each point individually and use the `UpdateMinMax` function to create a new AABB from these rotated points. Note that this process, shown in Listing 10.3, does not compute the minimal possible AABB of the underlying object after rotation. Thus, the game should save the original object space AABB to avoid error propagation after multiple rotations.

Listing 10.3   `AABB::Rotate` Implementation

```
void AABB::Rotate(const Quaternion& q)
{
    // Construct the 8 points for the corners of the box
    std::array<Vector3, 8> points;
    // Min point is always a corner
    points[0] = mMin;
    // Permutations with 2 min and 1 max
    points[1] = Vector3(mMax.x, mMin.y, mMin.z);
    points[2] = Vector3(mMin.x, mMax.y, mMin.z);
    points[3] = Vector3(mMin.x, mMin.y, mMax.z);
    // Permutations with 2 max and 1 min
    points[4] = Vector3(mMin.x, mMax.y, mMax.z);
    points[5] = Vector3(mMax.x, mMin.y, mMax.z);
    points[6] = Vector3(mMax.x, mMax.y, mMin.z);
    // Max point corner
    points[7] = Vector3(mMax);

    // Rotate first point
    Vector3 p = Vector3::Transform(points[0], q);
```

```
// Reset min/max to first point rotated
mMin = p;
mMax = p;
// Update min/max based on remaining points, rotated
for (size_t i = 1; i < points.size(); i++)
{
    p = Vector3::Transform(points[i], q);
    UpdateMinMax(p);
}
}
```

Oriented Bounding Boxes

An **oriented bounding box** (**OBB**) does not have the parallel restrictions of an AABB. This means that an OBB maintains the tightness of its bounds, regardless of the rotation of the underlying object, as in Figure 10.5. One way to represent an OBB is with a center point, a quaternion for the rotation, and the **extents** (width, height, and depth) of the box:

```
struct OBB
{
    Vector3 mCenter;
    Quaternion mRotation;
    Vector3 mExtents;
};
```

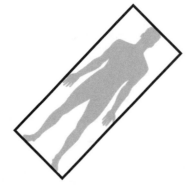

Figure 10.5 An oriented bounding box for a humanoid character that's rotated

Although it's tempting to use OBBs, the downside is that collision computations are far more expensive with OBBs than with AABBs.

Capsules

A **capsule** is a line segment with a radius:

```
struct Capsule
{
    LineSegment mSegment;
    float mRadius;
};
```

Capsules are popularly used for representing humanoid characters in a game, as in Figure 10.6. A capsule can also represent a sphere moving over a set period because there's a start point and an end point for the sphere's movement, and the sphere of course has a radius.

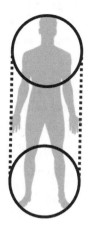

Figure 10.6 A capsule for a humanoid character

Convex Polygons

Sometimes, a game may need bounds for an object that are more accurate than any of the basic shapes. For a 2D game, the object might have bounds represented as a convex polygon. Recall that a polygon is **convex** if all its interior angles are less than 180°.

You can represent a convex polygon as a collection of vertices:

```
struct ConvexPolygon
{
   // Vertices have a clockwise ordering
   std::vector<Vector2> mVertices;
};
```

These vertices should have a set ordering, such as clockwise or counterclockwise along the polygon's edge. Without an ordering, intersections are more difficult to compute.

Note that this representation assumes that the developer correctly uses it, and it does no testing to make sure the polygon is convex and has vertices in a clockwise order.

Intersection Tests

Once the game is using geometric types to represent game objects, the next step is to test for intersections between these objects. This section looks at a series of useful tests. First, it explores whether an object contains a point. Then, it looks at intersections between different types of bounding volumes. Next, it looks at intersections between a line segment and other objects. Finally, this section covers how to handle dynamically moving objects.

Contains Point Tests

Testing whether a shape contains a point is useful by itself. For example, you might use this type of test for finding out whether a player is inside a region of the game world. In addition, some shape intersection algorithms rely on finding the point closest to an object and then figuring out if that point is inside the object. This section considers a point to be "contained" by a shape even if it's technically on one of the edges of that shape.

Sphere Contains Point Tests

To figure out if a sphere contains a point, first find the distance between the point and the center of the sphere. If this distance is less than or equal to the radius, then the sphere contains the point.

Because the distance and radius are both positive values, you can optimize this comparison by squaring both sides of the inequality. This way, you avoid the expensive square root operation and add only one multiplication, making it far more efficient:

```
bool Sphere::Contains(const Vector3& point) const
{
    // Get distance squared between center and point
    float distSq = (mCenter - point).LengthSq();
    return distSq <= (mRadius * mRadius);
}
```

AABB Contains Point Tests

Given a 2D axis-aligned box, a point is outside the box if any of the following cases are true: The point is to the left of the box, the point is to the right of the box, the point is above the box, or the point is below the box. If *none* of these cases are true, then the box *must* contain the point.

You can check for this by simply comparing components of the point to the min and max points of the box. For example, a point is to the left of the box if its x component is less than min.x.

This concept easily extends to a 3D AABB. However, instead of having four checks—one for each side of a 2D box—you have six checks because there are six faces for a 3D AABB:

```
bool AABB::Contains(const Vector3& point) const
{
    bool outside = point.x < mMin.x ||
        point.y < mMin.y ||
        point.z < mMin.z ||
        point.x > mMax.x ||
        point.y > mMax.y ||
        point.z > mMax.z;
    // If none of these are true, the point is inside the box
    return !outside;
}
```

Capsule Contains Point Tests

For testing whether a capsule contains a point, you first compute the minimum distance squared between the point and the line segment. To do so, you can use the existing `LineSegment::MinDistSq` function declared earlier. You know the capsule contains the point if that minimal distance squared is less than or equal to the radius squared:

```cpp
bool Capsule::Contains(const Vector3& point) const
{
    // Get minimal dist. sq. between point and line segment
    float distSq = mSegment.MinDistSq(point);
    return distSq <= (mRadius * mRadius);
}
```

Convex Polygon Contains Point (2D) Tests

There are multiple ways to test whether a 2D polygon contains a point. One of the simplest approaches is to construct vectors from the point to each pair of adjacent vertices. Then you can use the dot product and arccosine to find the angle formed by these vectors. If the sum of all these angles is close to 360°, then the point is inside the polygon. Otherwise, the point is outside the polygon. Figure 10.7 illustrates this concept.

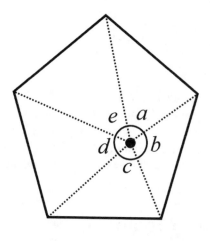

$$a + b + c + d + e = 360°$$

Figure 10.7 Angle summation test for whether a convex polygon contains a point

The code for this type of test, shown in Listing 10.4, relies on the fact that two adjacent vertices are also at adjacent indices in the convex polygon's vector.

Listing 10.4   `ConvexPolygon::Contains` Implementation

```
bool ConvexPolygon::Contains(const Vector2& point) const
{
    float sum = 0.0f;
    Vector2 a, b;
    for (size_t i = 0; i < mVertices.size() - 1; i++)
    {
        // From point to first vertex
        a = mVertices[i] - point;
        a.Normalize();
        // From point to second vertex
        b = mVertices[i + 1] - point;
        b.Normalize();
        // Add angle to sum
        sum += Math::Acos(Vector2::Dot(a, b));
    }
    // Compute angle for last vertex and first vertex
    a = mVertices.back() - point;
    a.Normalize();
    b = mVertices.front() - point;
    b.Normalize();
    sum += Math::Acos(Vector2::Dot(a, b));
    // Return true if approximately 2pi
    return Math::NearZero(sum - Math::TwoPi);
}
```

Unfortunately, this angle summation approach is not terribly efficient because it requires several square roots and arccosine calculations. Other, more complex, methods are more efficient. One such method is to draw an infinite ray starting at the point and to then count the number of edges the ray intersects. If the ray intersects an odd number of edges, the point is inside the polygon; otherwise, it's outside. This ray method works for both convex and concave polygons.

Bounding Volume Tests

It's very common to compute intersection tests between different bounding volumes. For example, imagine that both the player and the wall use AABBs for collision. When the player tries to move forward, you can test if the player's bounding volume intersects with the wall bounding volume. If they intersect, then you can fix the player's position so that they no longer intersect. (You will see how to do this later in this chapter.) This section doesn't cover all possible intersections between the different types of bounding volumes discussed earlier, but it touches on some important ones.

Sphere Versus Sphere Test

Two spheres intersect if the distance between their centers is less than or equal to the sum of their radii. As with the sphere contains point test, you can square both sides of the inequality for efficiency, using the following function:

```cpp
bool Intersect(const Sphere& a, const Sphere& b)
{
    float distSq = (a.mCenter - b.mCenter).LengthSq();
    float sumRadii = a.mRadius + b.mRadius;
    return distSq <= (sumRadii * sumRadii);
}
```

AABB Versus AABB Test

The logic for testing AABB intersection is like the logic for whether an AABB contains a point. You test for the cases where the two AABBs *cannot* intersect. If none of these tests are true, then the AABBs must intersect. For 2D AABBs, boxes A and B do not intersect if A is to the left of B, A is to the right of B, A is above B, *or* A is below B. You test this by leveraging the min and max points, as before. For example, A is to the left of B if the `max.x` of A is less than the `min.x` of B. Figure 10.8 illustrates these tests for 2D AABBs.

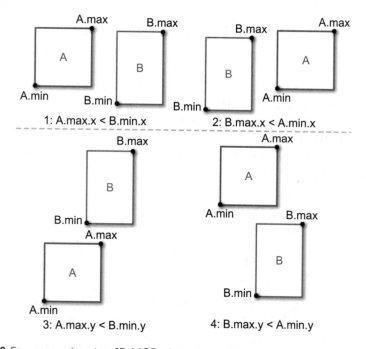

Figure 10.8 Four cases where two 2D AABBs do not intersect

As before, when switching from 2D AABBs to 3D AABBs, you must add two more checks, for a total of six:

```
bool Intersect(const AABB& a, const AABB& b)
{
    bool no = a.mMax.x < b.mMin.x ||
        a.mMax.y < b.mMin.y ||
        a.mMax.z < b.mMin.z ||
        b.mMax.x < a.mMin.x ||
        b.mMax.y < a.mMin.y ||
        b.mMax.z < a.mMin.z;
    // If none of these are true, they must intersect
    return !no;
}
```

This form of AABB intersection is an application of the **separating axis theorem**, which states that if two convex objects A and B do not intersect, then there must exist an axis that separates A from B. In the AABB case, you're testing the three coordinate axes to see if there is separation between the boxes on any of these axes. If the AABBs have separation on any coordinate axis, then, by the separating axis theorem, they cannot intersect. You can extend this approach to oriented bounding boxes, as discussed in Exercise 10.3 at the end of this chapter, and, in fact, to any set of convex objects.

Sphere Versus AABB Test

For sphere versus AABB intersection, you first need to calculate the minimum distance squared between the center of the sphere and the box. The algorithm for finding the minimum distance between a point and an AABB tests each component individually. For each component, there are three cases: The point's component is less than min, the point's component is between min and max, or the point's component is greater than max. In the middle case, the distance between the point and box for that axis is zero. In the other two cases, the distance between the point and the box for the axis is the distance to the closest edge (either min or max). Figure 10.9 illustrates this for a 2D AABB.

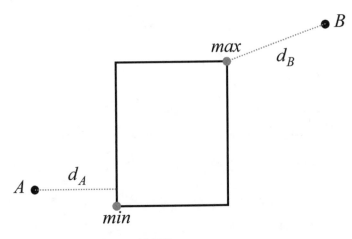

Figure 10.9 Distance between points and AABB

You can express this with multiple `Math::Max` function calls. For example, the distance in the x direction is as follows:

```
float dx = Math::Max(mMin.x - point.x, 0.0f);
dx = Math::Max(dx, point.x - mMax.x);
```

This works because if `point.x < min.x`, then `min.x - point.x` is the largest of the three values and the delta for the x-axis. Otherwise, if `min.x < point.x < max.x`, then zero is the highest. Finally, if `point.x > max.x`, then `point.x - max.x` is the highest. Once you have the delta for all three axes, you then use the distance formula to compute the final distance squared between the point and the AABB:

```
float AABB::MinDistSq(const Vector3& point) const
{
    // Compute differences for each axis
    float dx = Math::Max(mMin.x - point.x, 0.0f);
    dx = Math::Max(dx, point.x - mMax.x);
    float dy = Math::Max(mMin.y - point.y, 0.0f);
    dy = Math::Max(dy, point.y - mMax.y);
    float dz = Math::Max(mMin.z - point.z, 0.0f);
    dz = Math::Max(dy, point.z - mMax.z);
    // Distance squared formula
    return dx * dx + dy * dy + dz * dz;
}
```

Once you have the `MinDistSq` function, you can implement sphere versus AABB intersection. You find the minimal distance squared between the center of the sphere and the AABB. If it is less than or equal to the radius squared, then the sphere and AABB intersect:

```
bool Intersect(const Sphere& s, const AABB& box)
{
    float distSq = box.MinDistSq(s.mCenter);
    return distSq <= (s.mRadius * s.mRadius);
}
```

Capsule Versus Capsule Test

Intersecting two capsules is conceptually straightforward. Because both capsules are line segments with radii, you first find the minimal distance squared between these line segments. If the distance squared is less than or equal to the sum of radii squared, then the two capsules intersect:

```
bool Intersect(const Capsule& a, const Capsule& b)
{
    float distSq = LineSegment::MinDistSq(a.mSegment,
        b.mSegment);
    float sumRadii = a.mRadius + b.mRadius;
    return distSq <= (sumRadii * sumRadii);
}
```

Unfortunately, computing the minimal distance between two line segments is complex due to several edge cases. This chapter doesn't go into those details, but its source code provides an implementation of `MinDistSq` for two line segments.

Line Segment Tests

As mentioned earlier, line segments are versatile in collision detection. This chapter's game project uses line segment tests for testing whether the ball projectiles collide against objects. This section looks at a few key tests between line segments and other objects. For these tests, you want to know not only if the line segment intersects but the first such point of intersection.

This section relies heavily on the previously defined parametric equation of a line segment:

$$L(t) = Start + (End - Start)t \quad \text{where } 0 \leq t \leq 1$$

The approach for most line segment intersection tests is to first treat the segment as an infinite line—because if the infinite line does not intersect with the object, then there's no way the line segment will. Once you solve for the infinite line intersection, you then verify that t is within the [0, 1] bounds for the line segment.

Line Segment Versus Plane Test

To find the point of intersection between a line segment and a plane, you want to find whether there exists a t such that L(t) is a point on the plane:

$$L(t) \cdot \hat{n} + d = 0$$

You can solve this with some algebraic manipulation. First substitute for L(t):

$$\left(Start + (End - Start)t\right) \cdot \hat{n} + d = 0$$

Because the dot product is distributive over addition, you can rewrite this as follows:

$$Start \cdot \hat{n} + (End - Start) \cdot \hat{n}t + d = 0$$

Finally, you solve for t:

$$Start \cdot \hat{n} + (End - Start) \cdot \hat{n}t + d = 0$$
$$(End - Start) \cdot \hat{n}t = -Start \cdot \hat{n} - d$$
$$t = \frac{-Start \cdot \hat{n} - d}{(End - Start) \cdot \hat{n}}$$

Note that there's a potential for division by zero if the dot product in the denominator evaluates to zero. This will happen only in the case where the line is perpendicular to the normal of the plane, meaning the line is parallel to the plane. In this case, the line and plane intersect only if the line is entirely on the plane.

After you calculate the value of *t*, you then test whether it's within the bounds of the line segment, as in Listing 10.5. The `Intersect` function here returns the *t* value by reference, and the caller can use this to figure out the point of intersection if needed.

Listing 10.5 Line Segment Versus Plane Intersection

```
bool Intersect(const LineSegment& l, const Plane& p, float& outT)
{
   // First test if there's a solution for t
   float denom = Vector3::Dot(l.mEnd - l.mStart,
                              p.mNormal);
   if (Math::NearZero(denom))
   {
      // The only way they intersect if start/end are
      // points on the plane (P dot N) == d
      if (Math::NearZero(Vector3::Dot(l.mStart, p.mNormal) - p.mD))
      {
         outT = 0.0f;
         return true;
      }
      else
      { return false; }
   }
   else
   {
      float numer = -Vector3::Dot(l.mStart, p.mNormal) - p.mD;
      outT = numer / denom;
      // Validate t is within bounds of the line segment
      if (outT >= 0.0f && outT <= 1.0f)
      {
         return true;
      }
      else
      {
         return false;
      }
   }
}
```

Line Segment Versus Sphere Test

To find the point of intersection between a line segment and a sphere, you find if there's a *t* value such that the distance between the line and the center of the sphere *C* is equal to the radius of the sphere *r*:

$$\|L(t) - C\| = r$$
$$\|Start + (End - Start)t - C\| = r$$
$$\|Start - C + (End - Start)t\| = r$$

To simplify this equation, you introduce substitutions:

$$X = Start - C$$
$$Y = End - Start$$
$$\|X + Yt\| = r$$

To solve for t, you need some method to extract it from inside the length operation. To do this, you square both sides of the equation and replace the length squared operation with a dot product:

$$\|X + Yt\|^2 = r^2$$
$$(X + Yt) \cdot (X + Yt) = r^2$$

Because the dot product is distributive over vector addition, you can apply the FOIL (first, outside, inside, last) distribution rule:

$$(X + Yt) \cdot (X + Yt) = r^2$$
$$X \cdot X + 2X \cdot Yt + Y \cdot Yt^2 = r^2$$

You then rewrite this in the quadratic form:

$$Y \cdot Yt^2 + 2X \cdot Yt + X \cdot X - r^2 = 0$$
$$a = Y \cdot Y$$
$$b = 2X \cdot Y$$
$$c = X \cdot X - r^2$$
$$at^2 + bt + c = 0$$

Finally, you apply the quadratic equation to solve for t:

$$t = \frac{-b \pm \sqrt{b^2 - 4ac}}{2a}$$

The **discriminant** of the quadratic equation (the value under the radical) tells you the number and types of solutions to the equation. A negative discriminant means the solutions are imaginary. For the purposes of a game, you can assume that none of the objects have imaginary positions. Thus, you know that a negative discriminant means the line does not intersect with the sphere. Otherwise, there can be one or two solutions to the quadratic equation. A discriminant of zero means there's one solution because the line is tangential to the sphere. A discriminant greater than zero means the line has two points of intersection with the sphere. Figure 10.10 illustrates these three possibilities.

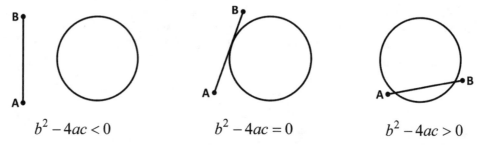

Figure 10.10 Possible discriminant values for line versus sphere intersection

Once you have solutions for *t*, you then validate that *t* is within the range [0, 1]. Because there are two possible solutions, you give preference to the lower value of *t*, which represents the first intersection. But if the line segment begins inside the sphere and exits the sphere, the higher value of *t* represents the point of intersection. Listing 10.6 gives this code for line segment versus sphere intersection. Note that this function returns `false` if the sphere wholly contains the line segment.

Listing 10.6   Line Segment Versus Sphere Intersection

```
bool Intersect(const LineSegment& l, const Sphere& s, float& outT)
{
    // Compute X, Y, a, b, c as per equations
    Vector3 X = l.mStart - s.mCenter;
    Vector3 Y = l.mEnd - l.mStart;
    float a = Vector3::Dot(Y, Y);
    float b = 2.0f * Vector3::Dot(X, Y);
    float c = Vector3::Dot(X, X) - s.mRadius * s.mRadius;
    // Compute discriminant
    float disc = b * b - 4.0f * a * c;
    if (disc < 0.0f)
    {
        return false;
    }
    else
    {
        disc = Math::Sqrt(disc);
        // Compute min and max solutions of t
        float tMin = (-b - disc) / (2.0f * a);
        float tMax = (-b + disc) / (2.0f * a);
        // Check whether either t is within bounds of segment
        if (tMin >= 0.0f && tMin <= 1.0f)
        {
            outT = tMin;
            return true;
        }
        else if (tMax >= 0.0f && tMax <= 1.0f)
        {
            outT = tMax;
            return true;
        }
        else
        {
            return false;
        }
    }
}
```

Line Segment Versus AABB Test

One approach for line segment versus AABB intersection is to construct planes for each edge of the box. In 2D, this yields four planes for the four different sides. Because the planes are infinite, simply intersecting with a side plane does not mean the segment intersects the box. In Figure 10.11(a), the line segment intersects the top plane at P_1 and the left plane at P_2. But because the box contains neither of these points, these points do not intersect the box. However, in Figure 10.11(b), the segment intersects the left plane at P_3. Because the box contains P_3, this is a point of intersection.

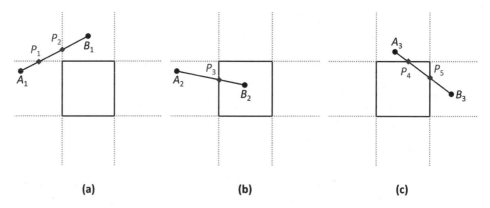

(a)   **(b)**   **(c)**

Figure 10.11 Intersection with the side planes but not the box (a), intersection with the box (b), and intersection with the box at two points (c)

Sometimes, the line segment may have multiple points of intersection, as in Figure 10.11(c). Both P_4 and P_5 intersect the box. In this case, the intersection should return the point closest to the start point, or the one at the lowest t value in the parametric formulation of the line segment.

For the segment tests versus each plane, recall that the equation for line segment versus plane intersection is as follows:

$$t = \frac{-Start \cdot \hat{n} - d}{(End - Start) \cdot \hat{n}}$$

However, because each plane is parallel to a coordinate axis (or, in 3D, a coordinate plane), you can optimize this equation because the normal of each plane will always have zeros for two components and a one for the third component. Thus, two of the three dot product components will always evaluate to zero.

For example, the normal of the left side plane points directly to the left or right; the direction doesn't matter for the purposes of the intersection test. In 2D, this is as follows:

$$\hat{n} = \langle 1, 0 \rangle$$

Because the min point for the box is on its left plane, the *d* value is as follows:

$$d = -P \cdot \hat{n} = -min \cdot \langle 1, 0 \rangle = -min_x$$

Similarly, the dot products in the segment versus plane intersection equation also simplify to their x components. This means the final equation solving for intersection against the left plane is as follows:

$$t = \frac{-Start \cdot \langle 1, 0 \rangle - d}{(End - Start) \cdot \langle 1, 0 \rangle} = \frac{-Start_x - (-min_x)}{End_x - Start_x} = \frac{-Start_x + min_x}{End_x - Start_x}$$

The equations for the other side planes have similar derivations. For 3D, there are a total of six planes to test. Listing 10.7 shows a helper function that encapsulates the behavior of testing a single side plane. Note that if the segment intersects with the plane, the function adds the *t* value to a supplied `std::vector`. The intersection function uses this `std::vector` to test all possible *t* values in order, from earliest to latest planar intersection.

Listing 10.7   Line Segment Versus AABB Helper Function

```
bool TestSidePlane(float start, float end, float negd,
    std::vector<float>& out)
{
    float denom = end - start;
    if (Math::NearZero(denom))
    {
        return false;
    }
    else
    {
        float numer = -start + negd;
        float t = numer / denom;
        // Test that t is within bounds
        if (t >= 0.0f && t <= 1.0f)
        {
            out.emplace_back(t);
            return true;
        }
        else
        {
            return false;
        }
    }
}
```

The `Intersect` function, shown in Listing 10.8, uses the `TestSidePlane` function to test the six different side planes of the AABB against the line segment. Each point of planar intersection has its *t* value stored in the `tValues` vector. Then, you sort this vector in ascending order and return the first intersection point contained by the AABB. If the AABB contains none of these points, the function returns `false`.

Listing 10.8   Line Segment Versus AABB Intersection

```
bool Intersect(const LineSegment& l, const AABB& b, float& outT)
{
   // Vector to save all possible t values
   std::vector<float> tValues;
   // Test the x planes
   TestSidePlane(l.mStart.x, l.mEnd.x, b.mMin.x, tValues);
   TestSidePlane(l.mStart.x, l.mEnd.x, b.mMax.x, tValues);
   // Test the y planes
   TestSidePlane(l.mStart.y, l.mEnd.y, b.mMin.y, tValues);
   TestSidePlane(l.mStart.y, l.mEnd.y, b.mMax.y, tValues);
   // Test the z planes
   TestSidePlane(l.mStart.z, l.mEnd.z, b.mMin.z, tValues);
   TestSidePlane(l.mStart.z, l.mEnd.z, b.mMax.z, tValues);

   // Sort the t values in ascending order
   std::sort(tValues.begin(), tValues.end());
   // Test if the box contains any of these points of intersection
   Vector3 point;
   for (float t : tValues)
   {
      point = l.PointOnSegment(t);
      if (b.Contains(point))
      {
         outT = t;
         return true;
      }
   }

   //None of the intersections are within bounds of box
   return false;
}
```

By testing each side of the box independently, you can modify the code to return which side intersects the line segment. This is useful if an object needs to bounce off the box (such as a ball bouncing as in this chapter's game project). While not shown here, this requires associating each call to `TestSidePlane` with a side of the box. Then, you add that side (or normal to the side) as a reference parameter that `Intersect` can write to.

You can optimize the segment versus AABB intersection by instead using **slabs**, which are infinite areas bounded by two planes. However, grasping this approach requires additional mathematical backing. It's one of the many topics discussed in Christer Ericson's book, listed in the "Additional Reading" section at the end of this chapter.

Dynamic Objects

The intersection tests covered thus far are **instantaneous** tests. In a game, this means that you test whether two objects intersect on the current frame. Although this might be sufficient for simple games, in practice there are issues.

Consider the case where a character fires a bullet at piece of paper. Suppose you use a bounding sphere for the bullet and a box for the paper. On each frame, you test whether the bullet intersects with the paper. Because the bullet travels quickly, it's unlikely that there's one specific frame where the bullet exactly intersects with the paper. This means that instantaneous tests will miss the intersection, as in Figure 10.12.

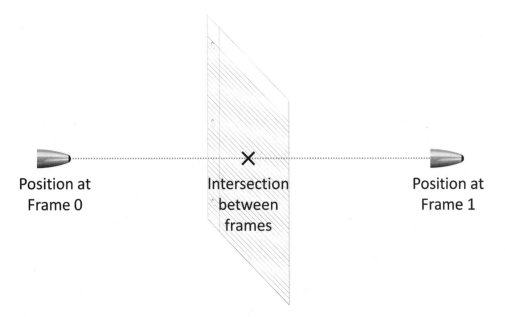

Position at
Frame 0

Intersection
between
frames

Position at
Frame 1

Figure 10.12 Instantaneous tests on frames 0 and 1 miss the collision between the bullet and paper

For the specific example of a bullet, you might solve this by representing the bullet as a line segment. The start point of the line segment is the position of the bullet in the last frame, and the end is the position of the bullet this frame. This way, you can detect whether the bullet intersects with the paper at any point between the last frame and this frame. However, this works only because the bullet is very small. You can't represent larger objects with a line segment.

For some types of moving objects, such as two moving spheres, you can solve directly for the time of intersection. However, this doesn't work well for cases such as boxes that rotate between two frames. For other types of moving objects, you might try to sample the intersection at multiple points between frames. The term **continuous collision detection** (**CCD**) can reference either directly solving the point of intersection or sampling the intersection.

To get a taste of how to solve directly for a time of intersection, consider the case of intersection between two moving spheres. This intersection, called **swept-sphere intersection**, also happens to commonly come up in video game companies' interview questions.

For each sphere, you have the center positions during the last frame and during this frame. You can represent these positions using the same parametric equation as for line segments, where the position last frame is $t = 0$ and the position this frame is $t = 1$. For sphere P, P_0 is the position last frame and P_1 is the position this frame. Similarly, the sphere Q has the positions Q_0 and Q_1. So, these are the parametric equations for the positions of spheres P and Q:

$$P(t) = P_0 + (P_1 - P_0)t$$
$$Q(t) = Q_0 + (Q_1 - Q_0)t$$

You want to solve for the value of t where the distance between the two spheres is equal to the sum of their radii:

$$\left\| P(t) - Q(t) \right\| = r_p + r_q$$

You now proceed in a manner similar to that used to test for line segment versus sphere intersection. You square both sides and replace the length squared with a dot product:

$$\left\| P(t) - Q(t) \right\|^2 = \left(r_p + r_q \right)^2$$
$$\left(P(t) - Q(t) \right) \cdot \left(P(t) - Q(t) \right) = \left(r_p + r_q \right)^2$$
$$\left(P_0 + (P_1 - P_0)t - Q_0 - (Q_1 - Q_0)t \right) \cdot \left(P_0 + (P_1 - P_0)t - Q_0 - (Q_1 - Q_0)t \right) = \left(r_p + r_q \right)^2$$

Then, you factor the terms and make substitutions:

$$\left(P_0 - Q_0 + ((P_1 - P_0) - (Q_1 - Q_0))t \right) \cdot \left(P_0 - Q_0 + ((P_1 - P_0) - (Q_1 - Q_0))t \right) = \left(r_p + r_q \right)^2$$
$$X = P_0 - Q_0$$
$$Y = (P_1 - P_0) - (Q_1 - Q_0)$$
$$(X + Yt) \cdot (X + Yt) = \left(r_p + r_q \right)^2$$

Finally, you distribute the dot product over addition, rewrite in the quadratic form, and solve the quadratic equation:

$$(X + Yt) \cdot (X + Yt) = \left(r_p + r_q \right)^2$$
$$a = Y \cdot Y$$
$$b = 2X \cdot Y$$
$$c = X \cdot X - \left(r_p + r_q \right)^2$$
$$at^2 + bt + c = 0$$
$$t = \frac{-b \pm \sqrt{b^2 - 4ac}}{2a}$$

As with line segment versus sphere, you use the discriminant to determine whether any real solutions exist. However, for swept-sphere intersection you only care about the first point of intersection, which is the lower of the two *t* values. As before, you must validate that *t* is within the range [0, 1]. Listing 10.9 gives the code for swept-sphere intersection. The function returns *t* by reference, so the caller can use this to determine the position of the spheres at the time of intersection.

Listing 10.9 Swept-Sphere Intersection

```
bool SweptSphere(const Sphere& P0, const Sphere& P1,
   const Sphere& Q0, const Sphere& Q1, float& outT)
{
   // Compute X, Y, a, b, and c
   Vector3 X = P0.mCenter - Q0.mCenter;
   Vector3 Y = P1.mCenter - P0.mCenter -
      (Q1.mCenter - Q0.mCenter);
   float a = Vector3::Dot(Y, Y);
   float b = 2.0f * Vector3::Dot(X, Y);
   float sumRadii = P0.mRadius + Q0.mRadius;
   float c = Vector3::Dot(X, X) - sumRadii * sumRadii;
   // Solve discriminant
   float disc = b * b - 4.0f * a * c;
   if (disc < 0.0f)
   {
      return false;
   }
   else
   {
      disc = Math::Sqrt(disc);
      // We only care about the smaller solution
      outT = (-b - disc) / (2.0f * a);
      if (outT >= 0.0f && outT <= 0.0f)
      {
         return true;
      }
      else
      {
         return false;
      }
   }
}
```

Adding Collisions to Game Code

The preceding sections discuss geometry objects used for collision and how to detect intersections between these objects. This section explores how to incorporate these techniques into game code. A new BoxComponent class adds AABBs for actors, and a PhysWorld class tracks boxes and detects intersections as needed. The character movement and new projectile firing code then leverage this new collision functionality.

The BoxComponent Class

The BoxComponent class declaration is much like the declaration of other components. However, instead of overriding the Update function, it overrides the OnUpdateWorldTransform function. Recall that the owning actor calls OnUpdateWorldTransform whenever it recomputes the world transform.

The member data of BoxComponent has two instances of the AABB struct: one AABB for the object space bounds, and one AABB for the world space bounds. The object space bounds shouldn't change after initialization of the BoxComponent, but the world space bounds change whenever the owning actor's world transform changes. Finally, BoxComponent has a Boolean for whether you want the BoxComponent to rotate based on the world rotation. This way, you can choose whether or not an actor's BoxComponent rotates when the actor rotates. Listing 10.10 shows the declaration of BoxComponent.

Listing 10.10 BoxComponent Declaration

```
class BoxComponent : public Component
{
public:
   BoxComponent(class Actor* owner);
   ~BoxComponent();
   void OnUpdateWorldTransform() override;
   void SetObjectBox(const AABB& model) { mObjectBox = model; }
   const AABB& GetWorldBox() const { return mWorldBox; }
   void SetShouldRotate(bool value) { mShouldRotate = value; }
private:
   AABB mObjectBox;
   AABB mWorldBox;
   bool mShouldRotate;
};
```

To get the object space bounds of mesh files, the Mesh class also adds an AABB in its member data. Then, when loading in a gpmesh file, Mesh calls AABB::UpdateMinMax on each vertex, ultimately yielding an object space AABB. Then actors using a mesh can grab the mesh's object space bounds and pass these bounds into the actor's BoxComponent:

```
Mesh* mesh = GetGame()->GetRenderer()->GetMesh("Assets/Plane.gpmesh");
// Add collision box
BoxComponent* bc = new BoxComponent(this);
bc->SetObjectBox(mesh->GetBox());
```

To convert from object bounds to world bounds, you need to apply scale, rotation, and translation to the bounds. As when constructing the world transform matrix, the order is important because rotation is about the origin. Listing 10.11 gives the code for OnUpdateWorldTransform. To scale the box, you multiply min and max by the scale of the owning actor. To rotate the box, you use the previously discussed `AABB::Rotate` function, passing in the quaternion of the owning actor. You do this rotation only if `mShouldRotate` is `true` (which it is by default). To translate the box, you add the position of the owning actor to both min and max.

Listing 10.11 `BoxComponent::OnUpdateWorldTransform` Implementation

```
void BoxComponent::OnUpdateWorldTransform()
{
   // Reset to object space box
   mWorldBox = mObjectBox;
   // Scale
   mWorldBox.mMin *= mOwner->GetScale();
   mWorldBox.mMax *= mOwner->GetScale();
   // Rotate
   if (mShouldRotate)
   {
      mWorldBox.Rotate(mOwner->GetRotation());
   }
   // Translate
   mWorldBox.mMin += mOwner->GetPosition();
   mWorldBox.mMax += mOwner->GetPosition();
}
```

The `PhysWorld` Class

Much as you have separate `Renderer` and `AudioSystem` classes, it's sensible to create a `PhysWorld` class for the physics world. You add a `PhysWorld` pointer to `Game` and initialize it in `Game::Initialize`.

`PhysWorld` has a vector of `BoxComponent` pointers and corresponding public `AddBox` and `RemoveBox` functions, as shown in the skeleton declaration in Listing 10.12. Then the constructor and destructor for `BoxComponent` can call `AddBox` and `RemoveBox`, respectively. This way, `PhysWorld` will have a vector of all box components, much like how `Renderer` has a vector of all sprite components.

Listing 10.12 Skeleton `PhysWorld` Declaration

```
class PhysWorld
{
public:
   PhysWorld(class Game* game);
   // Add/remove box components from world
   void AddBox(class BoxComponent* box);
```

```
   void RemoveBox(class BoxComponent* box);
   // Other functions as needed
   // ...
private:
   class Game* mGame;
   std::vector<class BoxComponent*> mBoxes;
};
```

Now that `PhysWorld` tracks all the box components in the world, the next step is to add support for collision tests against these boxes. You define a function called `SegmentCast` that takes in a line segment and returns `true` if the segment intersects with a box. In addition, it returns by reference information about the first such collision:

```
bool SegmentCast(const LineSegment& l, CollisionInfo& outColl);
```

The `CollisionInfo` struct contains the position of intersection, the normal at the intersection, and pointers to both the `BoxComponent` and `Actor` of the collision:

```
struct CollisionInfo
{
   // Point of collision
   Vector3 mPoint;
   // Normal at collision
   Vector3 mNormal;
   // Component collided with
   class BoxComponent* mBox;
   // Owning actor of component
   class Actor* mActor;
};
```

Because the segment potentially intersects with multiple boxes, `SegmentCast` assumes that the closest intersection is the most important one. Because the vector of box components has no ordering, `SegmentCast` can't simply return after the first intersection. Instead, the function needs to test against all boxes and return the intersection result with the lowest *t* value, as shown in Listing 10.13. This works because the lowest *t* value intersection is the one closest to the start of the line segment. `SegmentCast` uses the segment versus AABB intersection function discussed earlier but now modified to also return the normal of the side the line segment intersects with.

Listing 10.13 `PhysWorld::SegmentCast` Implementation

```
bool PhysWorld::SegmentCast(const LineSegment& l, CollisionInfo& outColl)
{
   bool collided = false;
   // Initialize closestT to infinity, so first
   // intersection will always update closestT
   float closestT = Math::Infinity;
   Vector3 norm;
```

```
    // Test against all boxes
    for (auto box : mBoxes)
    {
        float t;
        // Does the segment intersect with the box?
        if (Intersect(l, box->GetWorldBox(), t, norm))
        {
            // Is this closer than previous intersection?
            if (t < closestT)
            {
                outColl.mPoint = l.PointOnSegment(t);
                outColl.mNormal = norm;
                outColl.mBox = box;
                outColl.mActor = box->GetOwner();
                collided = true;
            }
        }
    }
    return collided;
}
```

Ball Collisions with `SegmentCast`

In the chapter game project, you use `SegmentCast` to determine whether the ball projectile the player fires hits something. If it does, you want the ball to bounce off the normal of the surface. This means that once the ball hits the surface, you must rotate it to face an arbitrary direction.

You first add a helper function to `Actor` that uses the dot product, cross product, and quaternions to adjust the actor's rotation to face the desired direction. Listing 10.14 shows the implementation of this helper function, `RotateToNewForward`.

Listing 10.14 `Actor::RotateToNewForward` Implementation

```
void Actor::RotateToNewForward(const Vector3& forward)
{
    // Figure out difference between original (unit x) and new
    float dot = Vector3::Dot(Vector3::UnitX, forward);
    float angle = Math::Acos(dot);

    // Are we facing down X?
    if (dot > 0.9999f)
    { SetRotation(Quaternion::Identity); }
    // Are we facing down -X?
    else if (dot < -0.9999f)
    { SetRotation(Quaternion(Vector3::UnitZ, Math::Pi)); }
```

```
    else
    {
        // Rotate about axis from cross product
        Vector3 axis = Vector3::Cross(Vector3::UnitX, forward);
        axis.Normalize();
        SetRotation(Quaternion(axis, angle));
    }
}
```

Next, you create a `BallActor` class and attach to it a new `MoveComponent` subclass called `BallMove`, which implements the movement code specific to `BallActor`. The `BallMove::Update` function, shown in Listing 10.15, first constructs a line segment in the direction the ball is traveling. If this segment intersects with anything in the world, you want it to bounce off the surface. You reflect the movement direction off the surface with `Vector3::Reflect` and then use `RoateToNewForward` to tell the ball to rotate to face this new direction.

Listing 10.15 Using `SegmentCast` for Ball Movement

```
void BallMove::Update(float deltaTime)
{
    // Construct segment in direction of travel
    const float segmentLength = 30.0f;
    Vector3 start = mOwner->GetPosition();
    Vector3 dir = mOwner->GetForward();
    Vector3 end = start + dir * segmentLength;
    LineSegment ls(start, end);

    // Test segment vs world
    PhysWorld* phys = mOwner->GetGame()->GetPhysWorld();
    PhysWorld::CollisionInfo info;
    if (phys->SegmentCast(ls, info))
    {
        // If we collided, reflect the direction about the normal
        dir = Vector3::Reflect(dir, info.mNormal);
        mOwner->RotateToNewForward(dir);
    }

    // Base class update moves based on forward speed
    MoveComponent::Update(deltaTime);
}
```

One thing to watch out for is what happens when you add a `BoxComponent` to the player, as you will do later in this section. You clearly don't want the ball to collide against the player because the player fires the ball! Luckily, you can leverage the fact that the `CollisionInfo` from `SegmentCast` has a pointer to the actor owning the box component. Thus, if you save a pointer to the player somewhere, you can make sure a ball doesn't collide against the player.

Testing Box Collisions in `PhysWorld`

Although not used in this chapter's game project, some game features may require testing all the boxes in the physics world against each other. A naïve implementation is to perform pairwise intersection tests between all combinations of boxes in the world. This basic approach, shown in Listing 10.16, uses an $O(n^2)$ algorithm because it tests every box against every other box. The `TestPairwise` function takes in a user-supplied function, `f`, and calls `f` on every intersection between boxes.

Listing 10.16 `PhysWorld::TestPairwise` Implementation

```
void PhysWorld::TestPairwise(std::function<void(Actor*, Actor*)> f)
{
    // Naive implementation O(n^2)
    for (size_t i = 0; i < mBoxes.size(); i++)
    {
        // Don't need to test vs. itself and any previous i values
        for (size_t j = i + 1; j < mBoxes.size(); j++)
        {
            BoxComponent* a = mBoxes[i];
            BoxComponent* b = mBoxes[j];
            if (Intersect(a->GetWorldBox(), b->GetWorldBox()))
            {
                // Call supplied function to handle intersection
                f(a->GetOwner(), b->GetOwner());
            }
        }
    }
}
```

Although `TestPairwise` is conceptually simple, it ends up making a lot of unnecessary calls to `Intersect`. It treats two boxes on opposite sides of the world the same as two boxes right next to each other. In the case of this chapter's game project, there are 144 boxes. `TestPairwise` makes over 10,000 calls to the `Intersect` function given these 144 boxes.

You can optimize this by observing that two 2D axis-aligned boxes do not intersect unless they overlap on both coordinate axes. For example, the interval `[min.x, max.x]` from one box must overlap with the `[min.x, max.x]` interval from another box if the two boxes are to intersect. The **sweep-and-prune** method takes advantage of this observation to reduce the number of box intersection tests. The sweep-and-prune method involves selecting an axis and testing only boxes that have overlapping intervals along that axis.

Figure 10.13 illustrates a handful of AABBs and considers their intervals along the x-axis. Box *A*'s and Box *B*'s x intervals overlap, so they may potentially intersect. Similarly, Box *B*'s and Box *C*'s x intervals overlap, so they may intersect. However, Box *A*'s and Box *C*'s x intervals do not overlap, so they cannot intersect. Similarly, Box *D*'s x interval overlaps with none of the other boxes, so it can't intersect with any of them. In this case, the sweep-and-prune algorithm calls `Intersect` only on the pairs (*A*, *B*) and (*B*, *C*) instead of on all six possible combinations.

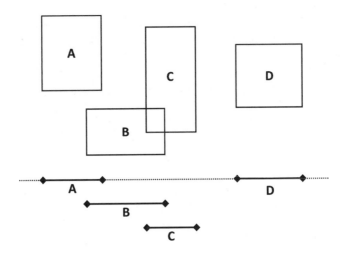

Figure 10.13 AABB intervals along the x-axis

Listing 10.17 gives the code for the sweep-and-prune method along the x-axis. You first sort the vector of boxes by their minimum x-value. Then, for every box, you grab the maximum x value and save it in `max`. In the inner loop, you only consider boxes whose `min.x` is less than `max`. Once the inner loop hits the first box with a `min.x` greater than `max`, there are no other boxes that overlap along the x-axis with the outer loop box. This means there are no other possible intersections against the outer loop box, so you break to the next iteration of the outer loop.

Listing 10.17 `PhysWorld::TestSweepAndPrune` Implementation

```
void PhysWorld::TestSweepAndPrune(std::function<void(Actor*, Actor*)> f)
{
    // Sort by min.x
    std::sort(mBoxes.begin(), mBoxes.end(),
        [](BoxComponent* a, BoxComponent* b) {
            return a->GetWorldBox().mMin.x <
                b->GetWorldBox().mMin.x;
    });
    for (size_t i = 0; i < mBoxes.size(); i++)
    {
        // Get max.x for box[i]
        BoxComponent* a = mBoxes[i];
        float max = a->GetWorldBox().mMax.x;
        for (size_t j = i + 1; j < mBoxes.size(); j++)
        {
```

```
            BoxComponent* b = mBoxes[j];
            // If box[j] min.x is past the max.x bounds of box[i],
            // then there aren't any other possible intersections
            // against box[i]
            if (b->GetWorldBox().mMin.x > max)
            {
                break;
            }
            else if (Intersect(a->GetWorldBox(), b->GetWorldBox()))
            {
                f(a->GetOwner(), b->GetOwner());
            }
        }
    }
}
```

In this chapter's game project, `TestSweepAndPrune` cuts down the number of calls to `Intersect` roughly by half in comparison to `TestPairwise`. The complexity of this algorithm is on average O(*n* log *n*). Even though sweep-and-prune requires a sort, it is generally more efficient than the naïve pairwise test—unless there are very few boxes. Some implementations of the sweep-and-prune algorithm do the pruning along all three axes, as in Exercise 10.2. This requires maintaining multiple sorted vectors. The advantage of testing all three axes is that after you prune for all three axes, the remaining set of boxes must intersect with each other.

Sweep-and-prune is one of a category of techniques called **broadphase** techniques. The broadphase tries to eliminate as many collisions as possible before the **narrowphase**, which tests the individual pairs of collisions. Other techniques use grids, cells, or trees.

Player Collision Against the Walls

Recall that `MoveComponent` uses the `mForwardSpeed` variable to move the character forward or backward. However, the current implementation allows the player to move through walls. To fix this, you can add a `BoxComponent` to each wall (encapsulated by `PlaneActor`), as well as a `BoxComponent` to the player. Because you only want to test the player against every `PlaneActor`, you don't use `TestSweepAndPrune`. Instead, you can just make a vector of `PlaneActor` pointers in `Game` and access this from the player's code.

The basic idea is that every frame, you test the player's collision against every `PlaneActor`. If the AABBs intersect, you adjust the player's position so that it no longer collides with the wall. To understand this calculation, it helps to visualize the problem in 2D.

Figure 10.14 illustrates a player's AABB colliding with a platform AABB. You calculate two differences per axis. For example, dx1 is the difference between the player's `max.x` and the platform's `min.x`. Conversely, dx2 is the difference between the player's `min.x` and the platform's `max.x`. Whichever of these differences has the lowest absolute value is the **minimum overlap** between the two AABBs. In Figure 10.14, the minimum overlap is dy1. If you then add dy1 to the player's y position, the player stands exactly on top of the platform. Thus, to correctly fix the collision, you can just adjust the position in the axis of the minimum overlap.

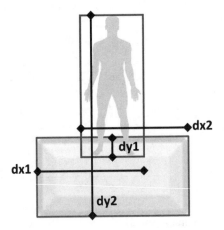

Figure 10.14 Calculating minimum overlap in 2D

In 3D, the principle is the same, except there are now six difference values because there are three axes. The FPSActor::FixCollisions function as shown in Listing 10.18 implements this minimum overlap test. Importantly, because changing the position of the player changes the player's BoxComponent, in between each intersect we must recompute the world bounds of the BoxComponent. You then call this function from UpdateActor, which means you call it after the MoveComponent updates the player's position every frame.

Listing 10.18 FPSActor::FixCollisions Implementation

```
void FPSActor::FixCollisions()
{
    // Need to recompute my world transform to update world box
    ComputeWorldTransform();

    const AABB& playerBox = mBoxComp->GetWorldBox();
    Vector3 pos = GetPosition();

    auto& planes = GetGame()->GetPlanes();
    for (auto pa : planes)
    {
        // Do we collide with this PlaneActor?
        const AABB& planeBox = pa->GetBox()->GetWorldBox();
        if (Intersect(playerBox, planeBox))
        {
            // Calculate all our differences
            float dx1 = planeBox.mMin.x - playerBox.mMax.x;
            float dx2 = planeBox.mMax.x - playerBox.mMin.x;
            float dy1 = planeBox.mMin.y - playerBox.mMax.y;
```

```
    float dy2 = planeBox.mMax.y - playerBox.mMin.y;
    float dz1 = planeBox.mMin.z - playerBox.mMax.z;
    float dz2 = planeBox.mMax.z - playerBox.mMin.z;

    // Set dx to whichever of dx1/dx2 have a lower abs
    float dx = (Math::Abs(dx1) < Math::Abs(dx2)) ? dx1 : dx2;
    // Ditto for dy
    float dy = (Math::Abs(dy1) < Math::Abs(dy2)) ? dy1 : dy2;
    // Ditto for dz
    float dz = (Math::Abs(dz1) < Math::Abs(dz2)) ? dz1 : dz2;

    // Whichever is closest, adjust x/y position
    if (Math::Abs(dx) <= Math::Abs(dy) &&
        Math::Abs(dx) <= Math::Abs(dz))
    {
        pos.x += dx;
    }
    else if (Math::Abs(dy) <= Math::Abs(dx) &&
             Math::Abs(dy) <= Math::Abs(dz))
    {
        pos.y += dy;
    }
    else
    {
        pos.z += dz;
    }

    // Need to set position and update box component
    SetPosition(pos);
    mBoxComp->OnUpdateWorldTransform();
    }
  }
}
```

Because you also use `PlaneActor` instances for the ground beneath the player, you can also leverage this code, with modification, to test whether the player lands on the platforms. In Exercise 10.1, you'll explore adding jumping to the player.

Game Project

This chapter's game project implements all the different types of intersections discussed in this chapter, as well as `BoxComponent` and `PhysWorld`. It also uses `SegmentCast` for the ball projectile and implements fixing the player colliding against the walls. The result is a first-person shooting gallery, as shown in Figure 10.15. The code is available in the book's GitHub repository, in the `Chapter10` directory. Open `Chapter10-windows.sln` in Windows and `Chapter10-mac.xcodeproj` on Mac.

The controls for this game project use the FPS-style controls implemented in Chapter 9. Recall that W/S move forward and back, A/D strafe, and the mouse rotates the character. In addition, clicking the left mouse button now fires a ball projectile in the direction of the vector derived from an unprojection (also discussed in Chapter 9). The ball projectile uses SegmentCast to test whether it intersects with a wall or target. In either case, the ball reflects its facing direction based on the normal of the surface, causing it to bounce. If the ball hits a target, the game plays a ding sound.

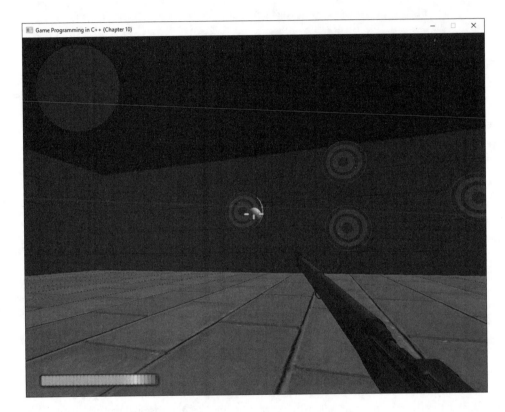

Figure 10.15 Chapter 10 game project

Summary

This chapter provides an in-depth introduction to collision detection techniques in games. Games might use many different geometric types for collision detection. A line segment has a start point and an end point. The representation of a plane is its normal and distance to the origin. Spheres are simple bounding volumes but may cause many false negatives for characters of different shapes. Axis-aligned bounding boxes have sides aligned with the axes, while oriented bounding boxes do not have this restriction.

For intersection tests, this chapter covers many different types of intersections. Contains point tests can say whether a shape contains a point. You can also test whether two bounding volumes (such as two AABBs) intersect with each other. This chapter also covers tests for whether a line segment intersects with objects including planes, spheres, and other boxes. For moving objects, you may need to use a form of continuous collision detection to ensure that the game doesn't miss collisions that occur between frames.

Finally, this chapter covers how to integrate collision detection into game code. The `BoxComponent` class has both object space bounds (derived from the mesh) and world space bounds that are updated based on the owning actor. `PhysWorld` keeps track of all box components in the world, and `SegmentCast` tests a line segment against all the boxes. For collisions between pairs of boxes, it's more efficient to use the sweep-and-prune broadphase algorithm. Sweep-and-prune exploits the fact that two boxes cannot intersect if their intervals along a coordinate axis do not overlap. This chapter shows how to use both segment cast and box component collisions to implement some game-specific features, such as the ball bouncing off objects or the player colliding with the wall.

Additional Reading

Christer Ericson provides extremely detailed coverage of collision detection, covering both the mathematical bases of the algorithms and usable implementations. Ian Millington doesn't have as much coverage of collision detection algorithms but explains how to incorporate collision in the context of physics engine movement, which is something this chapter does not discuss in detail.

Ericson, Christer. *Real-time Collision Detection*. San Francisco: Morgan Kaufmann, 2005.

Millington, Ian. *Game Physics Engine Development,* 2nd edition. Boca Raton: CRC Press, 2010.

Exercises

In this chapter's first exercise, you add jumping to the chapter's game project. In the second exercise, you improve upon the sweep-and-prune implementation covered in this chapter. In the last exercise you implement OBB versus OBB intersection between oriented bounding boxes.

Exercise 10.1

Add jumping to the player character. The ground objects already have corresponding axis-aligned bounding boxes. To implement jumping, select a key (such as the spacebar). When the player presses the jump key, set an additional velocity in the positive z direction. Similarly, add a negative z acceleration for gravity that slows down the jump velocity. After the player hits the apex of the jump, he or she starts falling. While they player is falling, you can detect in `FixCollisions` whether the player lands on top of a `PlaneActor` (because you know that the top is `dz2`). While the player is on the ground, disable gravity and set the z velocity back to zero.

To help keep the code modular, it's recommended that you use a simple state machine to represent the different states of the character: on the ground, jumping, and falling. As an additional feature, experiment with transitioning from the "on ground" state to the "falling" state. While in the "on ground" state, keep making downward `SegmentCasts` to detect whether the player has walked off the platform. If that happens, switch from "on ground" to "falling."

Exercise 10.2

Change the `SweepAndPrune` function to sweep and prune across all three coordinate axes. Have `PhysWorld` maintain three vectors of boxes and change it so that `AddBox` and `RemoveBox` touch all three vectors. Then sort each vector by its corresponding axis.

The sweep-and-prune code should then test along each axis independently and create a map of pairs of overlapping boxes along that axis. Once all three axes are complete, the code should compare the overlapping box vectors. The boxes that overlap along all three axes are the only boxes that intersect with each other.

Exercise 10.3

Implement OBB versus OBB intersection in a new `Intersect` function. As with AABBs, use the separating axis approach (that is, figure out whether they cannot intersect and then logically not the result). However, whereas there are 3 axes to test for AABBs, for OBBs there are a total of 15 different axes to test.

To implement this, first compute the 8 different corners of both OBBs. Each OBB has a total of 3 local axes corresponding to each side of the box. You can compute these by using vector subtraction between the correct set of points and normalizing the vectors. Because each box has three local axes, that yields the first 6 potential separating axes. The other 9 vectors are the combinations of cross products between the two OBBs' local axes. For example, OBB A's up vector crosses OBB B's up, right, and forward vectors.

To determine the interval of the box along an axis, compute the dot product of each corner of that box versus the axis. The lowest dot product result is the minimum value of the interval and, similarly, the highest dot product result is the maximum value. Then determine whether the [min, max] intervals of both boxes separate along the axis. If any of the 15 axes separate, then the boxes cannot intersect. Otherwise, they must intersect.

CHAPTER 11

USER INTERFACES

Most games include UI elements such as a menu
system and an in-game heads-up display (HUD). The
menu system allows the player to perform actions
such as starting and pausing the game. The HUD
includes elements that give information to the
player during gameplay. This can include elements
such as an aiming reticule or a radar.

This chapter looks at core systems needed to
implement user interfaces, including text rendering
with a font, a system for UI screens, and localization
for different languages. The chapter also explores
implementations of certain HUD elements.

Font Rendering

In the TrueType font format, straight line segments and Bézier curves form the outlines of individual characters (or **glyphs**). The SDL TTF library provides support for loading and rendering TrueType fonts. After initializing the library, the basic process is to load fonts at specific point sizes. Then SDL TTF takes in a string and renders the string to a texture, using the glyphs from the font. Once this texture exists, the game can render the texture just like any other 2D sprite.

Much as in other systems, the Game class initializes SDL TTF in Game::Initialize. The TTF_Init function returns 0 if successful, and -1 in the event of an error. Similarly, Game::Shutdown calls TTF_Quit to shut down the library.

Next, you declare a Font class to encapsulate any font-specific functionality, as shown in Listing 11.1. The Load function loads in a font from the specified file, and Unload frees all font data. The RenderText function takes in the provided string, color, and point size and creates a texture that contains the text.

Listing 11.1 Font Declaration

```
class Font
{
public:
   Font();
   ~Font();
   // Load/unload from a file
   bool Load(const std::string& fileName);
   void Unload();
   // Given string and this font, draw to a texture
   class Texture* RenderText(const std::string& text,
                 const Vector3& color = Color::White,
                 int pointSize = 30);
private:
   // Map of point sizes to font data
   std::unordered_map<int, TTF_Font*> mFontData;
};
```

The TTF_OpenFont function loads a font from a .ttf file at a specific point size and returns a pointer to the TTF_Font data corresponding to the font at that size. This means to support different-sized text in the game, you must call TTF_OpenFont multiple times. The Font::Load function, shown in Listing 11.2, first creates a vector of the desired point sizes, and then it loops over this vector, calling TTF_OpenFont once per size and adding each TTF_Font to the mFontData map.

Listing 11.2 Font::Load Implementation

```cpp
bool Font::Load(const std::string& fileName)
{
    // Support these font sizes
    std::vector<int> fontSizes = {
        8, 9, 10, 11, 12, 14, 16, 18, 20, 22, 24, 26, 28,
        30, 32, 34, 36, 38, 40, 42, 44, 46, 48, 52, 56,
        60, 64, 68, 72
    };
    // Call TTF_OpenFont once per every font size
    for (auto& size : fontSizes)
    {
        TTF_Font* font = TTF_OpenFont(fileName.c_str(), size);
        if (font == nullptr)
        {
            SDL_Log("Failed to load font %s in size %d", fileName.c_str(),
            size);
            return false;
        }
        mFontData.emplace(size, font);
    }
    return true;
}
```

As with other resources, you want to keep track of loaded fonts in a central place. In this case, the Game class adds a map where the key is the filename of the font, and the value is a Font pointer. You then add a corresponding GetFont function. As with GetTexture and similar functions, GetFont first tries to find the data in its map and, if it fails, it loads the font file and adds it to the map.

The Font::RenderText function, shown in Listing 11.3, creates a texture given a text string, using a font of the appropriate size. First, you convert the Vector3 color into an SDL_Color, where each component ranges from 0 to 255. Next, you look in the mFontData map to find the TTF_Font data corresponding to the font at the requested point size.

Next, you call the TTF_RenderText_Blended function, which takes in a TTF_Font*, the string of text to render, and a color. The Blended suffix means that the font will draw with alpha transparency around the glyphs. Unfortunately, TTF_RenderText_Blended returns a pointer to an SDL_Surface. OpenGL cannot directly draw an SDL_Surface.

Recall that in Chapter 5, "OpenGL," you created the Texture class to encapsulate a texture loaded for OpenGL usage. You can add a Texture::CreateFromSurface function to convert an SDL_Surface into a Texture. (This chapter omits the implementation of CreateFromSurface, but check the source code for the gameproject.) Once the SDL_Surface is converted into a Texture object, you can free the surface.

Listing 11.3 Font::RenderText Implementation

```cpp
Texture* Font::RenderText(const std::string& text,
   const Vector3& color, int pointSize)
{
   Texture* texture = nullptr;
   // Convert to SDL_Color
   SDL_Color sdlColor;
   sdlColor.r = static_cast<Uint8>(color.x * 255);
   sdlColor.g = static_cast<Uint8>(color.y * 255);
   sdlColor.b = static_cast<Uint8>(color.z * 255);
   sdlColor.a = 255;
   // Find the font data for this point size
   auto iter = mFontData.find(pointSize);
   if (iter != mFontData.end())
   {
      TTF_Font* font = iter->second;
      // Draw this to a surface (blended for alpha)
      SDL_Surface* surf = TTF_RenderText_Blended(font, text.c_str(),
                       sdlColor);
      if (surf != nullptr)
      {
         // Convert from surface to texture
         texture = new Texture();
         texture->CreateFromSurface(surf);
         SDL_FreeSurface(surf);
      }
   }
   else
   {
      SDL_Log("Point size %d is unsupported", pointSize);
   }
   return texture;
}
```

Because creating a texture is somewhat expensive, the UI code does not call RenderText every frame. Instead, it calls RenderText only when the text string changes and saves the resulting texture. Then on every frame, the UI code can draw the texture that contains the rendered text. For maximum efficiency, you could even render each letter in the alphabet to separate textures and then stich these letter textures together to form words.

UI Screens

Because a UI system might be used for many things, including the HUD and menus, flexibility is an important feature. Although there are data-driven systems that utilize tools such as Adobe Flash, this chapter instead focuses on a code-driven implementation. However, many of the ideas presented here can still apply to a more data-driven system.

It's useful to think of the UI as containing different layers. For example, during gameplay, the **heads-up display (HUD)** shows information relevant to the player, such as health or a score. If the player pauses the game, the game might show a menu that lets the player choose between different options. While the game shows the pause menu, you may still want the HUD elements to be visible under the pause menu.

Now suppose that one of the options in the pause menu is to quit the game. When the player selects this option, you might want to have the game show a confirmation dialog box that asks whether the player truly wants to quit. The player might still see parts of both the HUD and pause menu onscreen under this dialog box.

During this sequence, the player can typically interact with only the topmost layer of the UI. This naturally leads to the idea of using a stack to represent the different layers of the UI. You can implement the idea of a single UI layer with the `UIScreen` class. Each type of UI screen, such as the pause menu or HUD, is a subclass of `UIScreen`. After drawing the game world, the game draws all UI screens on the stack in a bottom-up order. At any point in time, only the `UIScreen` on top of the UI stack might receive input events.

Listing 11.4 shows the first iteration of the base `UIScreen` class. Notice that it has several virtual functions that subclasses can override: `Update` for updating the UI screen's state, `Draw` for drawing it, and the two input functions to handle different types of incoming input. You can also keep track of the state of a specific UI screen; in this case, you only need two states for whether the screen is active or closing.

The UI screen also might have a title, so the member data contains a pointer to the `Font`, a pointer to the `Texture` that contains the rendered title, and a position for the title onscreen. Subclasses can then call the `SetTitle` function, which uses `Font::RenderText` to set the `mTitle` member.

Finally, because a `UIScreen` is not an `Actor`, you cannot attach any types of components to it. Thus, the `UIScreen` class doesn't use the drawing functionality from `SpriteComponent`. Instead, you need a new helper function called `DrawTexture` that draws a texture at the specified position onscreen. Every UI screen can then call `DrawTexture` as needed.

Listing 11.4   Initial `UIScreen` Declaration

```
class UIScreen
{
public:
    UIScreen(class Game* game);
    virtual ~UIScreen();
    // UIScreen subclasses can override these
    virtual void Update(float deltaTime);
    virtual void Draw(class Shader* shader);
    virtual void ProcessInput(const uint8_t* keys);
    virtual void HandleKeyPress(int key);
```

```
      // Tracks if the UI is active or closing
      enum UIState { EActive, EClosing };
      // Set state to closing
      void Close();
      // Get state of UI screen
      UIState GetState() const { return mState; }
      // Change the title text
      void SetTitle(const std::string& text,
               const Vector3& color = Color::White,
               int pointSize = 40);
protected:
   // Helper to draw a texture
   void DrawTexture(class Shader* shader, class Texture* texture,
               const Vector2& offset = Vector2::Zero,
               float scale = 1.0f);
   class Game* mGame;
   // For the UI screen's title text
   class Font* mFont;
   class Texture* mTitle;
   Vector2 mTitlePos;
   // State
   UIState mState;
};
```

The UI Screen Stack

Adding the UI screen stack to the game requires connections in several places. First, you add a `std::vector` of `UIScreen` pointers to the `Game` class for the UI stack. You don't just use `std::stack` here because you need to iterate over the entire UI stack, which is not possible in `std::stack`. You also add functions to push a new `UIScreen` onto the stack (`PushUI`) and a function to get the entire stack by reference:

```
// UI stack for game
std::vector<class UIScreen*> mUIStack;
// Returns entire stack by reference
const std::vector<class UIScreen*>& GetUIStack();
// Push specified UIScreen onto stack
void PushUI(class UIScreen* screen);
```

Then the constructor of `UIScreen` calls `PushUI` and passes in its `this` pointer as the screen. This means that simply dynamically allocating a `UIScreen` (or subclass of `UIScreen`) automatically adds the `UIScreen` to the stack.

Updating the UI screens on the stack happens in `UpdateGame`, after updating all the actors in the world. This requires looping over the entire UI screen stack and calling `Update` on any active screens:

```
for (auto ui : mUIStack)
{
   if (ui->GetState() == UIScreen::EActive)
   {
      ui->Update(deltaTime);
   }
}
```

After updating all the UI screens, you also delete any screens whose state is `EClosing`.

Drawing the UI screens must happen in `Renderer`. Recall that `Renderer::Draw` first draws all the 3D mesh components by using the mesh shader and then draws all the sprite components by using the sprite shader. Because the UI comprises several textures, it's natural to draw them by using the same shader that sprites use. So, after drawing all sprite components, the `Renderer` gets the UI stack from the `Game` object and calls `Draw` on each `UIScreen`:

```
for (auto ui : mGame->GetUIStack())
{
   ui->Draw(mSpriteShader);
}
```

For testing purposes, you can create a subclass of `UIScreen` called `HUD`. You can create an instance of `HUD` in `Game::LoadData` and save it in an `mHUD` member variable:

```
mHUD = new HUD(this);
```

Because the constructor of `HUD` calls the constructor of `UIScreen`, this automatically adds the object to the game's UI stack. For now, `HUD` doesn't draw any elements to the screen or otherwise override any behavior of `UIScreen`. (Later in this chapter, you'll learn about supporting different functionality in the HUD.)

Handling input for the UI stack is a bit trickier. In most cases, a specific input action such as clicking the mouse should affect the game or the UI—but not both simultaneously. Thus, you first need a way to decide whether to route the input to the game or to the UI.

To implement this, you first add the `mGameState` variable to `Game` that supports three different states: gameplay, paused, and quit. In the gameplay state, all input actions route to the game world, which means you pass the input to each actor. On the other hand, in the paused state, all input actions go to the UI screen at the top of the UI stack. This means that `Game::ProcessInput` must call `ProcessInput` on either each actor or the UI screen, depending on this state:

```
if (mGameState == EGameplay)
{
   for (auto actor : mActors)
   {
      if (actor->GetState() == Actor::EActive)
      {
```

```
        actor->ProcessInput(state);
    }
  }
}
else if (!mUIStack.empty())
{
   mUIStack.back()->ProcessInput(state);
}
```

You can also extend this behavior so that the UI screen on top of the stack can decide whether it wants to process the input. If the UI screen decides it doesn't want to process the input, it can forward the input to the next topmost UI on the stack.

Similarly, when responding to SDL_KEYDOWN and SDL_MOUSEBUTTON events, you either send the event to the game world or to the UI screen at the top of the stack (via the HandleKeyPress function).

Because you added mGameState to track the state of the game, you also make changes to the game loop. The condition of the game loop changes to keep looping as long as the game is not in the EQuit state. You further update the game loop such that you call Update on all the actors in the world only if the game state is EGameplay. This way, the game doesn't continue to update the objects in the game world while in the paused state.

The Pause Menu

Once the game has support for a paused state, you can add a pause menu. First, you declare PauseMenu as a subclass of UIScreen. The constructor of PauseMenu sets the game state to paused and sets the title text of the UI screen:

```
PauseMenu::PauseMenu(Game* game)
    :UIScreen(game)
{
   mGame->SetState(Game::EPaused);
   SetTitle("PAUSED");
}
```

The destructor sets the game's state back to gameplay:

```
PauseMenu::~PauseMenu()
{
   mGame->SetState(Game::EGameplay);
}
```

Finally, the HandleKeyPress function closes the pause menu if the player presses the Escape key:

```
void PauseMenu::HandleKeyPress(int key)
{
   UIScreen::HandleKeyPress(key);
   if (key == SDLK_ESCAPE)
   {
      Close();
   }
}
```

This leads to the game deleting the `PauseMenu` instance, which calls the `PauseMenu` destructor, which sets the game state back to gameplay.

To show the pause menu, you need to construct a new `PauseMenu` object because the constructor automatically adds the `UIScreen` to the stack. You create the pause menu in `Game::HandleKeyPress` to have it appear when the player presses the Escape key.

The overall flow is that while in the gameplay state, the player can press Escape to see the pause menu. Constructing the pause menu object causes the game to enter the pause state, which means actors don't update. Then, if the player presses Escape when in the pause menu, you delete the pause menu and return to the gameplay state. Figure 11.1 shows the game paused with this simple version of the pause menu (which isn't really a menu yet because it has no buttons).

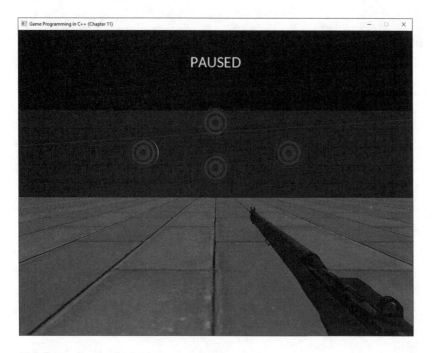

Figure 11.1 Game showing the basic pause menu

Buttons

Most menus in games also have buttons that the player can interact with. For example, a pause menu might have buttons for resuming the game, quitting the game, configuring options, and so on. Because different UI screens may need buttons, it makes sense to add this support to the base UIScreen class.

To encapsulate buttons, you can declare a Button class, as shown in Listing 11.5. You can assume that every button has a text name, and so it also needs a pointer to the Font that renders this text. In addition, the button has a position onscreen as well as dimensions (width and height). Finally, when the player clicks the button, some action should occur, depending on the button clicked.

To customize a button's action, Button uses the std::function class to encapsulate a callback function. This function can be a standalone function or, more likely, a lambda expression. When declaring a Button, the constructor takes in this function. Then, when the code detects a button click, you can call this function. This way, any arbitrary button you create for any arbitrary menu can call a corresponding arbitrary function.

Listing 11.5 Button Declaration

```cpp
class Button
{
public:
    // Constructor takes in a name, font,
    // callback function, and position/dimensions of button
    Button(const std::string& name, class Font* font,
        std::function<void()> onClick,
        const Vector2& pos, const Vector2& dims);
    ~Button();
    // Set the name of the button, and generate name texture
    void SetName(const std::string& name);

    // Returns true if the point is within the button's bounds
    bool ContainsPoint(const Vector2& pt) const;
    // Called when button is clicked
    void OnClick();
    // Getters/setters
    // ...
private:
    std::function<void()> mOnClick;
    std::string mName;
    class Texture* mNameTex;
    class Font* mFont;
    Vector2 mPosition;
    Vector2 mDimensions;
    bool mHighlighted;
};
```

Button has a ContainsPoint function that, given a point, returns true if the point is within the 2D bounds of the button. This function uses the same approach as in Chapter 10, "Collision Detection": You test for the four cases where the point is *not* within the bounds. If none of these four cases are true, then the button must contain the point:

```cpp
bool Button::ContainsPoint(const Vector2& pt) const
{
    bool no = pt.x < (mPosition.x - mDimensions.x / 2.0f) ||
        pt.x > (mPosition.x + mDimensions.x / 2.0f) ||
        pt.y < (mPosition.y - mDimensions.y / 2.0f) ||
        pt.y > (mPosition.y + mDimensions.y / 2.0f);
    return !no;
}
```

The Button::SetName function uses the previously discussed RenderText function to create the texture for the button's name, stored in mNameTex. The OnClick function simply calls the mOnClick handler, if it exists:

```cpp
void Button::OnClick()
{
    if (mOnClick)
    {
        mOnClick();
    }
}
```

You then add additional member variables to UIScreen to support buttons: a vector of Button pointers and two textures for the buttons. One texture is for unselected buttons, and the other is for selected buttons. Having different textures makes it easier for the player to differentiate between the selected and unselected buttons.

Next, you add a helper function to make it easy to create new buttons:

```cpp
void UIScreen::AddButton(const std::string& name,
    std::function<void()> onClick)
{
    Vector2 dims(static_cast<float>(mButtonOn->GetWidth()),
        static_cast<float>(mButtonOn->GetHeight()));
    Button* b = new Button(name, mFont, onClick, mNextButtonPos, dims);
    mButtons.emplace_back(b);
    // Update position of next button
    // Move down by height of button plus padding
    mNextButtonPos.y -= mButtonOff->GetHeight() + 20.0f;
}
```

The `mNextButtonPos` variable allows the `UIScreen` to control where the buttons draw. You could certainly add more customization with more parameters, but using the provided code is a simple way to get a vertical list of buttons.

Next, you add code in `UIScreen::DrawScreen` to draw the buttons. For each button, you first draw the button texture (which is either `mButtonOn` or `mButtonOff`, depending on whether the button is selected). Next, you draw the text for the button:

```
for (auto b : mButtons)
{
    // Draw background of button
    Texture* tex = b->GetHighlighted() ? mButtonOn : mButtonOff;
    DrawTexture(shader, tex, b->GetPosition());
    // Draw text of button
    DrawTexture(shader, b->GetNameTex(), b->GetPosition());
}
```

You also want the player to use the mouse to select and click on buttons. Recall that the game uses a relative mouse mode so that that mouse movement turns the camera. To allow the player to highlight and click on buttons, you need to disable this relative mouse mode. You can leave responsibility for this to the `PauseMenu` class; in the constructor, it disables relative mouse mode, and then it reenables it in the destructor. This way, when the player returns to gameplay, the mouse can once again rotate the camera.

The `UIScreen::ProcessInput` function, shown in Listing 11.6, handles highlighting buttons with the mouse. You first get the position of the mouse and convert it to the simple screen space coordinates where the center of the screen is (0, 0). You get the width and height of the screen from the renderer. You then loop over all the buttons in the `mButtons` vector and use the `ContainsPoint` function to determine whether the mouse cursor is within the bounds of the button. If the button contains the mouse cursor, its state is set to highlighted.

Listing 11.6 `UIScreen::ProcessInput` Implementation

```
void UIScreen::ProcessInput(const uint8_t* keys)
{
    // Are there buttons?
    if (!mButtons.empty())
    {
        // Get position of mouse
        int x, y;
        SDL_GetMouseState(&x, &y);
        // Convert to (0,0) center coordinates (assume 1024x768)
        Vector2 mousePos(static_cast<float>(x), static_cast<float>(y));
        mousePos.x -= mGame->GetRenderer()->GetScreenWidth() * 0.5f;
        mousePos.y = mGame->GetRenderer()->GetScreenHeight() * 0.5f
                    - mousePos.y;
```

```
      // Highlight any buttons
      for (auto b : mButtons)
      {
         if (b->ContainsPoint(mousePos))
         {
            b->SetHighlighted(true);
         }
         else
         {
            b->SetHighlighted(false);
         }
      }
   }
}
```

The mouse clicks are routed through `UIScreen::HandleKeyPress`. Because `ProcessInput` already determines which buttons are highlighted by the mouse, `HandleKeyPress` just calls the `OnClick` function on any highlighted buttons.

Using all this code, you can add buttons to `PauseMenu`. For now, you can add two buttons—one to resume the game and one to quit the game:

```
AddButton("Resume", [this]() {
   Close();
});
AddButton("Quit", [this]() {
   mGame->SetState(Game::EQuit);
});
```

The lambda expressions passed to `AddButton` define what happens when the player clicks the button. When the player clicks Resume, the pause menu closes, and when the player clicks Quit, the game ends. Both lambda expressions capture the `this` pointer so that they can access members of `PauseMenu`. Figure 11.2 shows the pause menu with these buttons.

Dialog Boxes

For certain menu actions, such as quitting the game, it's preferable to show the player a confirmation dialog box. This way, if the player clicks on the first button by mistake, he or she can still correct the mistake. Using a UI screen stack makes it easy to transfer control from one UI screen (such as the pause menu) to a dialog box. In fact, you can implement the dialog box with all the existing `UIScreen` functionality. To do this, you can make a new subclass of `UIScreen` called `DialogBox`.

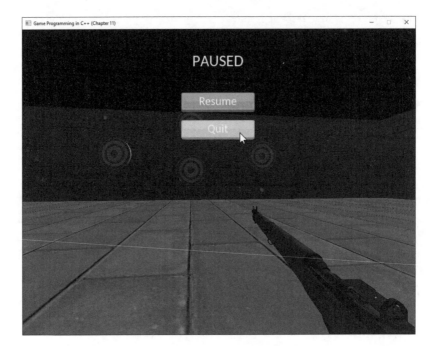

Figure 11.2 Pause menu with buttons

The `DialogBox` constructor takes in a string for the text shown, as well as a function to execute when the user clicks OK:

```
DialogBox::DialogBox(Game* game, const std::string& text,
    std::function<void()> onOK)
    :UIScreen(game)
{
    // Adjust positions for dialog box
    mBGPos = Vector2(0.0f, 0.0f);
    mTitlePos = Vector2(0.0f, 100.0f);
    mNextButtonPos = Vector2(0.0f, 0.0f);
    // Set background texture
    mBackground = mGame->GetRenderer()->GetTexture("Assets/DialogBG.png");
    SetTitle(text, Vector3::Zero, 30);
    // Setup buttons
    AddButton("OK", [onOK]() {
        onOK();
    });
    AddButton("Cancel", [this]() {
        Close();
    });
}
```

The constructor first initializes some of the position member variables for both the title and buttons. Notice that you also use a new member of UIScreen, mBackground, which is a texture for a background that appears behind the UIScreen. In UIScreen::Draw, you draw the background (if it exists) prior to drawing anything else.

Finally, DialogBox sets up both OK and Cancel buttons. You could add additional parameters to DialogBox so that the user can configure the text of the buttons, as well as callbacks for both buttons. However, for now you can just use the OK and Cancel text and assume that the Cancel button simply closes the dialog box.

Because DialogBox is also a UIScreen, you can add it to the UI stack by dynamically allocating an instance of DialogBox. In the case of the pause menu, you change the Quit button so that it creates a dialog box to confirm that the user wants to quit:

```
AddButton("Quit", [this]() {
    new DialogBox(mGame, "Do you want to quit?",
        [this]() {
            mGame->SetState(Game::EQuit);
    });
});
```

Figure 11.3 shows this dialog box for quitting the game.

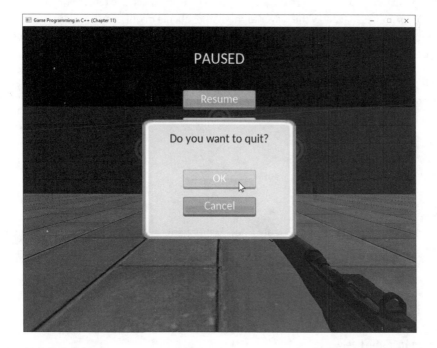

Figure 11.3 Quit dialog box

> **note**
>
> You could use the UI system as described to this point to also create a main menu screen. However, this also requires adding additional states to the Game class because the game can no longer spawn all the objects in the game world immediately; instead, you need to wait until the player progresses past the main menu.

HUD Elements

The types of elements in the HUD vary depending on the game. Such elements include showing hit points or ammo count, a score, or an arrow that points to the next objective. This section looks at two types of elements that are common for first-person games: a crosshair (or **aiming reticule**) and a radar that shows target positions.

Adding an Aiming Reticule

Most first-person games have some sort of aiming reticule (such as a crosshair) in the middle of the screen. As the player aims at different objects, the reticule might change appearance, with different textures. For example, if the player can pick up an object, the reticule might change to a hand. For games that allow the player to shoot, the reticule might change colors. If you implement the color change with a change of texture, then there isn't a difference between these two behaviors.

In this case, you can implement a reticule that changes to red when the player aims at one of the target objects in the game. To do this, you need to add member variables to HUD for the different textures, as well as a Boolean for whether the player is aiming at an enemy:

```
// Textures for crosshair
class Texture* mCrosshair;
class Texture* mCrosshairEnemy;
// Whether crosshair targets an enemy
bool mTargetEnemy;
```

To track what the targets are, you create a new component called `TargetComponent`. Then, you create a vector of `TargetComponent` pointers as a member variable in HUD:

```
std::vector<class TargetComponent*> mTargetComps;
```

You then add `AddTarget` and `RemoveTarget` functions that can add and remove from `mTargetComps`. You call these functions in the `TargetComponent` constructor and destructor, respectively.

Next, you create an `UpdateCrosshair` function, as shown in Listing 11.7. This function gets called by `HUD::Update`. You first reset `mTargetEnemy` back to `false`. Next, you use the `GetScreenDirection` function first described in Chapter 9, "Cameras." Recall that this function returns a normalized vector of the camera's current facing in the world. You use this vector and a constant to construct a line segment, and you use the `SegmentCast` function from Chapter 10 to determine the first actor that intersects with the segment.

Next, you see if this actor has a `TargetComponent`. The way you can check this for now is to find if any `TargetComponent` in `mTargetComps` has an owner corresponding to the actor that you collide against. You can optimize this significantly after you implement a method to figure out which components an actor has; you will do this in Chapter 14, "Level Files and Binary Data."

Listing 11.7 `HUD::UpdateCrosshair` Implementation

```
void HUD::UpdateCrosshair(float deltaTime)
{
    // Reset to regular cursor
    mTargetEnemy = false;
    // Make a line segment
    const float cAimDist = 5000.0f;
    Vector3 start, dir;
    mGame->GetRenderer()->GetScreenDirection(start, dir);
    LineSegment l(start, start + dir * cAimDist);
    // Segment cast
    PhysWorld::CollisionInfo info;
    if (mGame->GetPhysWorld()->SegmentCast(l, info))
    {
        // Check if this actor has a target component
        for (auto tc : mTargetComps)
        {
            if (tc->GetOwner() == info.mActor)
            {
                mTargetEnemy = true;
                break;
            }
        }
    }
}
```

Drawing the crosshair texture is straightforward. In `HUD::Draw`, you simply check the value of `mTargetEnemy` and draw the corresponding texture in the center of the screen. You pass in `2.0f` as the scale of the texture, as well:

```
Texture* cross = mTargetEnemy ? mCrosshairEnemy : mCrosshair;
DrawTexture(shader, cross, Vector2::Zero, 2.0f);
```

This way, as the player moves the aiming reticule to target an object, the reticule changes to the red crosshair texture, as shown in Figure 11.4.

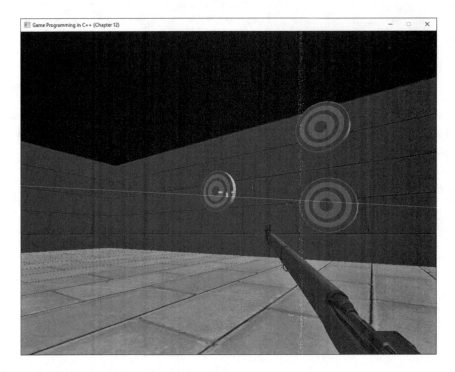

Figure 11.4 Red aiming reticule when aiming at a target

Adding Radar

A game may have a radar that displays nearby enemies (or other objects) within a certain radius of the player. You can represent these enemies on the radar with **blips** (which look like dots or circles on the radar). This way, the player can get a sense of whether there are enemies around. Some games always show enemies on the radar, while others show enemies only under certain conditions (such as if the enemy recently fired a weapon). However, these conditions would only be an extension of a basic approach that shows all enemies.

There are two parts to implementing a working radar. First, you need to track the actors that should appear on the radar. Then, on every frame you must update the blips on the radar based on the position of the actors relative to the player. The most basic approach is to represent the blips with a `Vector2` offset from the center of the radar, but you could also add other properties of blips, such as different textures.

You can leverage existing code and say that any actor that has a `TargetComponent` should also appear on the radar.

For this basic radar, you must add a few member variables to HUD:

```
// 2D offsets of blips relative to radar
std::vector<Vector2> mBlips;
// Adjust range of radar and radius
float mRadarRange;
float mRadarRadius;
```

The `mBlips` vector tracks the 2D offsets of the blips relative to the radar center. When updating the radar, you update `mBlips`. This way, drawing the radar simply means drawing the background and then the blip textures at the required offset.

Finally, the `mRadarRange` and `mRadarRadius` variables are parameters for the radar. The range is how far the radar sees in the world. For example, a range of 2000 means the radar has a range of 2000 units in world space. So, for every target that's within `mRadarRange` of the player, you create a blip on the radar. The radius variable is the radius of the 2D radar drawn onscreen.

Suppose a game has a radar with a range of 50 units. Now imagine that there's an object 25 units directly in front of the player. Because the object positions are in 3D, you need to convert both the position of the player and the object into 2D coordinates for the onscreen radar. In the case of a z-up world, this means the radar acts like a projection of the player and game objects on the x-y plane. This means your radar ignores the z components of both the player and the objects it tracks.

Because up on the radar usually denotes forward in world space, and your world is +x forward, just ignoring the z component is not enough. For both the player and any actors on the radar, you need to convert their (x, y, z) coordinates to the 2D vector (y, x) for the radar offsets.

Once both the player's and the object's positions are in 2D radar coordinates, you can construct a vector from the player to the object, which for clarity is the vector $\vec{a}$. The length of $\vec{a}$ determines whether the object is within the range of the radar. For the previous example with a range of 50 units and an object 25 units in front, the length of $\vec{a}$ is less than the maximum range. This means the object should appear on the radar halfway between the center of the radar and the edge. You can convert $\vec{a}$ to a scale relative to the radius of the radar by first dividing by the maximum range of the radar and then multiplying by the scale of the radar, saving the result in a new vector $\vec{r}$:

$$\vec{r} = RadarRadius\left(\vec{a} \,/\, RadarRange\right)$$

However, most radars rotate as the player rotates so that up on the radar always corresponds to forward in the game world. This means you can't just directly use $\vec{r}$ as the offset of the radar blip. Instead, you need to figure out the angle between the x-y projection of the player's facing vector and the world forward (unit x). Because you want the angle on the x-y plane, you can compute this angle θ with the atan2 function and construct a 2D rotation matrix given θ. Recall that given row vectors, the 2D rotation matrix is as follows:

$$Rotation2D(\theta) = \begin{bmatrix} \cos\theta & \sin\theta \\ -\sin\theta & \cos\theta \end{bmatrix}$$

Once you have the rotation matrix, the final blip offset is simply $\vec{r}$ rotated by this matrix:

$$BlipOffset = \vec{r}\ Rotation2D(\theta)$$

Listing 11.8 shows the code that computes the positions of all the blips. You loop over all the target components and test whether the owning actor is in range of the radar. If so, you compute the blip offset by using the preceding equations.

Listing 11.8 HUD::UpdateRadar Implementation

```
void HUD::UpdateRadar(float deltaTime)
{
    // Clear blip positions from last frame
    mBlips.clear();

    // Convert player position to radar coordinates (x forward, z up)
    Vector3 playerPos = mGame->GetPlayer()->GetPosition();
    Vector2 playerPos2D(playerPos.y, playerPos.x);
    // Ditto for player forward
    Vector3 playerForward = mGame->GetPlayer()->GetForward();
    Vector2 playerForward2D(playerForward.x, playerForward.y);

    // Use atan2 to get rotation of radar
    float angle = Math::Atan2(playerForward2D.y, playerForward2D.x);
    // Make a 2D rotation matrix
    Matrix3 rotMat = Matrix3::CreateRotation(angle);

    // Get positions of blips
    for (auto tc : mTargetComps)
    {
        Vector3 targetPos = tc->GetOwner()->GetPosition();
        Vector2 actorPos2D(targetPos.y, targetPos.x);

        // Calculate vector between player and target
        Vector2 playerToTarget = actorPos2D - playerPos2D;

        // See if within range
        if (playerToTarget.LengthSq() <= (mRadarRange * mRadarRange))
        {
            // Convert playerToTarget into an offset from
            // the center of the on-screen radar
            Vector2 blipPos = playerToTarget;
            blipPos *= mRadarRadius/mRadarRange;
```

```
        // Rotate blipPos
        blipPos = Vector2::Transform(blipPos, rotMat);
        mBlips.emplace_back(blipPos);
    }
  }
}
```

Drawing the radar is then just a matter of first drawing the background and then looping through each blip and drawing it as an offset of the center of the radar:

```
const Vector2 cRadarPos(-390.0f, 275.0f);
DrawTexture(shader, mRadar, cRadarPos, 1.0f);
// Blips
for (const Vector2& blip : mBlips)
{
    DrawTexture(shader, mBlipTex, cRadarPos + blip, 1.0f);
}
```

Figure 11.5 shows this radar in a game. The dots on the radar each correspond to a target actor in the game world. The arrow in the middle of the radar is just an extra texture drawn to show where the player is, but this always just draws at the center of the radar.

Figure 11.5 Radar in a game

Other extensions to the radar could include having different styles of blips depending on whether the enemy is above or below the player. Switching between such styles involves considering the z components of both the player and the object.

Localization

Localization is the process of converting a game from one region or **locale** to a different one. The most common items to localize include any voice-over dialogue as well as any text shown onscreen. For example, a game developer working in English may want to localize to Chinese if releasing the game in China. The biggest expense of localization is in the content: Someone must translate all the text and dialogue, and in the case of dialogue, different actors must speak the lines in different languages.

However, part of the responsibility of localization falls on the programmer. In the case of the UI, the game needs some system to easily show text from different locales onscreen. This means you can't hard-code strings such as "Do you want to quit?" throughout the code. Instead, you minimally need a map to convert between a key like `"QuitText"` and the actual text shown onscreen.

Working with Unicode

One issue with localizing text is that each ASCII character only has 7 bits of information (though it's stored internally as 1 byte). Only 7 bits of information means there is a total of 128 characters. Of these characters, 52 are letters (upper- and lowercase English), and the rest of the characters are numbers and other symbols. ASCII does not contain any glyphs from other languages.

To deal with this issue, a consortium of many different companies introduced the **Unicode** standard in the 1980s. At this writing, the current version of Unicode supports over 100,000 different glyphs, including glyphs in many different languages, as well as emojis.

Because a single byte can't represent more than 256 distinct values, Unicode must use a different byte encoding. There are several different byte encodings, including ones where each character is 2 bytes or 4 bytes. However, arguably the most popular encoding is **UTF-8**, in which each character in a string has a variable length between 1 and 4 bytes. Within a string, some characters may be only 1 byte, others may be 2 bytes, others may be 3, and others may be 4.

Although this seems more complex to handle than a fixed number of bytes for each character, the beauty of UTF-8 is that it's fully backward compatible with ASCII. This means that an ASCII sequence of bytes directly corresponds to the same UTF-8 sequence of bytes. Think of ASCII as a special case of UTF-8 in which each character in the UTF-8 string is 1 byte. The backward compatibility is likely the reason UTF-8 is the default encoding for the World Wide Web, as well as for file formats such as JSON.

Unfortunately, C++ does not have great built-in support for Unicode. For example, the `std::string` class is intended only for ASCII characters. However, you can use the `std::string` class to store a UTF-8 string. The catch is that if the string is UTF-8 encoded, the `length` member function no longer guarantees to specify the number of glyphs (or letters) in the string. Instead, the `length` is the number of bytes stored in the `string` object.

Luckily, both the RapidJSON library and SDL TTF support UTF-8 encoding. This, combined with storing the UTF-8 strings in `std::string`, means you can add support for UTF-8 strings without much additional code.

Adding a Text Map

In `Game`, you add a member variable called `mTextMap` that's a `std::unordered_map` with key and value types of `std::string`. This map converts a key such as `"QuitText"` to the displayed text "Do You Want to Quit?"

You can define this map in a simple JSON file format, as shown in Listing 11.9. Every language has its own version of this JSON file, which makes it easy to switch between different languages.

Listing 11.9 `English.gptext` Text Map File

```
{
    "TextMap":{
        "PauseTitle": "PAUSED",
        "ResumeButton": "Resume",
        "QuitButton": "Quit",
        "QuitText": "Do you want to quit?",
        "OKButton": "OK",
        "CancelButton": "Cancel"
    }
}
```

You then add a `LoadText` function to `Game` that parses in a `gptext` file and populates the `mTextMap`. (This function calls various RapidJSON functions to parse in the file, but we omit its implementation here for the sake of brevity.)

You likewise implement a `GetText` function in a game and, given a key, it returns the associated text. This just performs a find operation on the `mTextMap`.

You then make two modifications to `Font::RenderText`. First, rather than directly rendering the text string it takes in as a parameter, you have that text string looked up in the text map:

```
const std::string& actualText = mGame->GetText(textKey);
```

Next, instead of calling `TTF_RenderText_Blended`, you call `TTF_RenderUTF8_Blended`, which has the same syntax but takes in a UTF-8 encoded string instead of an ASCII string:

```
SDL_Surface* surf = TTF_RenderUTF8_Blended(font,
    actualText.c_str(), sdlColor);
```

Finally, any code that previously used a hard-coded text string instead uses the text key. For example, the title text for the pause menu is no longer `"PAUSED"` but `"PauseTitle"`. This way, when you eventually call `RenderText`, the correct text loads from the map.

> **tip**
>
> If the game code has finalized English text, a quick hack to localize the text is to use the finalized English text as the text key. This way, you don't have to track down every single non-localized string usage in the code. However, this can be dangerous if someone later changes the English strings in the code, thinking that this will change the text onscreen!

To demonstrate the functionality of this code, you can create a `Russian.gptext` file with a Russian translation of the strings in Listing 11.9. Figure 11.6 shows the Russian version of the pause menu with the Do You Want to Quit? dialog box.

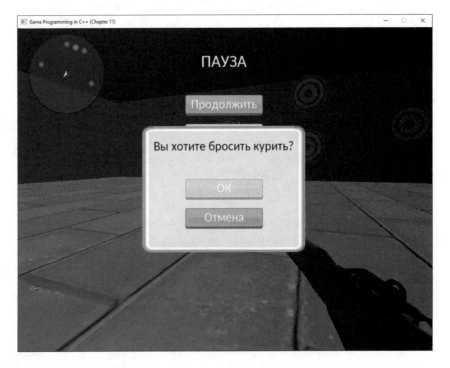

Figure 11.6 Pause menu in Russian

Other Localization Concerns

The code presented in this section works only if the TrueType font file supports all needed glyphs. In practice, it's common for a font file to include only a subset of glyphs. Some languages, such as Chinese, typically have a dedicated font file for the language. To solve this issue, you could add a font entry to the `gptext` file. When populating the `mTextMap`, you can also load the correct font. Then, the rest of the UI code needs to be sure to use this correct font.

Some issues with localization aren't clear at first glance. For example, German text is typically 20% longer than the equivalent English text. This means that if a UI element barely fits the English text, it likely won't fit the German text. Although this usually is a content issue, it may be an issue if the UI code assumes certain paddings or text sizes. One way to circumvent this is to always query the size of the rendered font texture and scale down the size of the text if it won't fit within the needed extents.

Finally, in some instances, content beyond text or dialogue might need a localization process. For example, in Germany, it is illegal to sell a product containing symbols associated with the Third Reich. So, a game set in World War II may show swastikas or other symbols in the English version, but the German version must replace these symbols with alternatives such as the iron cross. As another example, some games also have content restrictions in China (such as not showing too much blood). However, this type of issue usually can be solved without additional help from a programmer, since the artists can simply create alternative content for these regions.

Supporting Multiple Resolutions

For PC and mobile games, it's very common to have players with different screen resolutions. On a PC, common monitor resolutions include 1080p (1920×1080), 1440p (2560×1440), and 4K (3840×2160). On mobile platforms, there are a staggering number of different device resolutions. Although the `Renderer` class currently supports creating the window at different resolutions, the UI code in this chapter assumes a fixed resolution.

One way to support multiple resolutions is to avoid using specific pixel locations, or absolute coordinates, for UI elements. An example of using an absolute coordinate is placing a UI element precisely at the coordinate (1900, 1000) and assuming that this corresponds to the bottom-right corner.

Instead, you could use **relative coordinates**, where the coordinates are relative to a specific part of the screen, called an *anchor*. For example, in relative coordinates, you can say that you want to place an element at (−100,−100) relative to the bottom-right corner. This means the element would appear at (1820, 980) on a 1080p screen, while it would appear at (1580, 950) on a 1680×1050 screen (see Figure 11.7). You can express coordinates relative to key points on the screen (usually the corners or the center of the screen) or even relative to other UI elements. To implement this, you need to be able to specify the anchor points and relative coordinates for UI elements and then calculate the absolute coordinates dynamically at runtime.

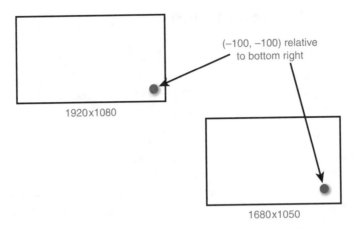

Figure 11.7 A UI element positioned relative to the bottom-right corner of the screen

Another refinement is to scale the size of UI elements depending on the resolution. This is useful because at very high resolutions, the UI might become too small and unusable. At higher resolutions, you could scale the size of the UI elements or even make the UI scale an option for the player.

Game Project

This chapter's game project demonstrates all the features discussed in this chapter except for supporting multiple resolutions. The Game class has a UI stack, along with a UIScreen class, a PauseMenu class, and a DialogBox class. The HUD demonstrates both the aiming reticule and the radar. The code also implements text localization. The code is available in the book's GitHub repository, in the Chapter11 directory. Open Chapter11-windows.sln in Windows and Chapter11-mac.xcodeproj on Mac.

In the game, use the standard first-person controls (WASD plus mouse look) to move around the world. Use the Escape key to enter the pause menu and the mouse controls to select and click on buttons in the menu. During gameplay, use the 1 and 2 key to switch between English (1) and Russian (2) text. Pressing these keys while the pause menu is showing doesn't do anything because the UI screen absorbs the game input.

Summary

This chapter provides a high-level overview of the challenges involved in implementing the user interface in code. Using the SDL TTF library is a convenient way to render fonts, as it can load in TrueType fonts and then render the text to a texture. In the UI stack system, you represent each unique UI screen as an element on the UI stack. At any point in time, only the topmost screen on the UI might receive input from the player. You can extend this system to support buttons as well as dialog boxes.

The HUD might contain many different elements, depending on the game. An aiming reticule that changes based on aiming at an object requires use of collision detection to determine what object the player is aiming at. If the player aims at a target object, the HUD can draw a different texture. For a radar, you can project the player and any enemy objects onto the x/y plane and use these converted coordinates to determine where to draw a blip on the radar.

Finally, the UI needs code to handle text for different locales. A simple map can convert between text keys and values. Using UTF-8 encoding of these text values makes it relatively painless to use. The RapidJSON library can load in JSON files encoded in UTF-8, and SDL TTF supports rendering UTF-8 strings.

Additional Reading

Desi Quintans' short article gives examples of good and bad game UI, from a design perspective. Luis Sempé, a UI programmer for games including *Deus Ex: Human Revolution*, has written the only book solely dedicated to programming UIs for games. (In the interest of full disclosure, I worked with the author many years ago.) Finally, Joel Spolsky's book is for UI design in general, but it provides insight into how to create an effective UI.

Quintans, Desi. "Game UI by Example: A Crash Course in the Good and the Bad." https://gamedevelopment.tutsplus.com/tutorials/ game-ui-by-example-a-crash-course-in-the-good-and-the-bad--gamedev-3943. Accessed September 10, 2017.

Sempé, Luis. *User Interface Programming for Games*. Self-published, 2014.

Spolsky, Joel. *User Interface Design for Programmers*. Berkeley: Apress, 2001.

Exercises

In this chapter's exercises, you explore adding a main menu as well as making changes to the game's HUD.

Exercise 11.1

Create a main menu. To support this, the game class needs a new state called `EMainMenu`. The game should first start in this state and display a UI screen with the menu options Start and Quit. If the player clicks Start, the game should switch to gameplay. If the player clicks Quit, the menu should show a dialog box confirming that the player wants to quit.

To add further functionality, consider spawning the actors only when first entering the gameplay state from the main menu. In addition, change the pause menu so that the Quit option deletes all actors and returns to the main menu rather than immediately quitting the game.

Exercise 11.2

Modify the radar so that it uses different blip textures, depending on whether the actor is above or below the player. Use the provided `BlipUp.png` and `BlipDown.png` textures to show these different states. Testing this feature may require changing the positions of some of the target actors in order to more clearly distinguish the height.

Exercise 11.3

Implement an onscreen 2D arrow that points to a specific actor. Create a new type of actor called `ArrowTarget` and place it somewhere in the game world. Then, in the HUD, compute the vector from the player to the `ArrowTarget`. Use the angle between this and the player's forward on the x-y plane to determine the angle to rotate the onscreen 2D arrow. Finally, add code to `UIScreen::DrawTexture` to supporting rotating a texture (with a rotation matrix).

CHAPTER 12

SKELETAL ANIMATION

Animating characters for a 3D game is very different from animating characters for a 2D game. This chapter looks at *skeletal animation*, the most common animation used in 3D games. This chapter first goes over the mathematical foundations of the approach and then dives into the implementation details.

Foundations of Skeletal Animation

As described in Chapter 2, "Game Objects and 2D Graphics," for 2D animation, games use a sequence of image files to yield the illusion of an animated character. A naïve solution for animating 3D characters is similar: Construct a sequence of 3D models and render those different models in rapid succession. Although this solution conceptually works, it's not a very practical approach.

Consider a character model composed of 15,000 triangles, which is a conservative number for a modern game. Assuming only 10 bytes per vertex, the total memory usage of this one model might be around 50 to 100 KB. A two-second animation running at 30 frames per second would need a total of 60 different models. This means the total memory usage for this single animation would be 3 to 6 MB. Now imagine that the game uses several different animations and several different character models. The memory usage for the game's models and animations will quickly become too high.

In addition, if a game has 20 different humanoid characters, chances are their movements during an animation such as running are largely the same. If you use the naïve solution just described, each of these 20 characters needs a different model set for its animations. This also means that artists need to manually author these different model sets and animations for each character.

Because of these issues, most 3D games instead take inspiration from anatomy: vertebrates, like humans, have bones. Attached to these bones are muscles, skin, and other tissue. Bones are rigid, while the other tissues are not. Thus, given the position of a bone, it's possible to derive the position of the tissue attached to the bone.

Similarly, in **skeletal animation**, the character has an underlying rigid skeleton. This skeleton is what the animator animates. Then, each vertex in the model has an association with one or more bones in the skeleton. When the animation moves the bones, the vertices deform around the associated bones (much the way your skin stretches when you move around). This means that there only needs to be a single 3D model for a character, regardless of the number of animations for the model.

> ## note
>
> Because skeletal animation has bones and vertices that deform along the bones, some call this technique **skinned animation**. The "skin" in this case is the model's vertices.
>
> Similarly, the terms *bone* and *joint*, though different in the context of anatomy, are interchangeable terms in the context of skeletal animation.

An advantage of skeletal animation is that the same skeleton can work for several different characters. For example, it's common in a game for all humanoid characters to share the same skeleton. This way, the animator creates one set of animations for the skeleton, and all characters can then use those animations.

Furthermore, many popular 3D model authoring programs such as Autodesk Maya and Blender support skeletal animations. Thus, artists can use these tools to author the skeletons and animations for characters. Then, as with 3D models, you can write exporter plugins to export into the preferred format for the game code. As with 3D models this book uses a JSON-based file format for the skeleton and animations. (As a reminder, the book's code on GitHub includes an exporter for Epic Games's Unreal Engine, in the `Exporter` directory.)

The remainder of this section looks at the high-level concepts and mathematics that drive skeletal animation. The subsequent section then dives into the details of implementing skeletal animation in game code.

Skeletons and Poses

The usual representation of a **skeleton** is as a hierarchy (or tree) of bones. The **root bone** is the base of the hierarchy and has no parent bone. Every other bone in the skeleton has a single parent bone. Figure 12.1 illustrates a simple skeletal hierarchy for a humanoid character. The spine bone is a child of the root bone, and then in turn the left and right hip bones are children of the spine bone.

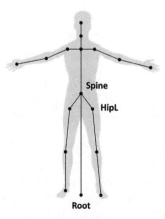

Figure 12.1 Character with a basic skeleton with some bones labeled

This bone hierarchy attempts to emulate anatomy. For example, if a human rotates her shoulder, the rest of the arm follows that rotation. With a game skeleton, you might represent this by saying the shoulder bone is the parent of the elbow bone, the elbow bone is the parent of the wrist bone, and the wrist bone is the parent of the finger bones.

Given a skeleton, a **pose** represents a configuration of the skeleton. For example, if a character waves hello in an animation, there is one pose during the animation where the character's hand bone is raised up to wave. An animation is then just a sequence of poses the skeleton transitions between over time.

The **bind pose** is the default pose of the skeleton, prior to applying any animation. Another term for bind pose is **t-pose** because, typically, the character's body forms a T shape in bind pose, as in Figure 12.1. You author a character's model so that it looks like this bind pose configuration.

The reason the bind pose usually looks like a T because it makes it easier to associate bones to vertices, as discussed later in this chapter.

In addition to specifying the parent/child relationships of the bones in the skeleton, you also must specify each bone's position and orientation. Recall that in a 3D model, each vertex has a position relative to the object space origin of the model. In the case of a humanoid character, a common placement of the object space origin is between the feet of the character in bind pose. It's not accidental that this also corresponds to the typical placement of the root bone of the skeleton.

For each bone in the skeleton, you can describe its position and orientation in two ways. A **global pose** is relative to the object space origin. Conversely, a **local pose** is relative to a parent bone. Because the root bone has no parent, its local pose and global pose are identical. In other words, the position and orientation of the root bone is always relative to the object space origin.

Suppose that you store local pose data for all the bones. One way to represent position and orientation is with a transform matrix. Given a point in the bone's coordinate space, this local pose matrix would transform the point into the parent's coordinate space.

If each bone has a local pose matrix, then given the parent/child relationships of the hierarchy, you can always calculate the global pose matrix for any bone. For example, the parent of the spine is the root bone, so its local pose matrix is its position and orientation relative to the root bone. As established, the root bone's local pose matrix corresponds to its global pose matrix. So multiplying the local pose matrix of the spine by the root bone's global pose matrix yields the global pose matrix for the spine:

$$[SpineGlobal] = [SpineLocal][RootGlobal]$$

With the spine's global pose matrix, given a point in the spine's coordinate space, you could transform it into object space.

Similarly, to compute the global pose matrix of the left hip, whose parent is the spine, the calculation is as follows:

$$[HipLGlobal] = [HipLLocal][SpineLocal][RootGlobal]$$
$$[HipLGlobal] = [HipLLocal][SpineGlobal]$$

Because you can always convert from local poses to global poses, it may seem reasonable to store only local poses. However, by storing some information in global form, you can reduce the number of calculations required every frame.

Although storing bone poses with matrices can work, much as with actors, you may want to separate the bone position and orientation into a vector for the translation and a quaternion for the rotation. The main reason to do this is that quaternions allow for more accurate interpolation of the rotation of a bone during an animation. You can omit a scale for the bones because scaling bones typically only sees use for cartoon-style characters who can stretch in odd ways.

You can combine the position and orientation into the following `BoneTransform` struct:

```
struct BoneTransform
{
    Quaternion mRotation;
    Vector3 mTranslation;
    // Convert to matrix
    Matrix4 ToMatrix() const;
};
```

The `ToMatrix` function converts the transform into a matrix. This just creates rotation and translation matrices from the member data and multiplies these matrices together. This function is necessary because even though many intermediate calculations directly use the quaternion and vector variables, ultimately the graphics code and shaders need matrices.

To define the overall skeleton, for each bone you need to know the name of the bone, the parent of the bone, and its bone transform. For the bone transform, you specifically store the local pose (the transform from the parent) when the overall skeleton is in the bind pose.

One way to store these bones is in an array. Index 0 of the array corresponds to the root bone, and then each subsequent bone references its parent by an index number. For the example in Figure 12.2, the spine bone, stored in index 1, has a parent index of 0 because the root bone is its parent. Similarly, the hip bone, stored in index 2, has a parent of index 1.

Index	0	1	2	3	4
Bone	Name: Root Parent: -1 Local Pose: ...	Name: Spine Parent: 0 Local Pose: ...	Name: HipL Parent: 1 Local Pose: ...	Name: HipR Parent: 1 Local Pose: ...	...

Figure 12.2 Representation of skeleton as an array of bones

This leads to the following `Bone` struct that contains the local bind pose transform, a bone name, and a parent index:

```
struct Bone
{
    BoneTransform mLocalBindPose;
    std::string mName;
    int mParent;
};
```

Then, you define a `std::vector` of bones that you can fill in based on the skeleton. The root bone sets its parent index to –1, but every other bone has a parent indexing into the array. To simplify later calculations, parents should be at earlier indices in the array than their children bones. For example, because the left hip is a child of spine, it should never be the case that left hip has a lower index than spine.

The JSON-based file format used to store the skeleton data directly mirrors this representation. Listing 12.1 gives a snippet of a skeleton file, showing the first two bones: root and pelvis.

Listing 12.1 The Beginning of a Skeleton Data File

```
{
    "version":1,
    "bonecount":68,
    "bones":[
        {
            "name":"root",
            "parent":-1,
            "bindpose":{
                "rot":[0.000000,0.000000,0.000000,1.000000],
                "trans":[0.000000,0.000000,0.000000]
            }
        },
        {
            "name":"pelvis",
            "parent":0,
            "bindpose":{
                "rot":[0.001285,0.707106,-0.001285,-0.707106],
                "trans":[0.000000,-1.056153,96.750603]
            }
        },
        // ...
    ]
}
```

The Inverse Bind Pose Matrix

With the local bind pose information stored in the skeleton, you can easily compute a global bind pose matrix for every bone by using matrix multiplication, as shown earlier. Given a point in a bone's coordinate space, multiplying by this global bind pose matrix yields that point transformed into object space. This assumes that the skeleton is in the bind pose.

The **inverse bind pose matrix** for a bone is simply the inverse of the global bind pose matrix. Given a point in object space, multiplying it by the inverse bind pose matrix yields that point transformed into the bone's coordinate space. This is actually very useful because the model's vertices are in object space, and the models' vertices are in the bind pose configuration. Thus, the inverse bind pose matrix allows you to transform a vertex from the model into a specific bone's coordinate space (in bind pose).

For example, you can compute the spine bone's global bind pose matrix with this:

$$[SpineBind] = [SpineLocalBind][RootBind]$$

Its inverse bind pose matrix is then simply as follows:

$$[SpineInvBind] = [SpineBind]^{-1} = ([SpineLocalBind][RootBind])^{-1}$$

The simplest way to compute the inverse bind pose matrix is in two passes. First, you compute each bone's global bind pose matrix using the multiplication procedure from the previous section. Second, you invert each of these matrices to get the inverse bind pose.

Because the inverse bind pose matrix for each bone never changes, you can compute these matrices when loading the skeleton.

Animation Data

Much the way you describe the bind pose of a skeleton in terms of local poses for each of the bones, you can describe any arbitrary pose. More formally, the current pose of a skeleton is just the set of local poses for each bone. An **animation** is then simply a sequence of poses played over time. As with the bind pose, you can convert these local poses into global pose matrices for each bone, as needed.

You can store this animation data as a 2D dynamic array of bone transforms. In this case, the row corresponds to the bone, and the column corresponds to the frame of the animation.

One issue with storing animation on a per-frame basis is that the frame rate of the animation may not correspond to the frame rate of the game. For example, the game may update at 60 FPS, but the animation may update at 30 FPS. If the animation code tracks the duration of the animation, then every frame, you can update this by delta time. However, it will sometimes be the case that the game needs to show the animation between two different frames. To support this, you can add a static `Interpolate` function to `BoneTransform`:

```
BoneTransform BoneTransform::Interpolate(const BoneTransform& a,
    const BoneTransform& b, float f)
{
    BoneTransform retVal;
    retVal.mRotation = Quaternion::Slerp(a.mRotation, b.mRotation, f);
    retVal.mTranslation = Vector3::Lerp(a.mTranslation,
    b.mTranslation, f);
    return retVal;
}
```

Then, if the game must show a state between two different frames, you can interpolate the transforms of each bone to get the current local pose.

Skinning

Skinning involves associating vertices in the 3D model with one or more bones in the corresponding skeleton. (This is different from the term *skinning* in a non-animation context.) Then, when drawing a vertex, the position and orientation of any associated bones **influence** the position of the vertex. Because the skinning of a model does not change during the game, the skinning information is an attribute of each vertex.

In a typical implementation of skinning, each vertex can have associations with up to four different bones. Each of these associations has a weight, which designates how much each of the four bones influences the vertex. These weights must sum to one. For example, the spine and left hip bone might influence a vertex on the lower-left part of the torso of the character. If the vertex is closer to the spine, it might have a weight of 0.7 for the spline bone and 0.3 for the hip bone. If a vertex has only one bone that influences it, as is common, then that one bone simply has a weight of 1.0.

For the moment, don't worry about how to add these additional vertex attributes for both the bones and skinning weights. Instead, consider the example of a vertex that has only one bone influencing it. Remember that the vertices stored in the vertex buffer are in object space, while the model is in bind pose. But if you want to draw the model in an arbitrary pose, P, you must then transform each vertex from object space bind pose into object space in the current pose, P.

To make this example concrete, suppose that the sole bone influence of vertex v is the spine bone. You already know the inverse bind pose matrix for the spine from earlier calculations. In addition, from the animation data, you can calculate the spine's global pose matrix for the current pose, P. To transform v into object space of the current pose, you first transform it into the local space of the spine in bind pose. Then you transform it into object space of the current pose. Mathematically, it looks like this:

$$v_{InCurrentPose} = v\left(\left[SpineBind\right]^{-1}\left[SpineCurrentPose\right]\right)$$

Now, suppose that v instead has two bone influences: The spine has a weight of 0.75, and the left hip has a weight of 0.25. To calculate v in the current pose in this case, you need to calculate each bone's current pose vertex position separately and then interpolate between them, using these weights:

$$v_0 = v\left(\left[SpineBind\right]^{-1}\left[SpineCurrentPose\right]\right)$$
$$v_1 = v\left(\left[HipLBind\right]^{-1}\left[HipLCurrentPose\right]\right)$$
$$v_{InCurrentPose} = 0.75 \cdot v_0 + 0.25 \cdot v_1$$

You could similarly extend the calculation for a vertex with four different bone influences.

Some bones, such as the spine, influence hundreds of vertices on the character model. Recalculating the multiplication between the spine's inverse bind pose matrix and the current pose matrix for each of these vertices is redundant. On a single frame, the result of this multiplication will never change. The solution is to create an array of matrices called the **matrix palette**. Each index in this array contains the result of the multiplication between the inverse bind pose matrix and the current pose matrix for the bone with the corresponding index.

For example, if the spine is at index 1 in the bone array, then index 1 of the matrix palette contains the following:

$$MatrixPalette[1] = \left[SpineBind\right]^{-1}\left[SpineCurrentPose\right]$$

Any vertex that's influenced by the spine can then use the precomputed matrix from the palette. For the case of the vertex solely influenced by the spine, its transformed position is as follows:

$$v_{InCurrentPose} = v\left(MatrixPalette[1]\right)$$

Using this matrix palette saves thousands of extra matrix multiplications per frame.

Implementing Skeletal Animation

With the mathematical foundations established, you can now add skeletal animation support to the game. First, you add support for the additional vertex attributes that a skinned model needs (bone influences and weights), and then you draw the model in bind pose. Next, you add support for loading the skeleton and compute the inverse bind pose for each bone. Then, you can calculate the current pose matrices of an animation and save the matrix palette. This allows you to draw the model in the first frame of an animation. Finally, you add support for updating the animation based on delta time.

Drawing with Skinning Vertex Attributes

Although drawing a model with different vertex attributes seems straightforward, several pieces of code written in Chapter 6, "3D Graphics," assume a single vertex layout. Recall that to this point, all 3D models have used a vertex layout with a position, a normal, and texture coordinates. To add support for the new skinning vertex attributes, you need to make a nontrivial number of changes.

First, you create a new vertex shader called `Skinned.vert`. Recall that you write shaders in GLSL, not C++. You don't need a new fragment shader in this case because you still want to light the pixels with the Phong fragment shader from Chapter 6. Initially, `Skinned.vert` is just a copy of `Phong.vert`. Recall that the vertex shader must specify the expected vertex layout of each incoming vertex. Thus, you must change the declaration of the vertex layout in `Skinned.vert` to the following:

```
layout(location = 0) in vec3 inPosition;
layout(location = 1) in vec3 inNormal;
layout(location = 2) in uvec4 inSkinBones;
layout(location = 3) in vec4 inSkinWeights;
layout(location = 4) in vec2 inTexCoord;
```

This set of declarations says that you expect the vertex layout to have three floats for position, three floats for the normal, four unsigned integers for the bones that influence the vertex, four floats for the weights of these bone influences, and two floats for the texture coordinates.

The previous vertex layout—with position, normal, and texture coordinates—uses single-precision floats (4 bytes each) for all the values. Thus, the old vertex layout has a size of 32 bytes. If you were to use single-precision floats for the skinning weights and full 32-bit integers for the skinned bones, this would add an additional 32 bytes, doubling the size of each vertex in memory.

Instead, you can limit the number of bones in a model to 256. This means you only need a range of 0 to 255 for each bone influence—or a single byte each. This reduces the size of `inSkinBones` from 16 bytes to 4 bytes. In addition, you can specify that the skinning weights will also be in a range of 0 to 255. OpenGL can then automatically convert this 0–255 range to a normalized floating-point range of 0.0–1.0. This reduces the size of `inSkinWeights` to 4 bytes, as well. This means that, in total, the size of each vertex will be the original 32 bytes, plus an additional 8 bytes for the skinned bones and weights. Figure 12.3 illustrates this layout.

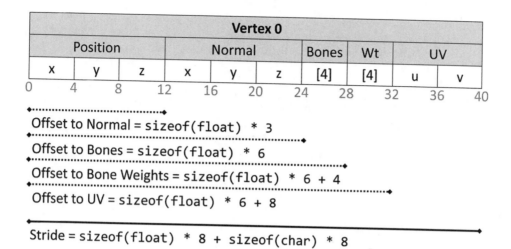

Figure 12.3 Vertex layout with bone influences and weights

To reduce the memory usage of `inSkinBones` and `inSkinWeights`, you don't need to make any further changes to the shader code. Instead, you need to specify the expected sizes of these attributes when defining the vertex array attributes in your C++ code. Recall from Chapter 5, "OpenGL," that the definition of the vertex array attributes occurs in the `VertexArray` constructor. To support different types of vertex layouts, you add a new enum to the declaration of the `VertexArray` class in `VertexArray.h`:

```
enum Layout
{
    PosNormTex,
    PosNormSkinTex
};
```

Then, you modify the `VertexArray` constructor so that it takes in a `Layout` as a parameter. Then, in the code for the constructor you check the layout to determine how to define the vertex array attributes. For the case of `PosNormTex`, you use the previously written vertex attribute code. Otherwise, if the layout is `PosNormSkinTex`, you define the layout as in Listing 12.2.

Listing 12.2   Declaring Vertex Attributes in the `VertexArray` Constructor

```
if (layout == PosNormTex)
{ /* From Chapter 6... */  }
else if (layout == PosNormSkinTex)
{
    // Position is 3 floats
    glEnableVertexAttribArray(0);
    glVertexAttribPointer(0, 3, GL_FLOAT, GL_FALSE, vertexSize, 0);
```

```
// Normal is 3 floats
glEnableVertexAttribArray(1);
glVertexAttribPointer(1, 3, GL_FLOAT, GL_FALSE, vertexSize,
    reinterpret_cast<void*>(sizeof(float) * 3));

// Skinning bones (keep as ints)
glEnableVertexAttribArray(2);
glVertexAttribIPointer(2, 4, GL_UNSIGNED_BYTE, vertexSize,
    reinterpret_cast<void*>(sizeof(float) * 6));
// Skinning weights (convert to floats)
glEnableVertexAttribArray(3);
glVertexAttribPointer(3, 4, GL_UNSIGNED_BYTE, GL_TRUE, vertexSize,
    reinterpret_cast<void*>(sizeof(float) * 6 + 4));

// Texture coordinates
glEnableVertexAttribArray(4);
glVertexAttribPointer(4, 2, GL_FLOAT, GL_FALSE, vertexSize,
    reinterpret_cast<void*>(sizeof(float) * 6 + 8));
}
```

The declarations for the first two attributes, position and normal, are the same as in Chapter 6. Recall that the parameters to `glVertexAttribPointer` are the attribute number, the number of elements in the attribute, the type of the attribute (in memory), whether OpenGL should normalize the value, the size of each vertex (or stride), and the byte offset from the start of the vertex to that attribute. So, both the position and normal are three float values.

Next, you define the skinning bones and weight attributes. For the bones, you use `glVertexAttribIPointer`, which is for values that are integers in the shader. Because the definition of `inSkinBones` uses four unsigned integers, you must use the `AttribI` function instead of the regular `Attrib` version. Here, you specify that each integer is an unsigned byte (from 0 to 255). For the weights, you specify that each is stored in memory as an unsigned byte, but you want to convert these unsigned bytes to a normalized float value from 0.0 to 1.0.

Finally, the declaration of the texture coordinates is the same as in Chapter 6, except that they have a different offset because they appear later in the vertex layout.

Once you have defined the vertex attributes, the next step is to update the `Mesh` file loading code to load in a gpmesh file with skinning vertex attributes. (This chapter omits the code for file loading in the interest of brevity. But as always, the source code is available in this chapter's corresponding game project.)

Next, you declare a `SkeletalMeshComponent` class that inherits from `MeshComponent`, as in Listing 12.3. For now, the class does not override any behavior from the base `MeshComponent`. So, the `Draw` function for now simply calls `MeshComponent::Draw`. This will change when you begin playing animations.

Listing 12.3 `SkeletalMeshComponent` Declaration

```
class SkeletalMeshComponent : public MeshComponent
{
public:
    SkeletalMeshComponent(class Actor* owner);
    // Draw this mesh component
    void Draw(class Shader* shader) override;
};
```

Then, you need to make changes to the `Renderer` class to separate meshes and skeletal meshes. Specifically, you create a separate `std::vector` of `SkeletalMeshComponent` pointers. Then, you change the `Renderer::AddMesh` and `RemoveMesh` function to add a given mesh to either the normal `MeshComponent*` vector or the one for `SkeletalMeshComponent` pointers. (To support this, you add a `mIsSkeletal` member variable to `MeshComponent` that says whether the mesh is skeletal.)

Next, you load the skinning vertex shader and the Phong fragment shaders in `Renderer::LoadShader` and save the resulting shader program in a `mSkinnedShader` member variable.

Finally, in `Renderer::Draw`, after drawing the regular meshes, you draw all the skeletal meshes. The code is almost identical to the regular mesh drawing code from Chapter 6, except you use the skeletal mesh shader:

```
// Draw any skinned meshes now
mSkinnedShader->SetActive();
// Update view-projection matrix
mSkinnedShader->SetMatrixUniform("uViewProj", mView * mProjection);
// Update lighting uniforms
SetLightUniforms(mSkinnedShader);
for (auto sk : mSkeletalMeshes)
{
    if (sk->GetVisible())
    {
        sk->Draw(mSkinnedShader);
    }
}
```

With all this code in place, you can now draw a model with skinning vertex attributes, as in Figure 12.4. The character model used in this chapter is the Feline Swordsman model created by Pior Oberson. The model file is `CatWarrior.gpmesh` in the `Assets` directory for this chapter's game project.

The character faces to the right because the bind pose of the model faces down the +y axis, whereas this book's game uses a +x axis as forward. However, the animations all rotate the model to face toward the +x axis. So, once you begin playing the animations, the model will face in the correct direction.

Figure 12.4 Drawing the Feline Swordsman model in bind pose

Loading a Skeleton

Now that the skinned model is drawing, the next step is to load the skeleton. The gpskel file format simply defines the bones, their parents, and the local pose transform for every bone in bind pose. To encapsulate the skeleton data, you can declare a `Skeleton` class, as shown in Listing 12.4.

Listing 12.4 `Skeleton` Declaration

```
class Skeleton
{
public:
    // Definition for each bone in the skeleton
    struct Bone
    {
        BoneTransform mLocalBindPose;
        std::string mName;
        int mParent;
    };
```

```
   // Load from a file
   bool Load(const std::string& fileName);

   // Getter functions
   size_t GetNumBones() const { return mBones.size(); }
   const Bone& GetBone(size_t idx) const { return mBones[idx]; }
   const std::vector<Bone>& GetBones() const { return mBones; }
   const std::vector<Matrix4>& GetGlobalInvBindPoses() const
       { return mGlobalInvBindPoses; }
protected:
   // Computes the global inverse bind pose for each bone
   // (Called when loading the skeleton)
   void ComputeGlobalInvBindPose();
private:
   // The bones in the skeleton
   std::vector<Bone> mBones;
   // The global inverse bind poses for each bone
   std::vector<Matrix4> mGlobalInvBindPoses;
};
```

In the member data of `Skeleton`, you store both a `std::vector` for all of the bones and a `std::vector` for the global inverse bind pose matrices. The `Load` function is not particularly notable, as it just parses in the gpmesh file and converts it to the vector of bones format discussed earlier in the chapter. (As with the other JSON file loading code, this chapter omits the code in this case, though it is available with the project code in the book's GitHub repository.)

If the skeleton file loads successfully, the function then calls the `ComputeGlobalInvBindPose` function, which uses matrix multiplication to calculate the global inverse bind pose matrix for every bone. You use the two-pass approach discussed earlier in the chapter: First, you calculate each bone's global bind pose matrix, and then you invert each of these matrices to yield the inverse bind pose matrix for each bone. Listing 12.5 gives the implementation of `ComputeGlobalInvBindPose`.

Listing 12.5 `ComputeGlobalInvBindPose` Implementation

```
void Skeleton::ComputeGlobalInvBindPose()
{
   // Resize to number of bones, which automatically fills identity
   mGlobalInvBindPoses.resize(GetNumBones());

   // Step 1: Compute global bind pose for each bone
   // The global bind pose for root is just the local bind pose
   mGlobalInvBindPoses[0] = mBones[0].mLocalBindPose.ToMatrix();

   // Each remaining bone's global bind pose is its local pose
   // multiplied by the parent's global bind pose
   for (size_t i = 1; i < mGlobalInvBindPoses.size(); i++)
   {
```

```
        Matrix4 localMat = mBones[i].mLocalBindPose.ToMatrix();
        mGlobalInvBindPoses[i] = localMat *
            mGlobalInvBindPoses[mBones[i].mParent];
    }

    // Step 2: Invert each matrix
    for (size_t i = 0; i < mGlobalInvBindPoses.size(); i++)
    {
        mGlobalInvBindPoses[i].Invert();
    }
}
```

Using the familiar pattern for loading in data files, you can add an `unordered_map` of `Skeleton` pointers to the `Game` class, as well as code to load a skeleton into the map and retrieve it from the map.

Finally, because each `SkeletalMeshComponent` also needs to know its associated skeleton, you add a `Skeleton` pointer to the member data of `SkeletalMeshComponent`. Then when creating the `SkeletalMeshComponent` object, you also assign the appropriate skeleton to it.

Unfortunately, adding the `Skeleton` code does not make any visible difference over just drawing the character model in bind pose. To see anything change, you need to do more work.

Loading the Animation Data

The animation file format this book uses is also JSON. It first contains some basic information, such as the number of frames and duration (in seconds) of the animation, as well as the number of bones in the associated skeleton. The remainder of the file is local pose information for the bones in the model during the animation. The file organizes the data into **tracks,** which contain pose information for each bone on each frame. (The term *tracks* comes from time-based editors such as video and sound editors.) If the skeleton has 10 bones and the animation has 50 frames, then there are 10 tracks, and each track has 50 poses for that bone. Listing 12.6 shows the basic layout of this gpanim data format.

Listing 12.6 The Beginning of an Animation Data File

```
{
    "version":1,
    "sequence":{
        "frames":19,
        "duration":0.600000,
        "bonecount":68,
        "tracks":[
            {
                "bone":0,
                "transforms":[
                    {
```

```
                    "rot":[-0.500199,0.499801,-0.499801,0.500199],
                    "trans":[0.000000,0.000000,0.000000]
                },
                {
                    "rot":[-0.500199,0.499801,-0.499801,0.500199],
                    "trans":[0.000000,0.000000,0.000000]
                },
                // Additional transforms up to frame count
                // ...
            ],
            // Additional tracks for each bone
            // ...
        }
    ]
  }
}
```

This format does not guarantee that every bone has a track, which is why each track begins with a bone index. In some cases, bones such as the fingers don't need to have any animation applied to them. In such a case, the bone simply would not have a track. However, if a bone has a track, it will have a local pose for every single frame in the animation.

Also, the animation data for each track contains an extra frame at the end that's a duplicate of the first frame. So even though the example above says there are 19 frames with a duration of 0.6 seconds, frame 19 is actually a duplicate of frame 0. So, there are really only 18 frames, with a rate in this case of exactly 30 FPS. This duplicate frame is included because it makes looping slightly easier to implement.

As is the case for the skeleton, you declare a new class called `Animation` to store the loaded animation data. Listing 12.7 shows the declaration of the `Animation` class. The member data contains the number of bones, the number of frames in the animation, the duration of the animation, and the tracks containing the pose information for each bone. As is the case with the other JSON-based file formats, this chapter omits the code for loading the data from the file. However, the data stored in the `Animation` class clearly mirrors the data in the gpanim file.

Listing 12.7 `Animation` Declaration

```
class Animation
{
public:
    bool Load(const std::string& fileName);

    size_t GetNumBones() const { return mNumBones; }
    size_t GetNumFrames() const { return mNumFrames; }
    float GetDuration() const { return mDuration; }
    float GetFrameDuration() const { return mFrameDuration; }

    // Fills the provided vector with the global (current) pose matrices
```

```
    // for each bone at the specified time in the animation.
    void GetGlobalPoseAtTime(std::vector<Matrix4>& outPoses,
        const class Skeleton* inSkeleton, float inTime) const;
private:
    // Number of bones for the animation
    size_t mNumBones;
    // Number of frames in the animation
    size_t mNumFrames;
    // Duration of the animation in seconds
    float mDuration;
    // Duration of each frame in animation
    float mFrameDuration;
    // Transform information for each frame on the track
    // Each index in the outer vector is a bone, inner vector is a frame
    std::vector<std::vector<BoneTransform>> mTracks;
};
```

The job of the GetGlobalPoseAtTime function is to compute the global pose matrices for each bone in the skeleton at the specified inTime. It writes these global pose matrices to the provided outPoses std::vector of matrices. For now, you can ignore the inTime parameter and just hard-code the function so that it uses frame 0. This way, you can first get the game to draw the first frame of the animation properly. The "Updating Animations" section, later in this chapter, circles back to GetGlobalPoseAtTime and how to properly implement it.

To compute the global pose for each bone, you follow the same approach discussed before. You first set the root bone's global pose, and then each other bone's global pose is its local pose multiplied by its parent's global pose. The first index of mTracks corresponds to the bone index, and the second index corresponds to the frame in the animation. So, this first version of GetGlobalPoseAtTime hard-codes the second index to 0 (the first frame of the animation), as shown in Listing 12.8.

Listing 12.8 First Version of GetGlobalPoseAtTime

```
void Animation::GetGlobalPoseAtTime(std::vector<Matrix4>& outPoses,
    const Skeleton* inSkeleton, float inTime) const
{
    // Resize the outPoses vector if needed
    if (outPoses.size() != mNumBones)
    {
        outPoses.resize(mNumBones);
    }

    // For now, just compute the pose for every bone at frame 0
    const int frame = 0;
    // Set the pose for the root
    // Does the root have a track?
```

```
if (mTracks[0].size() > 0)
{
   // The global pose for the root is just its local pose
   outPoses[0] = mTracks[0][frame].ToMatrix();
}
else
{
   outPoses[0] = Matrix4::Identity;
}

const std::vector<Skeleton::Bone>& bones = inSkeleton->GetBones();
// Now compute the global pose matrices for every other bone
for (size_t bone = 1; bone < mNumBones; bone++)
{
   Matrix4 localMat; // Defaults to identity
   if (mTracks[bone].size() > 0)
   {
      localMat = mTracks[bone][frame].ToMatrix();
   }

   outPoses[bone] = localMat * outPoses[bones[bone].mParent];
}
}
```

Note that because not every bone has a track, `GetGlobalPoseAtTime` must first check that the bone has a track. If it doesn't, the local pose matrix for the bone remains the identity matrix.

Next, you use the common pattern of creating a map for your data and a corresponding get function that caches the data in the map. This time, the map contains `Animation` pointers, and you add it to `Game`.

Now you need to add functionality to the `SkeletalMeshComponent` class. Recall that for each bone, the matrix palette stores the inverse bind pose matrix multiplied by the current pose matrix. Then when calculating the position of a vertex with skinning, you use this palette. Because the `SkeletalMeshComponent` class tracks the current playback of an animation and has access to the skeleton, it makes sense to store the palette here. You first declare a simple struct for the `MatrixPalette`, as follows:

```
const size_t MAX_SKELETON_BONES = 96;
struct MatrixPalette
{
   Matrix4 mEntry[MAX_SKELETON_BONES];
};
```

You set a constant for the maximum number of bones to 96, but you could go as high as 256 because your bone indices can range from 0 to 255.

You then add member variables to `SkeletalMeshComponent` to track the current animation, the play rate of the animation, the current time in the animation, and the current matrix palette:

```
// Matrix palette
MatrixPalette mPalette;
// Animation currently playing
class Animation* mAnimation;
// Play rate of animation (1.0 is normal speed)
float mAnimPlayRate;
// Current time in the animation
float mAnimTime;
```

Next, you create a `ComputeMatrixPalette` function, as shown in Listing 12.9, that grabs the global inverse bind pose matrices as well as the global current pose matrices. Then for each bone, you multiply these matrices together, yielding the matrix palette entry.

Listing 12.9   `ComputeMatrixPalette` Implementation

```
void SkeletalMeshComponent::ComputeMatrixPalette()
{
   const std::vector<Matrix4>& globalInvBindPoses =
      mSkeleton->GetGlobalInvBindPoses();
   std::vector<Matrix4> currentPoses;
   mAnimation->GetGlobalPoseAtTime(currentPoses, mSkeleton,
      mAnimTime);

   // Setup the palette for each bone
   for (size_t i = 0; i < mSkeleton->GetNumBones(); i++)
   {
      // Global inverse bind pose matrix times current pose matrix
      mPalette.mEntry[i] = globalInvBindPoses[i] * currentPoses[i];
   }
}
```

Finally, you create a `PlayAnimation` function that takes in an `Animation` pointer as well as the play rate of the animation. This sets the new member variables, calls `ComputeMatrixPalette`, and returns the duration of the animation:

```
float SkeletalMeshComponent::PlayAnimation(const Animation* anim,
                                           float playRate)
{
   mAnimation = anim;
   mAnimTime = 0.0f;
   mAnimPlayRate = playRate;

   if (!mAnimation) { return 0.0f; }
```

```
    ComputeMatrixPalette();

    return mAnimation->GetDuration();
}
```

Now you can load the animation data, compute the pose matrices for frame 0 of the animation, and calculate the matrix palette. However, the current pose of the animation still won't show up onscreen because the vertex shader needs modification.

The Skinning Vertex Shader

Recall from Chapter 5 that the vertex shader program's responsibility is to transform a vertex from object space into clip space. Thus, for skeletal animation, you must update the vertex shader so that it also accounts for bone influences and the current pose. First, you add a new uniform declaration for the matrix palette to `Skinned.vert`:

```
uniform mat4 uMatrixPalette[96];
```

Once the vertex shader has a matrix palette, you can then apply the skinning calculations from earlier in the chapter. Remember that because each vertex has up to four different bone influences, you must calculate four different positions and blend between them based on the weight of each bone. You do this before transforming the point into world space because the skinned vertex is still in object space (just not in the bind pose).

Listing 12.10 shows the main function for the skinning vertex shader program. Recall that `inSkinBones` and `inSkinWeights` are the four bone indices and the four bone weights. The accessors for x, y, and so on are simply accessing the first bone, the second bone, and so on. Once you calculate the interpolated skinned position of the vertex, you transform the point to world space and then projection space.

Listing 12.10 `Skinned.vert` Main Function

```
void main()
{
    // Convert position to homogeneous coordinates
    vec4 pos = vec4(inPosition, 1.0);

    // Skin the position
    vec4 skinnedPos = (pos * uMatrixPalette[inSkinBones.x]) *
inSkinWeights.x;
    skinnedPos += (pos * uMatrixPalette[inSkinBones.y]) * inSkinWeights.y;
    skinnedPos += (pos * uMatrixPalette[inSkinBones.z]) * inSkinWeights.z;
    skinnedPos += (pos * uMatrixPalette[inSkinBones.w]) * inSkinWeights.w;
```

```
// Transform position to world space
skinnedPos = skinnedPos * uWorldTransform;
// Save world position
fragWorldPos = skinnedPos.xyz;
// Transform to clip space
gl_Position = skinnedPos * uViewProj;

// Skin the vertex normal
vec4 skinnedNormal = vec4(inNormal, 0.0f);
skinnedNormal =
      (skinnedNormal * uMatrixPalette[inSkinBones.x]) * inSkinWeights.x
    + (skinnedNormal * uMatrixPalette[inSkinBones.y]) * inSkinWeights.y
    + (skinnedNormal * uMatrixPalette[inSkinBones.z]) * inSkinWeights.z
    + (skinnedNormal * uMatrixPalette[inSkinBones.w]) * inSkinWeights.w;
// Transform normal into world space (w = 0)
fragNormal = (skinnedNormal * uWorldTransform).xyz;
// Pass along the texture coordinate to frag shader
fragTexCoord = inTexCoord;
}
```

Similarly, you also need to skin the vertex normals; if you don't, the lighting will not look correct as the character animates.

Then, back in the C++ code for `SkeletalMeshComponent::Draw`, you need to make sure the `SkeletalMeshComponent` copies the matrix palette data to the GPU with the following:

```
shader->SetMatrixUniforms("uMatrixPalette", &mPalette.mEntry[0],
        MAX_SKELETON_BONES);
```

The `SetMatrixUniforms` function on the shader takes in the name of the uniform, a pointer to a `Matrix4`, and the number of matrices to upload.

You now have everything in place to draw the first frame of an animation. Figure 12.5 shows the first frame of the `CatActionIdle.gpanim` animation. This and other animations in this chapter are also by Pior Oberson.

Updating Animations

The final step to get a working skeletal animation system is to update the animation every frame, based on delta time. You need to change the `Animation` class so that it correctly gets the pose based on the time in the animation, and you need to add an `Update` function to `SkeletalMeshComponent`.

Figure 12.5 A character in the first frame of the "action idle" animation

For the `GetGlobalPoseAtTime` function, in Listing 12.11, you can no longer hard-code it to only use frame 0 of the animation. Instead, based on the duration of each frame and the current time, you figure out the frame before the current time (`frame`) and the frame after the current time (`nextFrame`). You then calculate a value from 0.0 to 1.0 that specifies where exactly between the two frames you are (`pct`). This way, you can account for the animation and game frame rates being different. Once you have this fractional value, you compute the global poses mostly the same as before. However, now instead of directly using a `BoneTransform` for a frame, you interpolate between the bone transforms of `frame` and `nextFrame` to figure out the correct in-between pose.

Listing 12.11   Final Version of `GetGlobalPoseAtTime`

```
void Animation::GetGlobalPoseAtTime(std::vector<Matrix4>& outPoses,
    const Skeleton* inSkeleton, float inTime) const
{
    if (outPoses.size() != mNumBones)
    {
        outPoses.resize(mNumBones);
    }
```

```
// Figure out the current frame index and next frame
// (This assumes inTime is bounded by [0, AnimDuration]
size_t frame = static_cast<size_t>(inTime / mFrameDuration);
size_t nextFrame = frame + 1;
// Calculate fractional value between frame and next frame
float pct = inTime / mFrameDuration - frame;

// Setup the pose for the root
if (mTracks[0].size() > 0)
{
    // Interpolate between the current frame's pose and the next frame
    BoneTransform interp = BoneTransform::Interpolate(mTracks[0][frame],
        mTracks[0][nextFrame], pct);
    outPoses[0] = interp.ToMatrix();
}
else
{
    outPoses[0] = Matrix4::Identity;
}

const std::vector<Skeleton::Bone>& bones = inSkeleton->GetBones();
// Now setup the poses for the rest
for (size_t bone = 1; bone < mNumBones; bone++)
{
    Matrix4 localMat; // (Defaults to identity)
    if (mTracks[bone].size() > 0)
    {
        BoneTransform interp =
            BoneTransform::Interpolate(mTracks[bone][frame],
                mTracks[bone][nextFrame], pct);
        localMat = interp.ToMatrix();
    }

    outPoses[bone] = localMat * outPoses[bones[bone].mParent];
}
}
```

Then, in `SkeletalMeshComponent`, you add an `Update` function:

```
void SkeletalMeshComponent::Update(float deltaTime)
{
    if (mAnimation && mSkeleton)
    {
        mAnimTime += deltaTime * mAnimPlayRate;
        // Wrap around anim time if past duration
```

```
      while (mAnimTime > mAnimation->GetDuration())
      { mAnimTime -= mAnimation->GetDuration(); }

      // Recompute matrix palette
      ComputeMatrixPalette();
   }
}
```

Here, all you do is update `mAnimTime` based on delta time and the animation play rate. You also wrap `mAnimTime` around as the animation loops. This works correctly even when transitioning from the last frame of the animation to the first because, as mentioned earlier, the animation data duplicates the first frame at the end of the track.

Finally, `Update` calls `ComputeMatrixPalette`. This function uses `GetGlobalPoseAtTime` to calculate the new matrix palette for this frame.

Because `SkeletalMeshComponent` is a component, the owning actor calls `Update` every frame. Then in the "generate outputs" phase of the game loop, the `SkeletalMeshComponent` draws with this new matrix palette as usual, which means the animation now updates onscreen!

Game Project

This chapter's game project implements skeletal animation as described in this chapter. It includes the `SkeletalMeshComponent`, `Animation`, and `Skeleton` classes, as well as the skinned vertex shader. The code is available in the book's GitHub repository, in the `Chapter12` directory. Open `Chapter12-windows.sln` in Windows and `Chapter12-mac.xcodeproj` on Mac.

This chapter's game project goes back to the follow camera discussed in Chapter 9, "Cameras," to make the character visible. The `FollowActor` class has a `SkeletalMeshComponent` component, and it thus uses the animation code. The player can use the WASD keys to move the character around. When the character is standing still, an idle animation plays. When the player moves the character, a running animation plays (see Figure 12.6). Currently, the transition between the two animations is not smooth, but you will change that in Exercise 12.2.

Figure 12.6 Character running through the game world

Summary

This chapter provides a comprehensive overview of skeletal animation. In skeletal animation, a character has a rigid skeleton that animates, and vertices act like a skin that deforms with this skeleton. The skeleton contains a hierarchy of bones, and every bone except for the root has a parent bone.

The bind pose is the initial pose of the skeleton, prior to any animations. You can store a local transform for each bone in bind pose, which describes the position and orientation of a bone relative to its parent. A global transform instead describes the position and orientation of a bone relative to object space. You can convert a local transform into a global one by multiplying the local pose by the global pose of its parent. The root bone's local pose and global pose are identical.

The inverse bind pose matrix is the inverse of each bone's global bind pose matrix. This matrix transforms a point in object space while in bind pose into the bone's coordinate space while in bind pose.

An animation is a sequence of poses played back over time. As with bind pose, you can construct a global pose matrix for the current pose for each bone. These current pose matrices can transform a point in a bone's coordinate space while in bind pose into object space for the current pose.

The matrix palette stores the multiplication of the inverse bind pose matrix and the current pose matrix for each bone. When computing the object space position of a skinned vertex, you use the matrix palette entries for any bones that influence the vertex.

Additional Reading

Jason Gregory takes an in-depth look at more advanced topics in animation systems, such as blending animations, compressing animation data, and inverse kinematics.

Gregory, Jason. *Game Engine Architecture,* 2nd edition. Boca Raton: CRC Press, 2014.

Exercises

In this chapter's exercises you will add features to the animation system. In Exercise 12.1 you add support for getting the position of a bone in the current pose, and in Exercise 12.2 you add blending when transitioning between two animations.

Exercise 12.1

It's useful for a game to get the position of a bone as an animation plays. For example, if a character holds an object in his hand, you need to know the position of the bone as the animation changes. Otherwise, the character will no longer hold the item properly!

Because the `SkeletalMeshComponent` knows the progress in the animation, the code for this system needs to go in here. First, add as a member variable a `std::vector` to store the current pose matrices. Then, when the code calls `GetGlobalPoseAtTime`, save the current pose matrices in this member variable.

Next, add a function called `GetBonePosition` that takes the name of a bone and returns the object space position of the bone in the current pose. This is easier than it sounds because if you multiply a zero vector by the current pose matrix for a bone, you get the object space position of that bone in the current pose. This works because a zero vector here means it is exactly at the origin of the bone's local space, and then the current pose matrix transforms it back to object space.

Exercise 12.2

Currently, `SkeletalMeshComponent::PlayAnimation` instantly switches to a new animation. This does not look very polished, and you can address this issue by adding blending to the animations. First, add an optional blend time parameter to `PlayAnimation`, which represents the duration of the blend. To blend between multiple animations, you must track each animation and animation time separately. If you limit blending to only two animations, you just need to duplicate those member variables.

Then, to blend between the animations, when you call `GetGlobalPoseAtTime`, you need to do so for both active animations. You need to get the bone transforms of every bone for each animation, interpolate these bone transforms to get the final transforms, and then convert these to the pose matrices to get the blended current pose.

CHAPTER 13

INTERMEDIATE GRAPHICS

There are a multitude of different graphical techniques used in games, which is why there are entire volumes and book series on the topic. This chapter explores a handful of intermediate graphics concepts: how to improve texture quality, rendering to textures, and a different method for lighting the scene, called *deferred shading*.

Improving Texture Quality

Recall from Chapter 5, "OpenGL," that bilinear filtering can improve the visual quality of a texture as it gets larger on the screen. For example, suppose a wall has a texture on it. As the player gets closer to the wall, the size of the texture becomes larger onscreen. Without bilinear filtering, the texture will look pixelated. However, bilinear filtering makes the image look smoother (although slightly blurry).

Also recall from Chapter 5 that images are just 2D grids of pixels, and each of these "texture pixels" is called a *texel*. Another way to look at the enlargement effect is that as the wall texture becomes larger onscreen, the size of every texel becomes larger onscreen. In other words, the ratio between a texel from the texture and a pixel onscreen decreases.

For example, if every 1 texel corresponds to 2 pixels onscreen, then that ratio is 1:2. **Texel density** is this ratio between pixels onscreen and texels. Ideally, you want the texel density to be as close to 1:1 as possible. As the density decreases, the image quality decreases. Ultimately, the texture appears either too pixelated (if using nearest-neighbor filtering) or too blurry (if using bilinear filtering).

If the texel density becomes too high, this means that each pixel onscreen corresponds to multiple texels in the texture. For example, a 10:1 texel density means that every pixel onscreen corresponds to 10 texels. Ultimately, each of these pixels needs to choose a single color to display. This means that the texture will appear to have texels missing when viewed onscreen; this is called a **sampling artifact**. In graphics, the term **artifact** refers to a graphical glitch that's a result of a graphics algorithm.

Figure 13.1 illustrates the different graphical artifacts caused by varying texel densities. Figure 13.1(a) shows a star texture at a texel density of roughly 1:1, meaning the texture appears onscreen with exactly the same ratio as the original image file. Figure 13.1(b) shows part of the star at a texel density of 1:5, which makes the edges appear blurry. Finally, Figure 13.1(c) shows the texture with a texel density of 5:1, which causes the edges of the star to disappear; to make the image easier to see, the figure illustrates it larger than the actual size.

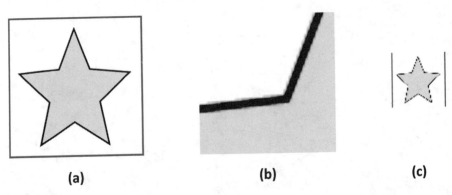

(a)   (b)   (c)

Figure 13.1 Star texture bilinear filtered with varying texel densities: (a) 1:1, (b) 1:5, (c) 5:1

Texture Sampling, Revisited

To understand why a high texel density causes texels to appear to be missing, we need to look more closely at how texture sampling works in general. Recall that textures use UV coordinates (also called texture coordinates) in the range of (0, 0) for the top-left corner and (1, 1) for the bottom-right corner. Suppose you have a texture that's a 4×4 square of texels. In this case, the UV coordinate for the center of the top-left texel is (0.125, 0.125). Similarly, the exact center of the texture corresponds to the UV coordinate (0.5, 0.5), as in Figure 13.2(a).

Now suppose you have a texel density of 1:2, and you draw the region of the texture from (0, 0) to (0.5, 0.5). This means that the top one-fourth of the texture appears at two times the size onscreen. When drawing this in the fragment shader, each fragment (pixel) gets a UV coordinate corresponding to the center of the pixel. For example, the top-left pixel in Figure 13.2(b) is sampling from the texture with a UV coordinate of (0.0625, 0.0625). However, in the original image, no texel's center directly corresponds to this coordinate. This is where a filtering algorithm comes in: It helps select what color to draw for these in-between UV coordinates.

In **nearest-neighbor filtering**, you simply select the texel whose center is the closest to that UV coordinate. So, because the top-left coordinate of (0.0625, 0.0625) is closest to the white texel at (0.125, 0.125), nearest-neighbor filtering selects white for that pixel. The result of this is that every texel is resized proportionally to the texel density, as in Figure 13.2(b). More plainly, in nearest-neighbor filtering, increasing the size of the texture onscreen increases the perceived size of each texel, making the image look pixelated.

In **bilinear filtering**, you find the four texel centers closest to a UV coordinate, and the sampled color at a UV coordinate is the weighted average between these four nearest texels. This yields a smoother transition as the image magnifies, though the image will appear blurry if magnified too much. Figure 13.2(c) illustrates bilinear filtering. Notice that there are fewer neighboring pixels with the same color, but instead the colors blend together.

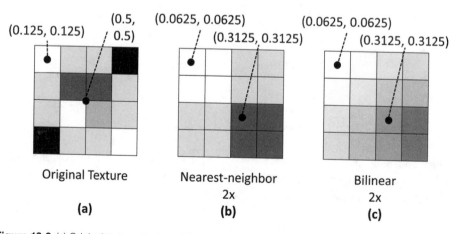

Figure 13.2 (a) Original texture; texture at 2x magnification with (b) nearest-neighbor filtering and (c) bilinear filtering

To understand how to calculate the weighted average in bilinear filtering, remember that you can treat a color as a 3D value and interpolate between colors the same way you interpolate other values. You then decompose the bilinear interpolation into the two separate axes' interpolations. Consider a point P that's nearest the four texels A, B, C, and D, as in Figure 13.3. First, you compute the interpolation between the colors at A and B in the u direction and, similarly, the interpolation between C and D in the u direction. This yields colors at the two points R and S, shown in Figure 13.3. Finally, you interpolate the colors at R and S in the v direction, which yields the final color at P.

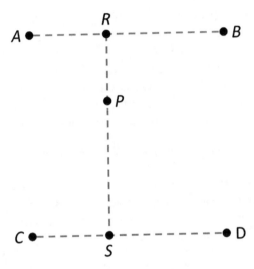

Figure 13.3 Bilinear interpolation of P relative to texels A, B, C, and D

Given the texture coordinates for A, B, C, D, and P, you can calculate this bilinear interpolation with the following set of equations:

$$uFactor = 1 - \frac{P.u - A.u}{B.u - A.u}$$

$$R_{color} = uFactor * A_{color} + (1 - uFactor) * B_{color}$$

$$S_{color} = uFactor * C_{color} + (1 - uFactor) * D_{color}$$

$$vFactor = 1 - \frac{P.u - A.u}{C.u - A.u}$$

$$P_{color} = vFactor * R_{color} + (1 - vFactor) * S_{color}$$

In these equations, *uFactor* determines the weighting in the u component direction, and *vFactor* determines the weighting in the v component direction. You then use these weightings to first calculate the colors at R and S and then, finally, the color at P.

These bilinear filtering calculations automatically occur on the graphics card if the texture has bilinear filtering enabled. And although this sounds like a lot of calculations to do for every fragment that samples the texture, modern graphics hardware can rapidly perform millions of such calculations per second.

As you've seen, magnifying the texture too much causes the image to appear either pixelated or blurry, depending on the technique used. The issue with reducing the size of the texture is that there aren't enough texture samples to maintain all the information stored in the texture. Returning to the example texture, if you reduce the size of the image by a factor of two, the filtering loses details from the texture, as in Figure 13.4(b). You no longer see the border, as in the original image. This example is especially dramatic because you have only four pixels left after the size reduction.

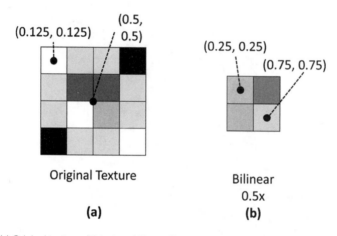

Figure 13.4 (a) Original texture; (b) texture bilinear filtered to half size

Mipmapping

In **mipmapping**, rather than having a single source texture, you generate a series of additional textures, called **mipmaps**, that are at lower resolutions than the source texture. For example, if the source texture has a resolution of 256×256, you may generate mipmaps of 128×128, 64×64, and 32×32. Then, when it's time to draw the texture onscreen, the graphics hardware can select the mipmap texture that yields a texel density closest to 1:1. While mipmapping doesn't improve texture quality when you're magnifying a texture to a resolution higher than the original resolution, it greatly improves the quality when you're reducing the size of a texture.

The main reason for the quality improvement is that you generate the mipmap textures only once—at the time the texture is loaded. This means that you can use more expensive algorithms that generate high-quality mipmaps (such as using a box filter). Thus, sampling from these high-quality mipmaps with a texel density close to 1:1 will look much better than sampling from the original texture with some higher texel density, such as 4:1.

Figure 13.5 illustrates sample mipmaps for the star texture. The highest-resolution texture is the original texture at 256×256, and the remaining textures are auto-generated mipmaps. Note how even the smallest mipmap maintains the border of the texture, which was missing previously when you directly sampled from the 256×256 texture at a low texel density.

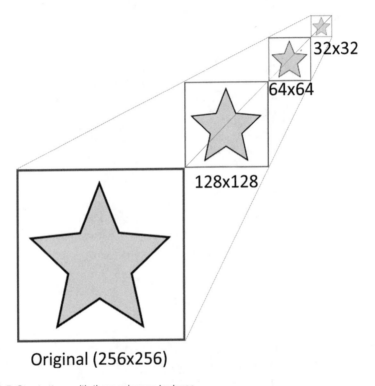

Figure 13.5 Star texture with three mipmap textures

Much as texture sampling can use nearest-neighbor filtering or bilinear filtering, there are two different approaches to applying mipmaps. In **nearest-neighbor mipmapping**, you simply select the mipmap that gives the texel density closest to 1:1. Although this works well in many cases, in some instances (such as with a floor texture), it may cause banding at the borders where the mipmap texture (or **mip level**) changes. In **trilinear filtering**, you sample the two mip levels closest to a 1:1 texel density separately (with bilinear filtering), and the final color is a blend between these two samples. This is "trilinear" because it blends now in three dimensions—the UV coordinates of the texture samples as well as the mip-level blend.

Enabling mipmapping for a texture in OpenGL is straightforward. After loading a texture with the code from Chapter 5, you simply add a call to `glGenerateMipmap`:

```
glGenerateMipmap(GL_TEXTURE_2D);
```

This automatically generates appropriate mip levels, using a high-quality filtering algorithm.

When setting texture parameters, you can set both the minimization filter (what happens when the texture becomes smaller onscreen) and the magnification filter (what happens when the texture becomes larger onscreen). This is what the `GL_TEXTURE_MIN_FILTER` and `GL_TEXTURE_MAG_FILTER` parameters reference.

After you've generated the mipmaps, you then change the texture parameter for the min filter to use mipmapping. To do trilinear filtering, you use these texture parameters:

```
glTexParameteri(GL_TEXTURE_2D, GL_TEXTURE_MIN_FILTER,
    GL_LINEAR_MIPMAP_LINEAR);
glTexParameteri(GL_TEXTURE_2D, GL_TEXTURE_MAG_FILTER,
    GL_LINEAR);
```

Note that you still use `GL_LINEAR` as the filtering function for magnification because mipmaps do not help with texel density lower than 1:1. To instead use nearest-neighbor mipmapping for minification, you would pass in `GL_LINEAR_MIPMAP_NEAREST` as the final parameter to the `GL_TEXTURE_MIN_FILTER` call.

Another advantage of mipmapping is that it improves the rendering performance due to the way that texture caching works. Much like a CPU cache, the graphics card has a cache for its memory. Small mip levels are very cache friendly, which means the overall rendering performance increases.

Anisotropic Filtering

Although mipmapping greatly reduces sampling artifacts in most instances, textures viewed at oblique angles relative to the camera will appear very blurry. This is noticeable especially with floor textures, as shown in Figure 13.6(b). **Anisotropic filtering** mitigates this by sampling additional points on the texture when it is viewed at an oblique angle. For example, 16x anisotropic filtering means that there are 16 different samples for the texel color.

The graphics hardware performs the anisotropic calculations, using a series of mathematical functions. This chapter does not cover these functions, but you can consult OpenGL Extensions Registry in the "Additional Reading" section at the end of this chapter for more information.

Although the newest specifications of OpenGL include anisotropic filtering as a default feature, anisotropic filtering is an extension in OpenGL 3.3. This means you should verify that the graphics hardware supports anisotropy before enabling the feature. For the most part, this is academic because every graphics card made in the past decade supports anisotropic filtering. But in general, it is a good idea to test whether an OpenGL extension is available before using said extension.

To turn on anisotropic filtering, you set the texture to use mipmapping and then add the following lines of code:

```
if (GLEW_EXT_texture_filter_anisotropic)
{
    // Get the maximum anisotropy value
    GLfloat largest;
    glGetFloatv(GL_MAX_TEXTURE_MAX_ANISOTROPY_EXT, &largest);
    // Enable it
    glTexParameterf(GL_TEXTURE_2D, GL_TEXTURE_MAX_ANISOTROPY_EXT,
    largest);
}
```

This code tests whether anisotropic filtering is available, and if it is, you ask OpenGL for the maximum anisotropy value. Then you set the texture parameter to use anisotropic filtering.

Figure 13.6 shows the ground from this chapter's game project with different settings. Figure 13.6(a) shows the ground using only bilinear filtering; note how the ground has many sampling artifacts on the edges of the bricks. Figure 13.6(b) shows trilinear filtering enabled; this is an improvement, but the distant ground is blurry. Finally, Figure 13.6(c) shows both trilinear filtering and anisotropic filtering enabled, which yields the best visual quality of the three choices.

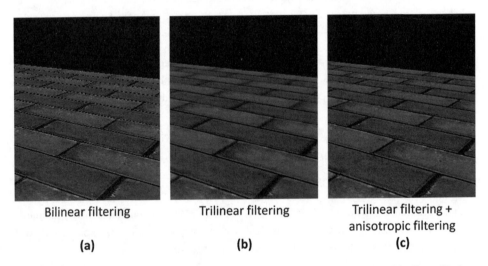

Bilinear filtering　　　　　Trilinear filtering　　　　Trilinear filtering +
anisotropic filtering

(a)　　　　　　　　　　(b)　　　　　　　　　(c)

Figure 13.6 Viewing the ground with different filtering methods: (a) bilinear filtering, (b) trilinear filtering, and (c) trilinear and anisotropic filtering

Rendering to Textures

To this point, you've always drawn polygons directly to the color buffer. However, this color buffer isn't special; it's just a 2D image that you write colors to at specific coordinates. It turns out you can also draw the scene to any arbitrary texture, or **render-to-texture**. Although this may seem unnecessary, there are many reasons you may want to render to a texture.

For example, a racing game might have a car with a rearview mirror. If you want the mirror to look accurate, you might render the game world from the perspective of the rearview mirror to a texture and then draw the texture on the mirror in the scene. Furthermore, some graphical techniques use textures as temporary storage before computing the final output to the color buffer.

This section explores how to render to a texture and then display this texture on the screen. This will require some changes to the overall rendering code, which previously assumed that everything writes directly to the color buffer. You also need to add support for rendering the scene from the perspectives of different cameras.

---

note

For high-quality reflections, such as for a large mirror, you must render the scene from the perspective of the surface. However, if the game scene contains many surfaces that need low-quality reflections, rendering the scene from the perspective of each of these surfaces is too expensive. In this case, you can instead generate a single **reflection map** of the entire scene. Then, for every low-quality reflective surface, you sample from this reflection map to give the illusion of a reflection. Although the quality is significantly lower than when rendering from the perspective of the reflective surface, it is sufficient for surfaces that only need low-quality reflections.

This book does not cover how to implement reflection maps, but you can consult the "Additional Reading" section at the end of this chapter for further information on the topic.

Creating the Texture

To render to a texture, you first need to create a texture. You can add a new function to the `Texture` class to support creating a texture for rendering. The code for creating a texture, shown in Listing 13.1, is like the code for creating textures from Chapter 5. However, rather than assuming that you want an RGBA format (which will result in 8 bits per component and 32 bits per pixel), you use a parameter to specify the format. Second, the texture has no initial data, which is why the last parameter to `glTexImage2D` is `nullptr`. If this last parameter is `nullptr`, then the second and third-to-last parameters are ignored. Finally, you purposefully do not enable mipmapping or bilinear filtering on the texture. You want the sampled data from the texture to precisely match the actual output.

Listing 13.1 Creating a Texture for Rendering

```
void Texture::CreateForRendering(int width, int height,
                                 unsigned int format)
{
   mWidth = width;
   mHeight = height;
```

```
// Create the texture id
glGenTextures(1, &mTextureID);
glBindTexture(GL_TEXTURE_2D, mTextureID);
// Set the image width/height with null initial data
glTexImage2D(GL_TEXTURE_2D, 0, format, mWidth, mHeight, 0, GL_RGB,
    GL_FLOAT, nullptr);

// For a texture we'll render to, just use nearest neighbor
glTexParameteri(GL_TEXTURE_2D, GL_TEXTURE_MIN_FILTER, GL_NEAREST);
glTexParameteri(GL_TEXTURE_2D, GL_TEXTURE_MAG_FILTER, GL_NEAREST);
}
```

Creating a Framebuffer Object

Much the way that OpenGL uses a vertex array object to contain all information about vertices (including the vertex buffer, vertex format, and index buffer), a **framebuffer object** (FBO) contains all information about a framebuffer. The FBO includes any textures associated with the framebuffer, an associated depth buffer (if it exists), and other parameters. You can then select which framebuffer to use for rendering. OpenGL provides a default framebuffer object with ID 0, which is the framebuffer that you've been drawing to up to this point. However, you can also create additional framebuffers and switch to other framebuffers as needed.

For now, you will use a custom framebuffer object for a rearview mirror that you display in the HUD onscreen. First, you must add two new member variables to the `Renderer` class:

```
// Framebuffer object for the mirror
unsigned int mMirrorBuffer;
// Texture for the mirror
class Texture* mMirrorTexture;
```

You store the ID of the framebuffer object you create in `mMirrorBuffer` and the texture object associated with the framebuffer in `mMirrorTexture`.

Next, you need a function that creates and configures the mirror framebuffer object, as shown in Listing 13.2. Several steps are necessary here. First, `glGenFrameBuffers` creates the framebuffer object and stores the ID in `mMirrorBuffer`. The `glBindFrameBuffer` call then sets this framebuffer as active. The next several lines of `CreateMirrorTexture` create a depth buffer and attach it to the current framebuffer object. This way, when rendering for the mirror, you still have a depth buffer to ensure that further objects appear behind closer objects.

Then you create the mirror texture, with a width and height one-quarter the size of the screen. You don't use the full screen size because you want the mirror to take up only part of the screen. You request a `GL_RGB` format for the texture because the mirror will contain the color output of the scene from the perspective of the mirror.

Next, the `glFramebufferTexture` call associates the mirror texture with the framebuffer object. Note how you specify `GL_COLOR_ATTACHMENT0` as the second parameter. This says that the mirror texture corresponds to the first color output of the fragment shader. Right now, your fragment shader writes only one output, but as you'll see later in this chapter, it's possible to write multiple outputs from the fragment shader.

The `glDrawBuffers` call then says that for this framebuffer object, you want to be able to draw to the texture in the `GL_COLOR_ATTACHMENT0` slot (which is the mirror texture). Finally, the `glCheckFrameBuffer` status call verifies that everything worked properly. If there was an issue, you delete the framebuffer object and mirror texture and return `false`.

Listing 13.2 Creating the Mirror Framebuffer

```
bool Renderer::CreateMirrorTarget()
{
    int width = static_cast<int>(mScreenWidth) / 4;
    int height = static_cast<int>(mScreenHeight) / 4;

    // Generate a framebuffer for the mirror texture
    glGenFramebuffers(1, &mMirrorBuffer);
    glBindFramebuffer(GL_FRAMEBUFFER, mMirrorBuffer);

    // Create the texture we'll use for rendering
    mMirrorTexture = new Texture();
    mMirrorTexture->CreateForRendering(width, height, GL_RGB);

    // Add a depth buffer to this target
    GLuint depthBuffer;
    glGenRenderbuffers(1, &depthBuffer);
    glBindRenderbuffer(GL_RENDERBUFFER, depthBuffer);
    glRenderbufferStorage(GL_RENDERBUFFER, GL_DEPTH_COMPONENT, width,
    height);
    glFramebufferRenderbuffer(GL_FRAMEBUFFER, GL_DEPTH_ATTACHMENT,
                              GL_RENDERBUFFER, depthBuffer);

    // Attach mirror texture as the output target for the framebuffer
    glFramebufferTexture(GL_FRAMEBUFFER, GL_COLOR_ATTACHMENT0,
        mMirrorTexture->GetTextureID(), 0);

    // Set the list of buffers to draw to for this framebuffer
    GLenum drawBuffers[] = { GL_COLOR_ATTACHMENT0 };
    glDrawBuffers(1, drawBuffers);

    // Make sure everything worked
    if (glCheckFramebufferStatus(GL_FRAMEBUFFER) != GL_FRAMEBUFFER_COMPLETE)
    {
        // If it didn't work, delete the framebuffer,
        // unload/delete the texture and return false
```

```
            glDeleteFramebuffers(1, &mMirrorBuffer);
            mMirrorTexture->Unload();
            delete mMirrorTexture;
            mMirrorTexture = nullptr;
            return false;
        }
        return true;
    }
```

In `Renderer::Initialize`, you add a call to `CreateMirrorTarget` and verify that the function returns `true`. Similarly, in `Renderer::Shutdown`, you delete the mirror framebuffer and mirror textures (using the same code that runs if the `glCheckFrameBuffer` call says the framebuffer is not complete).

Rendering to a Framebuffer Object

To support a mirror, you need to render the 3D scene twice: once from the perspective of the mirror and once from the perspective of the normal camera. Each time you render the scene is a render **pass**. To assist with drawing the 3D scene multiple times, you can create a `Draw3DScene` function, the skeleton of which is in Listing 13.3.

The `Draw3DScene` function takes in the ID of the framebuffer, the view matrix, the projection matrix, and the scale of the viewport. The viewport size lets OpenGL know the actual size of the framebuffer target that it's writing to. So, you need a viewport scale parameter here so that the normal framebuffer can use the full screen width and height, but the mirror can use its one-fourth size. You use the `glViewport` call to set the viewport to the correct size based on the screen width/height and the scale.

The code for drawing meshes is the same as in Chapter 6, "3D Graphics," and the code for drawing skinned meshes is the same as in Chapter 12, "Skeletal Animation." Other than the viewport code, the only other difference is that before drawing anything, the `glBindFramebuffer` call sets the active framebuffer to the requested one.

Listing 13.3   `Renderer::Draw3DScene` Helper Function

```
void Renderer::Draw3DScene(unsigned int framebuffer,
    const Matrix4& view, const Matrix4& proj,
    float viewportScale)
{
    // Set the current framebuffer
    glBindFramebuffer(GL_FRAMEBUFFER, framebuffer);

    // Set viewport size based on scale
    glViewport(0, 0,
        static_cast<int>(mScreenWidth * viewPortScale),
```

```
      static_cast<int>(mScreenHeight * viewPortScale)
   );

   // Clear color buffer/depth buffer
   glClearColor(0.0f, 0.0f, 0.0f, 1.0f);
   glClear(GL_COLOR_BUFFER_BIT | GL_DEPTH_BUFFER_BIT);

   // Draw mesh components
   // (Same code as Chapter 6)
   // ...

   // Draw any skinned meshes now
   // (Same code as Chapter 12)
   // ...
}
```

You then change the code in `Renderer::Draw` to call `Draw3DScene` twice, as in Listing 13.4. First, you draw using the mirror's view and rendering to the mirror framebuffer, and then you draw using the normal camera's view and rendering to the default framebuffer. Finally, you draw the sprites and UI screens using the code from Chapters 6 and 12.

Listing 13.4 `Renderer::Draw` Updated to Render Both Mirror and Default Passes

```
void Renderer::Draw()
{
   // Draw to the mirror texture first (viewport scale of 0.25)
   Draw3DScene(mMirrorBuffer, mMirrorView, mProjection, 0.25f);
   // Now draw the normal 3D scene to the default framebuffer
   Draw3DScene(0, mView, mProjection);

   // Draw all sprite components
   // (Same code as Chapter 6)
   // ...

   // Draw any UI screens
   // (Same code as Chapter 12)
   // ...

   // Swap the buffers
   SDL_GL_SwapWindow(mWindow);
}
```

Here, `mMirrorView` is a separate view matrix for the mirror. The specifics of the mirror view aren't anything new. You can create a `MirrorCamera` class that uses a basic follow camera, as in Chapter 9, "Cameras." However, the mirror camera is in front of the character, facing behind the character. This `MirrorCamera` then attaches to the player actor and updates `mMirrorView`.

Drawing the Mirror Texture in the HUD

Now that the drawing code is writing to the mirror texture, you can use it just like any other texture and draw it onscreen. Because the mirror in this case is just a HUD element, you can leverage the existing `DrawTexture` functionality in `UIScreen`.

However, drawing with the existing code results in a mirror that has a flipped y value from what is expected. This is because, internally, OpenGL places the UV origin at the bottom-left corner of the image instead of in the top-left corner (as is more typical). Luckily, this is easy enough to fix: When drawing the texture, you already create a scale matrix. If you negate the y-axis of this scale matrix, it will flip the texture in the y direction. To support this, you add a new `flipY` bool as an optional parameter to `UIScreen::DrawTexture`, as shown in Listing 13.5. You default `flipY` to `false` because the existing UI textures don't need their y-axis flipped.

Listing 13.5 Adding a `flipY` Option to `UIScreen::DrawTexture`

```
void UIScreen::DrawTexture(class Shader* shader, class Texture* texture,
    const Vector2& offset, float scale, bool flipY)
{
    // Scale the quad by the width/height of texture
    // and flip the y if we need to
    float yScale = static_cast<float>(texture->GetHeight()) * scale;
    if (flipY) { yScale *= -1.0f; }

    Matrix4 scaleMat = Matrix4::CreateScale(
        static_cast<float>(texture->GetWidth()) * scale,
        yScale,
        1.0f);


    // Translate to position on screen
    Matrix4 transMat = Matrix4::CreateTranslation(
        Vector3(offset.x, offset.y, 0.0f));

    // Set world transform
    Matrix4 world = scaleMat * transMat;
    shader->SetMatrixUniform("uWorldTransform", world);
    // Set current texture
    texture->SetActive();
    // Draw quad
    glDrawElements(GL_TRIANGLES, 6, GL_UNSIGNED_INT, nullptr);
}
```

Finally, you add two lines to `HUD::Draw` to display the mirror texture in the bottom-left corner of the screen, with a scale of 1.0 and `flipY` set to `true`:

```
Texture* mirror = mGame->GetRenderer()->GetMirrorTexture();
DrawTexture(shader, mirror, Vector2(-350.0f, -250.0f), 1.0f, true);
```

Figure 13.7 shows the mirror in action. Notice that the main view shows the normal perspective, which faces in the direction of the Feline Swordsman, but the mirror in the bottom left renders the scene in the opposite direction.

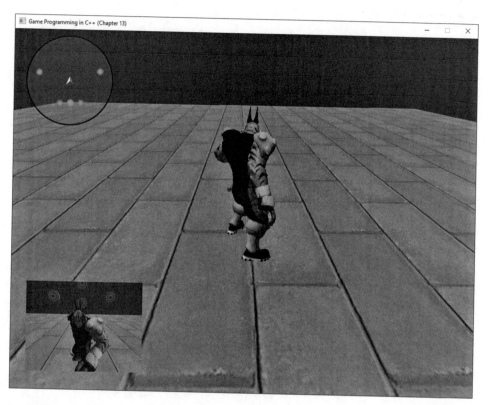

Figure 13.7 Game with a rearview mirror in the bottom left

Deferred Shading

Recall that the Phong lighting implemented in Chapter 6 performs the lighting calculations for each fragment when drawing a mesh. The pseudocode for this type of lighting calculation is as follows:

```
foreach Mesh m in Scene
    foreach Pixel p to draw from m
        if p passes depth test
            foreach Light li that effects p
                color = Compute lighting equation(li, p)
                Write color to framebuffer
```

This method of performing lighting calculations, called **forward rendering**, works well with a small number of lights. For example, the game currently has only one directional light, so forward rendering works perfectly fine. However, consider a game that takes place at night in a city. For such a game, a single directional light won't yield a believable nightscape. Instead, you would want dozens of lights for street lights, car headlights, lights inside buildings, and so on. Unfortunately, forward rendering doesn't scale well in this case. You need to compute lighting equations on the order of $O(m \cdot p \cdot li)$, which means adding several more lights increases the amount of lighting calculations significantly.

An alternative approach is to create a series of textures, collectively called the **G-buffer**, to store information about the visible surfaces in the scene. This G-buffer might contain the diffuse color (albedo), specular power, and normals of visible surfaces in the scene. You then render the scene in two passes. First, you go through every mesh and render the properties of their surfaces to the G-buffer. Then, in the second pass, you loop through every light and compute the lighting equations based on these lights and what is in the G-buffer. The following pseudocode accomplishes this:

```
foreach Mesh m in Scene
    foreach Pixel p1 to draw from m
        if p passes depth test
            Write surface properties of p1 to G-buffer

foreach Light li in the scene
    foreach Pixel p2 affected by li
        s = surface properties from the G-buffer at p2
        color = Compute lighting equation (l, s)
        Write color to framebuffer
```

Note how the complexity of this two-pass approach is $O(m \cdot p_1 + li \cdot p_2)$. This means that you can support far more lights in the scene than with forward rendering. Because there are two passes, and the shading of the fragment onscreen doesn't occur until the second pass, this technique is called **deferred shading** (or **deferred rendering**).

Implementing deferred shading requires several steps. First, you must set up a framebuffer object that supports multiple output textures. Then, you must create fragment shaders that write surface properties to the G-buffer. Next, you draw a quad that covers the entire screen and samples from the G-buffer to output the result of global lighting (such as directional and ambient light). Finally, you calculate the lighting for each non-global light (such as point lights or spotlights).

Creating a G-Buffer Class

Because the framebuffer object for the G-buffer is far more complex than the one for the mirror in the preceding section, it makes sense to encapsulate the FBO and all its associated textures into a new GBuffer class. Listing 13.6 shows the declaration of GBuffer. You declare an enum that defines the types of data stored in the different G-buffer textures. The G-buffer in this chapter stores the diffuse color, the normals, and the world position of each surface.

> **note**
>
> Storing the world position in the G-buffer makes your later calculations simpler—but at the expense of increased memory and rendering bandwidth usage.
>
> It's possible to reconstruct the world position at a pixel from the depth buffer and the view-projection matrix, which eliminates the need for the world position in the G-buffer. Consult Phil Djonov's article in the "Additional Reading" section at the end of the chapter to learn how to do these calculations.

One surface property missing from this G-buffer is the specular power. This means you currently cannot calculate the specular component of the Phong reflection model; in Exercise 13.1 you will fix this.

In the member data for `GBuffer`, you store the framebuffer object ID as well as a vector of the textures that serve as render targets.

Listing 13.6 `GBuffer` Declaration

```
class GBuffer
{
public:
    // Different types of data stored in the G-buffer
    enum Type
    {
        EDiffuse = 0,
        ENormal,
        EWorldPos,
        NUM_GBUFFER_TEXTURES
    };

    GBuffer();
    ~GBuffer();

    // Create/destroy the G-buffer
    bool Create(int width, int height);
    void Destroy();

    // Get the texture for a specific type of data
    class Texture* GetTexture(Type type);
    // Get the framebuffer object ID
    unsigned int GetBufferID() const { return mBufferID; }
    // Setup all the G-buffer textures for sampling
    void SetTexturesActive();
private:
    // Textures associated with G-buffer
    std::vector<class Texture*> mTextures;
    // Framebuffer object ID
    unsigned int mBufferID;
};
```

For the member functions of GBuffer, most of the work occurs in the Create function, which creates a G-buffer of the specified width and height. Listing 13.7 gives the truncated code for this function. The Create function first creates a framebuffer object and adds a depth buffer target, as was done in Listing 13.2.

Listing 13.7 GBuffer::Create Implementation

```
bool GBuffer::Create(int width, int height)
{
   // Create the framebuffer object and save in mBufferID
   // ...
   // Add a depth buffer to this target
   // ...

   // Create textures for each output in the G-buffer
   for (int i = 0; i < NUM_GBUFFER_TEXTURES; i++)
   {
      Texture* tex = new Texture();
      // We want three 32-bit float components for each texture
      tex->CreateForRendering(width, height, GL_RGB32F);
      mTextures.emplace_back(tex);
      // Attach this texture to a color output
      glFramebufferTexture(GL_FRAMEBUFFER, GL_COLOR_ATTACHMENT0 + i,
                 tex->GetTextureID(), 0);
   }

   // Create a vector of the color attachments
   std::vector<GLenum> attachments;
   for (int i = 0; i < NUM_GBUFFER_TEXTURES; i++)
   {
      attachments.emplace_back(GL_COLOR_ATTACHMENT0 + i);
   }
   // Set the list of buffers to draw to
   glDrawBuffers(static_cast<GLsizei>(attachments.size()),
          attachments.data());

   // Make sure everything worked
   if (glCheckFramebufferStatus(GL_FRAMEBUFFER) !=
   GL_FRAMEBUFFER_COMPLETE)
   {
      Destroy();
      return false;
   }
   return true;
}
```

Next, you loop over each type of texture desired in the G-buffer and create one Texture instance for each type of data (because they are separate render targets). Note that you request the GL_RGB32F format for each texture. This means there are three components per texel, and each of these components is a 32-bit single-precision floating-point value. You then attach each texture to a corresponding color attachment slot with the `glFramebufferTexture` call. The code takes advantage of the fact that the OpenGL definitions for the color attachments are consecutive numbers.

> **note**
>
> Although `GL_RGB32F` yields a lot of precision for the values in the G-buffer, the trade-off is that the G-buffer takes up a significant amount of graphics memory. Three `GL_RGB32F` textures at a resolution of 1024×768 (your screen resolution) takes up 27 MB of memory on the GPU. To reduce memory usage, many games instead use `GL_RGB16F` (three half-precision floats), which would cut the memory usage in half.
>
> You could further optimize the memory usage with other tricks. For example, because a normal is unit length, given the x and y components and the sign of the z component, you can solve for the z component. This means you could store the normals in `GL_RG16F` format (two half-precision floats) and later derive the z component. In the interest of simplicity, this chapter does not implement these optimizations, but you should know that many commercial games use such tricks.

You then create a vector of all the different color attachments and call `glDrawBuffers` to set the texture attachments for the G-buffer. Finally, you validate that creating the G-buffer succeeds. If it doesn't, the `Destroy` function deletes all associated textures and destroys the framebuffer object.

Next, you add a `GBuffer` pointer to the member data of `Renderer`:

```
class GBuffer* mGBuffer;
```

Then in `Renderer::Initialize`, you create the `GBuffer` object and set it to the width/ height of the screen:

```
mGBuffer = new GBuffer();
int width = static_cast<int>(mScreenWidth);
int height = static_cast<int>(mScreenHeight);
if (!mGBuffer->Create(width, height))
{
    SDL_Log("Failed to create G-buffer.");
    return false;
}
```

In `Renderer::Shutdown`, you add code that calls the `Destroy` member function on `mGBuffer`.

Writing to the G-buffer

Now that you have a G-buffer, you need to write data into it. Recall that mesh rendering currently uses the Phong fragment shader to write final (fully lit) colors to the default framebuffer. However, this is antithetical to the approach of deferred shading. You need to create a new fragment shader that writes surface properties into the G-buffer.

Another difference is that every previous fragment shader wrote only a single output value. However, fragment shaders can have multiple output values, or **multiple render targets**. This means that writing to each texture in the G-buffer is just a matter of writing to each of the correct outputs. In fact, the GLSL code for the main function of the fragment shader is relatively simple compared to the code for fragment shaders you've seen earlier in this book. You sample the diffuse color from the texture and simply pass along the normal and world position directly to the G-buffer.

Listing 13.8 gives the full GLSL code for `GBufferWrite.frag`. Note that you declare three different `out` values for the three different G-buffer textures. You also specify layout locations for each of the outputs; these numbers correspond to the color attachment indices specified when creating the G-buffer.

Listing 13.8 `GBufferWrite.frag` Shader

```
#version 330
// Inputs from vertex shader
in vec2 fragTexCoord; // Tex coord
in vec3 fragNormal;   // Normal (in world space)
in vec3 fragWorldPos; // Position (in world space)

// This corresponds to the outputs to the G-buffer
layout(location = 0) out vec3 outDiffuse;
layout(location = 1) out vec3 outNormal;
layout(location = 2) out vec3 outWorldPos;

// Diffuse texture sampler
uniform sampler2D uTexture;

void main()
{
    // Diffuse color is from texture
    outDiffuse = texture(uTexture, fragTexCoord).xyz;
    // Pass normal/world position directly along
    outNormal = fragNormal;
    outWorldPos = fragWorldPos;
}
```

You then change the shader loading code for the `mMeshShader` and `mSkinnedShader` to use `GBufferWrite.frag` as the fragment shader, instead of the previous `Phong.frag`.

Finally, in `Renderer::Draw`, you remove the call to `Draw3DScene`, which draws to the default framebuffer. You instead want to draw to the G-buffer:

```
Draw3DScene(mGBuffer->GetBufferID(), mView, mProjection, 1.0f, false);
```

The last Boolean parameter is new; it specifies that `Draw3DScene` should not set any lighting constants on the mesh shaders. This makes sense because the `GBufferWrite.frag` shader doesn't have any lighting constants to set in the first place!

Running the game at this point would yield an entirely black window other than the UI elements. This is because although you're writing surface properties to the G-buffer, you aren't drawing anything to the default framebuffer based on these surface properties. However, by using a graphics debugger such as RenderDoc (see the sidebar "Graphics Debuggers"), you can view the output to the different textures in the G-buffer. Figure 13.8 shows a visualization of the output to the different components of the G-buffer, including the depth buffer.

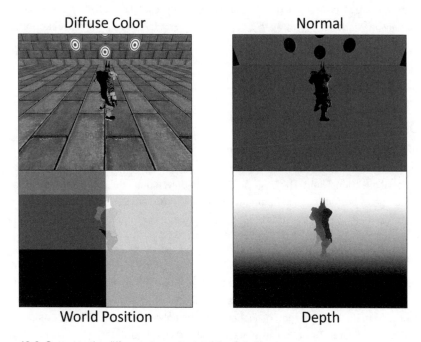

Figure 13.8 Output to the different components of the G-buffer

GRAPHICS DEBUGGERS

One difficulty with writing increasingly complex graphics code is that it is more difficult to debug than normal C++ code. With C++ code, if there is an issue, you can place a breakpoint and step through the execution of the code. However, if the game does not show the correct graphics output, it could be one of several issues. It might be that you're calling the wrong OpenGL functions, or the data passed to the shaders is wrong, or the GLSL shader code is wrong.

This difficulty in determining the source of problems led to the creation of graphics debuggers. There are several graphics debuggers available, some of which are proprietary to specific types of graphics hardware or consoles. At a minimum, these debuggers allow you to capture a frame of graphics data and step through the commands executed to see how the output to the framebuffer changes. They also allow you to view all the data sent to the GPU, including vertex data, textures, and shader constants. Some even allow you to step through the execution of a vertex or pixel shader to see where it goes wrong.

For Windows and Linux, the best graphics debugger that supports OpenGL is RenderDoc (https://renderdoc.org), an open source tool created by Baldur Karlsson. In addition to OpenGL, it supports debugging for Vulkan as well as Microsoft Direct3D 11 and 12 (the latter two only on Windows). Unfortunately, at this writing, RenderDoc has no macOS support.

For macOS users, Intel Graphics Performance Analyzers (GPA) is a great alternative. See https://software.intel.com/en-us/gpa.

Global Lighting

Now that the game is writing surface properties to the G-buffer, the next step is to use these properties to display a fully lit scene. This section focuses on global lights such as the ambient and a global directional light. The basic premise is to draw a quad the size of the screen to the default framebuffer. For each fragment in this quad, you sample surface properties from the G-buffer. Then, using these surface properties, you can compute the same Phong lighting equations from Chapter 6 to light the fragment.

First, you create a vertex and fragment shader in GLSL for global lighting from the G-buffer. Because you're ultimately drawing a quad to the screen, the vertex shader is identical to the sprite vertex shader from Chapter 5. The fragment shader, shown in Listing 13.9, has some differences from the Phong fragment shader. First, the only input from the vertex shader is the texture coordinates. This is because the normal and world positions at the fragment are in the G-buffer. Next, you add three `sampler2D` uniforms for the three different textures in the G-buffer (diffuse color, normal, and world position). In the main function for the fragment shader, you sample the diffuse color, normal, and world position from the G-buffer textures.

This, combined with the directional light uniforms (as in Chapter 6), gives all the information needed to light the fragment with the ambient and diffuse components of the Phong reflection model. You cannot calculate the specular component because this depends on the specular power of each surface, and you currently do not store the specular information in the G-buffer. (In Exercise 13.1 you explore adding the specular component.)

After calculating the Phong ambient and diffuse component, you multiply the diffuse color of the surface (from the G-buffer) to compute the final color at the pixel.

Listing 13.9 `GBufferGlobal.frag` Shader

```
#version 330
// Inputs from vertex shader
in vec2 fragTexCoord; // Tex coord

layout(location = 0) out vec4 outColor;

// Different textures from G-buffer
uniform sampler2D uGDiffuse;
uniform sampler2D uGNormal;
uniform sampler2D uGWorldPos;

// Lighting uniforms (as in Chapter 6)
// ...

void main()
{
    // Sample diffuse color, normal, world position from G-buffer
    vec3 gbufferDiffuse = texture(uGDiffuse, fragTexCoord).xyz;
    vec3 gbufferNorm = texture(uGNormal, fragTexCoord).xyz;
    vec3 gbufferWorldPos = texture(uGWorldPos, fragTexCoord).xyz;

    // Calculate Phong lighting (as in Chapter 6, minus specular)
    // ...

    // Final color is diffuse color times phong light
    outColor = vec4(gbufferDiffuse * Phong, 1.0);
}
```

With the global lighting vertex and fragment shader code written, the next step is to load these shaders in the `Renderer` class. You create a `Shader*` member variable called `mGGlobalShader` and instantiate it in the `LoadShader` function. In this code, shown in Listing 13.10, you first load the vertex and fragment shader files. Then, you set some of the uniforms for the shader.

The `SetIntUniform` calls associate each of the three `sampler2D` uniforms in the fragment shader with a specific texture index. The first `SetMatrixUniform` call sets the view-projection matrix to be identical to the sprite view-projection matrix (because you're drawing a quad). The second call sets the world transform to scale the quad to the entire screen and invert the y-axis (to solve the inverted y problem, as when drawing the mirror texture to the screen).

Listing 13.10   Loading the G-buffer Global Lighting Shader

```
mGGlobalShader = new Shader();
if (!mGGlobalShader->Load("Shaders/GBufferGlobal.vert",
    "Shaders/GBufferGlobal.frag"))
{
    return false;
}
// For the GBuffer, we need to associate each sampler with an index
mGGlobalShader->SetActive();
mGGlobalShader->SetIntUniform("uGDiffuse", 0);
mGGlobalShader->SetIntUniform("uGNormal", 1);
mGGlobalShader->SetIntUniform("uGWorldPos", 2);

// The view projection is just the sprite one
mGGlobalShader->SetMatrixUniform("uViewProj", spriteViewProj);
// The world transform scales to the screen and flips y
Matrix4 gbufferWorld = Matrix4::CreateScale(mScreenWidth,
    -mScreenHeight, 1.0f);
mGGlobalShader->SetMatrixUniform("uWorldTransform", gbufferWorld);
```

Next, you add a function to the `GBuffer` class that binds each texture in the G-buffer to a corresponding texture index:

```
void GBuffer::SetTexturesActive()
{
    for (int i = 0; i < NUM_GBUFFER_TEXTURES; i++)
    {
        mTextures[i]->SetActive(i);
    }
}
```

Here, the `SetActive` function called on each texture takes in an index, which corresponds to the indices set on the `sampler2D` uniforms in GLSL.

The final step is to add a function to `Renderer` that draws the G-buffer quad using the global lighting shader. You create a new `DrawFromGBuffer` function, as shown in Listing 13.11. Because the first step in `Renderer::Draw` is now to draw the scene to the G-buffer, `DrawFromGBuffer` is now the first code that draws to the default framebuffer. You need to disable depth testing for the quad, as you don't want it to affect the depth buffer. You then set the G-buffer shader and sprite quad vertices as active and call the `SetTexturesActive` function to activate all the G-buffer textures. You then use the `SetLightUniforms` function, created in Chapter 6, to set all the directional light uniforms in the G-buffer shader. Finally, you draw the quad, which invokes your G-buffer fragment shader for every fragment onscreen.

Listing 13.11 `Renderer::DrawFromGBuffer` Implementation

```
void Renderer::DrawFromGBuffer()
{
    // Disable depth testing for the global lighting pass
    glDisable(GL_DEPTH_TEST);
    // Activate global G-buffer shader
    mGGlobalShader->SetActive();
    // Activate sprite verts quad
    mSpriteVerts->SetActive();
    // Set the G-buffer textures to sample
    mGBuffer->SetTexturesActive();
    // Set the lighting uniforms
    SetLightUniforms(mGGlobalShader, mView);

    // Draw the triangles for the quad
    glDrawElements(GL_TRIANGLES, 6, GL_UNSIGNED_INT, nullptr);
}
```

Next, you change the code at the start of `Renderer::Draw` to first draw the 3D scene to the G-buffer, change the framebuffer to the default and finally call `DrawFromGBuffer`. After this, you render the sprites and UI screens as before:

```
// Draw the 3D scene to the G-buffer
Draw3DScene(mGBuffer->GetBufferID(), mView, mProjection, false);
// Set the framebuffer back to zero (screen's framebuffer)
glBindFramebuffer(GL_FRAMEBUFFER, 0);
// Draw from the GBuffer
DrawFromGBuffer();
// Draw Sprite/UI as before
// ...
```

With the global lighting shader code in place, the rendering code now draws the entire scene fully lit once again. Figure 13.9 shows the scene output. Note that because you are no longer calculating the specular component of the Phong lighting equation, the scene looks darker than before—even with a slightly higher ambient light value than you had previously. However, you can still see the entire scene, and other than the darkness, it looks like the forward-rendered scene. Also, note that the mirror still works properly, even though you still use forward rendering for the mirror (and because of the higher ambient light, the mirror looks brighter than before).

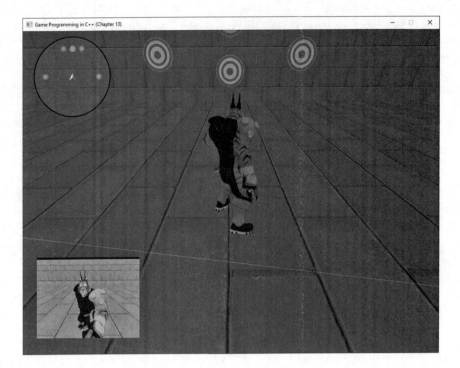

Figure 13.9 Scene with global lights calculated via deferred shading

Adding Point Lights

Recall that one of the main reasons to use deferred shading is that it scales very well as the number of lights in the scene increases. This section discusses how to add support for many non-global lights.

Suppose the game has 100 different point lights. You could create a uniform array in the shader that stores all the information about these point lights, including position, color, radius, and so on. Then in the GBufferGlobal.frag shader code, you could loop over these point lights. Using the G-buffer sampled world position, you could figure out whether a fragment is within range of a point light and, if so, compute the Phong equation for this.

Although this approach could work, there are some issues with it. You need to test every fragment against every point light, even for lights that are nowhere near the fragment. This means a lot of conditional checks in the shader code, which is expensive.

The solution to these problems is to instead use **light geometry**, or meshes that represent the lights. Because a point light has a radius, its corresponding light geometry is a sphere placed in the world. Drawing this sphere will then trigger a fragment shader call for every fragment the sphere touches. Using the world position information from the G-buffer, you can compute the intensity of the light to the fragment.

Adding a `PointLightComponent` Class

For point lights, you can create a component so that it's easy to attach to any actor to move the light. First, you declare the `PointLightComponent` class, as shown in Listing 13.12. For simplicity, you make its member variables public. The diffuse color is simply the diffuse color of the point light. The inner and outer radius variables determine the area of influence of the point light. The **outer radius** is the maximum distance from which the point light affects an object. The **inner radius** is the radius at which the point light applies its full intensity of light. Anything inside the inner radius has the full diffuse color, while the color intensity falls off when approaching the outer radius. The point light doesn't affect anything past the outer radius.

Listing 13.12 `PointLightComponent` Declaration

```
class PointLightComponent
{
public:
    PointLightComponent(class Actor* owner);
    ~PointLightComponent();

    // Draw this point light as geometry
    void Draw(class Shader* shader, class Mesh* mesh);

    // Diffuse color
    Vector3 mDiffuseColor;
    // Radius of light
    float mInnerRadius;
    float mOuterRadius;
};
```

You then add a vector of `PointLightComponent` pointers to the `Renderer` class called `mPointLights`. The constructor for `PointLightComponent` adds the light to `mPointLights`, and the destructor removes the light from the vector.

Point Light Fragment Shader

The next step is to create a `GBufferPointLight.frag` fragment shader file. As in the `GBufferGlobal.frag` shader, you need to declare three different `sampler2D` uniforms for the three different G-buffer textures. Unlike with the global lighting shader, however, you need to store information about a specific point light. You declare a `PointLight` struct and add a `uPointLight` uniform for this. You also add a uniform, `uScreenDimensions`, that stores the width/height of the screen:

```
// Additional uniforms for GBufferPointLight.frag
struct PointLight
{
    // Position of light
    vec3 mWorldPos;
```

```
   // Diffuse color
   vec3 mDiffuseColor;
   // Radius of the light
   float mInnerRadius;
   float mOuterRadius;
};
uniform PointLight uPointLight;
// Stores width/height of screen
uniform vec2 uScreenDimensions;
```

The shader's main function, given in Listing 13.13, is different from the global light shader in several ways. With the quad you drew for global lighting, you could simply use the texture coordinates of the quad to sample correctly into the G-buffer. However, using the texture coordinates from the point light's sphere mesh would not yield a correct UV coordinate to sample into the G-buffer. Instead, you can use `gl_FragCoord`, which is a built-in GLSL variable that contains the position in screen space of the fragment. In this instance, you only care about the x and y coordinates. However, because UV coordinates are in the range [0, 1], you need to divide the screen space coordinates by the dimensions of the screen. The division operator in this case is a component-wise division.

Once you have the correct UV coordinates, you use them to sample the diffuse, normal, and world positions from the G-buffer. Next, you compute the N and L vectors, much as in the previous Phong fragment shader.

Listing 13.13 `GBufferPointLight.frag` Main Function

```
void main()
{
   // Calculate the coordinate to sample into the G-buffer
   vec2 gbufferCoord = gl_FragCoord.xy / uScreenDimensions;

   // Sample from G-buffer
   vec3 gbufferDiffuse = texture(uGDiffuse, gbufferCoord).xyz;
   vec3 gbufferNorm = texture(uGNormal, gbufferCoord).xyz;
   vec3 gbufferWorldPos = texture(uGWorldPos, gbufferCoord).xyz;

   // Calculate normal and vector from surface to light
   vec3 N = normalize(gbufferNorm);
   vec3 L = normalize(uPointLight.mWorldPos - gbufferWorldPos);

   // Compute Phong diffuse component for the light
   vec3 Phong = vec3(0.0, 0.0, 0.0);
   float NdotL = dot(N, L);
   if (NdotL > 0)
   {
      // Get the distance between the light and the world pos
      float dist = distance(uPointLight.mWorldPos, gbufferWorldPos);
      // Use smoothstep to compute value in range [0,1]
```

```
         // between inner/outer radius
         float intensity = smoothstep(uPointLight.mInnerRadius,
                             uPointLight.mOuterRadius, dist);
         // The diffuse color of the light depends on intensity
         vec3 DiffuseColor = mix(uPointLight.mDiffuseColor,
                         vec3(0.0, 0.0, 0.0), intensity);
         Phong = DiffuseColor * NdotL;
    }
    // Final color is texture color times phong light
    outColor = vec4(gbufferDiffuse * Phong, 1.0);
}
```

However, when computing the diffuse color, you first calculate the distance between the point light's center and the fragment's world position. Then, the smoothstep function calculates a value in the range [0, 1]. The function returns 0 for distances less than or equal to the inner radius and 1 for distances greater than or equal to the outer radius. Distances in between yield some value in between. The smoothstep function uses a Hermite function (a type of polynomial) to calculate this in-between value. The resulting value corresponds to an intensity of the diffuse light; the value 0 means full intensity because the fragment is within the inner radius, whereas the value 1 means the point light should not affect the fragment.

You then compute the applied DiffuseColor based on the intensity value. Here, the mix function performs a linear interpolation between the point light's diffuse color and pure black. Remember that you do not calculate the specular component of the Phong reflection here because you currently do not have access to the specular power in the G-buffer.

It's important to understand that because point light rendering occurs after the global light G-buffer calculations, each fragment in the framebuffer already has a color. You don't want the point light shader to overwrite the colors that are already there. For example, if a fragment's world position says it's out of range of the point light, the shader will return black. If you just set the fragment to black, you lose all the color that was already there from the global lighting pass.

Instead, you want to *add* the output of the point light shader to whatever color is already there. Adding black to the color does not change any of the RGB values, which means it preserves the existing light. On the other hand, if you add a green value, that makes the fragment greener. Adding the output color to the existing color doesn't require any changes to the fragment shader code itself; instead, you can do this on the C++ side of things.

Drawing Point Lights

You need to add some glue code to Renderer and PointLightComponent before you can draw the point lights in DrawFromGBuffer. First, you add a new shader member variable called mGPointLightShader. You then load this shader in LoadShaders. For the vertex shader, you use the BasicMesh.vert shader from Chapter 6 because the point light's sphere mesh doesn't need any special behavior. For the fragment shader, you use the GBufferPointLight.frag shader.

As with the global lighting shader, you need to set the uniforms for the different samplers to bind them to specific G-buffer textures. You also set the uScreenDimensions uniform to the width and height of the screen.

You also add a mPointLightMesh member variable that simply points to the mesh you want to use for the point lights. You load the mesh when initializing the Renderer and save it in the variable; the mesh in question is a sphere.

Now you add additional code to DrawFromGBuffer, shown in Listing 13.14. This code goes after all the code that drew the full-screen quad that applied global lighting. The first part of this code copies the depth buffer from the G-buffer to the default framebuffer's depth buffer. Because you're drawing the 3D scene to the G-buffer, its depth buffer contains the actual depth information for every fragment. Because you want to depth test the point light spheres, you need to copy over this information to the default depth buffer.

Listing 13.14 Drawing Point Lights in Renderer::DrawFromGBuffer

```
// Copy depth buffer from G-buffer to default framebuffer
glBindFramebuffer(GL_READ_FRAMEBUFFER, mGBuffer->GetBufferID());
int width = static_cast<int>(mScreenWidth);
int height = static_cast<int>(mScreenHeight);
glBlitFramebuffer(0, 0, width, height,
    0, 0, width, height,
    GL_DEPTH_BUFFER_BIT, GL_NEAREST);

// Enable depth test, but disable writes to depth buffer
glEnable(GL_DEPTH_TEST);
glDepthMask(GL_FALSE);

// Set the point light shader and mesh as active
mGPointLightShader->SetActive();
mPointLightMesh->GetVertexArray()->SetActive();
// Set the view-projection matrix
mGPointLightShader->SetMatrixUniform("uViewProj",
    mView * mProjection);
// Set the G-buffer textures for sampling
mGBuffer->SetTexturesActive();

// The point light color should add to existing color
glEnable(GL_BLEND);
glBlendFunc(GL_ONE, GL_ONE);

// Draw the point lights
for (PointLightComponent* p : mPointLights)
{
    p->Draw(mGPointLightShader, mPointLightMesh);
}
```

Next, you reenable the depth test (because you disabled it when drawing the full-screen quad for the global lighting), but you disable the depth mask. This means that when you try to draw fragments for each point light's sphere, they need to pass the depth test, *but* these fragments do not write new depth values to the depth buffer. This ensures that the point light sphere meshes do not interfere with the existing depth buffer values. Because you're disabling depth buffer writes here, you add a corresponding call to the beginning of `Draw3DScene` that reenables writes to the depth buffer. (Otherwise, you can't clear the depth buffer!)

Then you activate the shader for the point lights as well as the corresponding point light mesh. You need to set the view-projection matrix just as for any other object rendered in the world to make sure the point light has the correct location onscreen. You also need to bind the G-buffer textures to their respective slots.

Because you want to add to the colors already in the color buffer, you enable blending. The blend function with `GL_ONE` as both parameters says that you just want to directly add the two colors, without considering the alpha values or any other parameters.

Finally, you loop over all the point lights and call the `Draw` function on each point light. The code for `PointLightComponent::Draw`, shown in Listing 13.15, doesn't look that much different from the code for drawing any other mesh. For the world transform matrix, you need to scale based on the outer radius of the light. You divide by the radius of the mesh because the point light mesh does not have a unit radius. The translation is just based on the position of the light, which comes from the owning actor.

Furthermore, you need to set the different uniforms for this specific point light, which isn't different from how you've set the uniforms before. Finally, the `glDrawElements` call draws the light geometry for the point light, which is your sphere mesh. You don't need to set the vertex array as active because the `Renderer` does this before calling `Draw`.

Once you draw all the point light meshes, for every fragment you calculate the contribution of the point light to the color of the fragment. You then add this additional light color to the already existing color from the global lighting pass.

Listing 13.15 `PointLightComponent::Draw` Implementation

```
void PointLightComponent::Draw(Shader* shader, Mesh* mesh)
{
    // Scale world transform to the outer radius (divided by
    // the mesh radius) and positioned to the world position
    Matrix4 scale = Matrix4::CreateScale(mOwner->GetScale() *
        mOuterRadius / mesh->GetRadius());
    Matrix4 trans = Matrix4::CreateTranslation(mOwner->GetPosition());
    Matrix4 worldTransform = scale * trans;
    shader->SetMatrixUniform("uWorldTransform", worldTransform);
```

```
// Set point light shader constants
shader->SetVectorUniform("uPointLight.mWorldPos",
mOwner->GetPosition());
shader->SetVectorUniform("uPointLight.mDiffuseColor", mDiffuseColor);
shader->SetFloatUniform("uPointLight.mInnerRadius", mInnerRadius);
shader->SetFloatUniform("uPointLight.mOuterRadius", mOuterRadius);

// Draw the sphere
glDrawElements(GL_TRIANGLES, mesh->GetVertexArray()->GetNumIndices(),
    GL_UNSIGNED_INT, nullptr);
}
```

To demonstrate the point light rendering, this chapter's game project creates several point lights with different colors along the floor. Figure 13.10 illustrates these point lights, powered by deferred shading.

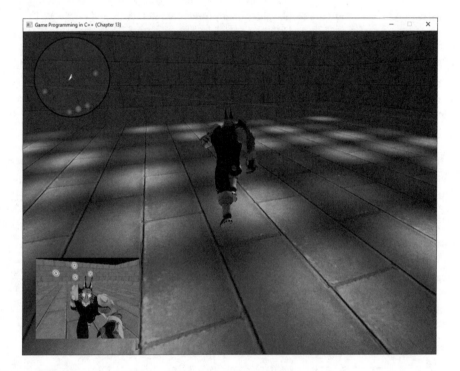

Figure 13.10 Numerous point lights in the game project

Improvements and Issues

Although deferred shading is a very powerful rendering technique used by many modern games, it isn't perfect. One problem is that it can't handle partially transparent objects such as windows. Because the G-buffer can only store a single surface's properties, drawing such an object into the G-buffer would overwrite the objects behind it. The solution for this case is to draw transparent objects in a separate pass after drawing the rest of the scene.

Also, for some types of games, the overhead of setting up the G-buffer and rendering to multiple targets is not worth it. If a game takes place largely during the day or has a very small number of lights, the cost of the deferred shading setup every frame might be higher than the cost of a forward-rendering approach. Many virtual-reality games, which need a very high frame rate, use forward rendering for this reason.

Another issue is that the light geometry has many edge cases to consider and fix. For example, if the point light sphere partially intersects with a wall, the point light will affect both sides of the wall in the current approach. Also, if you create a very big point light but place the camera inside the light, you don't see the effect of that light. To fix these light geometry issues, you need to use a stencil buffer, which is a different type of output buffer.

Game Project

This chapter's game project provides the full implementation of deferred shading. In addition, it uses both mipmapping and anisotropic aliasing to improve texture quality. The project includes the mirror texture that's forward rendered. The code is available in the book's GitHub repository, in the `Chapter13` directory. Open `Chapter13-windows.sln` in Windows and `Chapter13-mac.xcodeproj` on Mac.

There are no changes to the controls or character from the previous chapter. The player still uses the `WASD` keys to move the character around. To demonstrate the point lights, several point lights are provided in `Game::LoadData`.

Summary

This chapter covers a handful of intermediate graphics techniques. First, it looks at how texture filtering works—both nearest-neighbor filtering and bilinear filtering. Mipmapping can reduce sampling artifacts when reducing the size of textures because it generates several lower-resolution textures. However, for oblique surfaces, mipmapping may appear blurry. In this case, anisotropic filtering improves the quality of the textures.

Another powerful technique is rendering the scene to textures. OpenGL allows creation of arbitrary framebuffer objects associated with textures. Then, you can choose to draw the 3D scene to this texture. One use of this technique is to draw a high-quality reflection, such as for a mirror.

Finally, this chapter explores deferred shading, which is a two-pass approach to lighting. In the first pass, you write the object's surface properties, such as diffuse color, normals, and world position, into a G-buffer. In the second pass, you read from the G-buffer to calculate lighting equations. For lights with limited ranges, such as point lights, you render lighting geometry to ensure that the light affects only the fragments in range. Deferred shading is an excellent approach when there are many lights in the scene, though there are some issues, such as the inability to handle partially transparent objects.

Additional Reading

As mentioned in Chapter 6, *Real-Time Rendering* by Thomas Akenine-Moller et al. is the go-to book when it comes to rendering techniques and games. Jason Zink et al. give a good overview of many techniques, including deferred shading, even though the book focuses on Direct3D 11 instead of OpenGL. Matt Pharr et al. cover physically based rendering, which is a newer technique games use to achieve more realistic lighting. Wolfgang Engel's books are always on the cutting edge of what graphics programmers in the video game industry are using. Phil Djonov discusses how to eliminate the need for the world position in the G-buffer. Finally, sometimes to understand how various OpenGL extensions work, you need to read the official registry.

Akenine-Moller, Thomas, Eric Haines, and Naty Hoffman. *Real-Time Rendering*, 3rd edition. Natick: A K Peters, 2008.

Djonov, Phil. "Deferred Shading Tricks." Shiny Pixels. Accessed November 26, 2017. http://vec3.ca/code/graphics/deferred-shading-tricks/.

Engel, Wolfgang, ed. *GPU Zen: Advanced Rendering Techniques*. Encinitas: Black Cat Publishing, 2017.

Khronos Group. *OpenGL Extensions Registry*. Accessed October 16, 2017. https://github.com/KhronosGroup/OpenGL-Registry.

Pharr, Matt, Wenzel Jakob, and Greg Humphreys. *Physically Based Rendering: From Theory to Implementation,* 3rd edition. Cambridge: Elsevier, 2017.

Zink, Jason, Matt Pettineo, and Jack Hoxley. *Practical Rendering and Computation with Direct3D 11*. Boca Raton: CRC Press, 2012.

Exercises

In this chapter's exercises, you explore improving the deferred shading techniques covered in the latter half of the chapter.

Exercise 13.1

Add support for the specular component to both the global G-buffer lighting (the directional light) and the point lights. To do this, first you need a new texture in the G-buffer that stores the specular power of the surface. Add this new texture to the relevant parts of code (both in C++ and in GLSL).

Next, change the PointLightComponent class, the PointLightComponent::Draw function, and the shader code for point lights and the global light. For the point lights, use the intensity to interpolate the specular color, as is done for the diffuse color. Calculate the specular component according to the Phong equations, as before.

Exercise 13.2

Adding a new type of light to deferred shading requires a new type of light geometry. Add support for spotlights. To do so, you need to create a SpotLightComponent as well as a corresponding shader to draw these lights after the point lights.

Use the provided SpotLight.gpmesh file (which is a cone) as the mesh for spotlights. A spotlight should have parameters like those of a point light, but it also needs a variable for its angle. To be able to change the angle, the mesh needs to also scale non-uniformly. The default mesh has a half angle of 30 degrees.

CHAPTER 14

LEVEL FILES AND BINARY DATA

This chapter explores how to load and save JSON-based level files representing the game world. These level files store global properties as well as properties of all the actors and components in the game.

In addition, this chapter explores the trade-offs of using text-based file formats versus binary file formats. As an example, it discusses an implementation of a binary mesh file format.

Level File Loading

To this point, this book hasn't used a data-driven approach to the placement of objects in the game world. Instead, the `Game::LoadData` function code dictates the actors and components in the game, as well as global properties, such as the ambient light. The current approach has several disadvantages, most notably that even small changes, such as placement of a cube in a level, requires recompilation of the source code. A designer who wants to change the placement of objects in the game shouldn't have to change the C++ source code.

The solution is to create a separate data file for the level. This data file should be able to specify which actors the level contains and which properties and, optionally, adjust the components of these actors. This level file should also include any needed global properties.

For a 2D game, using a basic text file works perfectly well. You can simply define different ASCII characters for different objects in the world and create a text grid of these objects. This makes the level file look like ASCII art. Unfortunately, this approach doesn't work very well for a 3D game because each object in the game world could be at some arbitrary 3D coordinate. Furthermore, in the game object model used in this book, actors can have components, so you may need to also save properties of each attached component.

For all the reasons just listed, you need a file format that's more structured. As with the rest of the book, in this chapter you once again use a text-based JSON format for data. However, this chapter also explores the trade-offs that any text format makes, as well as techniques needed for binary file formats.

This section explores building up a JSON-level file format. You start with global properties and slowly add additional features to the file so that the `Game::LoadData` function has barely any code other than a function call that specifies the level file to load. Unlike earlier chapters, this chapter explores the usage of the RapidJSON library to parse in the JSON file.

Loading Global Properties

The only global properties the game world really has are the lighting properties—the ambient light and the global directional light. With such a limited number of properties, this is a good starting point for defining the JSON level file format. Listing 14.1 shows how you might specify the global lighting properties in the level file.

Listing 14.1 Level with Global Lighting Properties (`Level0.gplevel`)

```
{
    "version": 1,
    "globalProperties": {
        "ambientLight": [0.2, 0.2, 0.2],
        "directionalLight": {
```

```
        "direction": [0.0, -0.707, -0.707],
        "color": [0.78, 0.88, 1.0]
      }
    }
}
```

Listing 14.1 shows several constructs that you commonly encounter in a level file. First, at its core, a JSON document is a dictionary of key/value pairs (or **properties**) called a **JSON object**. The key name is in quotes, and then the value follows the colon. Values can be of several types. The basic types are strings, numbers, and Booleans. The complex types are arrays and JSON objects. For this file, the globalProperties key corresponds to a JSON object. This JSON object then has two keys: one for the ambient light and one for the directional light. The ambientLight key corresponds to an array of three numbers. Similarly, the directionalLight key corresponds to another JSON object, with two additional keys.

This nesting of JSON objects and properties drives the implementation of the parsing code. Specifically, you can see common operations where, given a JSON object and a key name, you want to read in a value. And in your C++ code, the types you have are far more varied than the JSON format, so you should add code to assist with parsing.

To parse these global properties in code, you begin by declaring a LevelLoader class. Because loading the level from a file affects the state of the game, but not the level loader itself, you declare the LoadLevel function as a static function, as follows:

```
class LevelLoader
{
public:
    // Load the level -- returns true if successful
    static bool LoadLevel(class Game* game, const std::string& fileName);
};
```

Note that in addition to the filename, the LoadLevel function takes in the pointer to the Game object. This is necessary because creating or modifying anything requires access to the game.

The first step in LoadLevel is to load and parse the level file into a rapidjson::Document. The most efficient approach is to first load the entire file into memory and then pass this buffer to the Parse member function of the Document. Because loading a JSON file into a Document is a common operation, it makes sense to create a helper function. This way, gpmesh, gpanim, and any other asset types that need to load in a JSON file can also reuse this function.

Listing 14.2 shows the implementation of LoadJSON. This function is also a static function. It takes in the filename and a reference to the output document. The first step loads the file into an ifstream. Note that you load the file in binary mode instead of text mode. This is for efficiency purposes because all you need to do is load the entire file into a character buffer (array) and pass that buffer directly to RapidJSON. You also use the `std::ios::ate` flag to specify that the stream should start at the end of the file.

If the file loads successfully, you use the `tellg` function to get the current position of the file stream. Because the stream is at the end of the file, this corresponds to the size of the entire file. Next, you have the `seekg` call set the stream back to the beginning of the file. You then create a vector with enough space to fit the entire file plus a null terminator and have the `read` function read the file into the vector. Finally, you call the `Parse` function on `outDoc` to parse the JSON file.

Listing 14.2 `LevelLoader::LoadJSON` Implementation

```
bool LevelLoader::LoadJSON(const std::string& fileName,
                           rapidjson::Document& outDoc)
{
    // Load the file from disk into an ifstream in binary mode,
    // loaded with stream buffer at the end (ate)
    std::ifstream file(fileName, std::ios::in |
                       std::ios::binary | std::ios::ate);
    if (!file.is_open())
    {
        SDL_Log("File %s not found", fileName.c_str());
        return false;
    }

    // Get the size of the file
    std::ifstream::pos_type fileSize = file.tellg();
    // Seek back to start of file
    file.seekg(0, std::ios::beg);

    // Create a vector of size + 1 (for null terminator)
    std::vector<char> bytes(static_cast<size_t>(fileSize) + 1);
    // Read in bytes into vector
    file.read(bytes.data(), static_cast<size_t>(fileSize));

    // Load raw data into RapidJSON document
    outDoc.Parse(bytes.data());
    if (!outDoc.IsObject())
    {
        SDL_Log("File %s is not valid JSON", fileName.c_str());
        return false;
    }

    return true;
}
```

You then call `LoadJSON` at the start of `LoadLevel`:

```
rapidjson::Document doc;
if (!LoadJSON(fileName, doc))
{
    SDL_Log("Failed to load level %s", fileName.c_str());
    return false;
}
```

Given a JSON object, you need to read in keys and extract their corresponding values. You shouldn't assume that a given key will always be there, so you should first validate that the key exists and matches the expected type. If it does, you read in the value. You can implement this behavior in another class with a static function called `JsonHelper`. Listing 14.3 shows the `JsonHelper::GetInt` function. It tries to find the property, validates that it matches the expected type, and then returns `true` if successful.

Listing 14.3 `JsonHelper::GetInt` Implementation

```
bool JsonHelper::GetInt(const rapidjson::Value& inObject,
                        const char* inProperty, int& outInt)
{
    // Check if this property exists
    auto itr = inObject.FindMember(inProperty);
    if (itr == inObject.MemberEnd())
    {
        return false;
    }

    // Get the value type, and check it's an integer
    auto& property = itr->value;
    if (!property.IsInt())
    {
        return false;
    }

    // We have the property
    outInt = property.GetInt();
    return true;
}
```

You can then use the `GetInt` function in `LoadLevel` to validate that the loaded file's version matches the expected version:

```
int version = 0;
if (!JsonHelper::GetInt(doc, "version", version) ||
    version != LevelVersion)
{
    SDL_Log("Incorrect level file version for %s", fileName.c_str());
    return false;
}
```

Here, the JSON object in question is the overall document (the root JSON object). You first make sure that `GetInt` returns a value and, if it does, you check that its value matches the expected value (a `const` called `LevelVersion`).

You also add similar functions to `JsonHelper` to extract other basic types: `GetFloat`, `GetBool`, and `GetString`. However, where this paradigm really becomes powerful is for non-basic types. Specifically, many properties in this game are of type `Vector3` (such as `ambientLight`), so having a `GetVector3` function is very useful. The overall construction of the function is still the same, except you need to validate that the property is an array with three members that are floats. You can similarly declare a `GetQuaternion` function.

Ambient and Directional Lights

With the helper functions in place, you can create a function to load in the global properties. Because the global properties are varied and may not necessarily need the same class types, you must manually query the specific properties you need. The `LoadGlobalProperties` function in Listing 14.4 demonstrates how to load the ambient light and directional light properties. Notice that for the most part, you call the helper functions you've created for these properties.

Note that you can access a property as a `rapidjson::Value&` directly through `operator[]`. The `dirObj["directionalLight"]` call gets the value with the `directionalLight` key name, and then the `IsObject()` call validates that the type of the value is a JSON object.

Another interesting pattern for the directional light is to have direct access to variables you want to set. In this case, you do not need to add any conditional checks on the `GetVector3` calls. This is because if the property requested does not exist, the `Get` functions guarantee not to change the variable. If you have direct access to a variable and don't care if the property is unset, then this reduces the amount of code.

Listing 14.4 `LevelLoader::LoadGlobalProperties` Implementation

```
void LevelLoader::LoadGlobalProperties(Game* game,
   const rapidjson::Value& inObject)
{
   // Get ambient light
   Vector3 ambient;
   if (JsonHelper::GetVector3(inObject, "ambientLight", ambient))
   {
      game->GetRenderer()->SetAmbientLight(ambient);
   }

   // Get directional light
   const rapidjson::Value& dirObj = inObject["directionalLight"];
```

```
    if (dirObj.IsObject())
    {
        DirectionalLight& light = game->GetRenderer()->GetDirectionalLight();
        // Set direction/color, if they exist
        JsonHelper::GetVector3(dirObj, "direction", light.mDirection);
        JsonHelper::GetVector3(dirObj, "color", light.mDiffuseColor);
    }
}
```

You then add a call to `LoadGlobalProperties` in `LoadLevel`, immediately after the valida-
tion code for the level file version:

```
// Handle any global properties
const rapidjson::Value& globals = doc["globalProperties"];
if (globals.IsObject())
{
    LoadGlobalProperties(game, globals);
}
```

You can then add a call to `LoadLevel` in `Game::LoadData`, which loads in the `Level0.
gplevel` file:

```
LevelLoader::LoadLevel(this, "Assets/Level0.gplevel");
```

Because you're now loading in the light properties from the level file, you can also remove the
code in `LoadData` that hard-coded the ambient light and directional light.

Loading Actors

Loading in the actors means the JSON file needs an array of actors, and each actor has property
information for that actor. However, you need some way to specify which type of `Actor` you
need (because there are subclasses). In addition, you want to avoid having a long set of conditional checks in the level loading code to determine which `Actor` subclass to allocate.

As before, it helps to first visualize what the data might look like. Listing 14.5 shows one
method to specify the actors in the JSON file. This example only shows actors of type
`TargetActor`, but the type can easily specify any other `Actor` subclass. Note that in addition
to the type are any other properties to specify for that actor. Here, the only properties set are
position and rotation, but these could conceivably be any property the actor has.

Listing 14.5 Level with Actors (`Level1.gplevel`)

```
{
    // Version and global properties
    // ...

    "actors": [
        {
```

```
        "type": "TargetActor",
        "properties": {
            "position": [1450.0, 0.0, 100.0]
        }
    },
    {
        "type": "TargetActor",
        "properties": {
            "position": [0.0, -1450.0, 200.0],
            "rotation": [0.0, 0.0, 0.7071, 0.7071]
        }
    },
    {
        "type": "TargetActor",
        "properties": {
            "position": [0.0, 1450.0, 200.0],
            "rotation": [0.0, 0.0, -0.7071, 0.7071]
        }
    }
    ]
}
```

Assuming for a moment that you have a method to construct an actor of a specific type, you also need to be able to load properties for the actor. The simplest approach is to create a virtual LoadProperties function in the base Actor class, shown in Listing 14.6.

Listing 14.6 `Actor::LoadProperties` Function

```cpp
void Actor::LoadProperties(const rapidjson::Value& inObj)
{
    // Use strings for different states
    std::string state;
    if (JsonHelper::GetString(inObj, "state", state))
    {
        if (state == "active")
        {
            SetState(EActive);
        }
        else if (state == "paused")
        {
            SetState(EPaused);
        }
        else if (state == "dead")
        {
            SetState(EDead);
        }
    }
}
```

```
    // Load position, rotation, and scale, and compute transform
    JsonHelper::GetVector3(inObj, "position", mPosition);
    JsonHelper::GetQuaternion(inObj, "rotation", mRotation);
    JsonHelper::GetFloat(inObj, "scale", mScale);
    ComputeWorldTransform();
}
```

Then, for some subclass of `Actor`, you can override the `LoadProperties` function to load any additional properties, as needed:

```
void SomeActor::LoadProperties(const rapidjson::Value& inObj)
{
    // Load base actor properties
    Actor::LoadProperties(inObj);

    // Load any of my custom properties
    // ...
}
```

Now that you have a way to load properties, the next step is to solve the issue of constructing an actor of the correct type. One approach is to create a map where the key is the string name of the actor type, and the value is a function that can dynamically allocate an actor of that type. The key is straightforward because it's just a string. For the value, you can make a static function that dynamically allocates an actor of a specific type. To avoid having to declare a separate function in each subclass of `Actor`, you can instead create a template function like this in the base `Actor` class:

```
template <typename T>
static Actor* Create(class Game* game, const rapidjson::Value& inObj)
{
    // Dynamically allocate actor of type T
    T* t = new T(game);
    // Call LoadProperties on new actor
    t->LoadProperties(inObj);
    return t;
}
```

Because it's templated on a type, it can dynamically allocate an object of the specified type and then call `LoadProperties` to set any parameters of the actor type, as needed.

Then, back in `LevelLoader`, you need to create the map. The key type is `std::string`, but for the value, you need a function that matches the signature of the `Actor::Create` function. For this, you can once again use the `std::function` helper class to define the signature.

First, you use an **alias declaration** (which is like a typedef) to create an `ActorFunc` type specifier:

```
using ActorFunc = std::function<
   class Actor*(class Game*, const rapidjson::Value&)
>;
```

The template parameters to `std::function` specify that the function returns an `Actor*` and takes in two parameters: `Game*` and `rapidjson::Value&`.

Next, you declare the map as a static variable in `LevelLoader`:

```
static std::unordered_map<std::string, ActorFunc> sActorFactoryMap;
```

Then in `LevelLoader.cpp`, you construct the `sActorFactoryMap` to fill in the different actors you can create:

```
std::unordered_map<std::string, ActorFunc> LevelLoader::sActorFactoryMap
{
   { "Actor", &Actor::Create<Actor> },
   { "BallActor", &Actor::Create<BallActor> },
   { "FollowActor", &Actor::Create<FollowActor> },
   { "PlaneActor", &Actor::Create<PlaneActor> },
   { "TargetActor", &Actor::Create<TargetActor> },
};
```

This initialization syntax sets up entries in the map with a key as the specified string name and the value as the address of an `Actor::Create` function, templated to create the specific type of `Actor` subclass. Note that you don't call the various create functions here. Instead, you just get the memory address of a function and save it for later use.

With the map set up, you can now create a `LoadActors` function, as in Listing 14.7. Here, you loop over the `actors` array in the JSON file and get the type string for the actor. You use this type to then look up in `sActorFactoryMap`. If you find the type, you call the function stored as the value in the map (`iter->second`), which in turn calls the correct version of `Actor::Create`. If you don't find the type, you have a helpful debug log message output.

Listing 14.7 `LevelLoader::LoadActors` Implementation

```
void LevelLoader::LoadActors(Game* game, const rapidjson::Value& inArray)
{
   // Loop through array of actors
   for (rapidjson::SizeType i = 0; i < inArray.Size(); i++)
   {
      const rapidjson::Value& actorObj = inArray[i];
```

```
    if (actorObj.IsObject())
    {
        // Get the type
        std::string type;
        if (JsonHelper::GetString(actorObj, "type", type))
        {
            // Is this type in the map?
            auto iter = sActorFactoryMap.find(type);
            if (iter != sActorFactoryMap.end())
            {
                // Construct with function stored in map
                Actor* actor = iter->second(game, actorObj["properties"]);
            }
            else
            {
                SDL_Log("Unknown actor type %s", type.c_str());
            }
        }
    }
}
```

You then add a call to LoadActors inside LoadLevel, immediately after loading in the global properties:

```
const rapidjson::Value& actors = doc["actors"];
if (actors.IsArray())
{
    LoadActors(game, actors);
}
```

With this code, you're now loading in actors and setting their properties. However, you are not yet able to adjust properties of components nor add additional components in the level file.

Loading Components

Loading data for components involves many of the same patterns as for actors. However, there is one key difference. Listing 14.8 shows a snippet of the declaration of two different actors with their components property set. The base Actor type does not have any existing components attached to it. So in this case, the MeshComponent type means that you must construct a new MeshComponent for the actor. However, the TargetActor type already has a MeshComponent, as one is created in the constructor for TargetActor. In this case, the properties specified should update the existing component rather than create a new one. This means the code for loading components needs to handle both cases.

Listing 14.8 Actors with Components in JSON (Excerpt from the Full File)

```
"actors": [
    {
        "type": "Actor",
        "properties": {
            "position": [0.0, 0.0, 0.0],
            "scale": 5.0
        },
        "components": [
            {
                "type": "MeshComponent",
                "properties": { "meshFile": "Assets/Sphere.gpmesh" }
            }
        ]
    },
    {
        "type": "TargetActor",
        "properties": { "position": [1450.0, 0.0, 100.0] },
        "components": [
            {
                "type": "MeshComponent",
                "properties": { "meshFile": "Assets/Sphere.gpmesh" }
            }
        ]
    }
]
```

To determine whether Actor already has a component of a specific type, you need a way to search through an actor's component vector by type. While you might be able to use the built-in type information in C++, it's more common for game programmers to use their own type information (and disable the built-in functionality). This is mainly because of the well-documented downsides of the built-in C++ Run-type type information (RTTI) not obeying the "you only pay for what you use" rule.

There are many ways to implement your own type information; this chapter shows a simple approach. First, you declare a TypeID enum in the Component class, like so:

```
enum TypeID
{
    TComponent = 0,
    TAudioComponent,
    TBallMove,
    // Other types omitted
    // ...
    NUM_COMPONENT_TYPES
};
```

Then, you add a virtual function called `GetType` that simply returns the correct `TypeID` based on the component. For example, the implementation of `MeshComponent::GetType` is as follows:

```
TypeID GetType() const override { return TMeshComponent; }
```

Next, you add a `GetComponentOfType` function to `Actor` that loops through the `mComponents` vector and returns the first component that matches the type:

```
Component* GetComponentOfType(Component::TypeID type)
{
    Component* comp = nullptr;
    for (Component* c : mComponents)
    {
        if (c->GetType() == type)
        {
            comp = c;
            break;
        }
    }
    return comp;
}
```

The disadvantage of this approach is that every time you create a new `Component` subclass, you must remember to add an entry to the `TypeID` enum and implement the `GetType` function. You could automate this somewhat by using macros or templates, but the code here does not do so for the sake of readability and understanding.

Note that this system also assumes that you won't have multiple components of the same type attached to one actor. If you wanted to have multiple components of the same type, then `GetComponentOfType` would potentially have to return a collection of components rather than just a single pointer.

Also, the type information does not give inheritance information; you can't figure out `SkeletalMeshComponent` is a subclass of `MeshComponent`, as `GetType` for `SkeletalMeshComponent` just returns `TSkeletalMeshComponent`. To support inheritance information, you would need an approach that saves some hierarchy information as well.

With the basic type system in place, you can move on to more familiar steps. As with `Actor`, you need to create a virtual `LoadProperties` function in the base `Component` class and then override it for any subclasses, as needed. The implementations in the various subclasses are not necessarily straightforward. Listing 14.9 shows the implementation of `LoadProperties` for `MeshComponent`. Recall that `MeshComponent` has an `mMesh` member variable that's a pointer to the vertex data to draw. You don't want to specify the vertex directly in the JSON file; instead, you want to reference the gpmesh file. The code first checks for the `meshFile` property and then gets the corresponding mesh from the renderer.

Listing 14.9 `MeshComponent::LoadProperties` Implementation

```cpp
void MeshComponent::LoadProperties(const rapidjson::Value& inObj)
{
    Component::LoadProperties(inObj);

    std::string meshFile;
    if (JsonHelper::GetString(inObj, "meshFile", meshFile))
    {
        SetMesh(mOwner->GetGame()->GetRenderer()->GetMesh(meshFile));
    }

    int idx;
    if (JsonHelper::GetInt(inObj, "textureIndex", idx))
    {
        mTextureIndex = static_cast<size_t>(idx);
    }

    JsonHelper::GetBool(inObj, "visible", mVisible);
    JsonHelper::GetBool(inObj, "isSkeletal", mIsSkeletal);
}
```

The next step is to add a static templated `Create` function for `Component`, which is very similar to the one in `Actor` except that the parameters are different. (It takes in `Actor*` as the first parameter instead of `Game*`.)

You then need a map in `LevelLoader`. You use `std::function` again to create a helper type called `ComponentFunc`:

```cpp
using ComponentFunc = std::function<
    class Component*(class Actor*, const rapidjson::Value&)
>;
```

Then, you declare the map. However, unlike with the `sActorFactoryMap`, which has only a single value, in this case, you need a pair of values. The first element in the pair is an integer corresponding to the `TypeID` of the component, and the second element is the `ComponentFunc`:

```cpp
static std::unordered_map<std::string,
    std::pair<int, ComponentFunc>> sComponentFactoryMap;
```

Then, in `LevelLoader.cpp`, you instantiate the `sComponentFactoryMap`:

```cpp
std::unordered_map<std::string, std::pair<int, ComponentFunc>>
LevelLoader::sComponentFactoryMap
{
    { "AudioComponent",
        { Component::TAudioComponent, &Component::Create<AudioComponent> }
    },
```

```
    { "BallMove",
      { Component::TBallMove, &Component::Create<BallMove> }
    },
    // Other components omitted
    // ...
};
```

You then implement a `LoadComponents` helper function in `LevelLoader`, as shown in
Listing 14.10. As with `LoadActors`, it takes in an array of the components to load and loops
through this array. You then use the `sComponentFactoryMap` to find the component type.
If it is found, you then check if the actor already has a component of the type. The `iter->`
`second.first` accesses the first element of the value pair, which corresponds to the type ID.
If the actor doesn't already have a component of the requested type, then you create one by
using the function stored in the second element of the value pair (`iter->second.second`).
If the component already exists, you can then just directly call `LoadProperties` on it.

Listing 14.10 `LevelLoader::LoadComponents` Implementation

```
void LevelLoader::LoadComponents(Actor* actor,
   const rapidjson::Value& inArray)
{
   // Loop through array of components
   for (rapidjson::SizeType i = 0; i < inArray.Size(); i++)
   {
      const rapidjson::Value& compObj = inArray[i];
      if (compObj.IsObject())
      {
         // Get the type
         std::string type;
         if (JsonHelper::GetString(compObj, "type", type))
         {
            auto iter = sComponentFactoryMap.find(type);
            if (iter != sComponentFactoryMap.end())
            {
               // Get the typeid of component
               Component::TypeID tid = static_cast<Component::TypeID>
                  (iter->second.first);
               // Does the actor already have a component of this type?
               Component* comp = actor->GetComponentOfType(tid);
               if (comp == nullptr)
               {
                  // It's a new component, call function from map
                  comp = iter->second.second(actor, compObj["properties"]);
               }
               else
               {
                  // It already exists, just load properties
                  comp->LoadProperties(compObj["properties"]);
               }
            }
         }
      }
   }
}
```

```
            else
            {
                SDL_Log("Unknown component type %s", type.c_str());
            }
        }
    }
}
```

Finally, you add code in `LoadActors` that accesses the `components` property, if it exists, and calls `LoadComponents` on it:

```
// Construct with function stored in map
Actor* actor = iter->second(game, actorObj["properties"]);
// Get the actor's components
if (actorObj.HasMember("components"))
{
    const rapidjson::Value& components = actorObj["components"];
    if (components.IsArray())
    {
        LoadComponents(actor, components);
    }
}
```

With all this code in place, you can now load the entire level from a file, including the global properties, actors, and any components associated with each actor.

Saving Level Files

Saving to a level file is conceptually simpler than loading from a file. First, you write the global properties for the level. Then, you loop through every actor in the game and every component attached to every actor. For each of these, you need to write out the relevant properties.

The implementation details are bit involved because the RapidJSON interface is slightly more complicated for creating JSON files than for reading in files. However, overall you can use techniques like those used for loading the level file.

First, you create helper `Add` functions in `JsonHelper` so that you can quickly add additional properties to an existing JSON object. For example, the `AddInt` function has the following syntax:

```
void JsonHelper::AddInt(rapidjson::Document::AllocatorType& alloc,
    rapidjson::Value& inObject, const char* name, int value)
{
    rapidjson::Value v(value);
    inObject.AddMember(rapidjson::StringRef(name), v, alloc);
}
```

The last three parameters are identical to the parameters of the `GetInt` function, except the `Value` is now not `const`. The first parameter is an allocator that RapidJSON uses when needing to allocate memory. Every call to `AddMember` requires an allocator, so you must pass one in. You can get the default allocator just from a `Document` object, but you could conceivably use a different allocator if desired. You then create a `Value` object to encapsulate the integer and use the `AddMember` function to add a value with the specified name to `inObject`.

The rest of the `Add` functions are similar, except for `AddVector3` and `AddQuaternion`, for which you must first create an array and then add float values to that array. (You'll see this array syntax when looking at the global properties.)

You then create a skeleton for the `LevelLoader::SaveLevel` function, as shown in Listing 14.11. First, you create the RapidJSON document and make an object for its root via `SetObject`. Next, you add the version integer. Then, you use the `StringBuffer` and `PrettyWriter` to create a pretty-printed output string of the JSON file. Finally, you use a standard `std::ofstream` to write out the string to a file.

Listing 14.11   `LevelLoader::SaveLevel` Implementation

```
void LevelLoader::SaveLevel(Game* game,
   const std::string& fileName)
{
   // Create the document and root object
   rapidjson::Document doc;
   doc.SetObject();

   // Write the version
   JsonHelper::AddInt(doc.GetAllocator(), doc, "version", LevelVersion);

   // Create the rest of the file (TODO)
   // ...

   // Save JSON to string buffer
   rapidjson::StringBuffer buffer;
   // Use PrettyWriter for pretty output (otherwise use Writer)
   rapidjson::PrettyWriter<rapidjson::StringBuffer> writer(buffer);
   doc.Accept(writer);
   const char* output = buffer.GetString();

   // Write output to file
   std::ofstream outFile(fileName);
   if (outFile.is_open())
   {
      outFile << output;
   }
}
```

For now, this function only writes out the version to the output file. But with this skeleton code, you can start adding the remaining output.

Saving Global Properties

Next, you need to add a `SaveGlobalProperties` function to `LevelLoader`. We omit the implementation here, as it's very similar to the other functions written thus far. You simply need to add the properties for the ambient light and the directional light object.

Once this function is complete, you integrate it into your `SaveLevel` function as follows:

```
rapidjson::Value globals(rapidjson::kObjectType);
SaveGlobalProperties(doc.GetAllocator(), game, globals);
doc.AddMember("globalProperties", globals, doc.GetAllocator());
```

Saving Actors and Components

To be able to save actors and components, you need a way to get a string name of the type, given an `Actor` or `Component` pointer. You already have a `TypeID` for components, so to get a corresponding string, you need only declare a constant array of the different names in `Component`. You declare this array in `Component.h` as follows:

```
static const char* TypeNames[NUM_COMPONENT_TYPES];
```

And then in `Component.cpp`, you fill in the array. It's important that you maintain the same ordering as the `TypeID` enum:

```
const char* Component::TypeNames[NUM_COMPONENT_TYPES] = {
    "Component",
    "AudioComponent",
    "BallMove",
    // Rest omitted
    // ...
};
```

By maintaining the ordering, you make it easy to get the name of a component, given the type, using a snippet like this:

```
Component* comp = /* points to something */;
const char* name = Component::TypeNames[comp->GetType()];
```

To do the same thing for the `Actor` and its subclasses, you need to add a `TypeID` enum to `Actor` as well. This is essentially the same as the code for `TypeID`s in components earlier in this chapter, so we omit it here.

You then need to create a virtual `SaveProperties` function in both `Actor` and `Component` and then override it in every subclass that needs to do so. This ends up playing out very similarly to the `LoadProperties` functions written when loading in the level files. As an example, Listing 14.12 shows the implementation of `Actor::SaveProperties`. Note that you liberally use the `Add` functions in `LevelLoader`, and you need to pass in the allocator because all the `Add` functions need it.

Listing 14.12 `Actor::SaveProperties` Implementation

```
void Actor::SaveProperties(rapidjson::Document::AllocatorType& alloc,
    rapidjson::Value& inObj) const
{
    std::string state = "active";
    if (mState == EPaused)
    {
        state = "paused";
    }
    else if (mState == EDead)
    {
        state = "dead";
    }

    JsonHelper::AddString(alloc, inObj, "state", state);
    JsonHelper::AddVector3(alloc, inObj, "position", mPosition);
    JsonHelper::AddQuaternion(alloc, inObj, "rotation", mRotation);
    JsonHelper::AddFloat(alloc, inObj, "scale", mScale);
}
```

With all these pieces in place, you can then add `SaveActors` and `SaveComponents` functions to `LevelLoader`. Listing 14.13 shows the `SaveActors` function. First, you get the vector of actors from the game by `const` reference. Then, you loop through every actor and create a new JSON object for it. You then add the string for the type by using the `TypeID` and `TypeNames` functionality. Next, you create a JSON object for the properties and call the actor's `SaveProperties` function. You then create an array for the components before calling `SaveComponents`. Finally, you add the actor's JSON object into the JSON array of actors.

Listing 14.13 `LevelLoader::SaveActors` Implementation

```
void LevelLoader::SaveActors(rapidjson::Document::AllocatorType& alloc,
    Game* game, rapidjson::Value& inArray)
{
    const auto& actors = game->GetActors();
    for (const Actor* actor : actors)
    {
        // Make a JSON object
        rapidjson::Value obj(rapidjson::kObjectType);
        // Add type
        AddString(alloc, obj, "type", Actor::TypeNames[actor->GetType()]);
```

```
        // Make object for properties
        rapidjson::Value props(rapidjson::kObjectType);
        // Save properties
        actor->SaveProperties(alloc, props);
        // Add the properties to the JSON object
        obj.AddMember("properties", props, alloc);

        // Save components
        rapidjson::Value components(rapidjson::kArrayType);
        SaveComponents(alloc, actor, components);
        obj.AddMember("components", components, alloc);

        // Add actor to inArray
        inArray.PushBack(obj, alloc);
    }
}
```

You similarly implement a `SaveComponents` function. With all this code implemented, you can now save all the actors and components to the file. For testing purposes, pressing the R key in this chapter's game project saves to the `Assets/Save.gplevel` level file.

> **note**
> With some work, you could create a single serialize function that both load and saves properties. This way, you could avoid having to update two different functions every time you add a new property to an actor or a component.

While this code will save almost everything in the game, it doesn't quite fully capture the current state of the game at a specific point in time. For example, it does not save the state of any active FMOD sound events. To implement this, you would need to ask FMOD for the current timestamp of the sound events, and then when loading the game from the file, you would need to restart the sound events with those timestamps. It takes some additional work to go from saving a level file to being usable as a save file for the player.

Binary Data

You've used JSON file formats throughout this book: for meshes, animations, skeletons, text localization, and now for level loading. The advantages of using a text-based file format are numerous. Text files are easy for humans to look at, find errors in, and (if needed) manually edit. Text files also play very nicely with source control systems such as Git because it's very easy to see what changed in a file between two revisions. During development, it's also easier to debug loading of assets if they are text files.

However, the disadvantage of using text-based file formats is that they are inefficient, both in terms of disk and memory usage as well as in terms of performance at runtime. Formats such as JSON or XML take up a lot of space on disk simply because of the formatting characters they use, such as braces and quotation marks. On top of this, parsing text-based files at runtime is slow, even with high-performance libraries such as RapidJSON. For example, on my computer, it takes about three seconds to load in the `CatWarrior.gpmesh` file in a debug build. Clearly, this would lead to slow load times for a larger game.

For the best of both worlds, you may want to use text files during development (at least for some members of the team) and then binary files in optimized builds. This section explores how to create a binary mesh file format. To keep things simple, in the code that loads in the gpmesh JSON format, you will first check if a corresponding `gpmesh.bin` file exists. If it does, you'll load that in instead of the JSON file. If it doesn't exist, the game will create the binary version file so that next time you run the game, you can load the binary version instead of the text version.

Note that one potential downside of this approach is that it may lead to bugs that occur only with the binary format but not the text one. To avoid this, it's important that you continue to use both formats throughout development. If one of the two formats becomes stale, then there's a greater chance that format will stop working.

Saving a Binary Mesh File

With any binary file format, an important step is to decide on a layout for the file. Most binary files begin with some sort of **header** that defines the contents of the file as well as any specific size information that's needed to read in the rest of the file. In the case of a mesh file format, you want the header to store information about the version, the number of vertices and indices, and so on. Listing 14.14 shows the `MeshBinHeader` struct that defines the layout of the header. In this example, the header is not **packed** (reduced in size as much as possible), but it gives the general idea of what you might want to store in a header.

Listing 14.14 `MeshBinHeader` Struct

```
struct MeshBinHeader
{
    // Signature for file type
    char mSignature[4] = { 'G', 'M', 'S', 'H' };
    // Version
    uint32_t mVersion = BinaryVersion;
    // Vertex layout type
    VertexArray::Layout mLayout = VertexArray::PosNormTex;
    // Info about how many of each you have
    uint32_t mNumTextures = 0;
```

```
    uint32_t mNumVerts = 0;
    uint32_t mNumIndices = 0;
    // Box/radius of mesh, used for collision
    AABB mBox{ Vector3::Zero, Vector3::Zero };
    float mRadius = 0.0f;
};
```

The `mSignature` field is a special 4-byte magic number that specifies the file type. Most popular binary file types have some sort of signature. The signature helps you figure out what a file type is from its first few bytes without knowing anything other than the signature to look for. The rest of the data is information you need to reconstruct the mesh data from the file.

After the header is the main data section of the file. In this case, there are three main things to store: the filenames for associated textures, the vertex buffer data, and the index buffer data.

With the file format decided on, you can then create the `SaveBinary` function, as shown in Listing 14.15. This function takes in a lot of parameters because there's a lot of information needed to create the binary file. In total, you need the filename, a pointer to the vertex buffer, the number of vertices, the layout of these vertices, a pointer to the index buffer, the number of indices, a vector of the texture names, the bounding box of the mesh, and the radius of the mesh. With all these parameters, you can save the file.

Listing 14.15 `Mesh::SaveBinary` Implementation

```
void Mesh::SaveBinary(const std::string& fileName, const void* verts,
    uint32_t numVerts, VertexArray::Layout,
    const uint32_t* indices, uint32_t numIndices,
    const std::vector<std::string>& textureNames,
    const AABB& box, float radius)
{
    // Create header struct
    MeshBinHeader header;
    header.mLayout = layout;
    header.mNumTextures =
        static_cast<unsigned>(textureNames.size());
    header.mNumVerts = numVerts;
    header.mNumIndices = numIndices;
    header.mBox = box;
    header.mRadius = radius;

    // Open binary file for writing
    std::ofstream outFile(fileName, std::ios::out
        | std::ios::binary);
    if (outFile.is_open())
    {
        // Write the header
        outFile.write(reinterpret_cast<char*>(&header), sizeof(header));
```

```
   // For each texture, we need to write the size of the name,
   // followed by the string, followed by a null terminator
   for (const auto& tex : textureNames)
   {
      uint16_t nameSize = static_cast<uint16_t>(tex.length()) + 1;
      outFile.write(reinterpret_cast<char*>(&nameSize),
         sizeof(nameSize));
      outFile.write(tex.c_str(), nameSize - 1);
      outFile.write("\0", 1);
   }

   // Figure out number of bytes for each vertex, based on layout
   unsigned vertexSize = VertexArray::GetVertexSize(layout);
   // Write vertices
   outFile.write(reinterpret_cast<const char*>(verts),
      numVerts * vertexSize);
   // Write indices
   outFile.write(reinterpret_cast<const char*>(indices),
      numIndices * sizeof(uint32_t));
   }
}
```

The code in Listing 14.15 does quite a lot. First, you create an instance of the `MeshBinHeader` struct and fill in all its members. Next, you create a file for output and open it in binary mode. If this file successfully opens, you can write to it.

Then you write the header of the file with the `write` function call. The first parameter `write` expects is a `char` pointer, so in many cases it's necessary to cast a different pointer to a `char*`. This requires a `reinterpret_cast` because a `MeshBinHeader*` cannot directly convert to a `char*`. The second parameter to write is the number of bytes to write to the file. Here, you use `sizeof` to specify the number of bytes corresponding to the size of `MeshBinHeader`. In other words, you are writing `sizeof(header)` bytes starting at the address of `header`. This is a quick way to just write the entire struct in one fell swoop.

> ### warning
>
> **WATCH OUT FOR ENDIANNESS**   The order in which a CPU platform saves values larger than 1 byte is called endianness. The method used here to read and write `MeshBinHeader` will not work if the endianness of the platform that writes out the `gpmesh.bin` file is different from the endianness of the platform that reads the `gpmesh.bin` file.
>
> Although most platforms today are little endian, endianness can still be a potential issue with code of this style.

Next, you loop through all the texture names and write each of them to the file. For each file-name, you first write the number of characters in the filename (plus one for the null terminator) and then write the string itself. Note that this code assumes that a filename can't be larger than 64 KB, which should be a safe assumption. The reason you write the number of characters and the name is for loading. The header only stores the number of textures and not the size of each string. Without storing the number of characters, at load time you would have no way of knowing how many bytes to read for the filename.

After writing all the filenames, you then write all the vertex and index buffer data directly to the file. You don't need to include the sizes here because they already appear in the header. For the vertex data, the number of bytes is the number of vertices times the size of each vertex. Luckily, you can use a `VertexArray` helper function to get the size of each vertex based on layout. For the index data, you have a fixed size (32-bit indices), so the total number of bytes is easier to calculate.

Then in `Mesh::Load`, if the binary file doesn't exist, the code loads the JSON file and creates the corresponding binary file.

Loading a Binary Mesh File

Loading a binary mesh file is like writing to it but in reverse. The steps are to load in the header, check the validity of the header, load in the textures, load in the vertex and index data, and finally create the actual `VertexArray` (which will upload the data to the GPU via OpenGL). Listing 14.16 shows the outline of the code for `Mesh::LoadBinary`.

Listing 14.16 `Mesh::LoadBinary` Outline

```
void Mesh::LoadBinary(const std::string& filename,
   Renderer* renderer)
{
   std::ifstream inFile(fileName, /* in/binary flags ... */);
   if (inFile.is_open())
   {
      MeshBinHeader header;
      inFile.read(reinterpret_cast<char*>(&header), sizeof(header));

      // Validate the header signature and version
      char* sig = header.mSignature;
      if (sig[0] != 'G' || sig[1] != 'M' || sig[2] != 'S' ||
         sig[3] != 'H' || header.mVersion != BinaryVersion)
      {
         return false;
      }

      // Read in the texture file names (omitted)
      // ...
```

```
    // Read in vertices/indices
    unsigned vertexSize = VertexArray::GetVertexSize(header.mLayout);
    char* verts = new char[header.mNumVerts * vertexSize];
    uint32_t* indices = new uint32_t[header.mNumIndices];
    inFile.read(verts, header.mNumVerts * vertexSize);
    inFile.read(reinterpret_cast<char*>(indices),
        header.mNumIndices * sizeof(uint32_t));

    // Now create the vertex array
    mVertexArray = new VertexArray(verts, header.mNumVerts,
        header.mLayout, indices, header.mNumIndices);

    // Delete verts/indices
    delete[] verts;
    delete[] indices;

    mBox = header.mBox;
    mRadius = header.mRadius;

    return true;
    }

    return false;
}
```

First, you open the file for reading in binary mode. Next, you read in the header via the `read` function. Much as with `write`, `read` takes in a `char*` for where to write and the number of bytes to read from the file. Next, you verify that the signature and version in the header match what is expected; if they don't, you can't load the file.

After this, you read in all the texture filenames and load them, though we omit that code from Listing 14.16 to save space. Next, you allocate memory to store the vertex and index buffers, and you use `read` to grab the data from the file. Once you have the vertex and index data, you can construct the `VertexArray` object and pass in all the information it needs. You need to make sure to clean up the memory and set the `mBox` and `mRadius` members before returning.

Note that `LoadBinary` returns `false` if the file fails to load. This way, the `Mesh::Load` code first tries to load the binary file. If it succeeds, that's it. Otherwise, it can proceed using the JSON parsing code from before:

```
bool Mesh::Load(const std::string& fileName, Renderer* renderer)
{
    mFileName = fileName;
    // Try loading the binary file first
    if (LoadBinary(fileName + ".bin", renderer))
    {
        return true;
    }
    // ...
```

With the switch to binary mesh file loading, the performance improves significantly in debug mode. The `CatWarrior.gpmesh.bin` file now loads in one second as opposed to three—meaning a 3x performance gain over the JSON version! This is great because you'll spend most of your development time running in debug mode.

Unfortunately, in an optimized build, the performance of both the JSON and binary path is almost identical. This could be due to several factors, including the RapidJSON library being very optimized or other aspects being the primary overhead, such as transferring the data to the GPU or loading in the textures.

On the disk space side of things, you save space. While the JSON version of the Feline Swordsman is around 6.5 MB on disk, the binary version is only 2.5 MB.

Game Project

This chapter's game project implements the systems discussed in this chapter. Everything loads from a `gplevel` file, and pressing the R key saves the current state of the world into `Assets/Saved.gplevel`. The project also implements the binary saving and loading of mesh files in the `.gpmesh.bin` format. The code is available in the book's GitHub repository, in the `Chapter14` directory. Open `Chapter14-windows.sln` in Windows and `Chapter14-mac.xcodeproj` on Mac.

Figure 14.1 shows the game project in action. Notice that it looks identical to the game project from Chapter 13, "Intermediate Graphics." However, the entire contents of the game world now load directly from the `Assets/Level3.gplevel` file, which was in turn created by saving the level file. The first time the game runs, it creates a binary mesh file for every mesh loaded. Subsequent runs load meshes from the binary files instead of JSON.

Figure 14.1 Chapter 14 game project

Summary

This chapter explores how to create level files in JSON. Loading from a file requires several systems. First, you create helper functions that wrap the functionality of the RapidJSON library to easily be able to write the game's types to JSON. You then add code to set global properties, load in actors, and load in components associated with the actors. To do this, you need to add some type information to components, as well as maps that associate names of types to a function that can dynamically allocate that type. You also need to create virtual LoadProperties functions in both Component and Actor.

You also need to create code to save the game world to JSON, and you create helper functions to assist with this process. At a high level, saving the file requires saving all the global properties first and then looping through all the actors and components to write their properties. As with file loading, you have to create virtual SaveProperties functions in both Component and Actor.

Finally, this chapter discusses the trade-offs involved in using a text-based file format instead of a binary one. While a text format is often more convenient to use in development, it comes at a cost of inefficiency—both in performance and disk usage. This chapter explores how to design a binary file format for mesh files, which involves writing and reading from files in binary mode.

Additional Reading

There are no books devoted specifically to level files or binary data. However, the classic *Game Programming Gems* series has some articles on the topic. Bruno Sousa's article discusses how to use resource files, which are files that combine several files into one. Martin Brownlow's article discusses how to create a save-anywhere system. Finally, David Koenig's article looks at how to improve the performance of loading files.

Brownlow, Martin. "Save Me Now!" *Game Programming Gems 3*. Ed. Dante Treglia. Hingham: Charles River Media, 2002.

Koenig, David L. "Faster File Loading with Access Based File Reordering." *Game Programming Gems 6*. Ed. Mike Dickheiser. Rockland: Charles River Media, 2006.

Sousa, Bruno. "File Management Using Resource Files." *Game Programming Gems 2*. Ed. Mark DeLoura. Hingham: Charles River Media, 2001.

Exercises

In this chapter's first exercise, you need to reduce the size of the JSON files created by `SaveLevel`. In the second exercise you convert the `Animation` file format to binary.

Exercise 14.1

One issue with the `SaveLevel` code is that you write every property for every actor and all its components. However, for a specific subclass like `TargetActor`, few if any of the properties or components change after construction.

To solve this problem, when it's time to save the level, you can create a temporary `TargetActor` and write out the JSON object for that actor by using the normal writing techniques. This JSON object serves as the template, as it's the state of `TargetActor` when it's originally spawned. Then, for each `TargetActor` to save in the level, compare its JSON object to the template one and write only the properties and components that are different.

You can then use this process for all the different types of actors. To assist with this, RapidJSON provides overloaded comparison operators. Two `rapidjson::Value`s are equal only if they have the same type and contents. This way, you can eliminate setting at least most of the components (because they won't change). It will require a bit more work to do this on a granular (per-property) level.

Exercise 14.2

Applying the same binary file techniques you used for the mesh files, create a binary file format for the animation files. Because all the tracks of bone transforms are the same size, you can use a format where, after writing the header, you write the ID for each track followed by the entire track information. For a refresher on the animation file format, refer to Chapter 12, "Skeletal Animation."

INTERMEDIATE C++ REVIEW

This appendix provides a quick review of intermediate C++ concepts used throughout the book. The concepts roughly correspond to typical topics in Computer Science 1 and 2 courses. If you are rusty with C++, you should spend extra time reviewing this material.

References, Pointers, and Arrays

Although references, pointers, and arrays might seem like separate concepts, they are closely related. Furthermore, because pointers are often stumbling points for C++ programmers, it's worthwhile to spend some time reviewing their intricacies.

References

A **reference** is a variable that *refers* to another variable that already exists. To denote a variable as a reference, add an & immediately after the type. For example, here is how you can declare r as a reference to the already existing integer i:

```
int i = 20;
int& r = i; // r refers to i
```

By default, functions pass parameters by value (**pass-by-value**), meaning that when you call a function, the parameter copies to a new variable. When passing by value, modifications to parameters do not persist beyond the function call. For example, here is an (incorrect) implementation of a Swap function that swaps two integers:

```
void Swap(int a, int b)
{
    int temp = a;
    a = b;
    b = temp;
}
```

The problem with Swap is that a and b are copies of the parameters, which means the function cannot truly swap the parameters as desired. To solve this problem, you should instead declare the parameters of Swap as *references* to integers:

```
void Swap(int& a, int& b)
{
    // (The body of the function is identical to the previous)
}
```

When passing a parameter by reference (**pass-by-reference**), any changes made to that parameter within the function will persist after the function ends.

One caveat is that because a and b are now references to integers, they must reference existing variables. You can't pass in temporary values for the parameters. For example, Swap(50,100) is invalid because 50 and 100 are not declared variables.

> ### warning
>
> **PASS-BY-VALUE IS DEFAULT**   By default, all parameters in C++, even objects, pass by value. In contrast, languages like Java and C# default to passing objects by reference.

Pointers

To understand pointers, it first helps to remember the way computers store variables in memory. During program execution, entering a function automatically allocates memory for local variables in a segment of memory called the **stack**. This means that all local variables in a function have memory addresses known to the C++ program.

Table A.1 shows code snippets and possible locations of their variables in memory. Notice that each variable has an associated memory address. The table shows the memory addresses in hexadecimal simply because that's the typical notation for memory addresses.

Table A.1   Variable Storage

Code	Variable	Memory Address	Value
`int x = 50;`	x	0xC230	50
`int y = 100;`	y	0xC234	100
`int z = 200;`	z	0xC238	200

The **address-of** operator (also `&`) queries the address of a variable. To get the address of a variable, place a `&` in front of the variable. For example, given the code in Table A.1, the following code outputs the value `0xC234`:

```
std::cout << &y;
```

A **pointer** is a variable that stores an integral value corresponding to a memory address. The following line declares the pointer `p` that stores the memory address of the variable `y`:

```
int* p = &y;
```

The `*` after the type signifies a pointer. Table A.2 shows the pointer `p` in action. Note that, just like any other variable, `p` has both a memory address and a value. But because `p` is a pointer, its value corresponds to the memory address of `y`.

Table A.2 Variable Storage (with Pointers)

Code	Variable	Memory Address	Value
`int x = 50;`	x	0xC230	50
`int y = 100;`	y	0xC234	100
`int z = 200;`	z	0xC238	200
`int* p = &y;`	p	0xC23C	0xC234

The * operator also dereferences a pointer. Dereferencing a pointer accesses the memory "pointed to" by the pointer. For example, the last line in Table A.3 changes the value of y to 42. This is because dereferencing p goes to the memory address 0xC234, which corresponds to the location of y in memory. Thus, writing the value 42 at this memory address overwrites the value of y.

Table A.3 Variable Storage (with Dereferencing)

Code	Variable	Memory Address	Value
`int x = 50;`	x	0xC230	50
`int y = 100;`	y	0xC234	42
`int z = 200;`	z	0xC238	200
`int* p = &y;`	p	0xC23C	0xC234
`*p = 42;`			

Unlike references, which must refer to something, pointers can point to nothing. A pointer that points to nothing is a **null pointer**. To initialize a pointer as null, use the `nullptr` keyword, as in the following code:

```
char* ptr = nullptr;
```

Dereferencing a null pointer crashes the program. The error message varies depending on the operating system, but typically "access violation" or "segmentation fault" errors occur when dereferencing a null pointer.

Arrays

An **array** is a collection of multiple elements of the same type. The following code declares an array of 10 integers called a and then sets the first element in the array (index 0) to 50:

```
int a[10];
a[0] = 50;
```

By default, the elements in an array are uninitialized. While you could manually initialize each element in an array, it's more convenient to use either the initializer syntax or a loop. The initializer syntax uses braces, like this:

```
int fib[5] = { 0, 1, 1, 2, 3 };
```

Alternatively, you could use a loop. The following initializes each of the 50 elements in `array` to 0:

```
int array[50];
for (int i = 0; i < 50; i++)
{
   array[i] = 0;
}
```

> ## warning
>
> **ARRAYS DON'T BOUND CHECK**   Requesting invalid indices can lead to memory corruption and other errors. Several tools exist to help find bad memory accesses, such as the AddressSanitizer tool available in Xcode.

C++ stores arrays contiguously in memory. This means that the data for index 0 is right next to the data for index 1, which is right next to index 2, and so on. Table A.4 shows an example of a five-element array in memory. Keep in mind that the variable `array` (without the subscript) references the memory address of index 0 (in this case, `0xF2E0`). Because of this, you can pass a single-dimensional array to a function via a pointer.

Table A.4   An Array in Memory

Code	Variable	Memory Address	Value

`int array[5] = {`
`   2, 4, 6, 8, 10`
`};`
	`array[0]`	`0xF2E0`	2

	`array[1]`	`0xF2E4`	4
	`array[2]`	`0xF2E8`	6
	`array[3]`	`0xF2EC`	8
	`array[4]`	`0xF2F0`	10

A POINTER BY ANY OTHER NAME...

The C programming language (the precursor to C++) does not support references. Thus, the concept of passing by reference does not exist in C. Instead of using references, you must use pointers. For example, in C, you would write the `Swap` function as follows:

```
void Swap(int* a, int* b)
{
    int temp = *a;
    *a = *b;
    *b = temp;
}
```

Calling this version of `Swap` then requires the address-of operator:

```
int x = 20;
int y = 37;
Swap(&x, &y);
```

At program execution time, there is no difference between how references and pointers work. However, keep in mind that a reference *must* refer to something, whereas a pointer can be `nullptr`.

In C++, many developers prefer passing by reference over passing by pointer. This is because passing by pointer implies that `nullptr` is a valid parameter. However, for stylistic reasons, this book typically passes dynamically allocated objects by pointer, even in cases where references would work.

You also can declare multidimensional arrays. For example, the following code creates a 2D array of floats with four rows and four columns:

```
float matrix[4][4];
```

To pass a multidimensional array into a function, you must explicitly specify the dimensions, like this:

```
void InvertMatrix(float m[4][4])
{
    // Code here...
}
```

Dynamic Memory Allocation

As discussed earlier, memory allocation for local variables is automatic in C++. These variables end up in memory on the stack. This is great for temporary variables and function parameters. However, local variables are sometimes not enough.

First, the stack has a limited amount of memory available—typically much less than the amount of memory an average program might want to use. For example, the Microsoft Visual C++ compiler has a default stack size of 1 MB. Such a small amount of memory won't be enough for all but the simplest games.

Second, local variables have a fixed lifetime. They are only available from the point of declaration until the end of the containing scope. This scope is typically within a function, as global variables are stylistically undesirable.

In **dynamic memory allocation**, the programmer controls allocation and deallocation of variables in memory. Dynamic allocations go into the **heap**, which is a separate part of memory. The heap is much larger in size compared to the stack (several gigabytes on current machines), and data on the heap persists until either the programmer deletes the data or the program ends.

Recall that in C++, the `new` and `delete` operators allocate and deallocate memory on the heap. The `new` operator allocates memory for the requested type of variable, and for classes and structs, it calls the constructor. The `delete` operator performs the opposite: It calls the destructor for class/struct types and deallocates the memory for the variable.

For example, this code dynamically allocates memory for a single `int` variable:

```
int* dynamicInt = new int;
```

To free the memory of a dynamically allocated variable, use `delete`:

```
delete dynamicInt;
```

Forgetting to delete a dynamically allocated variable causes a **memory leak**, meaning that the memory is unusable for the remaining life span of the program. For programs that run for a long time, small memory leaks accumulate over time and eventually cause the heap to run out of memory. If the heap runs out of memory, the program will almost always crash soon afterward.

Of course, dynamically allocating just a single integer doesn't take advantage of all the available memory on the heap. You can also dynamically allocate arrays:

```
char* dynArray = new char[4*1024*1024];
dynArray[0] = 32; // Set the first element to 32
```

Note that when dynamically allocating an array, you place square brackets immediately after the type and specify the size there. Unlike with a statically allocated array, with a dynamically allocated array, you can specify a size at runtime.

To delete a dynamically allocated array, use `delete[]`:

```
delete[] dynArray;
```

Assorted Class Topics

Recall that C++ supports object-oriented programming through classes. This section assumes familiarity with the basics of classes in C++: classes versus objects, how to declare a class with member variables and functions, the constructor, and inheritance and polymorphism. It instead focuses on certain topics that cause some issues when using classes in C++.

References, `const`, and Classes

Passing objects by value to functions is inefficient. This is because copying the object can be expensive, especially if the object has a lot of data. Thus, a best practice is to pass objects by reference.

However, one issue with references is that they allow the function to modify the parameter. For example, suppose an `Intersects` function takes in two `Circle` objects and returns whether these circles intersect. If the function takes in these circles by reference, it could choose to modify the centers or radii of the circles.

The solution is to instead use a constant (`const`) reference. A **`const` reference** guarantees that the function can only read from the reference but not write to it. So, a more correct declaration of `Intersects` uses `const` references:

```
bool Intersects(const Circle& a, const Circle& b);
```

You can also mark member functions as **`const` member functions** to guarantee that a member function does not modify member data. For example, a `GetRadius` function for `Circle` shouldn't modify member data, which means it should be a `const` member function. To denote that a member function is `const`, add the `const` keyword immediately after the closing parenthesis of the function declaration, as in Listing A.1.

Listing A.1 `Circle` Class with `const` Member Function

```
class Circle
{
public:
   float GetRadius() const { return mRadius }
   // Other functions omitted
   // ...
private:
   Point mCenter;
   float mRadius;
};
```

To summarize, the best practices when it comes to references, `const`, and classes are as follows:

- Pass non-basic types by reference, `const` reference, or pointers, to avoid making copies.
- Pass by `const` reference when a function does not need to modify a reference parameter.
- Mark member functions that don't modify data as `const`.

Dynamic Allocation of Classes

Just as with any other type, you can dynamically allocate classes. Listing A.2 shows a declaration for a `Complex` class that encapsulates a real part and an imaginary part.

Listing A.2   A `Complex` Class

```
class Complex
{
public:
   Complex(float real, float imaginary)
      : mReal(real)
      , mImaginary(imaginary)
   { }
private:
   float mReal;
   float mImaginary;
};
```

Notice how the constructor for `Complex` takes two parameters. To dynamically allocate an instance of `Complex`, you must pass in these parameters:

```
Complex* c = new Complex(1.0f, 2.0f);
```

As with dynamic allocation of other types, the `new` operator returns a pointer to the dynamically allocated object. Given a pointer to an object, the `->` operator accesses any public members. For example, if the `Complex` class had a public `Negate` member function that takes no parameters, the following would call the function on the object `c`:

```
c->Negate();
```

You can also dynamically allocate arrays of objects. This works only if the class has a **default constructor** (a constructor that takes in no parameters). This is because there's no way to specify constructor parameters when dynamically allocating an array. If you don't define any constructors for a class, C++ automatically creates a default constructor for you. However, if you declare a constructor that takes in parameters, then C++ will not automatically create a default constructor. In this case, if you want a default constructor you must declare it yourself. In the case of `Complex`, because you declared a non-default constructor, there is no default constructor.

Destructors

Suppose you needed to dynamically allocate arrays of integers several times throughout a program. Rather than manually write this code repeatedly, it might make sense to encapsulate this functionality inside a `DynamicArray` class, as in Listing A.3.

Listing A.3   A Basic Declaration for `DynamicArray`

```
class DynamicArray
{
public:
    // Constructor takes in size of element
    DynamicArray(int size)
        : mSize(size)
        , mArray(nullptr)
    {
        mArray = new int[mSize];
    }
    // At function used to access an index
    int& At(int index) { return mArray[index]; }
private:
    int* mArray;
    int mSize;
};
```

With this `DynamicArray` class, you could create a dynamic array with 50 elements by using the following code:

```
DynamicArray scores(50);
```

However, as previously discussed, every call to `new` must have a matching call to `delete`. In this case, `DynamicArray` dynamically allocates an array in its constructor, but there's no matching `delete[]` anywhere. This means that when the `scores` object goes out of scope, there is a memory leak.

The solution is to use another special member function called the **destructor**. The destructor is a member function that automatically runs when destroying the object. For objects allocated on the stack, this happens when the object goes out of scope. For dynamically allocated objects, the `delete` call on the object also invokes the destructor.

The destructor always has the same name as the class, except prefaced with a tilde (~). So for `DynamicArray`, this is the destructor:

```
DynamicArray::~DynamicArray()
{
    delete[] mArray;
}
```

If you add this destructor, when `scores` goes out of scope, the destructor deallocates `mArray`, eliminating the memory leak.

The Copy Constructor

The **copy constructor** is a special constructor that creates an object as a copy of another object of the same type. For example, suppose you declare the following `Complex` object:

```
Complex c1 = Complex(5.0f, 3.5f);
```

You could then instantiate a second instance of `Complex` as a copy of `c1`:

```
Complex c2(c1);
```

In most cases, C++ provides a copy constructor implementation if the programmer doesn't declare one. This default copy constructor directly copies all member data from the original object to the new object. For `Complex`, this works perfectly fine; for example, it means that `c2.mReal` and `c2.mImaginary` directly copy from the corresponding members of `c1`.

However, for classes with pointers to data, such as `DynamicArray`, directly copying member data doesn't give the desired result. Suppose you run the following code:

```
DynamicArray array(50);
DynamicArray otherArray(array);
```

With the default copy constructor, you directly copy the `mArray` pointers rather than copying the underlying dynamically allocated array. This means that if you next modify `otherArray`, you also modify `array` at the same time! Figure A.1 illustrates this problematic behavior, called a **shallow copy**.

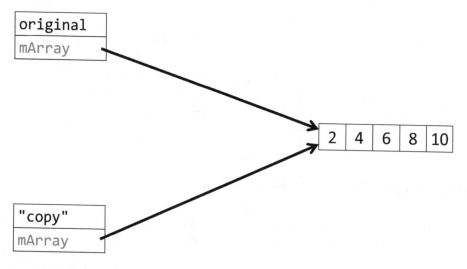

Figure A.1 A shallow copy of `mArray`

If the default copy constructor is insufficient, as is the case for `DynamicArray`, you must declare a custom copy constructor:

```
DynamicArray(const DynamicArray& other)
    : mSize(other.mSize)
    , mArray(nullptr)
{
    // Dynamically allocate my own data
    mArray = new int[mSize];
    // Copy from other's data
    for (int i = 0; i < mSize; i++)
    {
        mArray[i] = other.mArray[i];
    }
}
```

Note that the only parameter to the copy constructor is a `const` reference to another instance of the class. The implementation in this case dynamically allocates a new array and then copies over the data from the other `DynamicArray`. This is as a **deep copy** because the two objects now have separate underlying dynamically allocated arrays.

In general, classes that dynamically allocate data should implement the following member functions:

- A destructor to free the dynamically allocated memory
- A copy constructor to implement deep copies
- An assignment operator (discussed in the next section), also to implement deep copies

If it's necessary to implement any of these three functions, then you should implement all three. This problem is so common in C++ that developers coined the term **rule of three** to remember it.

> ### note
> In the C++11 standard, the rule of three expands to the rule of five, as there are two additional special functions (the move constructor and the move assignment operator). While this book does use some C++11 features, it does not use these additional functions.

Operator Overloading

C++ gives programmers the ability to specify the behavior of built-in operators for custom types. For example, you can define how the arithmetic operators work for the `Complex` class. In the case of addition, you can declare the + operator as follows:

```
friend Complex operator+(const Complex& a, const Complex& b)
{
    return Complex(a.mReal + b.mReal,
                   a.mImaginary + b.mImaginary);
}
```

Here, the `friend` keyword means that `operator+` is a standalone function that can access `Complex`'s private data. This is a typical declaration signature for binary operators.

After overloading the + operator, you can use it to add two complex objects, like so:

```
Complex result = c1 + c2;
```

You can also override binary comparison operators. The only difference is that these operators return a `bool`. For example, the following code overloads the `==` operator:

```
friend bool operator==(const Complex& a, const Complex& b)
{
    return (a.mReal == b.mReal) &&
        (a.mImaginary == b.mImaginary);
}
```

You can also overload the = operator (or **assignment operator**). As with the copy constructor, if you don't specify an assignment operator, C++ gives you a default assignment operator that performs a shallow copy. So, you usually only need to overload the assignment operator in the "rule of three" case.

There's one big difference between an assignment operator and a copy constructor. With a copy constructor, you're constructing a new object as a copy of an existing one. With an assignment operator, you're overwriting an *already existing instance* of an object. For example, the following code invokes the assignment operator for `DynamicArray` on the third line because the first line previously constructed `a1`:

```
DynamicArray a1(50);
DynamicArray a2(75);
a1 = a2;
```

Because the assignment operator overwrites an already existing instance with new values, it needs to deallocate any previously dynamically allocated data. For example, this is the correct implementation of the assignment operator for `DynamicArray`:

```
DynamicArray& operator=(const DynamicArray& other)
{
    // Delete existing data
    delete[] mArray;
    // Copy from other
    mSize = other.mSize;
    mArray = new int[mSize];
```

```
for (int i = 0; i < mSize; i++)
{
    mArray[i] = other.mArray[i];
}
// By convention, return *this
return *this;
}
```

Note that the assignment operator is a member function of the class, not a standalone friend function. Also, by convention, the assignment operator returns a reference to the reassigned object. This allows for code (albeit ugly code) that chains assignments, such as the following:

```
a = b = c;
```

You can override nearly every operator in C++, including the subscript [] operator, new, and delete. However, with great power comes great responsibility. You should try to overload an operator only when it's clear what the operator does. It makes sense that the + operator does addition, but you should avoid reassigning the meaning of an operator.

For example, some math libraries override | and ^ for the dot and cross products, even though | and ^ are the bitwise OR and bitwise XOR for integral types. Overusing operator overloading in this manner leads to code that is difficult to understand. Amusingly, the C++ library itself breaks this best practice: Streams overload the >> and << operators for input and output (which are bitshift operators for integral types).

Collections

A **collection** provides a way to store elements of data. The C++ Standard Library (STL) provides many different collections, and so it's important to understand when to utilize which collections. This section discusses the most commonly used collections.

Big-O Notation

Big-O notation describes the rate at which an algorithm scales as the problem size scales. This rate is also known as the **time complexity** of the algorithm. You can use Big-O to understand the relative scaling of specific operations on collections. For example, an operation with a Big-O of $O(1)$ means that regardless of the number of elements in the collection, the operation will always take the same amount of time. On the other hand, a Big-O of $O(n)$ means that the time complexity is a linear function of the number of elements.

Table A.5 lists the most common time complexities, from the fastest to the slowest. Algorithms that are exponential or slower are too slow to see real use beyond very small problem sizes.

Table A.5 Common Time Complexities in Big-O Notation (Fastest to Slowest)

Big-O	Described As	Examples
$O(1)$	Constant	Insertion into the front of a linked list, array indexing
$O(\log n)$	Logarithmic	Binary search (given an already sorted collection)
$O(n)$	Linear	Linear search
$O(n \log n)$	"n log n"	Merge sort, quick sort (average case)
$O(n^2)$	Quadratic	Insertion sort, bubble sort
$O(2^n)$	Exponential	Integer factorization
$O(n!)$	Factorial	Brute-forcing the traveling salesperson problem

Although Big-O notation says how an algorithm scales, for certain problem sizes, algorithms with worse time complexity may perform better. For example, a quick sort has an average time complexity of $O(n \log n)$, while an insertion sort has a time complexity of $O(n^2)$. However, for small problem sizes (such as $n<20$), the insertion sort has a faster execution time because it does not use recursion. Thus, it's as important to consider the actual execution performance of an algorithm as its specific use case.

Vector

A **vector** is a dynamic array that automatically resizes based on the number of elements in the collection. To insert elements into a vector, use the `push_back` (or `emplace_back`) member function. This adds an element to the end (back) of the vector. For example, the following code declares a vector of floats and then adds three elements at the end of the vector:

```
// #include <vector> to use std::vector
std::vector<float> vecOfFloats;
vecOfFloats.push_back(5.0f);  // Contents: { 5.0f }
vecOfFloats.push_back(7.5f);  // Contents: { 5.0f, 7.5f }
vecOfFloats.push_back(10.0f); // Contents: { 5.0f, 7.5f, 10.0f }
```

Once the vector has elements, you can use array subscript notation to access specific elements in the vector. So given the vector from the preceding snippet, `vecOfFloats[2]` accesses the third element in the vector, yielding `10.0f`.

In the long run, insertion into the back of a vector averages out to O(1). However, because a vector exists in one contiguous block of memory, as in Figure A.2, insertion at an arbitrary position in the vector is O(n). Because of this, you should avoid arbitrary insertion into a vector. But an advantage of this contiguous memory layout is that accessing an element at an index is O(1).

Figure A.2 The internal memory layout of a vector is contiguous, as with arrays

Linked List

A **linked list** is a collection that stores each element at a separate location in memory and links them together with pointers. The `std::list` collection allows for insertion to both the front and the back of the list. Use the `push_front` (or `emplace_front`) function to insert into the front, and `push_back` (or `emplace_back`) for the back. The following code creates a linked list of integers and inserts a handful of elements:

```
// #include <list> to use std::list
std::list<int> myList;
myList.push_back(4);
myList.push_back(6);
myList.push_back(8);
myList.push_back(10);
myList.push_front(2);
```

Figure A.3 illustrates `myList` after completing all the insertions. Note that, by definition, the elements in the linked list are not next to each other in memory. One advantage of a linked list is that insertion to either end of the list is O(1). If you have a pointer to an element in the list, you can also insert before or after that element in O(1) time.

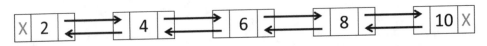

Figure A.3 `myList` with elements inserted into it

However, one disadvantage of a linked list is that accessing the *n*th element of the list is O(n). For this reason, the implementation of `std::list` does not allow indexing via array subscripting.

EFFICIENCY: LINKED LIST OR VECTOR?

In cases where each individual element in the collection is small (less than 64 bytes), a vector almost always outperforms a linked list. This is because of the way a CPU accesses memory.

Reading values from memory is very slow for the CPU, so when it needs to read a value from memory, it also loads neighboring values into a high-speed cache. Because elements in a vector are contiguous in memory, accessing an element at a specific index also loads its neighboring indices into the cache.

However, because elements in a linked list are not contiguous, loading one element also loads unrelated memory into the cache. Thus, operations such as looping over an entire collection are much more efficient with a vector than with a linked list, even though both operations have a time complexity of $O(n)$.

Queues

A **queue** exhibits **first-in, first-out** (**FIFO**) behavior, much like waiting in a line at a store. With a queue, you cannot remove elements in any arbitrary order. With a queue, you must remove elements in the same order in which they were added. Although many books use **enqueue** to reference insertion into a queue and **dequeue** to reference removal from a queue, the implementation of `std::queue` uses `push` (or `emplace`) for insertion and `pop` for removal. To access the element at the front of the queue, use `front`.

The following code inserts three elements into a queue and then removes each element from the queue, outputting the values:

```
// #include <queue> to use std::queue
std::queue<int> myQueue;
myQueue.push(10);
myQueue.push(20);
myQueue.push(30);
for (int i = 0; i < 3; i++)
{
    std::cout << myQueue.front() << ' ';
    myQueue.pop();
}
```

Because queues operate in a FIFO manner, the above code outputs the following:

```
10 20 30
```

The `std::queue` implementation guarantees $O(1)$ time complexity for insertion, accessing the front element, and removal.

Stack

A **stack** exhibits **last-in, first-out (LIFO)** behavior. For example, if you add the elements A, B, and C to a stack, you can only remove them in the order C, B, A. You use the `push` (or `emplace`) function to add an element onto the stack and the `pop` function to remove an element from the stack. The `top` function accesses the element on the "top" of the stack. The following code shows `std::stack` in action:

```
// Include <stack> to use std::stack
std::stack<int> myStack;
myStack.push(10);
myStack.push(20);
myStack.push(30);
for (int i = 0; i < 3; i++)
{
    std::cout << myStack.top() << ' ';
    myStack.pop();
}
```

Because of the LIFO behavior of a stack, the above code outputs the following:

```
30 20 10
```

As with `queue`, the major operations for `std::stack` all have constant time complexity.

Maps

A **map** is an ordered collection of {key, value} pairs, sorted by key. Each key in the map must be unique. Because a map has both a key type and a value type, you must specify both types when declaring a map. The recommended way to add an element to a map is with the `emplace` function, which takes in the key and values as parameters. For example, the following code creates a `std::map` of months, where the key is the number of the month and the value is the string name of the month:

```
// #include <map> to use std::map
std::map<int, std::string> months;
months.emplace(1, "January");
months.emplace(2, "February");
months.emplace(3, "March");
// ...
```

The easiest way to access an element from a map is by using the `[]` operator and passing in the key. For example, the following would output `February`:

```
std::cout << months[2];
```

However, this syntax works as expected only if the key is in the map. To determine if a key is in a map, use the `find` function. This returns an iterator to the element, if found. (We discuss iterators in a moment.)

Internally, the `std::map` implementation uses a balanced binary search tree. This means that `std::map` can find an element by key in $O(\log n)$ (logarithmic) time. Insertion and removal from the map are also logarithmic. Furthermore, due to the binary search tree, looping over the contents of a map is in ascending order of the keys.

Hash Maps

While a regular map maintains an ascending order of the keys, a **hash map** is unordered. In exchange for the lack of ordering, insertion, removal, and search are all $O(1)$. Thus, in cases where you need a map but don't need ordering, a hash map yields better performance than a regular map.

The C++ hash map `std::unordered_map` has the same functions as `std::map`, just without any guaranteed ordering. To use the hash map class, use `#include <unordered_map>`.

Iterators, Auto, and Range-Based For Loops

For looping over all the elements in a vector you can use the same syntax as for looping over an array. However, many of the other C++ STL collections, such as `list` and `map`, do not support this array syntax.

One way to loop over these other containers is with an **iterator**, which is an object that helps traverse the collection. Every C++ STL collection supports iterators. Each collection has a `begin` function that returns an iterator to the first element and an `end` function that returns an iterator to the last element. The type of the iterator is the type of the collection followed by `::iterator`. For example, the following code creates a list and then uses an iterator to loop over each element in the list:

```
std::list<int> numbers;
numbers.emplace_back(2);
numbers.emplace_back(4);
numbers.emplace_back(6);
for (std::list<int>::iterator iter = numbers.begin();
    iter != numbers.end();
    ++iter)
{
    std::cout << *iter << std::endl;
}
```

Note that the iterator is dereferenced with *, the same way a pointer is dereferenced. The syntax for looping over other collections with iterators is similar.

In the case of a map, the iterator actually points to a `std::pair`. So, given an iterator to an element in a map, you must use `first` and `second` to access the key and value, respectively. Returning to the `months` map from earlier, you can get an iterator to an element and output its data with the following code:

```cpp
// Get an iterator to the element with the key 2
std::map<int, std::string> iter = months.find(2);
if (iter != months.end()) // This is only true if found
{
    std::cout << iter->first << std::endl; // Outputs 2
    std::cout << iter->second << std::endl; // Outputs February
}
```

Typing out the long type names for iterators is annoying. C++11 provides the `auto` keyword to help reduce this pain. `auto` tells the compiler to deduce the type of a variable for you, based on the assigned value. For example, because the `begin` function returns an iterator of a very specific type, `auto` can deduce that correct type. There is no performance penalty for using `auto`, though some programmers find the code harder to understand.

Using `auto`, you can rewrite the list loop as follows:

```cpp
// auto is deduced to be std::list<int>::iterator
for (auto iter = numbers.begin();
    iter != numbers.end();
    ++iter)
{
    std::cout << *iter << std::endl;
}
```

The code in this book uses `auto` only when it provides a benefit in readability.

Even with `auto`, the code for looping via iterators is clunky. Many other programming languages provide a `foreach` construct for looping over collections. C++11 has a similar construct called a **range-based** for **loop**. To loop over the `numbers` list with a range-based for loop, use the following syntax:

```cpp
for (int i : numbers)
{
    // i stores the element for the current loop iteration
    std::cout << i << std::endl;
}
```

This loop makes a copy of each element in the list as it iterates over it. However, you can also pass by reference if you want to modify elements in the collection. Similarly, you can use `const` references.

You can also use `auto` for the type when writing a range-based `for` loop. However, as with using an explicit type, this makes a copy of each element. However, you can also use `const` and `&` with `auto`, if needed.

One disadvantage of a range-based `for` loop is that you can't add or remove elements in the collection during the loop. So, if you need this behavior, you must use another type of loop.

Additional Reading

There are many excellent resources available online to help you learn and practice the fundamentals of C++. One such website is LearnCPP.com, which contains a very in-depth progression of topics. If you prefer traditional books, you should see Stephen Prata's book, which provides coverage of the basics. Eric Roberts's book covers both the fundamentals of C++ and relevant data structures.

Both of Scott Meyers's books are great resources for best practices in C++. They are short reads that provide many tips on how to achieve maximum effectiveness from C++ code.

There is also a great deal of information available on the C++ Standard Library. Bjarne Stroustrup, the creator of C++, devotes a large section of his book to the C++ collection implementations.

LearnCpp.com. Last modified April 28, 2016. http://www.learncpp.com.

Meyers, Scott. *Effective C++*, 3rd edition. Boston: Addison-Wesley, 2005.

Meyers, Scott. *Effective Modern C++*. Sebastopol: O'Reilly Media, 2014.

Prata, Stephen. *C++ Primer Plus,* 6th edition. Upper Saddle River: Addison-Wesley, 2012.

Roberts, Eric. *Programming Abstractions in C++*. Boston: Pearson, 2014.

Stroustrup, Bjarne. *The C++ Programming Language,* 4th edition. Upper Saddle River: Pearson, 2013.

INDEX